ASIATIC MYTHOLOGY

A DETAILED DESCRIPTION AND EXPLANATION OF THE MYTHOLOGIES OF ALL THE GREAT NATIONS OF ASIA

HEAD OF A STATUE OF BUDDHA
British Museum.

ASIATIC MYTHOLOGY

A DETAILED DESCRIPTION AND EXPLANATION OF THE MYTHOLOGIES OF ALL THE GREAT NATIONS OF ASIA

J. HACKIN: CLEMENT HUART: RAYMONDE LINOSSIER
H. DE WILMAN-GRABOWSKA: CHARLES-HENRI MARCHAL
HENRI MASPERO : SERGE ELISEEV

WITH AN INTRODUCTION BY
PAUL-LOUIS COUCHOUD

WITH 15 PLATES AND 354 OTHER ILLUSTRATIONS

GYAN

Published by

GYAN

Gyan Publishing House
5, Ansari Road
Daryaganj, New Delhi-110002
Phone: 011-47034999, 9811692060
E-mail: books@gyanbooks.com

Distribution Network
gyanbooks.com
India, USA, Canada, UK, Australia, France

ISBN : 9788121231398 (PB)
First Published, London, 1932

2nd Impression 2020

Printed at: Gyan Press, Delhi.

Asiatic Mythology
Author: J. Hackin

ASIATIC MYTHOLOGY

A DETAILED DESCRIPTION AND EXPLANATION OF THE MYTHOLOGIES OF ALL THE GREAT NATIONS OF ASIA

J. HACKIN : CLEMENT HUART : RAYMONDE LINOSSIER
H. DE WILMAN-GRABOWSKA : CHARLES-HENRI MARCHAL
HENRI MASPERO : SERGE ELISEEV

WITH AN INTRODUCTION BY
PAUL-LOUIS COUCHOUD

WITH 15 PLATES AND
354 OTHER ILLUSTRATIONS

ASIAN EDUCATIONAL SERVICES
NEW DELHI ★ MADRAS ★ 1994

ASIAN EDUCATIONAL SERVICES
* 31, HAUZ KHAS VILLAGE, NEW DELHI-110016.
CABLE: ASIA BOOKS, PH.: 660187, 668594, FAX: 011-6852805
* 5, SRIPURAM FIRST STREET, MADRAS-600014

AES
Rs 2300.
First Published. London, 1932
AES Reprint: New Delhi, 1994
ISBN: 81-206-0920-4

Published by J. Jetley
for ASIAN EDUCATIONAL SERVICES
C-2/15, SDA New Delhi-110 016
Processed by APEX PUBLICATION SERVICES
New Delhi-110 016
Printed at Nice Printing Press
Delhi-110 051

ASIATIC MYTHOLOGY

A Detailed Description and Explanation of the Mythologies of All the Great Nations of Asia

BY

J. HACKIN : CLEMENT HUART : RAYMONDE LINOSSIER
H. DE WILMAN-GRABOWSKA : CHARLES-HENRI MARCHAL
HENRI MASPERO : SERGE ELISEEV

WITH AN INTRODUCTION BY
PAUL-LOUIS COUCHOUD

WITH 15 PLATES IN COLOUR AND
354 OTHER ILLUSTRATIONS

LONDON
GEORGE G. HARRAP & CO. LIMITED
BOMBAY & SYDNEY

TRANSLATOR'S NOTE

THE preparation of an English version of this widely comprehensive work on the mythologies of Asia presented many problems, and the fullest and most grateful acknowledgment is due to the authorities in the various departments of the British Museum Library for their invaluable and ungrudging assistance. More especially the translator's heartiest thanks are herewith recorded to Dr Lionel Giles and to Mr J. V. S. Wilkinson, whose help was unfailing at all times.

F. M. ATKINSON

Devils hurling the Wicked into the Flames
Fragment of a *makimono* by the monk Kaïteï from the collection of Baron Rynetchi Kuki, Tokio.

CONTENTS

CONTENTS

CONTENTS

THE MYTHOLOGY OF JAPAN—*continued*

CONTENTS

VISHṆU AS A CHILD

One of the Four Excursions
From Borobodur.

ILLUSTRATIONS

PLATES IN COLOUR

ILLUSTRATIONS IN THE TEXT

ASIATIC MYTHOLOGY

THE MYTHOLOGY OF PERSIA

THE MYTHOLOGY OF THE KĀFIRS

THE MYTHOLOGY OF BUDDHISM IN INDIA

ILLUSTRATIONS

BRAHMANIC MYTHOLOGY

THE MYTHOLOGY OF LAMAISM

THE MYTHOLOGY OF INDO-CHINA AND JAVA

ASIATIC MYTHOLOGY

BUDDHIST MYTHOLOGY IN CENTRAL ASIA

THE MYTHOLOGY OF MODERN CHINA

ILLUSTRATIONS

THE MYTHOLOGY OF JAPAN

The Loosing of Buddha, from the Episode of the Dove
From Borobodur.

INTRODUCTION

Until our present day the gods of vast Asia have remained all but unknown to the cultured European. They were all confused together in a sort of queer and quaint Olympus. Their names, seldom pronounced, seemed unpronounceable.

But now to-day these gods are drawing closer to us. Seen from nearer at hand, they ceased to be monstrous or inert. For many Europeans they are already clear and distinct, alive and kind, almost friends. There is a desire to learn their legends, to recognize their attributes, to follow their avatars.

And this curiosity is no mere passing fashion. It is linked up with a great spiritual current, the deepest and strongest that has touched the Western world since the Renaissance.

In the sixteenth century Europe all at once found the ancient gods anew. Jupiter and Juno, Apollo and Diana, Mars and Venus, the Satyrs and the Muses, were hideous demons no longer. They dwelt in the imagination of poets and the palaces of princes. And they brought in their train a whole dancing world of ideas, of fancies, of shapes. It was like a sudden growth of the spirit. Man was vividly enlarged by a whole human past that had been thought to be utterly abolished. Three centuries did not exhaust this prodigious enrichment.

To-day begins another enrichment, more prodigious still. The Western man has a new inheritance to garner, or rather to share, vaster than that of the classical antique world, less accessible, stranger, not buried deep in the past, but far away in space, ripening and maturing to infinity under the early rays of the sun—the spiritual dowry of old Asia, venerable mother of the peoples.

The distance that lies between us has been shrunken, and in certain ways annihilated. What takes place in Delhi, in Pekin, in Tokyo, is known the same day in London, in Paris, in New York. A continuous stream of images and sounds comes from thence to eddy about our heads. It is an inevitable coming together. Whether humanity likes or dislikes it, a mechanical process is forcing it to assemble within the same enclosure.

Mechanical coming together would be nothing if it did not prepare the way for an exchange of secret treasures.

A new humanism is on the horizon. This time it will take in humanity entire. Can the men of to-day call themselves cultivated if they are nurtured on Europe alone? Can they still disregard the thought, the dreams, the experience, of one-half of humanity?

How many are saying with Romain Rolland: "There are a certain number of us in Europe for whom the civilization of Europe is no longer enough."

Or with Hermann Keyserling: "Europe no longer makes me react. This world is too familiar to me to give new shapes to my being; it is too limited. Europe to-day has no more than a single spirit. I wish to escape to spaces where my life must needs be transformed if it is to survive."

Maeterlinck sets over against each other what he calls the "Western lobe" and the "Eastern lobe" of the human brain:

> The one here produces reason, science, consciousness; the other yonder secretes intuition, religion, the subconscious. . . . More than once they have endeavoured to penetrate one another, to mingle, to work together; but the Western lobe, at any rate on the most active expanse of our globe, has heretofore paralysed and almost annihilated the efforts of the other. We owe to it extraordinary progress in all material sciences, but also catastrophes, such as those we are undergoing to-day. . . . It is time to awaken the paralysed Eastern lobe.

To bring the two halves of humanity face to face will be the great work of this century.

Let us incline our ear. A faint prelude heralds an event whose very immensity hides it from our senses. In the human symphony new, full-sounding instruments have just come in. A few harmonies, unheard before, make themselves felt. A concert is beginning in which the lute and the flute of Asia will play their part.

Let us open our eyes. Perhaps we shall see what has never yet been seen. Humanity has not yet known itself. It has unfolded itself upon two terraces. There were two showers of bright sparks, two rockets soaring in the night. For the first time, from one end of the vast earth to the other, man is the spectator of man. For this new festival how high will the rockets go?

On the very long and very winding road that by a slow ascent will lead us to the knowledge of Asia the study of mythology is the first stage, the indispensable rudiment, the ABC.

The Daughters of Māra, from the Episode of the Temptation
From Borobodur.

It is through art that Asia first of all shows herself to us. Thousands of figured objects — prints, scrolls, statues—obsess our eyes. Through these we find ourselves in contact with an unknown world.

All art is thought.

The first condition necessary to understand a work of art in which a theme is treated is to know that theme. In Asia, as elsewhere, three-fourths of the subjects represented are religious. Hence we must begin by deciphering the mythology that inspires them.

In order to interpret the white statues resurrected from the earth the men of the Renaissance feverishly studied the history of the ancient gods. Even so must we spell out that of the gods of Asia. Kwannon, Ṣiva, Gaṇeṣa, Jizô, must be as familiar to us as Ceres, Hercules, Silenus, were to them.

Inasmuch as henceforward the art and the thought of Asia are part of the patrimony of humanity, inasmuch as every well-bred person must needs be capable of appreciating a Khmer or Chinese masterpiece no less than an ancient marble or a Quattrocento bronze, he must have at least a quarter of the knowledge possessed by every street-urchin in Cambodia or in China.

It is a lazy fallacy to think that art can be appreciated apart from its subject. Indifference to the subject is the mark of an ageing art. It appears among a sophisticated public to whom every subject has become commonplace and trite. It does not apply to periods of spontaneous and popular art. There everything is significant, everything speaks.

To take but a single example, could we enjoy to the full the beauty of a tympanum or a stained-glass window of the Middle Ages if Émile Mâle had not taught us to disentangle and construe its meaning? The Indian, Khmer, or Javanese artist is brother to the artist of Chartres. He has the same frankness, the same piety, the same eagerness to narrate, to edify. He deserves the same audience.

To penetrate to the heart of a civilization we ought to begin with a knowledge of its gods. And in the very end that is what we come back to.

The creation of the gods is the most natural, the most secret, the slowest, the loftiest, of the works of man. It is the supreme achievement of his profound experiences. It is the mysterious fruit of minds in the mass.

How many thoughts and accumulated desires must go to make a god? The gods have no reality save a spiritual one, but this reality is superior to that of all the humble worshippers who give them life. In the orchard of humanity they are the golden apples to which all saps flow and concentrate.

THE MONK BODHIDHARMA RETURNING TO THE PARADISE OF AMITĀBHA
Japanese carving.

We Western peoples, with our spirits still barbarian and too much caught up with what the philosophers call realism, we find it hard to comprehend the genesis of the gods. An invincible prepossession leads us to believe that God, the gods, the demons, are in things and outside ourselves.

They are no such thing. India, more subtle than we, knows this. " It is the high distinction of this race," says Michelet, " that while continually adoring they always know that they have made their gods themselves."

"The mortal made the immortal," says the *Ṛigveda*. The Indian monk Bodhidharma,[1] in the sixth century of our era, said before the Emperor Leang Wu Ti: " There is no Buddha outside the heart. Save the reality of the heart all is imaginary. The heart is Buddha, and Buddha is the heart. To imagine a Buddha outside the heart, to conceive that he is seen in an external place, is but delirium."

It is good for us to give ear to the lesson of the monk Bodhidharma.

In vast Asia there are great religious provinces.

Persia is the one least a stranger to us. Twice the Persian gods all but conquered the West. They were stopped at Salamis. Eight centuries later the god Mithra insinuated himself into the Roman world.

[1] Bodhidharma is the founder of the Dhyāna school. The pilgrim Sung-Yün, when on his way back from India, met him, after his death, among the Mountains of the Onions: " He was departing barefoot, carrying a sandal in his hand and making his way to the West, returning to the Paradise of Amitābha." (See the section entitled " The Mythology of Modern China," p. 380.)

Under the Severi there were more Mithraists than Christians in the West. In the well-known phrase of Renan, "If Christianity had been stopped in its growth by some deadly disease the world would have been Mithraist." The possibility is one to dream over. Perhaps our civilization would not have followed a very different path. The cathedrals would have been built. In the apse the Bull would have supplanted the Cross.

Land of eternal thought, India is the most religious country in the universe. Certain countries have a dazzling pre-eminence in some particular direction: China in porcelain, Japan in drawing, India in religion. Porcelain is made everywhere; China alone has made

VISHṆU NARA-SIṂHA AND HIRAṆYA-KAṢIPU
Fragment of a chariot in the Musée Guimet.

VISHṆU NARA-SIṂHA AND LAKSHMĪ
Fragment of a chariot in the Musée Guimet.

it a marvel. Men draw everywhere; only in Japan are men 'drawing-mad.' Even so man is everywhere religious. In India alone has he gone to the farthest limit of his religious faculty.

India has carried the two opposite types of religion, the dynamic and the ascetic, to their abstract absolute, the religions that exalt man's force and those that are founded upon renunciation, "the religions of masters" and "the religions of slaves," to speak in the words of Nietzsche. The cult of Ṣiva is the most vigorous, the most jubilant, the most unrestrained, the most pitiless of paganisms. And Buddhism is, before Christianity, a logical Christianity which pursues detachment to the last fibre of the soul. Beside these pure forms the other religions of the world have something bastard and diluted about them.

After having been intoxicated and etiolated with Buddhism India swung violently back to Ṣiva, completing the entire cycle of religious metamorphoses. When we see at Ellora, cut successively in the same cliff mass, the Buddhist monasteries where the monks performed prodigies of self-denial and the monolithic Paradise of Ṣiva, an eternal hymn to the Dance, to Carnage, to Virility, we compass in a glance the religious history of India, an epitome of that of humanity.

All Asia received its religious education from India. The Buddhism that India discarded pursued its destiny all around her.

It was above all in the Lamaism of Thibet that it flowered most luxuriantly in legend, and that its iconography was evolved. It was in Indo-China, in Java, in China, in Japan, that it found its loveliest and most highly developed artistic expression.

It is the great controller of the arts of Asia. And it has given men's souls that simplicity and delicacy and resonance that make all Asia one single landscape of the heart.

Honest China offers the example of a living popular religion in which Buddhism, Taoism, and Confucianism were finally all fused together. Christianity would have been fused into it too if the Jesuits in the time of the Emperor Kang Hsi had succeeded in establishing themselves.

Nowhere better than in this teeming hive, set in the midst and centre of humanity, may we observe the elementary religious needs of the people, the simple efficacious methods with which it satisfies them.

Japan, the museum of Asia, has sifted and refined all the exquisite productions of the meditation of China and India. And on its own part it preserves strong, intact, alive, a prehistoric religion.

With its neolithic legends, its ritual belonging to the time of the fairies, Shintô is a unique example on this scale of a religion pursuing its career since the origins of mankind.

As for Japanese Buddhism, it is, I verily believe, the most exquisite blossom of religion upon this earth.

Up to the present there has been no general mythology of Asia. The pioneer work was still to be done. No single person could hope to perform the task. Collaboration was necessary.

Naturally enough the savants who have written this work are all connected with the Musée Guimet of Paris, that incomparable museum of religions.

The keeper, or we might more properly say the active commander, of the Musée Guimet, M. J. Hackin, who by his explorations and by his archæological labours has added so much to our knowledge of Thibet, Nepal, and Afghanistan, drew up the plan of the book, and co-ordinated the various tasks and the illustrations. He chose for his own share Lamaism and Central Asia, contributing also the section on Kāfiristān.

His colleague at the Musée Guimet, Mlle Raymonde Linossier, has dealt with Buddhist India, patiently collecting and commenting on its iconography in a most illuminating fashion.

Brahmanic India was assigned to Mme de Wilman-Grabowska, Professor of Sanskrit in the École des Hautes Études, a pupil and colleague of Sylvain Lévi.

The deeply regretted President of the Académie des Inscriptions, Clément Huart, kept Persia for himself, a domain he had made peculiarly his own by a life of research.

The keeper and enlarger of Angkor, M. Henri Marchal, lays before us Indo-China and Java, so rich in architecture and statuary. Mlle Sapho Marchal has adorned her father's monograph with the drawings she made at Angkor.

China has M. Henri Maspero for its accredited and sage interpreter. The name he inherits has shed lustre upon Egypt. The reader will see that China too has to-day its own Maspero.

Japan fell to the greatest of French students of that country, Claude Maitre. Death

MAITREYA AND THE EIGHTEEN ARHATS
Fourteenth-century rock-carving from Hang-kow.

cut the stem before the harvest. Claude Maitre wished to write the two sections on Japan. He entrusted them, before he died, to his worthy successor in the lore of Japan, M. Serge Eliseev, formerly Professor in the University of Petrograd.

Reader, before entering into the dark and enchanted forest of the mythologies of Asia, take two talismans—patience and sympathy.

Do not be afraid of strange names. Do not lose the thread of tangled and repeated legends. The faces that at first appear to be louring, look long at them until you see them smile.

For reward of your efforts you will perhaps feel, approaching you above and over the words and the images, something of the terrible prestige of Mahādeva or the mystic grace of Our Lord Buddha.

PAUL-LOUIS COUCHOUD

Fig. 1. Ahura Mazda
From a bas-relief.

THE MYTHOLOGY OF PERSIA

Persia has a long past to look back upon—twenty-five centuries of history. She began, in the middle of the sixth century before our era, with a dynasty that created her as a new state, the foundations of whose astounding successes had been laid by its first kings as a result of certain events of which we know nothing. The Persian clan of the Hakhamanish, who spoke an Indo-European dialect, had seized Susa and overthrown a native dynasty that had enjoyed a lengthy period of rule over Susiana, the Elam of the Bible. One of its kings, Cyrus (558–528 B.C.), blazed forth as a great conqueror: he destroyed the empire of the Medes, a people akin, as a matter of fact, to the Persians, who had managed with the help of Babylon to take and to ruin Nineveh, the proud Semitic city that dominated Upper Asia; he conquered Crœsus, the King of Phrygia, and seized Asia Minor; he took Babylon by assault. Nothing survived of those states, all annexed without any great resistance, for the Persian policy, hitherto unknown among those cruel and barbarous peoples, consisted in allowing the conquered peoples to live in peace, retaining their religions, their gods, and even at times their own kings. That was how the statues of divinities previously conquered were restored to their former owners, and how the Israelites, in accordance with this principle, recovered possession of the treasures of the Temple of Jerusalem, their gratitude for which appears in the Book of Esdras. It was enough that they should remain in obedience and provide the satraps, or governors, of the newly made provinces with the sums of money or the tribute in kind exacted by the central power. Darius I, after subduing the districts that revolted upon the death of Cambyses, organized that enormous empire which stretched from Egypt to the Indus. This dynasty, which strove against Greece and had the worst of it, is known as the Achæmenids (546–330 B.C.).

Alexander the Great brought the colossus down, but palace revolutions had for long years before been undermining its foundations. Hellenism invaded the East; after the death of the conqueror his lieutenants founded new states, with varying political fortunes; but Greek art penetrated very far into the vast Asiatic continent, and created in Gandhāra, on the Indian border, the recently rediscovered Græco-Buddhist sculpture, in which Buddha figures in Greek costume. Persia recovered her autonomy before very long with the almost feudal *régime* established by the Parthians, an Iranian tribe from the North, and maintained by the dynasty of the Arsacids (250 B.C.–A.D. 224), so called from its founder Arsaces.

In the third century of the Christian era an attempt was made to re-establish the old empire by a new revolution: the Arsacids were overthrown by Ardashīr, son of Pāpak, the founder of the dynasty of the Sasanids, who derived their name from a supposed ancestor. To maintain the unity of the empire it had a powerful weapon in the religion of Zoroaster, set forth in a book, the *Avesta*, written in a tongue already dead, the sister to the ancient Persian of the Achæmenian inscriptions, but interpreted by the commentaries in Pehlevi, the official language of the period. This dynasty, which struggled against Rome with varying fortune, and which included four remarkable monarchs, the two Sapors and the two Chosroes, was destroyed by the Arab conquests, which spread Islam, the religion recently founded by Muḥammad (A.D. 642–651).

Persia did not become Muhammadan immediately: frequent revolts showed that the natives were unwilling to endure a foreign yoke, but these risings were smothered; the Khalifs, first of Madina, then of Damascus, and lastly of Baghdad, proved that they were strong enough to hold the subdued territories under control. Little by little, by the infection of example, by the pressure of authority, by the advantages offered to new converts, Islam spread deeper and deeper through the country; the fire shrines were closed one by one, and to-day there remain on the soil of Persia only a few feeble groups of Zoroastrians; but, on the other hand, those who exiled themselves into India, finding a welcome from the local authorities, founded at Sanjān, close to what became later the flourishing city of Bombay, the powerful Parsee community, rich in influence and intellect, some members of which have succeeded in amassing very considerable fortunes.

Among the numerous schismatic sects that sprang up on Muhammadan soil, certain Persian groups had adopted Shī'ism, which asserted the violation of the right of 'Alī, the Prophet's cousin and son-in-law, to succeed him; but the governors (with the single exception of the Buwaihids), being all Turks, and therefore Sunnīs, had prevented the schism from spreading; in fact the Persians, especially the cultured classes, were Shāfi'ites, and consequently Sunnīs. This was completely altered with the revolution that at the beginning of the sixteenth century placed upon the throne a family of dervishes from Ardabil who made Shī'ism the national religion. These were the Safavids, Ismā'īl I, who was defeated by the Ottomans at Chāldirān, 'Abbās the Great, and 'Abbās II, who knew our European travellers Pietro della Valle, Chardin, and Tavernier. From that time Persia was Shī'ite.

Mythology in the Time of the Achæmenids

In the huge Persian Empire every people preserved its own religion; here we are concerned only with that held by the Medo-Persian group, the conquering group that provided the satraps, or governors of provinces, but made no encroachments upon the religious territory of the subjugated peoples. It appears that this group comprised three religions: that of the King and the royal family, that of the people, and that of the Magians.

Darius I seems to have a special devotion for Ahura Mazda, whom he calls "the great god," "the greatest of the gods." True, he knows other deities, but he uses the phrase "other gods" almost casually, and seems to assign little importance to them. In the bas-reliefs of Persepolis we find a representation of Ahura Mazda hovering in the air above the altar of fire, the symbol of divinity. The god wears exactly the same costume as the King—the cap, the long beard, the wide-sleeved tunic; the feet, however, are not seen; the long robe with full flounces hides them, or perhaps he needs none, since he is poised in air on his great outspread wings. His waist is girdled by a circle that represents the sun's disk; two ribbons with scrolled-up ends complete the costume.

Fig. 2. Darius slaying an Evil Genius
Bas-relief from Persepolis.

Another Persepolis bas-relief shows the King standing, grasping with his left hand the horn of a winged fantastic monster that stands upright on its hind legs while its right forepaw is warding off the King's arm and the left set against his breast; the royal combatant is thrusting the sword in his right hand into the entrails of the dreadful beast (Fig. 2). We have not the key to the correct interpretation of this episode, for explanatory texts are lacking. Is it an Assyrian type preserved by the artists employed by the Persians to decorate the magnificent palaces built by their kings? Might it not be a personification of falsehood (*drauga*), as quoted in the great inscription of Bisitun? Or, indeed, in allusion to Darius' wars against the rebellious, a representation of the genius of insurrection, as in the expression largely employed a hundred years ago, though now dropped into disuse, and even into ridicule, "the hydra of anarchy"? It is difficult to see in it the principle or genius of evil, to which the Persepolitan inscriptions nowhere allude, a clear proof that the kings were not Zoroastrians. It is exceedingly difficult to ascertain the royal religion, which may have been influenced by the milieu of Susa, in which the fortunes of the Achæmenids developed.

The capitals of the pillars in the Palace of Susa present bulls' heads, which have certain affinities with creeds of which we have no information (Fig. 3).

In the time of Artaxerxes Mnemon two new divinities appear, Mithra—that is to say, the Sun (known as *Sol invictus* and compared with Apollo in the Roman period)—and Anāhitā, who is Venus. The latter seems to come from Chaldean astrology.

Fig. 3. Capital from Susa
Louvre. *A.G. photo.*

The religion of the kings was not that of the Persian people. The latter has been described to us by Herodotus, who was not aware of the former. The Persian people adored the four elements: light, which was of two kinds, the light of the day, the sun, the light of the night, the moon; next water, earth, the wind. This religion allowed the sacrifice of animals, but these sacrifices could only be made in the presence of a Magian. Now, the Magians were Medes, as we are about to see. How the Medes, beaten and conquered as they were, had succeeded in rooting themselves in Persian soil is a puzzle. The sacrificer always brought the victim to a pure spot; he covered the tiara on his head with a myrtle crown; he invoked the deity and prayed for the prosperity of the King and all Persians; he cut up the victim into pieces, boiling the flesh and laying the cut-up pieces upon a bed of tender herbs, such as clover. Then the Magian chanted what Herodotus calls a *Theogony*, a "genealogy of the gods," probably a kind of hymn in which the different gods of the Pantheon were enumerated. A fragment of a bas-relief representing a sacrifice of this kind has been found in Asia Minor.

The Magians were one of those tribes that were banded together to re-establish the empire of the Medes destroyed, or rather absorbed, by Cyrus. It seems that they had an ancient ritual that preserved a mass of traditions and beliefs going back to the prehistoric epoch when the Indians and the Iranians were still a single people. It was these traditions of great antiquity, maintained throughout the ages by colleges of priests, that were the basis of the *Avesta*, which was only reduced to the form in which we have it in the third century of the Christian era; but it is incontestably the echo of primitive beliefs that take us very far back. It was the Magians who buried their dead only after the corpses had been worried and torn by birds or dogs, a practice maintained by the Parsees of our own days in the Towers of Silence (*dakhmas*), huge circles enclosed by high walls in which bodies are exposed to the open air and devoured by vultures. The bones alone are preserved in the ossuaries.

Mythology under the Arsacids

The royal Court was placed under the influence of Hellenistic ideas; the coinage bore Greek inscriptions; the kings had the tragedies of Euripides and the great classic dramatists played before them. We have no means of knowing what the religion of the people was under the Parthian kings, whose reigns were disturbed by home and foreign wars. At the same time, numismatic studies have revealed that in Fars there persisted a series of priest-kings, vassals to the Arsacids, who seem to have kept up the national traditions; on the reverse of their coins the kings are represented standing bow in hand in front of the fire altar, recalling the attitude of Darius on the sculptures of Naqsh-i-Rustam. Beside the altar stands the national standard, which can only be the well-known banner of the period, the flag of the smith Kāva, who raised the people against the tyranny of Zahhāk, the foreign conqueror, and placed the mythical King Farīdūn upon the throne. It is difficult to refrain from the belief that it was under these local dynasts, or in similar circumstances, that colleges of the Magians managed to preserve the traditions that when the Sasanids were restored served as the basis for the *Avesta*.

Fig. 4. Bas-relief from Nimrūd-Dagh: Antiochus and Mithra

Under the dynasty of the Arsacids, about the first century B.C., we must place a singular phenomenon, the expansion of the cult of Mithra throughout the Roman world (Fig. 6). This ancient divinity of Cappadocia (we find him mentioned in cuneiform inscriptions in the fourteenth century before our era) had been the object of a particular cult with Artaxerxes II; the campaigns of Pompey in the East introduced it among the Roman soldiers, and it remained more or less a military religion; the garrisons carried it to the western confines of the Empire; its monuments have been found in Paris. It was a secret cult; in order to take part in it an initiation with seven degrees was necessary. In the ceremonies the adepts wore masks representing the various types fixed by tradition. The oldest monument is the bas-relief of Nimrūd-Dagh, in which is shown King Antiochus Commagenes: he is face to face with Mithra, who has a Phrygian cap and his head surrounded with rays, and holds out his hand to him in sign of alliance (Fig. 4). But the most popular episode, which has been represented in hundreds of copies, is that of Mithra *Tauroktonos*, or "slayer of the bull": with a Phrygian cap on his head, his left knee pressing on the victim's shoulder, the god is burying a dagger in the heart of the bull; from the beast's body springs every kind of vegetable growth. A dog licks the flowing blood; a snake crawls at his feet (Fig. 5). The setting is a cavern; as a matter of fact, the faithful generally met to practise their rites in rocky excavations, near a spring or running water. The starting-point of Mithraism was Persia; but, formed in Asia Minor and in Mesopotamia, it admitted elements borrowed from Babylonia; it has almost no other Iranian touches in it.

Fig. 5. MITHRA
At the top the chariots of the Sun and the Moon.
Louvre. *A.G. photo.*

Fig. 6. MITHRA SACRIFICING THE BULL
A.G. photo.

Mythology in the Time of the Sasanids

Now we have a more certain guide, the actual text of the *Avesta*, which Anquetil-Duperron had gone to India to find among the Parsees of Bombay, and the first known manuscripts of which, preserved to-day in the Bibliothèque Nationale, he brought back with him. Thanks to this sacred book, we know what made up the mythology of this State religion, which was the main prop of the throne of the Sasanids and lost its importance with the downfall of that *régime*, for it is no longer represented to-day, except by a few adepts in Persia and by an important community established in Bombay and its environs.

Ahura Mazda is no longer the one god whom Darius revered; he is the personification of light and good, but over against him he has a formidable adversary, the spirit of darkness and evil, Angra Mainyu (Ahriman). The foundation of the teaching of Zoroaster is in fact the existence of two principles, light and darkness: the first is good, the second evil. These two are engaged in a perpetual contest, with alternating success and defeat for one as well as the other. The universe is divided in two by an immense abyss; on either side fight the forces of the two enemies. Ahura Mazda (Ormazd) creates all good; Ahriman all evil. This struggle will last for twelve thousand years, divided into periods of three thousand each; each of the two principles is to dominate in turn during one of these periods; we are at present in that in which evil predominates. In the end good will vanquish evil, the light will conquer the darkness; that will be, and this time finally, the triumph of Ahura Mazda.

The spirit of good and the spirit of evil are not the only combatants; each is at the head of an army, the army of heaven and the army of hell; the two forces are opposed to one another in a perfect parallelism. Ahura Mazda is, as he must be, the head of the army of heaven; he is surrounded by a council of six ministers, of which he is president. These are the six Amshaspands, Amesha Spentas ("immortal saints"), abstractions without any real existence; they are the archangels who stand before the throne of God, the ministers charged with the execution of his orders. Vohu-Manah (Bahman) is "right thought"; Asha-Vahishta (Ardabahisht) "supreme virtue"; Khshathra Vairya (Shahrevar) "desired empire"; Spentā Ārmaiti (Asfandarmad) "generous surrender"; Haurvatāt (Khurdād) "health"; Ameretāt (Murdād) "immortality."

The Amshaspands are the protectors of various categories of creatures. Thus Vohu-Manah has under his charge useful animals; Asha-Vahishta controls fire; Khshathra Vairya has metals under his care; Spentā Ārmaiti rules over the land; Haurvatāt and Ameretāt protect waters and plants. Certain months of the calendar and certain days of the week are consecrated to them.

In the celestial hierarchy there come on a lower plane the Yazatas, "those who merit worship"; these are kinds of genii of incalculable numbers, and may be reckoned in thousands. They are the tutelary genii of the sun, the moon, the stars, the earth, the air, fire and water, or personifications of abstract ideas—victory, truth, peace, power. Ātar ("fire") is the son of Ahura Mazda, whether it is the fire of the sky, the thunderbolt, or the fire that is shut up within the veins of the wood and that friction forces to appear. To him are attached Hvaranah ("glory"), a halo of light that surrounds the person of kings and indicates them to their subjects (*farr*), exactly what painters call a 'glory' in religious art; the terrestrial fires, Frobāgh, in a mountain near Kabul; Adhar-Gushnasp, near Ardabil; Burzīn, in Khurasan, genii who are the protectors of priests, warriors, and husbandmen.

Apō ("water") is the object of particular devotion, for he is of heavenly origin, as the rain shows. There is a male genius of the waters, who creates and shapes man, defends and protects the royal glory, and a female genius, who is no other than Anaitis, or Venus, who assists women in labour, giving men courageous companions and strong horses. Hvarekhshaēta ("the brilliant sun") is Ahura Mazda's eye; he is drawn by swift horses, like the car of Apollo. Māh is the moon invoked beside the sun; her light favours the growing of plants. The star Tishtrya is no other than Sirius, as Plutarch already knew. She is the inspector of the other stars, in close relations with rainwater, the seed of which she contains. Every ten days she changes her shape; she is now a youth, now a cow, now a horse; in return for the sacrifices made to her she assures mankind numerous progeny, abundance of cattle and horses, and above all, the purification of the soul; her weapon against the attack of the demons is the lightning. Beside Tishtrya we find three other stars or constellations quoted—Haptō-iringa (the Great Bear), Satavaēsa and Vanant (both unidentified), the twelve Akhtar, or zodiacal constellations, considered as the generals of Ahura Mazda's army.

Dervāspā, or Gosh, is the soul of the bull (*Geus urvan*), an object of respect and veneration, guardian of cattle. Mithra is the god of light and of truth. In the *Gāthās*, ancient hymns partly preserved in the text of the *Avesta*, he is the god of the contract, which he defends against those who would violate its sanctity; warriors call him to their aid; in later times he will be one of the judges of the dead.

Sraosha ("the obedient") is the guardian angel of the world; with Mithra and Rashnu, he will be one of the judges of the other world. A compassionate genius, he feeds the poor. The Fravashis are guardian angels of men; they exist in heaven before birth; they are united to the soul after death; they are Ahura Mazda's auxiliaries in the war against evil.

Verethraghna, the genius of victory, became the name of the planet Mars, the Bahrām of the modern Persians; he is naturally invoked by war leaders not only against men, but also against the demons; he shows himself under very varied forms—horse, camel, wild boar, or bird. Rāma (or Vayu) is the genie who gives dishes their savour. Vāta ("the wind"), Āsmān ("the sky"), Zem ("the earth"), are so many Yazatas.

One of the principal ceremonies of Zoroastrianism is the drinking by the priest of a liquor prepared from the *haoma*, a plant the leaves and stems of which are pressed to give a juice that is passed through a strainer. In view of the part it plays in this species of communion, this plant, the same as the *soma* of the Indians, has been made divine; it too is a Yazata. It was known to Plutarch, who calls it ὅμωμι. It grows only on high mountains, and heals both body and soul.

Such is the army of good. The parallel demands that the army of evil should stand in opposition, the infernal forces that fight to conquer Ahura Mazda. These are commanded by a general whose name we have seen above, Angra Mainyu, "the spirit of anguish," the Ahriman of more recent times; his part is that of Satan, the inspirer of evil works. Under his command are the mob of the demons, the *dīv* (*daēvas*) who people hell; among them are six principal ones who play the part of ministers of Satan and balance the six Amshaspands with Ahura Mazda. Just as *daēva* is the same word as in Sanskrit is applied to the gods (Latin *divus*), and in Persian to the demons, three of these demons are Indian divinities, Indra, Sarva, Nāsatyā, who are easily recognized in the names of Indra, Sauru, Nāonhaithya. Aka-Manah ("evil thought") is naturally opposed to Vohu-Manah ("good thought"). Indra is the adversary of Asha-Vahishta; it is he who awaits the souls of the dead on the bridge Chinvat, makes it shrink as they are passing over, and hurls them into the abyss; he torments them in hell. He seeks to implant in the living cares and distress of heart; he takes possession of natures penetrated with gloom. Sauru is the enemy of Khshathra Vairya; he inspires kings with tyranny, incites common men to theft and brigandage. He fills them with hardness of heart, he seeks to destroy metals. Nāonhaithya, opposed to Spentā Ārmaiti, inspires men with pride, ingratitude, incapacity to endure misfortune, obstinacy. The history of Aēshma, the demon of anger, fury, devastation, is very interesting: besides the fact that the Persian language has preserved the word *khashm* in the sense of anger, the complete expression Aēshma-daēva became Asmodeus in the Book of Tobit, and thence passed into Christian dæmonology, where Lesage found it. One of the Yazatas has the task of fighting him, and will bring him to nought at the end of time; this is Sraosha, already mentioned above, the incarnation of religious obedience, of devotion.

Besides the *dīv*, there are also the *drujs*, whose name serves to form the word *darvant* (*dragvant*), which signifies the wicked, the unjust, the servants of Satan. The principal *druj* is falsehood (*drauga*, the Persian *durūgh*), already fought against by Darius I in the cuneiform inscription of Bisitun; but there are others, like Būshyanstā, the demon of sleep, who prevents men from engaging in acts of devotion, distinguished by his long hands, and the Nasu, the female demon who represents the corruption of corpses, the chief impurity recognized by Zoroastrian rites. She introduces herself into the dead body in the shape of a fly; she can be driven away by the glance of a dog, which always figures in funerals; this rite is called *sag-dīd* ("dog-sight"). The living body can be freed from her by the ceremonies of the Barashnūm, a purification which continues for nine days.

Another demon of this kind is Azhi-Dahāka, a monster with three heads, six eyes, and three mouths, later personified as a King of Babylon who is completely mythical, Zahhāk, surnamed Bīvar-asp "of the ten thousand horses," who is represented in Firdausī's *Book of Kings* with a serpent coming out of each shoulder and fed daily with human brains (Fig. 7). It was he who was overthrown by Farīdūn (Thraētaona), the hero of the Iranian revival, whom the Smith Kāva had gone to seek in order to place him on the throne of Persia as legitimate descendant of the ancient kings.

The Yātus are the magicians, the sorcerers. The Paris (Pairikas) are fairies, sirens, whose evil influence is applied to earth, water, fire, cattle, plants; they cast spells upon the stars to prevent rain, and make them fall in the form of shooting-stars or meteors. Dragons and monsters are created by the evil spirit to destroy the human race (Fig. 8). Happily there are heroes, like Hercules and many Christian saints, courageous enough to go out and fight with these enemies of mankind and rid the world of them. These diabolical creations are destined to thwart the efforts of good; hence they are called *paityāra*, or "adverse moves."

Fig. 7. Zahhāk, King of Babylon
From a lithographed edition of *The Book of Kings*.

The rule of moral conduct laid down by Zoroaster for his adherents is to have the spirit continually aiming after perfection as formulated in three words: good thought, good word, good action. After death the soul is carried away to the bridge Chinvat, thrown across hell between the mountain-chain of the Alburz and the Daityā peak; there it finds the three judges already mentioned, who weigh in a balance the deeds of the man in his lifetime. Upon their judgment, which follows the movement of the balance, depends the dead man's future fate. The bridge Chinvat is wide and easy for the soul of the just, narrow and

Fig. 8. Dragons and Monsters
From a bas-relief.

increasingly slender for the soul of the wicked, who ends by stumbling and being swallowed up by an abyss where the darkness is so thick that it can be grasped by the hands.

The part played in epic by the fabulous bird, the Sīmurgh, makes it impossible to omit him. It is the vulture Saēna of the *Avesta*: near his nest in the Alburz Mountains Sām exposes his son Zāl (later to be Rustam's father); the vulture is about to feed his young with the child's flesh when a voice from the skies prevents him. He brings Zāl up in his nest; he gives Sām one of his feathers, bidding him throw it into the fire whenever he finds himself in any pressing need, he will then fly to Sām's rescue. He is the protector of Rustam's family: summoned by Rustam, he heals the wounds of the hero and his horse Rakhsh. He carries him in a single night to the China Sea, where the *gaz* tree (the tamarisk) is found, a branch of which is to provide the arrow with which he will slay his enemy Isfandiyār.

Mythology of the Manichæans

It was in the Persian empire of the Sasanids that Manichæism was born, the new religion invented by a man whose name we know under its Greek form Manes, but who was really called Mani. He was born in A.D. 215, on Babylonian territory, and at the age of thirteen, and later at twenty-five, received divine revelations enjoining upon him to preach the true religion. This was a compromise between the Zoroastrian dogmas and the teaching of the Gnostics, which was spread among all the Christian subjects of the King of Persia who spoke Aramaic. The opposition of the two principles, the dualism of light and darkness, for him was something more drastic and systematic than in the official religion. Evil existed from all eternity. He recognized two natures, one good, one bad, in the elements—water, air, earth, fire. Beside these borrowings from Zoroastrianism, which he modified in accordance with his beliefs, he gave a large place to the teaching of Jesus, which for a long time caused him to be considered by Western historians as a Christian heresiarch; but recent discoveries in Central Asia give us reason to modify this point of view. The works he composed were adorned with miniatures, which according to St Ephraim represented the virtues of light and the powers of darkness "in the lineaments most proper to cause those to be loved and these hated, in order thus to complete the written doctrine for those persons who have been taught and to supply it for others." The adepts took great pains to multiply manuscript copies of these works; and this is beyond question, for St Augustine, who began his career as a Manichæan, saw in the hands of the faithful large numbers of manuscripts, decorated in various coloured inks and sumptuously bound; none of these, unhappily, has come down to us.

For Mani the two contrary principles were both eternal and irreconcilable. The kingdom of God, light, extends infinitely to the north, the east, and the west, while the empire of the demon stretches only in the direction of the south. War broke out one day between the two states, for the demon conceived the notion of conquering the realm of light; the Father of Greatness—that is to say, God—created, in order to resist this sudden attack, the Mother of Life, who gave birth to the first man. This first man was at first overthrown by Satan, from which arose a universal confusion in which good found itself mingled with ill; but Satan's attack was broken by this chaos. The creation of the living Spirit delivered man, and the world was created.

Mani in like manner recognized two souls in man: a good soul, whence proceeded thought, feeling, the luminous intellect, and an evil soul—that is to say, the same phenomena in their dark phase; from the first proceeded pity, good faith, patience, wisdom, in a word all the virtues; from the second came hatred, lust, wrath, folly, the sins and vices.

Mythology of the Mazdakites

Mazdak, the founder of this sect, born in Khurasan, was a disseminator of communistic ideas who found an adept in the person of a King of Persia, Kavād (488–531). He preached not only community of property but also community of women, the abolition of all privileges, and prohibition against killing any living creature for food. His teaching derived from that of Mani; he believed in the existence of the two principles, but admitted differences between them: the light acted freely, was sensitive and intelligent; darkness acted by chance, was ignorant and blind. Their intermingling and the consequent creation of the world were the outcome of chance, without preconceived plan; it was to be the same with regard to their severing, bringing about the end of the universe. Three elements composed this universe: water, fire, and earth; from their intermingling proceeded good and evil, the first deriving from the pure parts of the elements, the second from their turbid parts. God sat upon his throne like a sovereign; in front of him were four forces: discernment, intelligence, memory, and joy. Seven ministers directed the affairs of the world by the intermediary of twelve powers, or spiritual beings.

Mythology of Muhammadan Persia

Islam is a religion with rigid dogmas, which does not (at any rate in recent times) admit any representation of any living thing, through fear of seeing the old vanquished paganism revive and the worship of idols. It would seem, then, that it must be devoid of all mythology, and this is true of the sects that lay claim to represent primitive Islam, such as the Kharijites in Oman, the Mzab in Algeria, the island of Jerba and the Jebel-Nufūsa in Tunisia, the island of Zanzibar, or the Wahabis in Central Arabia. But the Persians had too much imagination, were people too fundamentally artistic for mythology not to recover part of its rights before long. It is especially after the sixteenth century, when Persia became altogether Shī'ite, and when the native dynasty of the Safavids produced a real renaissance of the arts (miniatures in manuscripts, mural paintings, sumptuous walls of enamelled bricks from Kāshān), that, except in the mosques, the representation of living creatures recovered the place that could not fail to come to it again among a beauty-loving people.

The Shī'ites are, in principle, followers of 'Alī, and claim that the first three Khalifs (Abu-Bakr, 'Umar, and 'Uthmān) wrongfully seized from him his genuine right to succeed Muḥammad in both spiritual and temporal power. The "sect of the Twelve," to which the Persians of our own day belong, recognize a special and peculiar character not only in 'Alī but in his descendants as well—*i.e.*, his eldest son Ḥasan, his younger son Ḥusain, and in Ḥusain's line in direct descent from father to son—Zain al-'Abidīn, Muḥammad

MAHOMET AND ALI APPEARING IN THE FORM OF FLAME
(Bibliothèque Nationale.)

al-Bāqir, Ja'far aṣ-Ṣādiq, Mūsā al-Kādhim, 'Alī ar-Rizā, Muḥammad at-Taqī, 'Alī an-Naqī, Ḥasan al-'Askarī az-Zakī, and lastly Muḥammad al-Mahdī, who disappeared suddenly, and will return at the end of time to announce the last judgment and the resurrection of the dead—which makes up, counting 'Alī, twelve *imāms*, or directors, considered impeccable and the objects of particular devotion. They are like so many divinities. And there we have mythology re-established in the heart of Muhammadanism.

Sunday is reserved for 'Alī, and also for his wife Fātima, the daughter of the Prophet; prayer addressed to him on this day wipes out sins. 'Alī is given the surnames of Murtaẓā ("the approved"); Ḥaidar ("the Lion of God"); Abu-Turāb ("the man of the dust"); this last name was given him by Muḥammad, who had found him asleep at the door of his house and had dragged him by the lappet of his mantle. He was born under the ascendancy of Mars, the sign of a bellicose temperament. In the moment between daybreak and sunrise a special prayer is said to him. His miracles are reckoned by thousands, but sixty are especially quoted.

Fig. 9. Jupiter and the Sign of the Lion
Below Saturn, Mercury, Jupiter, Venus, Mars.
Abu Ma'shar, "Treatise on Astrology" (Bibliothèque Nationale).

Fātima, surnamed "the pure," "the best of women," spoke already, before her birth, in her mother's womb. When she appeared in the world the earth was covered with flowers, tulips, and basil. The last hour of the night, the hour before daybreak, is sacred to her. Sunday also, as for 'Alī, is assigned to her.

The *imām* Ḥasan, the eldest son of the pair already named, is called Valī ("tutor"), Vazīr ("burden-carrier"), Zakī ("pure from all defect"), Sayyid ("lord"), etc. The second hour of the day is assigned to him, from sunrise to the disappearing of the ruddy gleams of dawn. He is strong to protect from unpleasantness, to help in achieving vengeance on enemies, in escaping from tyranny. Monday is reserved to him, and to his brother Ḥusain. This latter is the martyr of Karbalā, surnamed "the father of the poor." The time assigned to him is the third hour, at the moment of sunrise. Thanks to his interposition, divine compassion and forgiveness of sins may be attained; this ministry he shares with the Prophet and with Fātima.

The fourth *imām*, 'Alī, is named Zain al-'Abidīn ("the ornament of the devout") and *sajjād* ("the prostrate"); he displayed such ardour in prayer that one day Satan, having taken the form of a serpent, bit his toe without his interrupting his devotions. His mother was, they say, Shahrbānū, the daughter of the last Sasanid King of Persia, Yazdagird III, the son of Shahryār; hence the special veneration of the Persian Shī'ites for the lineage of the *imāms* descended from Ḥusain by this marriage, which seemed to them to carry on the dynasty of the ancient kings. The hour that falls to him is the fourth, from the rising of the sun until midday; Tuesday is his chosen day. He is invoked to obtain safety against a sultan's tyranny, or to become honoured at Court.

Muḥammad al-Bāqir, "the midwife of the sciences," so called because he brought them to birth, is the man of the fifth hour, and is invoked to aid in obtaining knowledge. Tuesday is assigned to him, as to his father and his son Ja'far. Ja'far aṣ-Ṣādiq ("the sincere") is the sixth *imām*; the sixth hour, noon, belongs to him; he is invoked to aid in accomplishing acts of devotion. His day is Tuesday, the same as for his father and grandfather. The seventh *imām* is Mūsā al-Kādhim ("who bridles back his wrath"); his is the seventh hour, when the midday prayer is ended; this is the moment when it is proper to comb the hair and the beard, invoking him the while. His mediation is sought for the healing of maladies internal and external.

Fig. 10. MARS AND THE RAM IN CONJUNCTION WITH JUPITER
On the right is the Sun. Below the five 'Stupefied planets.'
Abu Ma'shar, "Treatise on Astrology" (Bibliothèque Nationale).

The eighth *imām*, 'Alī, is named Riẓā ("satisfaction of God"). The eighth hour, that of the afternoon prayer, belongs to him. It is his to guarantee, when involved in prayer, a prosperous journey by land and by sea, a happy return to one's native land, and deliverance from home sickness. Muḥammad at-Taqī ("God-fearing") has the ninth hour, from the afternoon prayer to the end of the third quarter of the day. His intervention brings the boon of satisfaction with little, successive benefits, riches, gifts.

To the tenth *imām*, 'Alī an-Naqī ("the pure"), falls the tenth hour, from the beginning of the fourth quarter of the day until one hour before the yellow of twilight. His intervention is exercised for the securing of the rights of true believers, the doing of supererogatory works, the setting aside of the oppression of men, and the obtaining of old desires; Wednesday is the day reserved to him.

'Abdallah Ḥasan, called Zakī ("the pure"), is also called 'Askarī ("the soldier"), from a miracle in which he displayed a huge army between his two fingers. The eleventh hour is reserved for him, the hour that comes before the yellow hue of twilight. His intervention governs religious and worldly affairs, prevents all error in these matters, and makes men glad at all times. Thursday is his peculiar day.

Fig. 11. The Sun

Muḥammad al-Mahdī ("the well directed"), the twelfth and last *imām*, disappeared in a subterranean chamber that formed part of the house he lived in at Samarra, north of Baghdad, when he was between six and ten years of age. His intervention is efficacious to obtain victory over enemies and to repay loans. Friday is his day; and it will be on a Friday that he will return to announce the end of the world.

A few Shī'ite sects have gone still further; they are described by writers as "extreme"; among others there are the Ismailians, who gained notoriety in the time of the Crusades under the title of Assassins (*hashshāshīn*, eaters of hashish, or Indian hemp), the Druses, whom we have come to know in Syria, the Nuṣairīs, who are now called 'Alawīs, in the mountains of Latakia. These all united in admitting the incarnation of divinity in the person of the *imāms*.

Fig. 12. Jupiter

Let us keep to Persian soil. However bold the artists were, they never went so far as to represent 'Alī's countenance; his face is always modestly covered by a veil; as for the rest of his body, it is clothed in the same fashion as other Muslims of the period of the artist himself, who gave very little heed to local colour. According to native belief, such was the brightness of his countenance that onlookers could not endure his presence; besides, even had it been possible, men would not have been worthy of such a favour. The other *imāms*, his descendants, are treated similarly.[1]

There is another method also of getting round the difficulty, which is to make with interlaced letters the drawing of an animal to which exception cannot be taken, because it is merely letters. In this way figures of horses, eagles, lions, are drawn; the lion is

[1] See Muḥammad and 'Alī as flames and the veiled *imāms* in the colour plate facing p. 46.

especially in demand with regard to 'Alī, whose surname is "the lion of God." It is formed with the following Arabic verses:

> Call upon 'Alī, the object of the greatest marvels,
> Thou wilt find him a present help in trouble.
> All ills and all griefs will be scattered
> By thy holiness, O 'Alī! O 'Alī! O 'Alī!

These verses among others figure on certain little round disks made of a clay found near the tombs of 'Alī (at Mashhad-'Alī, in 'Irāq, the ancient Najat) and other saints, upon which the Persians place their foreheads when they pray.

Fig. 13. Venus

Like the rest of the Muslims, the Persians believe in judicial astrology, in the influence of the planets, among which they reckon the sun and the moon, because of their apparent movement in the heavens (Figs. 9 and 10). The sun is the principle of heat; the moon is the principle of moisture; the other planets give birth to cold and dryness. The sun's influence is fortunate, but this effect may be counterbalanced by the other planets. The most favourable among them is Jupiter, who presents an equable mixture of hot and moist; he is a cause of prosperity for the creatures under his care, he is "the great star of fortune." Venus is "the little star of fortune"; the conjunction of these two planets is an extremely favourable sign. On the contrary, Saturn and Mars are sinister; the first is "the great misfortune," deadly to all nature; he presents a mixture of cold and dry; the second follows him close; mingled hot and dry, he is "the little misfortune." Mercury is remarkable for the ease with which he changes his nature according to the environment in which he finds himself; hence he is called "the hypocrite."

Fig. 14. Saturn

The Muslims knew nothing of the polytheism of the Greeks and the Romans; when they quote, as we have just seen, the names of pagan divinities they merely refer to the stars of the same name; but by a kind of rebound they have personified the planets in their own fashion, and thus in turn constituted a very curious pantheon. The Moon presides over thieves and spies (Fig. 16); Mars over executioners, butchers, and all whose profession leads them to shed blood (Fig. 15); Mercury over authors and scribes (Fig. 17); Jupiter over magistrates, preachers in the mosques, men of religion, and all who profess to live grave and sober lives (Fig. 12); Venus has under her dancing-girls, female musicians, and almahs (Fig. 13);

Saturn is the patron of thieves and swindlers (Fig. 14); the Sun has in his care princes, sultans, and financiers (Fig. 11). In the Hofbibliothek at Vienna there is a manuscript that reproduces the attributes of these planets turned into divinities. Representations of angels are sometimes met with in the illuminated manuscripts; we give here (Fig. 18)

Fig. 15. MARS

Fig. 16. THE MOON

Fig. 17. MERCURY

figures of angels carved in half-relief on the ancient walls (now demolished) of Konia, in Asia Minor, and preserved in the museum of that town. These sculptures go back to the thirteenth century A.D.

The Persians believe in the existence of various supernatural beings more or less maleficent. Between Teheran and Ispahan there is an accursed region called Malak al-

Fig. 18. ANGELS FROM THE KONIA MUSEUM

Maut Dara ("Valley of the Angel of Death"), which can only be compared with the Hazār-Dara ("the Thousand Vales") to the south of Ispahan for sinister notoriety. A host of tales centre round these two places. There one is exposed to encounter with the *ghūls* and the *ifrīts*, the commonest and the most dangerous of the genii. They first endeavour to get the traveller away from the caravan; taking the shape of a friend or a relative, they call out for help, and if the traveller yields to these entreaties they take him off into a secluded place, suddenly resume their real shape, and tear him to pieces and devour him.

The *nasnās* is another monster, which appears in the shape of a feeble old man; he is generally met with seated on the bank of a stream, which he is unable to cross. When he sees the traveller coming up he asks him to help him over the water; if the traveller consents he gets up on his shoulders; but once they have reached midstream he winds his long legs round his bearer's neck and throws him down in the water, where he soon perishes.

Another kind of gnome is the *pā-līs* ("foot-licker"), who attacks only those who fall asleep in the desert. He kills his victim by licking the soles of his feet until he has sucked all the blood out of him. Two mule-drivers of Ispahan once found a way to be safe from his wickedness. Surprised by night in the desert, they lay down foot to foot on the ground and covered themselves over with their clothes. The foot-licker arrived and began to go round the sleepers to discover where their feet were, but as they had the soles of their feet planted against one another the demon circled round them in vain; he found nothing but their heads. In despair he gave up the search, muttering this verse:

> "I have travelled a thousand valleys and thirty-three, but never met a man with two heads."

The demon Al is dreaded by women, who do not hesitate to invoke him against their companions when they are angry. He attacks women in labour and tries to rend and devour their liver. Various precautions are taken against this calamity: sabres and other weapons are placed under the woman's pillow, and she is not allowed to sleep for several hours after her child is born; she is watched over by her friends, who cry "Yā Maryam!" ("O Mary!") whenever she seems to be sinking into a doze. We may note that the demon Al, like his *confrères*, is supposed to be fair-haired.

Men must be careful not to offend the *jinn*, for they would torment you to swooning; hence you must be on your guard. It is dangerous to fling a stone without pronouncing the name of God, for that stone might hit an invisible *jinnī* and blind him or injure him in some way. The *jinn* never forgive such an injury, and punish the guilty sooner or later. We may recall the tale of the *Thousand and One Nights* in which a careless fellow throws date-stones behind him as he eats; a stone knocks out the eye of the son of a *jinnī*, who seeks to be avenged upon the man who has unwittingly blinded his child. Rustam was able to fight and vanquish the *dīv*, notably the white demon (*dīv-i safīd*) in the mountains of Tabaristan (Fig. 19). Yet there was one more cunning than the rest, the demon Akwan, who took advantage of the hero's slumbers to snatch him up from the earth and hurl him into the sea (Fig. 20), an episode, however, that turned out far from ill for the legendary champion of Iran.

Among the *dīv* there are some the Persians call *nar*, *nara*, or males, because they are the most terrible and the wickedest of all. The most celebrated, the ones who did most harm to men in ancient times, are Damrukh Nara, Shelān Nara, Mardash Nara, Kahmaraj Nara, who made war upon the ancient kings (Fig. 21); one of these kings, Tahmurath, was named *dīv-band*, "gaoler of demons," for having vanquished them, taken them prisoner, and shut them up in dreadful mountain caves, where he kept them under guard.

Side by side with the *jinn* the Qur'ān knows the *jānn*, created before Adam; he is accordingly a pre-Adamite, such as La Peyrère thought he had discovered. His nature was that of the fire of the simoom, whence he had been drawn. To the Persians Jānn is the father of the *jinn*; he is called Tārnush in the *Book of Adam*. When his descendants had grown numerous upon the earth God granted them a religious law, to which he made them subject; they remained obedient to it until the end of one revolution of the fixed

Fig. 19. Rustam fighting the White Demon
From a lithographed edition of the *Shāh-nāma*.

stars, the duration of which is thirty-six thousand, or, according to others, eighty thousand two hundred years; but after this time they rebelled through pride; for punishment God caused them all to perish save the poor and the humble who had remained in the way of obedience; for governor he gave these one of themselves named Hilyaish.

After the expiration of another revolution of the fixed stars these also in turn rebelled; God destroyed them all save a small number that remained faithful, over whom he set a chief named Maliqā. At the end of the third revolution once more the children of Jann left the straight path and fell victims to the wrath of the Most High; the few that remained steadfast became in sequence of time an immense people ruled over by Hāmūs, celebrated

Fig. 20. The Demon Akwān hurling Rustam into the Sea
From a lithographed edition of the *Shāh-nāma*.

for his merits, his learning, and his uprightness; he spent his life in upholding the reign of justice and good. After his death the wicked disobeyed, and God sent them prophets to give them good counsel, but they would not hearken. At the end of the fourth revolution God sent a legion of angels to war upon them; they descended from heaven and fought against the children of Jānn, and slew the greater part of them; the remnant scattered through the islands and ruined places; some that had not reached years of discernment were made prisoners by the angels. Among these was Iblīs (the Devil, Satan), who accompanied the angels on their return to heaven, and was brought up among them; his education progressed so far that he was in turn appointed to teach them. The place where he engaged in preaching was at the foot of the throne of God; he was mounted

Fig. 21. THE PERSIAN KING KAI KĀŪS, HELD CAPTIVE BY THE WHITE DEMON, IS DELIVERED BY RUSTAM

From a copy of the *Shāh-nāma* in the Bibliothèque Nationale.

upon a pulpit of ruby, and over his head flew a banner of light. So numerous were his hearers that only the Deity could count them.

After many years the children of Jānn, having multiplied anew, came forth from the islands, from the ruins and desert places, took possession of the habitable earth, and abandoned the path of uprightness. Iblīs begged and obtained permission to go to them and preach sound doctrine to them; he came down from heaven upon the earth accompanied by a troop of angels; a small number of the sons of Jānn, who had remained faithful, hastened to enrol in his service. The archangel 'Azāzīl sent them as ambassador one Sahlūb, the son of Mulātib, to bring the people to the right path; but the rebels slew him without Iblīs knowing of it.

Seeing that the messenger was long in coming back, 'Azāzīl dispatched another, who found the same fate; then he entrusted this mission to certain of their own kin, but those impure beings treated them in the same fashion. Finally he sent to them Yūsuf ibn Waṣif, who by clever devices succeeded in escaping from them, and returned to bring back news of the situation. Iblīs, after obtaining authority to do so, set out at the head of a legion of angels to fight against them; he slew them nearly all, and scattered the survivors over the various regions of the earth. Become independent, he raised the standard of autocracy and claimed to be sole sovereign. "If the Creator," he said to himself, "entrusts the power to another I will refuse to recognize him." In a word, he saw himself perfect in theory and practice, and judged no one more worthy than himself to fulfil these high functions. Infatuated with himself, sometimes he was upon the earth and anon he set forth for heaven.

In these circumstances one day a group of angels went to contemplate the Tablet of the Divine Decrees; on their return Iblīs perceived the melancholy that darkened their brows. He inquired the reason. "We found," said they, "in the Tablet of the Divine Decrees that soon one of the archangels would be expelled from heaven and laid under an eternal curse; we are concerned over the fate that is awaiting one of us. We implore of you to entreat the Supreme King not to try any of us by this dreadful calamity; we are in the very depths of terror and affright." "Take no thought for this," rejoined Iblīs, "for this thing touches neither me nor you. I have known of this future project for many years, and I have never spoken of it to anyone." In his pride Iblīs paid no heed to the words of the angels, and thought neither of humbling himself nor of submission. And thus it was he earned everlasting condemnation.

At this moment there thundered forth in the ears of the inhabitants of the earth the divine word of the Qur'ān. God said: "I will appoint me a vicar upon the earth," and the creation of Adam was determined. "What," cried Iblīs, "could a creature created out of slime pretend to be above me, who was created out of fire? Earth is dense and dark, while fire is subtle and light." Thus he persisted in his fault and was damned.

CLÉMENT HUART

Fig. 22. SASANID DRAGON

Fig. 1. Idols of Easter Island

THE MYTHOLOGY OF THE KĀFIRS

Kāfiristān (the country of the unbelievers, the pagans) is that little-known part of Afghanistan which is bounded on the north by the Badakshan, on the south by the valley of Laghman (the ancient Lampāka) and Bajaur, on the east by the country of Dīr, on the west by Kohistān.

The inhabitants of Kāfiristān, whom certain writers regard as the descendants of the Greek settlers established in the country by Darius Hystaspes, belong racially and linguistically to the Indo-European family.

Thanks to its geographical position, Kāfiristān long remained isolated from the rest of the world; only at the end of the nineteenth century did a few travellers, mostly English, penetrate to the interior of the country and explore it. According to them, the Kāfirs, about 200,000 in number, are divided into three great tribes living in the most perfect harmony with one another. Commerce and industry are unknown in this region. The chief, and in a manner of speaking the only, occupation of the natives is cattle-breeding. They own enormous flocks of goats, eating the flesh and drinking the milk. The same animals' skin serves them for garments, the dark colour of which has caused them to be called by the Muslims round them the *Simposh*, which means " clad in black."

Down to recent years the Kāfirs practised a religion with mysterious rites that the Muslim conquest (1898) caused to disappear almost completely.

" Their religion," reports Sir Mountstuart Elphinstone,

> does not resemble any other with which I am acquainted. They believe in one God, whom the Caufirs of Caumdaish call Imra and those of Tsokooee Dagun; but they also worship numerous idols, which they say represent great men of former days, who intercede with God in favour of their worshippers.
>
> These idols are of stone or wood, and always represent men or women, sometimes mounted and

sometimes on foot. Moollah Nujeeb had an opportunity of learning the arts which obtain an entrance to the Caufir Pantheon. In the public apartment of the village of Caumdaish was a high wooden pillow on which sat a figure, with a spear in one hand and a staff in the other. This idol represented the father of one of the great men of the village, who had erected it himself in his lifetime, having purchased the privilege by giving several feasts to the whole village; nor was this the only instance of men deified for such reasons, and worshipped as much as any other of the gods. The Caufirs appear, indeed, to attach the utmost importance to the virtues of liberality and hospitality. It is they which procure the easiest admission to their paradise, which they call Burry Le Boola, and the opposite vices are the most certain guides to Burry Duggur Boola, or Hell.

Fig. 2. EQUESTRIAN IDOL
Kabul Museum.

General Court, in his unpublished papers, confirms the particulars given by Elphinstone:

> When the Kāfirs invoke the Supreme Being they give him the name of Amra (Imra or Yamri). Kassir and Bekassir are their idols; they are of stone, with metal masks. . . .
>
> The idols worshipped at Kattar by the Tarkhemes are different; they are called Boruk and Dirkhel. To their idols they sacrifice animals like oxen, sheep, and goats, which they fell and slaughter as we do; sometimes they kill them with the sword.
>
> They have four principal feasts. The first, which they call Katche, takes place in autumn. The second, called Taskhe, corresponds to the Qurbān of the Muslims; each family must sacrifice a goat. The third, which they call Manrouh, is looked upon as the New Year. The fourth, called Neminide, takes place in the spring.

Fig. 3. CARVING MOUNTED ON A STAKE PLANTED ON THE TOMB OF A WARRIOR
Kabul Museum.

Sir George Scott Robertson, the Political Agent at Gilgit, penetrated into Kāfiristān in 1890; he saw a great number of idols. All these images, he tells us, "are carved on conventional models, and are made solely with axes and with knives. The more ponderous kinds are roughly fashioned in the forest, and are then brought into the village to be finished."

We have no precise information about the images of the divinities properly so called—Imra, Boruk, Dirkhel. The Kāfiristān idols now in the Kabul Museum represent deified ancestors, and may be linked up with Iranian archetypes. The clothes are very coarsely and crudely indicated; no attempt at individualization is to be observed in those flat, round, or rectangular faces (Fig. 4), which remind us in a surprising fashion of those of the colossal statues on Waihu (Easter Island). An equestrian statue of slightly more careful execution belongs to the same type (Fig. 2). (Note the decoration of the costume and compare the dagger fixed on the breast with the arms of

KAFIR FAMILY
(From a drawing in the possession of Comte Philipon.)

Fig. 4. IDOLS FROM KĀFIRISTĀN
Kabul Museum.

the Kāfir warriors in the colour plate facing p. 58.) A piece of wood (Fig. 3) rudely squared out is surmounted by the representation of two men facing one another; their legs cross, and they are holding each other by the shoulders. This piece was on a warrior's tomb. Sir George Scott Robertson saw a great number of these, of the same type, in the valleys of Bashgul and Dungul. After the country of the heathen became Nūristān (the country of light) the representations of the old gods almost completely disappeared. The idols in the Kabul Museum represent all that survives of the ancient pantheon of the Kāfirs.

J. HACKIN

Fig. 1. FRIEZE
Amarāvatī.

THE MYTHOLOGY OF BUDDHISM IN INDIA

BUDDHISM was born on the banks of the Ganges; and it was on the banks of the Ganges that it was most rapidly forgotten.

This doctrine, preached by its founder, the Buddha Ṣākyamuni (563–483 B.C.?), spread rapidly through Northern India, thanks to the conquests of King Aṣoka (274–237 B.C.), one of the Maurya dynasty, a fervent adherent of the new religion. The same potentate sent missionaries to spread the gospel in Kashmir and Gandhāra in the west, in the Himalayan regions, in Southern India, and as far as Ceylon. He raised pillars and monuments bearing inscriptions that have enabled us to identify the holy places of Buddhism, and to recognize the site of vanished townships whose names, associated with that of the Master, are venerated in Buddhist countries.

The Emperor Kanishka, of the Indo-Scythian dynasty of the Kushāns, continued Aṣoka's work in the second century of our era (A.D. 120–162, according to V. A. Smith). His sway extended over Bactria, a part of Central Asia, the Panjab, Gandhāra, and the western part of Northern India. The Buddhist texts ascribe to him the part of Protector of the Faith; he convened a council to put an end to heresies that had newly sprung up. The monuments in the region of Gandhāra bear witness to the prosperity of Buddhism during his reign. It was there that under the sway of the Greek satraps there arose a school of Hellenistic art, the influence of which extended as far as the Far East.

Thereafter Buddhism endured the vicissitudes due to changing dynasties. Vanished, or nearly so, in Gandhāra after the invasion of the Ephthalite Huns, led by Toramāna and the ferocious Mihiragula, it was maintained by King Harsha Ṣīlāditya of Kanauj (606–647). The advent of the Pāla dynasty in Bengal (eighth to eleventh centuries) retarded its decline.

There were left only a few great religious centres, such as the famous university of Nālanda, when the Muslim conquests ruined its last sanctuaries and drove out the last of the monks.

Buddhism is now forgotten in the India of to-day, except in the kingdom of Nepal and the island of Ceylon. But the Far East still remains under its sway.

We must distinguish, in considering the mythology and the pantheon of Buddhism, the elements borrowed from pre-existing religions, the contribution of the primitive Buddhism and the creations of the school of the Mahāyāna.

From Brahmanism the new religion retained, while developing and modifying them, the belief in transmigration and the idea of a world peopled with gods, creatures half

Fig. 2. LOKAPĀLA
Sānchī. *Photo Goloubev.*

divine, inferior genii in constant intercourse with men. The gods (*devas*) live in paradises of sensuous pleasures or intellectual delight. Shorn of their prestige, inferior to the saints, they play in the legend a part comparable to that of the ancient chorus in the drama. They frequently descend to earth, accompany the Buddha, exhort him to preach his Law, listen to his sermons, are present at his miracles, strew celestial flowers over the gathering of the monks. They are often to be seen on the bas-reliefs, hovering in air, holding garlands above the head of the Master.

Brahmā and Indra are the only two who have kept their individuality. But they are now nothing more than simple acolytes of the Buddha. Brahmā, come down from his paradise, Brahmalōka, takes on the aspect of a Brahman ascetic. Wearing the chignon of plaited tresses, he holds the waterpot in his hand. Indra, under the name of Ṣakra, presides over the heaven of the thirty-three gods. He figures frequently in the story of the previous lives of the Buddha. When supernatural intervention becomes necessary the throne of Ṣakra grows burning hot. The attention of the god is thereupon drawn to terrestrial happenings, and he hastens to the aid of the Bodhisattva. He is richly clad, covered

Fig. 3. Nāga worshipping a Stūpa
Amarāvatī. *Photo Goloubev.*

with jewels, and has a high tiara or a turban on his head. Sometimes he carries his Vedic attribute, the thunderbolt.

Māra is the tempter, the Satan of the Buddhist legend. God of love and death, derived from the Mṛityu and Kāma of the *Vedas*, his part is to delay the coming and the preaching of the Law. He reigns over the sphere of the pleasures of sense: the earth, the underworld, and the first six storeys of the heavens. He commands an army of demons. His three daughters are Thirst, Sexual Pleasure, Carnal Desire.

Below the gods are the Lokapālas, or the "four great kings," the guardians of the cardinal points of the compass; they watched at the doors of the *stūpas* of Barhut and Sānchī (Fig. 2). Kuvera, or Vaiṣravaṇa, the chief of the Yakshas, good or evil genii, reigns over the region of the North. Virūdhaka is the sovereign of the South. His subjects, the Kumbhāṇḍas, are pot-bellied gnomes with short limbs. Dhṛitarāshṭra, in the East, leads the Gandharvas, who are celestial musicians. Virūpāksha, in the West, is the King of the Nāgas, those fantastic creatures which play one of the most important parts in the legend.

They are the snakes that live at the bottom of lakes in marvellous palaces with fabulous treasures. A precious stone imbedded in their throat or their skull gives them magical powers. Masters of the rains, they determine the prosperity of a whole region. Frequently they assume a human shape. But a broad cobra hood spreads above their head. Sometimes their human torso ends in the folds of a serpent's tail. Generally they are devout and grieve for their fall; for in spite of their supernatural powers they are inferior to man. They can be dangerous; a subtle poison emanates from their body. Certain evildoing Nāgas were converted by the Buddha.

Their enemies are the Garuḍas, giant birds that feed upon them. The carrying off of the Nāgas by the Garuḍa is often represented in art, and had a great vogue in Cambodia as a decorative theme. In India the Garuḍa gradually assumed a human shape, retaining nothing of the bird of prey but the wings and the beak turned into a hooked nose.

Over against these powerful beings we must set the damned. Some are wandering spectres, the Pretas. Their mouth, tiny as the eye of a needle, does not allow them to eat or drink, and they have the balloon-like bellies of the starving. The others are scattered through the hells, which are arranged in storeys according to the tortures inflicted in them. The infinite variety of these torments bears witness to the imaginative powers of the authors of the legend.

All these creatures live, die, and transmigrate. None of them is immortal. None knows in what wretched condition he will have to be reborn, by way of expiation of the forgotten transgressions he committed in a previous existence. This instability, this perpetual change, is figured by the Buddhist image of Bhavachakra. The creature swings round that "wheel of life" whose spokes enfold the worlds divine, human, animal, and infernal. The treatises on discipline enjoined that it should be painted at the entrance of monasteries to inspire the monks with the desire for Nirvāna. A few fragments survive in the veranda of the seventeenth cave at Ajanta.

The primitive doctrine added to the category of already known deities only the Buddhas and the Bodhisattvas.

The Buddhas are men. They have lived lives of charity, devotion, and serenity. Their merits in previous lives, in accordance with the law of retribution for deeds, have allowed them to attain to absolute wisdom. They are omniscient, freed from passions, assured, at their death, of escape from transmigration; they will not be born again; they will enter into Nirvāna. The last Buddha was Gautama, or Ṣākyamuni. Later the Buddha Maitreya will come and preach the doctrine, renew the dying faith.

Fig. 4. THE FIRST PREACHING
Sānchī. *Photo Goloubev.*

This latter is still only a Bodhisattva. The term indicates a stage in the career of absolute sanctity. A Bodhisattva is one who will attain perfect knowledge (Bodhi) in the course of his next human existence. The texts give this title to Ṣākyamuni up to the night of the Enlightenment, the night during which his meditation attained the absolute, during which he became a Buddha.

About the first century of our era the Mahāyāna created a whole new pantheon. To the human Buddhas it opposes celestial Buddhas, or " Buddhas of meditation " (Dhyāni-Buddhas). They reign in the Paradises that in the Far East, more than Nirvāna, become the goal of the believer. The cult of the female divinities spread. Under the influence of the magic doctrines men learned to invoke the terrible forms of these ancient representatives of absolute charity.

Fig. 5. THE ENLIGHTENMENT
Sānchī. *Photo Goloubev.*

LIFE OF THE BUDDHA ṢĀKYAMUNI

To understand the illustrations of the scenes of the life of Buddha a few iconographic notes will be useful.

The ancient Indian school never depicted the founder of the religion. On the bas-reliefs of Bharhut, of Bodh-Gayā, of Sānchī, and sometimes of Amarāvatī the place of Ṣākyamuni is taken by a symbol that indicates his presence in the scene portrayed. But merely accessory details would not have sufficed for recognition of the legend illustrated, in the absence of the principal personage. A series of conventions therefore were evolved in the school, which remedied this difficulty. They are known to us from the explanatory inscriptions of the Bharhut carvings.

These symbols were adapted to the acts of the Buddha. The wheel surmounting an empty throne or a pillar indicated a preaching scene. The bas-reliefs showing worshippers in adoration before this emblem represent the first preaching, although the persons composing the congregation are rarely in accordance with the texts (Fig. 4).

The tree was more especially reserved for the meditation. The fig-tree is the symbol of

Fig. 6. THE BUDDHAS OF TIMES PAST (FRAGMENT)
Sānchī. *Photo Goloubev.*

the Enlightenment of Ṣākyamuni. This episode, one of the most important of the Buddhist legend, is portrayed in the same way as the preceding one: the worshippers pay homage to the tree under which the Blessed One attained to perfect knowledge (Fig. 5).

Fig. 7. THE PARINIRVĀNA
Sānchī. *Photo Goloubev.*

This rule, however, is not an absolute one, and mistakes are possible unless the species of the tree represented is noted. In actual fact tradition has attributed to each one of Ṣākyamuni's predecessors a special tree in the shadow of which he attained to Bodhi. The sculptures of Bharhut have preserved the names of these trees for us, and the aspect of their foliage. At Sānchī the seven Buddhas "of time past" were often represented by a line of trees surrounded by worshippers (Fig. 6), or by alternate trees and *stūpas*. The future Buddha, Maitreya, may be reçognized by the flowerets among the foliage of the *champaka*.

In the actual life of Ṣākyamuni other trees are met with besides the fig. The *jambu* symbolizes the first meditation of the adolescent youth in the shade of the rose-apple-tree (see Fig. 8). The *ṣāla* is found in the scenes of the Parinirvāna.

The *stūpa* was a commemorative monument often raised over relics. Its funerary character caused it to be accepted as a substitute for the image of the dying Buddha. While in certain bas-reliefs it still represents a building, it is more frequently employed to symbolize the death of Ṣākyamuni (Fig. 7).

Lastly, in episodes referring neither to meditation nor to preaching the Indian artists made use of other emblems. A rectangular flagstone stood for the ambulatory (*chankrama*) where the Buddha walked (see Fig. 25: "The ambulatory in the midst of the waters"). The empty throne, the footprints, the parasol above an empty space, are also frequent. They

Fig. 8. THE GREAT DEPARTURE
Sānchī. *Photo Goloubev.*

may be brought together on the same bas-relief. Indeed, the artists often grouped several episodes in the same panel. This habit continued in the Gandhāra school; it is found also in the composition of the Ajanta paintings.

Thus on the lintel of a door at Sānchī (Fig. 8) we see the departure from home (the groom holds a parasol above the riderless horse), the arrival in the forest, the farewell of Ṣākyamuni to his servant (the footprint symbol), the groom's return to Kapilavastu, while a *jambu*-tree, the emblem of the first meditation, evokes the dawning of the religious vocation. Sometimes an episode is inserted into a panel with the sole object of assigning a place to the scenes in the midst of which it figures. On a pillar at Sānchī the dream of Māyā placed above a royal *cortège* indicates that it is setting out from Kapilavastu.

Fig. 9. THE NATIVITY
Sānchī. *Photo Goloubev.*

There is one motif in the repertory of the ancient school in which no substitute appears for the image of Buddha. That is the Nativity. Māyā is sitting or standing upon a lotus, the emblem of miraculous births. Two wild elephants (*nāgas*) are sprinkling her from waterpots which they hold with their trunks. The infant Buddha is absent (Fig. 9). This picture has passed into Brahman iconography like that of Ṣrī, the goddess of fortune. In the Gandhāra school the formula of the Nativity was completely changed.

To this school was due the creation of the plastic type of the Buddha, according to the view put forward by M. Foucher and generally accepted (Fig. 10).

Quite recently M. Coomaraswamy has tried to restore to the Indian school of Mathurā the honour of having been the first to portray the features of the Blessed One.

Symbolism, however, did not disappear. In Buddhist art, as in Hindu art, we find many conventional elements a knowledge of which is indispensable for the understanding

Fig. 10. INDO-GREEK BUDDHA
Foucher Collection, Louvre.

and identification of the scenes. With the attributes, which after the fashion of the Brahman divinities the Bodhisattvas hold in their multiple hands, we must note the *mudrās* (ritual gestures) and the *āsanas* (postures of the lower limbs).

The legend of the last human Buddha, as it has come down to us, evidently enshrines incidents that are historical. But is seems impossible to discriminate between the myth and the facts whose memory was transmitted by tradition. Folklore, stories of miracles,

THE BIRTH OF THE BUDDHA
(Musée Guimet.)

the intervention of the gods, and the creation of the Buddhist pantheon have 'embellished' and distorted the primitive legend from which in any case supernatural elements can never have been lacking.

Thus the first episode of the life of the Buddha is not placed in the world of men, but in the Tushita heaven. There the Bodhisattva completes his last existence but one. He preaches the Law to the assembly of the gods, consecrates his successor, Maitreya, the human Buddha of the future, and proceeds to the four great scrutinies: what age, what continent, what country, what family will be worthy of his birth.

The family chosen is that of the Rajah Ṣuddhodana, of the caste of the Kshatriyas, the King of the Ṣākyas. The texts delight in describing the splendour of this monarch and the beauty of his capital, Kapilavastu, situated in the region of India bordering on Nepal. Yet he seems to have been only a petty sovereign, the chief of an aristocratic principality.

Fig. 11. Descent from the Tushita Heaven
Amarāvatī. *Photo Goloubev.*

His wife Māyā saw one night in a dream a white elephant with six tusks enter into her through her right side. This dream, which figures in the bas-reliefs, became, both in tradition and in the texts that came later, the true incarnation. Fig. 11 shows us the descent from the Tushita heaven. The Bodhisattva, in the shape of an elephant, is carried in a palanquin by dwarf, pot-bellied genii, in the midst of a *cortège* of *devas* flying in the air and making the gesture of adoration. The upper panel of the same bas-relief represents the Preaching in the Tushita heaven. The Bodhisattva is portrayed in it, according to the ancient custom, by symbols—the print of his feet upon an empty throne before a tree.

Around the bed of Māyā, who lies on her right side in accordance with the formula of the ancient school, the four Lokapālas mount guard. The queen's serving-women sleep in careless attitude (Fig. 12). The elephant, which usually appears above Māyā, does not figure on this bas-relief. The Gandhāra school, more careful of verisimilitude, represented Māyā lying on the left side; thus the Bodhisattva could enter through her right flank, as the texts have it. Amazons armed with pikes took the place of the Lokapālas.

On the morrow Brahmans interpreted Māyā's dream. A son would be born to her who would bear upon his body the signs of great monarchs. If he would consent to reign he would be a *Chakravartin* (sovereign of the world); but if he should abandon his wealth to adopt the life of the wandering ascetics he would become a Buddha and deliver men from the sufferings caused by old age, sickness, and death.

The birth of the Bodhisattva was no less miraculous than his conception.

The queen, feeling the end of her pregnancy drawing near, went to the Lumbinī Garden, outside the enclosure of the city. The exact site of this garden (the present village of Rummindeī) has been discovered, thanks to the commemorative pillar set up by King Aṣoka. Here it was that in the posture in which every mother of a Buddha must give birth, standing, and holding the branch of a *ṣāla* in her raised right hand, she brought into the world Siddhārtha,[1] who issued from her right hip without wounding her. Indra received the babe upon a celestial cloth (Fig. 13).

Fig. 12. THE CONCEPTION
Amarāvatī. *Photo Goloubev.*

Two Nāgas, Nanda and Upananda, appearing half out of the sky, made two streams of water, cold and hot, for the new-born babe's bath. According to another tradition, the bath was given by the gods Indra and Brahmā.

Then the babe took seven paces in the direction of each of the points of the compass, proclaiming his future glory. Lotus-flowers sprang up under his feet.

The different phases of the birth are often grouped together in the same bas-relief. In representations of the old Indian school the print of the feet is visible on the cloth held by the gods, and a lotus cross on the ground indicates that the Bodhisattva has walked in the four directions.

Fig. 13. BIRTH AND ADOLESCENCE OF THE FUTURE BUDDHA
Foucher Collection, Louvre.

Siddhārtha was taken back to Kapilavastu. There a Brahman sage, the *ṛishi* Asita, came

[1] Siddhārtha is the name the Bodhisattva bore "in the age." When he had renounced the world he was called Gautama and Ṣākyamuni.

to visit him. This sage came hastening down from the mountains, where he led a life of meditation, to honour the superhuman being of whose birth he had learned. Accompanied by his nephew Naradatta, Asita went to the palace, recognized on the infant's body the thirty-two signs of a "great man" and the eighty secondary marks that indicated his vocation for the religious life. The king and the queen, sitting on a throne, listened to the horoscope, while Asita, holding the Bodhisattva on his lap, expressed by a gesture his grief that he must die without hearing the Buddha preach.

Māyā died seven days after Siddhārtha's birth, in accordance with the destiny of all mothers of the Buddhas. Their hearts would break if they saw their sons renounce the world to adopt the life of wandering ascetics. She was born again in the heaven of the thirty-three gods.

It was Mahāprajāpatī, Māyā's sister and Ṣuddhodana's second wife, who brought the boy up. A few episodes of his youth have remained famous.

One of them is the manifestation in school. The Bodhisattva, sitting in the midst of his fellow-pupils, with a writing-tablet placed upon his knees, astonishes his teacher by his intuitive knowledge. Games and physical exercises were equally occasions for prodigies.

It was at an uncertain period, varying, according to the text, from infancy to manhood, that Siddhārtha for the first time gave himself up to meditation. He was in the country and saw ploughing.

> Seeing the young grass torn up and scattered by the share, covered with the eggs and the young of the slain insects, he was seized with profound grief as though it had been the massacre of his own kin. And seeing the ploughers, their faces withered with dust, the fierce sun and the wind . . . the most noble of men felt the utmost compassion.[1]

Fig. 14. Indo-Greek Bodhisattva
Foucher Collection, Louvre.
A.G. photo.

He sat down in the shade of a rose-apple-tree, in the prescribed attitude, and "concentrated his thought." The hours went by; he still continued to meditate. His companions found him fixed and immobile; and in spite of the progress of the sun, though the shadow of the other trees had shifted round, the shade of the rose-apple-tree continued to protect the youth. This scene is distinguished from the other meditations by the rich lay costume worn by the Bodhisattva: scarves, necklaces, bracelets, earpendants, turban or tiara adorned with precious stones. This costume he was to retain through the whole of his worldly life (Fig. 14).

Meanwhile Siddhārtha continued his career as royal prince. The marriage hour arrived. But the father of the lovely Gopā, or Yaṣodharā, refused to give his daughter to an "idle fellow," a stranger to the noble arts of fencing, of boxing, of wrestling, etc. . . . A tourney was arranged in which Gopā was the prize. The Bodhisattva triumphed over all his opponents. One difficulty arose in the archery contest: every bow broke when Siddhārtha sought to bend them. The bow of his grandfather Simhahanu, that no man had ever availed to bend, was sent for. The Bodhisattva, "without rising from his seat, seized

[1] *Buddha Charita*, Book V, pp. 5–6.

it with his left hand and bent it with a single finger of his right hand."[1] The arrow pierced through a series of iron drums and buried itself in the earth twenty miles away (Fig. 15: "The contests and the marriage").

The Bodhisattva thereafter led a life of pleasure in his palace, surrounded by his women,

Fig. 15. The Contests and the Marriage
Foucher Collection, Louvre.

musicians, and dancers. He knew nothing of real life, of its sufferings, and even of its brevity. But the religious vocation was to awake in him under the influence of certain visions that taught the young man the sadness of human life.

These are the four celebrated encounters, a theme that never attained in Indian art the success that might have been expected from its dramatic power.

Fig. 16. The Life of Pleasure in the Women's Quarters
Louvre.

The prince desires to go to the pleasure-garden. Stringent orders are given by the king to keep away from his route "everything that might not delight the eye of the young man or might be disagreeable to him." But chance, or the will of the gods, sets in his path an old man, "broken and decrepit, with veins and sinews standing out all over his body, with teeth falling out, his body covered with wrinkles, bald, stooped, back bent like the joists of a roof."[2] The driver of his carriage tells the prince that all men are subject to decrepitude, "that there is no other way out for created beings." Siddhārtha, troubled by this revelation, returns to the palace.

In the course of two other excursions the Bodhisattva discovers the existence of sickness and death: finally, an encounter with a wandering ascetic inspires him with the desire to seek in the religious life a serenity exempt from the passions.

The idea of departure haunts him. The king's surveillance becomes closer. Armed

[1] *Lalita-Vistara*, Chapter 12. [2] *Lalita-Vistara*, Chapter 14.

soldiers keep guard upon the gates of the city. The women are ordered to keep the prince amused (Fig. 16). In vain; the prince sleeps through concerts and dances. His final resolution is reached in a night of sleeplessness. Siddhārtha, fully awake, sits upon his bed and contemplates the women of his harem, the musicians, the attendants all sunk in slumber. "Some are dribbling, smeary with spittle; others grinding their teeth; others snoring, talking in their sleep. Their mouths lie wide open, their garments all disordered" [1] (Fig. 17). He seems to be in a graveyard among corpses rotting away.

Fig. 17. THE SLEEP OF THE WOMEN
Louvre.

The Bodhisattva calls for his horse Kaṇṭhaka. He leaves the palace accompanied by his faithful squire Chhandaka. The gods cast the guards into sleep, open the massy iron gates, and form a triumphal *cortège* for the prince. The Lokapālas place their hands under his horse's hoofs and deaden the sound of his steps (Fig. 18).

This scene forms part of a unit comprising the four principal episodes of the life of the Buddha, frequently reproduced upon steles. They are: (1) "The Great Departure or the Birth"; (2) "Enlightenment" (passing of the Bodhisattva into Buddhahood); (3) "The First Preaching"; (4) "The Entry into Nirvāna."

Fig. 18. THE GREAT DEPARTURE
Amarāvatī. *Photo Goloubev.*

When he has come to a sufficient distance from Kapilavastu Siddhārtha strips off his princely array. He gives over his jewels to Chhandaka, cuts with his sword the knot of his hair and flings it to the wind. The Trayastrimṣas gather it up and preserve it piously in their paradise.

Then the Bodhisattva changes his garment of "Benares muslin" for the coarse, russet-coloured garb of a hunter. Henceforward he will lead the solitary, roaming life of the wandering devotees, living on alms, covered with the long tunic of the monks, which he will wear until his death.

The search for truth led him to become the disciple of Brahman ascetics. But their learning appeared to him empty and vain; it did not lead to emancipation. Ṣākyamuni sought a practical solution to the problems of which he caught a fleeting glimpse in the four encounters. They taught him a most subtle philosophy. But the path of deliverance, the remedy for old age, for sickness, for death, was not to be found amid these hair splittings.

[1] *Nidāna-Kathā.*

He went, then, from master to master, until the day when he determined to induce revelation by the practice of asceticism. Accompanied by five disciples, he withdrew to Uruvilvā, on the banks of the river Nairañjanā. There, for six years, he gave himself up to terrible austerities, living exposed to the sun, to the rain, without change of posture, reducing his daily food to one single grain of rice.

This trial established the defeat of the Brahman theories then in favour. Many sects vaunted asceticism. The Buddha, in the sequel, enjoined upon his disciples to follow the "middle way," equally far from the easy life of the Brahmans who remained "in the world" and from barren and exaggerated penances.

As a matter of fact, Ṣākyamuni perceived that he was going farther away from the end he sought. With weakness of body came lassitude of spirit. His meditation was no longer strong enough to arrive at perception. He decided to take more food, to recover his vanished strength. A girl, Sujāta, had prepared a dish of rice cooked in milk as a pious offering. She brought it to the Bodhisattva in a golden bowl. He accepted it, and went down to the river-bank and bathed. (See the section entitled "Javanese Mythology," p. 240.)

He now goes in the direction of Bodh-Gayā. From his body proceeds a light of such radiance that a Nāga king, Kālika, is disturbed by it in the deeps of his underground dwelling. He comes out with his wife from the pond he lives in, and, bowing respectfully, hands joined in the gesture of adoration, he pays homage to the Bodhisattva.

Ṣākyamuni spreads a truss of grass under the fig-tree of Wisdom. Seated upon this carpet of sward, he pronounces the following prayer:

> "Here upon this seat may my body wither, may my skin, my bones, my flesh, dissolve, if before I have obtained the understanding hard to obtain in the space of many *kalpas*, I raise my body from this seat." [1]

But the evil powers are on the watch. Māra assembles his army of demons and sends it to disturb the Blessed One's meditation. They have grimacing faces, bodies out of proportion, animal's muzzles, sometimes a second face in their bellies. On foot or mounted upon elephants they brandish various weapons without succeeding in inspiring fear in the Bodhisattva (Fig. 20). He is protected by the 'perfection' of his wisdom. The earth itself bears witness to it when, stretching out his right hand to it, he asks it to be his surety.

Sensual temptation by the daughters of Māra fails in like manner. Placed near Ṣākyamuni, they show him the thirty-two magics of women. They display modest or provoking attitudes, they dance and sing for his pleasure (Fig. 19). They try the sixty-four magics of desire. They say to him, "Behold these women with faces like unto the moon, with mouths like unto the new lotus, with the sweet, ravishing voices, with teeth like silver and snow." He replied, "I see the body filled with impure matters and a family of worms, soon attacked by destruction and infirmities." [2]

The Bodhisattva, left alone, meditates during the three watches of the night. This is the supreme moment of the legend, the acquiring of Buddhahood. His spirit, completely freed from all impure elements, goes about the world, sees beings living, dying, transmigrating. He recalls his previous existences, discovers the chain of causes and effects,

[1] *Lalita-Vistara*, Chapter 19.

[2] *Lalita-Vistara*, Chapter 21.

and conceives pain, the production of pain, the annihilation of pain, and the way that leads to the annihilation of pain.

This "Enlightenment" could not but be a common theme for Buddhist artists. It forms part of the four great ritual scenes. But the impossibility of distinguishing it from the other meditations led the artists to adopt, as the symbol of the passing to complete Buddhahood, one of the episodes immediately before or after: the assailing of Māra, the temptation of the flesh, the "taking to witness" indicated by the gesture of the hand (*bhūmisparṣa mudrā*), or the devotion of the Nāga Muchilinda, who protects the meditating Buddha from the storm by making a seat for him with his own folded body and by sheltering him under his expanded hood.

Fig. 19. THE TEMPTATION
Amarāvatī. *Photo Goloubev.*

It is now time for the Blessed One to eat. The four great kings bring him bowls. He accepts them, and by his supernatural power transforms them into one. The religious devotee, in fact, must own nothing beyond the necessary.

Two paths then offer themselves to the Buddha. He can now enter into Nirvāna or put off his own deliverance and dwell upon earth to spread the gospel. Thus he will bring salvation to suffering humanity. Māra urges him to leave this life. He hesitates. The gods hasten to him. Grouped about Ṣākyamuni, they implore him, beg him, to preach his Law. The Blessed One yields to their supplications.

He determines to convert, in the first place, the five disciples who had borne him

Fig. 20. THE ASSAILING OF MĀRA
Sānchī. *Photo Goloubev.*

company in the years of his asceticism. They had abandoned their master when he had renounced his penances. Since then they have lived at Sārnāth, near Benares, in the Deer Park (*Mrigadāva*).

At the sight of the Buddha they plot among themselves :

"Here comes the Ṣramana Gautama, that flabby one, that glutton, spoiled by his slackness. We must have nothing to do with him; we must neither go to meet him with respect, nor rise up;

neither take his monk's garments from him nor his begging-bowl; we must not give him a mat, nor a prepared beverage, nor where to set his feet." [1]

But a supernatural impulse constrains them to rise, to make room for him, to show their respect. The Buddha preaches to them the doctrine he has elaborated during the night of Enlightenment. They are to be the first members of the community of monks.

Fig. 21. THE FIRST PREACHING AND THE PARINIRVANA
Amarāvatī. *Photo Goloubev.*

This first preaching is distinguished from similar scenes by the presence of two gazelles, which places it in the park at Benares. Small matter, then, if the disciples are few or many, or if, as in Fig. 21, their place is taken by a group of *devas*. It is always the sermon at Benares that is intended.

Sometimes a wheel is placed between the gazelles. This indicates that the Buddha " is setting the Wheel of the Law in motion," the Buddhist expression for the expounding of the doctrine.

Now begins the cycle of the Preaching, which was to continue four-and-forty years. The Buddha, followed by his disciples, goes from city to city, from village to village, preaching, converting, according to the texts, all his hearers. The community of monks expands. They accompany the Master, clad like him in the russet-coloured tunic. But they are distinguished from him by the absence of the signs of the Buddha: the protuberance on the skull (*ushṇīsha*), the woolly tuft between the eyebrows (*ūṛnā*) (Fig. 22).

Certain episodes of the career of Ṣâkyamuni as Buddha were very popular in Indian art.

These are first of all the accessory miracles, which, with the four principal scenes described above, form a group frequently reproduced.

The Submission of the Elephant. This episode forms part of the cycle of Deva-

[1] *Lalita-Vistara,* Chapter 26.

datta, the cousin and enemy of the Buddha. On two occasions he had sought to slay the Blessed One. He prepares a new snare for him with the help of Ajātaṣatru, the King of Rājagṛiha. The royal elephant Nalagiri is made drunk, to make him furious; he is let loose in the city at the hour when the Buddha makeṣ his customary round of almsgiving. The inhabitants flee in terror. The drunken beast demolishes houses, smashes carts to matchwood, tramples upon the passers-by. In vain do the disciples of the Blessed One

Fig. 22. HEAD OF THE BUDDHA
Musée Guimet.

implore him to go back to the monastery. " This Nalagiri is a cruel and untamable beast. Of a surety he knows nought of the merit of the Buddhas. Let the Blessed One withdraw." The venerable Ṣāriputra entreats the Master: " Lord, it is laid upon the eldest son that he should do service to the father. I will triumph over this animal." Then Ananda, the beloved disciple, moved by his deep affection for the Master, exclaims: " Let this elephant slay me first! " and throws himself in front of the Blessed One. But Nalagiri is conquered by the power of the benevolence of the Buddha. His intoxication falls away from him. He prostrates himself at the feet of Ṣākyamuni.

The Great Miracle of Ṣravasti. King Prasenajit had organized a contest of prodigies between the Buddha and the Tīrthyas, in order to confound this heretical sect.

Fig. 23. THE SUBMISSION OF THE ELEPHANT
Amarāvatī. *Photo Goloubev.*

The various miracles accomplished by the Blessed One are enumerated in a lengthy narrative. Two episodes of this struggle of supernatural powers have been perpetuated by the Buddhist artists.

The first is known by the name of the "twin miracles," miracles of fire and water.

Bhagavat entered into a meditation in such wise that as soon as his spirit gave itself to it he disappeared from the place where he had been sitting, and, soaring into the air toward the West, he then appeared in the four attitudes of decency—that is to say, he walked, he stood upright, he sate, he lay down. He next attained the region of light, and no sooner was he therein than divers lights escaped from his body, blue lights, yellow, red, white, and others having the most beautiful hues of the crystal. He caused also many marvels to appear: from the lower part of his body there gushed forth flames, from the upper part issued a rain of cold water. That which he did in the West he accomplished likewise in the South, and the same he repeated in the four points of space.[1]

We sometimes meet with representations of Buddha in the Great Miracle. Flames come out of the shoulders and water flows from the feet in sinuous waves; for it is the rule that the prodigy is reproduced several times. The flames and the water jet out alternately from the upper and lower parts of the body.

The second episode is that of the multiplication of the Buddhas. Indra and his gods are placed on the Buddha's left hand; Brahmā is on his right.

The two Nāgas, Nanda and Upananda, created a lotus of a thousand leaves, large as a chariot-wheel, entirely of gold, and its stalk of diamond, and came to present it to Bhagavat. And Bhagavat sat on the pericarp of this lotus, with legs crossed, body upright, and applying his mind to recollection. Above this lotus he created another; and upon this lotus Bhagavat appeared similarly seated. And in like mannner before him, behind him, around him, appeared masses of Blessed Buddhas created by him, who, elevating themselves even to the heaven of the Akanishthas, formed an assembly of Buddhas, all created by the Blessed One.[2]

The Indian artists have given the most varied interpretations of this prodigy. Sometimes the magic Buddhas, in serried ranks, cover the whole wall of a sanctuary. Sometimes, reduced to two, they enframe the central Buddha. Sometimes even they have disappeared, and only the huge lotus upon which Ṣākyamuni sits in meditation informs us that it is still the Great Miracle.

The Monkey's Offering. A monkey came and offered the Buddha a bowl of honey. In his joy at seeing it accepted by the Master "he began to leap and dance here and there, so much that he tumbled into a hole, lost his life, and was immediately reborn as the son of a Brahman." [3]

The Conversion of the Kāṣyapas. Among the innumerable conversions recounted by the texts we shall refer only to that of the famous Brahman ascetics, the three Kāṣyapa brothers. They lived at Uruvilvā, with a thousand disciples. A series of miracles was needed to bring them to the Buddhist faith.

In the room where Kāṣyapa tended the sacred fire there was a poisonous Nāga. The Buddha obtained permission to spend the night there. A struggle in magic powers began between the serpent and the Blessed One. By turns the opponents emitted clouds of smoke and flames; the temple seemed to be on fire. The ascetics, grouped outside, grieved for the monk delivered over to the Nāga's wrath.

In the morning the Buddha came forth and held out to Kāṣyapa his begging-bowl in

[1] Burnouf, *Introduction à l'histoire du Bouddhisme indien*, pp. 162–163. [2] Burnouf, pp. 164–165.

[3] Foucher, *Art gréco-bouddhique du Gandhāra*, p. 513.

which lay the serpent deprived of his venom. "Indeed and in truth," thought the Brahman, "the great Ṣramana possesses vast magic powers and supernatural faculties. But I am holier than he" (Fig. 24: The temple of the fire. Behind the altar the Nāga spreads out his cobra hood. The ascetics gathered about the temple. The Buddha is not shown, as is the rule with the ancient school).

Fig. 24. The Miracle of the Fire
Sānchī. *Photo Goloubev.*

The hermits were unable to cleave the wood for the sacrifice. At the Buddha's order it split of itself. The fire of the altar could not be lit without his permission; then it became unquenchable. (See p. 95.)

"Nevertheless," said Kāṣyapa, "I am a greater saint."

The rains made the river overflow. Ṣākyamuni turned the waters back. In the midst of the flooded plain he reserved for himself a place "of dry land covered with dust." He was walking up and down this when a boat came up full of ascetics who had come to rescue him. Then Kāṣyapa recognized his superiority and was converted with all his disciples. He was subsequently one of the heads of the community (Fig. 25).

The Buddha and his Family. Ṣākyamuni's family no longer plays anything but a very subordinate part in the legend. He felt no need to see his native land again, and it was at the express request of Ṣuddhodana that he came to Kapilavastu, several years after the Enlightenment. Then for the first time he saw his son Rāhula, born, according to the texts, on the very day of the great departure, or some time after.

Fig. 25. The Water Miracle
Sānchī. *Photo Goloubev.*

The Buddha enters within the city. He begs from door to door, like a true monk. A meal is offered him at the royal palace. Yaṣodharā, the abandoned wife, dresses her son in his handsomest clothes and shows him the Blessed One: "That monk is thy father. He possessed great treasures that we have not seen since he renounced the world. Go thou and claim thy heritage." The boy attaches himself to the Buddha's heels and follows him throughout the city, crying: "Monk, give me my heritage!" Arrived at the Nyagrodha grove, where the community was, Ṣākyamuni confers upon his son the ordination of the religious (Fig. 26).

It was with a joyful heart, full of filial love, that Rāhula became a monk. It was otherwise with Nanda, the Buddha's half-brother. His marriage had just been celebrated with the most beautiful woman of the land. The Blessed One came to his door to beg. Nanda hastened to fill the begging-bowl, but the Buddha refused to take it, and in silence went away to his hermitage. Out of respect for the Master Nanda dared not ask him to relieve him of that encumbering bowl, and he followed him therefore till they came among the monks. Then the Buddha called a barber, caused his brother's head to be shaved, and constrained him to put on the religious habit (Fig. 27: Below to the left Nanda and his wife; on the right the Buddha refuses to take the bowl; above is the ordination of Nanda).

Fig. 26. THE CARRYING OFF OF RĀHULA
Amarāvatī. *Photo Goloubev.*

He was unhappy. The thought of his wife haunted him. He dreamed of escaping. One day he was entrusted with the charge of guarding the monastery. He resolved to flee away after carefully closing the doors of the house. "But when he would have shut the doors, scarcely had he closed one leaf when the other leaf sprang open again; hardly had he closed a single-leafed door when another door flew open." The hour of the monks' return drew near; he set off. On the way he saw from afar the Buddha coming; he hid himself behind a tree. "But the god of the tree raised the tree into the air, so that Nanda stood there in the full light." His attempt at escape had failed.

Some time after that Ṣākyamuni led him up on the mountain, where they beheld an old blind monkey. The Blessed One asked his brother: "Hath thy wife a face as beautiful as this monkey's?" Nanda thought indignantly within himself: "My wife is so lovely that she has few peers among humankind; why does the Buddha now compare her to this monkey?"

Then the Buddha led him to the heaven of the thirty-three gods, to a magnificent palace inhabited by five hundred *devīs*. They explained to the monk: "In Jambūdvīpa there is a disciple of the Buddha named Nanda; the Buddha has constrained him to leave the world; because he has left the world he must after his death be born into this celestial palace to be our *deva*." [1]

Nanda recognized the fact that his wife was no more than an ugly ape beside these *devīs*; and, returning to the monastery, he redoubled his zeal in order to ensure his rebirth

[1] Chavannes, *Contes*, No. 409.

into the heaven of the thirty-three gods. But the Buddha took him into hell, where he saw a cauldron of boiling water that was reserved for him. Because of his carnal desires he was to fall into this at the termination of his divine existence. Terrified, he studied the doctrine and became a saint (*Arhat*).

Fig. 27. THE CONVERSION OF NANDA
Amarāvatī. *Photo Goloubev.*

Numerous members of the family of Buddha entered into the community. His adoptive mother Mahāprajāpatī was the first Buddhist nun; but her giving up of the life of the world does not seem to have brought her into intimacy with Ṣākyamuni.

The one who appears constantly at the Buddha's side, accompanies him in his travels, tends him, surrounds him with an affection very far from compatible with the detachment prescribed for a disciple, is Ananda, the Blessed One's cousin. His life of devotion is summed up in these words of Buddha, when Ananda wept for the approaching death of his master: "Be not disturbed; weep not. . . . Long hast thou been close to me, Ananda, by thy acts, thy words, thy thoughts of love and tenderness infinite that never changed. Thou hast done well, Ananda!"[1] And, addressing the monks, the Blessed One said: "All the Buddhas of times past have had disciples as devoted as Ananda. And all the Buddhas to come will have disciples as devoted as Ananda. Ananda is a sage."[1]

It is Ananda whom we shall find tending the Buddha in his last moments.

The Parinirvāna Cycle. This includes the period of preparation for entry into Nirvāna, the journey from Rājagriha to Kūṣinàgara, the last sermons, sickness, death, the obsequies.

The Buddha, accompanied by Ananda, leaves Rājagriha, where he dwelt on the Vulture's Peak. He takes the road again, but no longer wanders taking chance roads or meeting chance adventures. He passes again through the cities he had most specially frequented—Nālanda, which had a university famous in the Middle Ages, Pātaliputra, the future capital of the Maurya kings, Vaiṣālī. Everywhere he convenes his disciples to leave them his last instructions: rules of "spiritual life" to the monks, of practical morals to the lay faithful.

Ṣākyamuni withdraws to Beluva during the rainy season. He falls seriously ill, but by an effort of the will he triumphs over his sickness. He must not die without taking leave of the order of monks. The old man's lassitude appears in a discourse to Ananda: "I am

[1] *Mahāparinibbāna-Sutta,* Chapter 5.

old, Ananda; my journey draws to an end; I have reached the bounds of my life; I am eighty years old. And just as a worn-out old cart can only be made to run at the cost of infinite care, so the body of the Tathāgata can keep itself in life only by a great effort." Henceforth the community is self-sufficing; the Wheel of the Law has been set in motion; the Buddha may die.

But he is tempted to live, and in this tale the man appears through the saint. It is within his power to stay on earth, to put off death. He tries to move Ananda to an entreaty to which he would willingly yield. Sitting at the foot of a tree, he addresses his disciple:

> "Beautiful, O Ananda, is the land of Vaiṣālī, the land of the Vrijis; beautiful is the Chaitya Chāpāla, of the seven mango-trees, of the many young men, the fig-tree of Gautama, the grove of the *Ṣālas* the place where the burden is laid down, the Chaitya where the Mallas hang up their hair. Varied is Jambūdvīpa; life there is sweet for men. That being, Ananda, whosoever he may be, who has sought out, understood, given out, the four principles of supernatural power can, if anyone asks him to do so, live either through a whole kalpa or until the end of the kalpa. Now, O Ananda, the four principles of supernatural power are possessed by the Tathāgata." [1]

Fig. 28. THE WAR FOR THE RELICS
Sānchī. *Photo Goloubev.*

But Māra perturbs the disciple's mind. Ananda fails to divine the Buddha's meaning; he does not make the longed-for response. Three times Ṣākyamuni repeats the phrase. Ananda remains dumb, silent. The Buddha is to die. It is at Kūṣinagara he succumbs to dysentery caused by an indigestible dish eaten at the house of the smith Chunda of Pāvā.

Ananda had made ready his bed between two *sāla*-trees. It was not the season of flowers, yet these trees were covered with blossoms that shed themselves upon the Blessed One. The Gandharvas make the skies resound with melody. Ananda weeps, forgetting the Master's teachings. The Mallas of Kūṣinagara file past before the dying saint. He meditates, and from trance passes into Nirvāna. He dies lying on his right side, his legs laid out at length one upon the other, surrounded by his disciples in tears.

[1] Burnouf, p. 66.

The next day the Mallas make all ready for the funeral ceremonies. They wrap up the corpse according to the royal rites. A pyre is built. The fire lights of itself when the venerable Mahākāṣyapa arrives. A divine rain extinguishes it when the body is entirely consumed.

Fig. 29. THE DISTRIBUTION OF THE RELICS—DEPARTURE OF THE AMBASSADORS
Amarāvatī. *Photo Goloubev.*

As soon as the tidings of the death of the Buddha reach the places of his preachings the kings and the heads of governments claim a share of his ashes. The Mallas of Kūṣinagara put forward their demand to keep the relics of the Master. A war is imminent. The armies of the princes are about to besiege the city; troops of fighting elephants, horsemen, archers, arrive at the foot of the walls. Resistance is organized. Armed soldiers watch on the battlements of the citadel, and even at the windows of the houses (Fig. 28). The Brahman Drona invokes the pacifist doctrine of the Buddha to advise the sharing of the relics. The ambassadors carry away in urns the ashes of the Blessed One (Fig. 29).

Seven *stūpas* will be erected on Indian soil above the sacred relics. The eighth, at Rāmagrāma, will be entrusted to the Nāgas. Later, King Aṣoka sought to deprive

Fig. 30. THE VISIT OF AṢOKA TO THE STŪPA OF RĀMAGRĀMA
Sānchī. *Photo Goloubev.*

them of their wardship, but he was obliged to leave it to them, so much did the Nāgarāja's offerings to the *stūpa* surpass those that could have been made by men (Fig. 30). Long, long after, travellers lost in the jungle that had overrun Rāmagrāma saw wild elephants sweep and water the sacred soil, and decorate the ruined *stūpa* with garlands of flowers. The animals, more faithfully devout than men, preserved the memory of the Master.

THE JĀTAKAS

Often it befell that the disciples gathered about the Master would question him upon the practice of a virtue or upon the causes of an event such as a recent snare laid for him by Devadatta. " It is not the first time," he would reply, " that Devadatta shows himself to be treacherous," and he would tell a story of the past.

This story would unwind itself, a long narrative or a brief apologue, a legend fantastic or very simple. The heroes were gods, Nāgas, or men; animals in many cases. His discourse at an end, the Buddha would indicate the moral lesson enshrined in it, and identify the principal characters; for it would be no fable, but a true tale from one of his previous existences. In fact, when a sage attains Bodhi he acquires at once the gift of

Fig. 31. Vessantara-Jātaka
Sānchī. *Photo Goloubev.*

memory. Man knows not whence he comes, while all his acts are ineluctably determined by the merits or the sins accumulated in the course of the ages. He is rich because he gave alms in a preceding life. He is hunchbacked for having mocked at an ascetic. He will suffer through the one he has ill-treated. Only a Buddha knows the linking of causes and effects.

Nothing could be more edifying than the recital of these " Jātakas." Ṣākyamuni had given unrivalled examples in them of the practice of the virtues, and the great law of retribution appeared there in its mechanical operation, freed from the veil with which death and forgetting cover it.

The hearer learned from these how he himself could fix the frame in which his future destiny would be set. By virtue of a wish uttered at the moment of performing a good action he might obtain the privilege of being reborn into such and such a family, of becoming reincarnated in a magnificent body like Anupama the " incomparable." Further still, he might prevent death from severing the ties of affection. The united household is formed anew in another existence, and throughout the ages Yaṣodharā was the wife of the Buddha.

After a dry exposition of the doctrine the devout layman was entertained with the wiles by which the virtuous Amarādevī succeeded in shutting up the four great persons who were laying siege to her in a basket from which they came forth, after a woeful night, only to be the butt of the sarcasms of the King and the Court. He was moved by the devotion shown by animals. He trembled at the tales of the adventurous journeys of merchants, through the jungle peopled with brigands and ghouls, or over the seas, exposed to shipwrecks, to the rage of the fabulous monsters and the demons that inhabit the unknown islands.

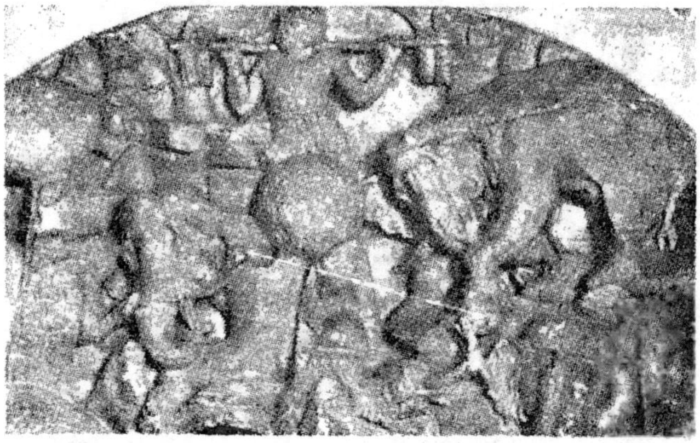

Fig. 32. SHADDANTA-JĀTAKA. THE ELEPHANT PULLS OUT HIS TUSKS
Amarāvatī. *Photo Goloubev.*

Shaddanta-Jātaka. A herd of wild elephants lived by a lake in the Himalayas. Their leader, the Bodhisattva, was a royal elephant with six tusks (Shaddanta), his body white as snow, his head and feet red. One day as he roamed with his two wives he knocked against a blossoming tree. Chance sent the pollen and the petals showering over one of the wives, while the other received only twigs and dead leaves. Devoured with jealousy, she sought some way of being revenged. A pious offering to an ascetic gave her the opportunity to make this prayer: " May I be reborn in a royal family and have this elephant killed." She allowed herself to die of hunger. Her wish was fulfilled. Becoming the chief wife of the King of Benares, she pretended that she had seen in a dream an elephant so beautiful that she could not live without a pair of his tusks. An unscrupulous hunter set out for the forest. He dug a trench on the edge of the lake and placed himself in ambush in it, bow in hand, disguised as a holy man.

The Bodhisattva was struck by a poisoned arrow. " So great was his anguish that he came near to killing his foe." But he recognized the yellow robe of the monks, " emblem of holiness sacred in the eye of the sage." He asked the hunter the explanation of his deed, and at once understood the cause of the queen's strange desire. He knelt down to let the man saw off his tusks; but the saw could not bite on the ivory. The Bodhisattva had to take the tool with his trunk and help his slayer. Then only did he die (Fig. 32).

Fig. 33. MAHĀKAPI-JĀTAKA
Sānchī. *Photo Goloubev.*

Returned to Benares, the hunter brought the tusks to the queen. She laid them on her knees and thought of the one she had loved so greatly in her previous existence. Then such grief flooded over her that her heart broke, and she died the same day.

Mahākapi-Jātaka. This tale exalts " the perfection of energy." The Bodhisattva was a monkey-king. He was accustomed to go with his suite of eighty thousand monkeys to disport themselves in a mango-tree. The King's archers were ordered to surround it and exterminate the marauders.

They could only escape by crossing the Ganges. A bamboo rope was fastened to the branch of a great tree. The Bodhisattva tied the other end to his girdle and with a prodigious leap cleared the river, but the rope was too short to allow him to reach the bank. He could only seize a tree with both hands, and over this living bridge the eighty thousand monkeys passed safely (Fig. 33).

Now the traitor Devadatta was one of the Blessed One's following. Animated by his habitual malevolence, he dropped on his back and broke his spine. The King of Benares received the Bodhisattva on a quilt. Before he died the latter had time to set forth certain moral verses and enlighten the King upon the conduct fitting for a monarch.

Fig. 34. VESSANTARA-JĀTAKA
Sānchī. *Photo Goloubev.*

Vessantara-Jātaka. The generous nature of Prince Vessantara showed itself on the very day of his birth. He was born with his eyes open, and immediately stretched forth his hand and declared: " Mother, I desire to do charity."

At the age of sixteen he married the princess Madrī, by whom he had a son and a daughter.

The Bodhisattva distributed all his goods in alms. " Those who wished to eat were fed; those who desired clothes were given them; those who wished to have gold, silver, or jewels were given as much as they would; every man was granted according to his desire, and no wish was denied."

Now the prosperity of the realm depended upon the possession of a white elephant, born the same day as the prince, and endowed with power to cause rain.

The king of a neighbouring country sent Brahmans to Vessantara to beg the gift of this luck-bringing animal. Disguised as holy men, they betook themselves to the house of almsgiving, and, holding out their hands, they entreated the prince. At once he had a ewer brought to perform the prescribed rites of donation. The people were indignant, and insisted on the banishment of Vessantara. He went forth accompanied by Madrī and his children, not before he had exhausted his wealth by the " gift of the seven hundreds " (seven hundred elephants, seven hundred chariots, seven hundred girls, seven hundred slaves of both sexes). They met four Brahmans who had not been able to get to the city in time for the distribution of alms. To each of them the Bodhisattva gave one of his horses, and he yoked himself to the chariot (Fig. 34). Before long he gave this up to another beggar. Madrī carrying their daughter and Vessantara their son, they went on toward the Himalayas on foot. They built hermit huts on Mount Vanka, and there lived

Fig. 35. VESSANTARA-JĀTAKA
Sānchī. *Photo Goloubev.*

the ascetic life. The Bodhisattva gave himself up to meditation. Madrī went out every morning to look for wild fruit and roots, their only food.

Now there was, in the kingdom of Kalinga, an old Brahman afflicted with the twelve kinds of ugliness. He was too poor to buy the slave that his young, lazy, ill-natured wife demanded to help her in the tasks of the household. Knowing Vessantara's generosity, he set out to find him. Arriving in the forest, he waited for Madrī to be away, and approached the Bodhisattva. In barbarous language he asked him to give him his children as servants. Terrified by his brutality, the children fled and took refuge in a lake, hiding their heads under the leaves of the water-lilies.

Fig. 36. CAPITAL
Sānchī.

But Vessantara called them back. Their entreaties, their rebellion, could not soften him, so supremely did he possess the " perfection of benevolence." He saw the Brahman drag them away, striking them with a withy; and only when they had disappeared from sight he wept bitterly (Fig. 35).

Madrī returned late; the gods, in order to spare her this painful scene, had taken the shapes of lions and tigers and barred the path to the hermitage from her. Huge was her despair: but another trial awaited her. On the morrow it was she herself that Ṣakra, disguised as a Brahman, came to ask for, and obtained, from the charitable prince (Fig. 37).

It would have been cruel to put off till another existence the reward of this incomparable generosity. Hence Ṣakra, at the moment when he was taking Madrī away, disclosed his identity. The children were ransomed by their grandfather; the sentence of banishment was revoked, and Vessantara returned to his kingdom with great state.

Ṣibi-Jātaka. The King of the Ṣibis was more generous still. A dove, pursued by a sparrow-hawk, flew down upon his knees and implored his protection. The two birds were no other than Ṣakra and one of his *devas*, seeking to test the King's charity. For he had made a vow to save all living things. But was he not condemning the hawk to death

Fig. 37. VESSANTARA-JĀTAKA
Sanchī. *Photo Goloubev.*

in depriving it of "freshly killed" flesh, its customary food? The Bodhisattva redeemed the dove with an equal quantity of his own flesh.

He himself cut the flesh from one of his thighs.

> The King sent for a pair of scales and put his flesh over against the dove; but the body of the dove became heavier and heavier, while the King's flesh grew lighter and lighter; the King gave command to cut the flesh off both his thighs; but when all had been taken it was still too light and insufficient. They cut away successively his two buttocks, his two breasts, his chest and back, and when all the flesh of his body had gone the body of the dove outweighed it still. The King then gave his whole body as offering, and it weighed exactly as much as the dove.[1]

Ṣakra, resuming his divine shape, sent a celestial physician to heal the wounds of the Bodhisattva. (Fig. 38: The dove in the King's lap. At the foot of the disk the flesh is being cut from an arm. The balance is at the side.)

Champeyya-Jātaka. The King of the Magadhas, fleeing before the foe, plunges into a river. He falls before the palace of the King of the Nāgas. A treaty of alliance is concluded; every year the Nāgarāja comes up from his home in great state and joins his friend on the bank.

The Bodhisattva was then a poor man. Envious of the serpent's splendour, he accumulates meritorious deeds so that he may be born again into the aquatic world. His prayers are granted, and he becomes the Nāgarāja Champeyya. Yet he feels regrets at the sight of his body "like a great garland of jasmine." His wife, the young Nāgī Sumanā, cannot console him for this. And in fact a serpent cannot observe the Law and attain to Emancipation.

[1] Chavannes, *Contes*, No. 197.

On the days fixed by previous Buddhas for fasting Champeyya leaves his palace and returns to the world of men. He stations himself on an ant-heap, which he lights up with the radiance from his body. His coils are white like silver; his head is like a red woollen hood.

A serpent-charmer sees him. He culls magic herbs and draws near, uttering a sacred formula. At once the ears of the Bodhisattva are as though transpierced by burning brands. Nevertheless he takes care not to turn his poisonous breath in the direction of the Brahman. The man wounds him. He spits out one of his herbs upon the serpent; and at every point of his body touched by the herb a blister forms. He strikes him with his cudgel, breaks his fangs, and shuts him up in a wicker basket. Henceforth the Nāga must obey his master's orders—dance, unfold his hood, perform tricks on the public streets.

Fig. 38. Ṣibi-Jātaka
Photo Goloubev.

At Benares they give a performance to the King. The entertainment is interrupted by Sumanā, the Nāgī. A supernatural sign had warned her of her husband's fate. Hovering aloft in the air above the royal palace, she begins to moan. The story of Champeyya is related to the King of Benares. The Bodhisattva is set free. "Then he glides into the calyx of a flower, where he abandons his serpent shape and reappears in the guise of a young man magnificently attired." He takes the King of Benares to his palace and offers him his treasures. Hundreds of chariots are laden with these, and since that time the soil of India has retained the colour of gold.

Story of the One-horned Ṛishi. There are several versions of this Jātaka. One of these, which is preserved in a Chinese translation, might be found carved on a Gothic capital. It is, as a matter of fact, constructed on the theme of the *Lay of Aristotle.*

The *ṛishi* One-horn (Ekaṣṛinga) was the son of an ascetic and a doe. Born in the forest, brought up by his father, he knew nothing of the world save his hermitage. He had no trouble, therefore, in devoting all his time to the study of the sacred books. By the practice of ecstatic trance he obtained supernatural faculties.

> One day when he was descending the mountain-side heavy rain was falling and the soil was muddy and slippery; as his feet were not wholly in keeping with his person he fell and hurt his foot; at once, in great anger, he ordered, by means of a magic formula, the rain to cease; by the effect of the happiness-producing virtue of the hermit all the Nāga divinities caused that there should be no more rain. As there was no more rain the cereals and fruits were no longer produced: the people were at the end of their resources and had no more means of subsistence.[1]

The King of Benares took counsel with his ministers upon the causes of this drought. There was only one way to remedy it: to reduce the sage Ekaṣṛinga to the condition of an ordinary man. If he committed a sin the effect of his magic formula would cease at once.

A courtesan offered to seduce him; she even engaged to return to the city mounted astride of the ascetic's neck. She set out for the forest accompanied by five hundred women. There they built huts of branches beside One-horn's dwelling, and clad in bark presented themselves to him as anchorites.

Now the young man had never seen a woman. Gladly he accepted the good clear wine, which they said was water, the cakes they christened fruits.

> When the hermit had eaten and drunk to repletion he said to the women: "Since I was born I never found fruits nor water like to these." The women said to him: "We practise good with all our heart; that is why heaven grants our desires and we find these fruits and this water." The hermit asked the women: "Whence comes it that the colour of your skin is so gleaming and so fresh?" They replied: "It is because we always eat of these good fruits and drink of this excellent water." The hermit rejoined: "Why do you not establish yourselves here?" They replied: "We can well remain here."

At once a great rain fell, which lasted for seven days. Ekaṣṛinga had lost his magic power.

The provisions were exhausted; the *ṛishi* found the forest fruits and the mountain water most insipid. He agreed to go with the courtesan to the place where those succulent fruits were grown. Some distance from the city she feigned fatigue and pretended she could go no farther. One-horn proposed that she should get up astride of his neck. And thus they came into the city, where the anchorite remained for a few days. But the desire for the life of contemplation laid hold of him again, and he went back to his hermitage. He presently recovered his supernatural faculties.

Ṣyāma-Jātaka. Ṣyāma also lived in the Himalayas with his blind parents. The poisonous breath of a serpent had deprived them of sight. As a matter of fact, in a previous existence Ṣyāma's father had been an oculist by profession; at his wife's instigation he had destroyed one eye of a patient who was a bad payer. As punishment for this sin they lost the use of their two eyes.

Every day the Bodhisattva went to look for wild fruits, drew the water, swept the hermitage. He never ate until his parents were full fed, and he got up thrice every night to find out "if they were too hot or too cold."

Now the King of Benares came to hunt in the forest. He saw Ṣyāma go down to the brink of the river, fill his jar, put it back on his shoulder. and call together the train of

[1] Chavannes, *Contes*, No. 453.

stags that always accompanied him as he went. The King, surprised to encounter a man in these deserted regions, asked himself: " Is this a god or a Nāga? If I show myself he will take flight if he is a god, or will bury himself in the earth if he is a Nāga. But I shall not always be remaining in the Himalayas. Soon my servants will be asking me if I have not seen any marvels in my journey. If I describe this being without being able to name him they will reproach me for my ignorance. I will therefore wound him so that he may not escape me."

He sent a poisoned arrow that struck Ṣyāma in the right side and came out by the left side. The King questioned the young man. He replied without anger and described the condition of his parents. " Their life is near to extinction. Their provisions will be exhausted. They will go here and go there in the forest, uneasy because I am belated. In vain they will imagine they hear the sound of my steps and feel my caresses."

The King, deeply touched, promised the Bodhisattva to devote his life to the old people and to serve them as though he were their own son. Then he went to tell the hermits of Ṣyāma's death. In spite of their despair they did not reproach him. Led to the lifeless body of the young man, they mourned and lamented.

But there is one resource for the Sage, the testimony of his virtues. The mother proclaimed: " If it is true that Ṣyāma has done none but virtuous acts, let the poison in his veins lose its strength and become harmless! If he has never uttered a lie, and has tended his parents night and day, let the poison be conquered and dispersed! May the merits we have accumulated, his father and I, triumph over the violence of the poison. Let Ṣyāma live again! "

This invocation was repeated by the father, and by a *devī*, Bahusodarī, who had given birth to the Bodhisattva in a previous existence. The young man rose up, and his parents recovered their sight.

BUDDHAS AND BODHISATTVAS

We have lingered a little to tell the legend of Ṣākyamuni. His predecessors, the Buddhas of past time, are in Indian literature what they were in Indian art—mere names occasionally quoted. Bas-reliefs or paintings show us the group of the last seven Buddhas accompanied by Maitreya. They are recognizable only by the place they occupy or by the foliage of their Bodhi-tree.

Only the Buddha Dīpankara is represented individually. But he owes this favour to the vow he received from the young Sumati, the future Ṣākyamuni, the vow to attain Bodhi (*Pranidhāna*). His legend therefore comes from the cycle of the Jātakas.

The Dhyāni-Buddhas of the school of the Great Vehicle (Mahāyāna) are very different from the saints of primitive Buddhism. They bear the imprint of the evolution of the doctrine in a more philosophic and more emotional direction. A new cosmology also appears. In infinite space and time innumerable Buddhas coexist. They rule over " Lands of Buddha " (*Buddha-Kshetra*), including millions of worlds which they illumine by their radiance.

The elect of their Paradises, myriads of Bodhisattvas, proclaim their glory eternally.

They are veritable gods, according to our Western conceptions. They receive and grant the prayers of the faithful.

If we except the Nepalese representations, we do not find in India portrayals of the Dhyāni-Buddhas singly. Often they adorn the faces of a *stūpa* in groups of four. But they appear more often in little figurines decorating the tiara of the Bodhisattvas, who are their spiritual sons.

The most celebrated of the Dhyāni-Buddhas is Amitābha (Infinite Light), or Amitāyus (Infinite Life). He governs, in the West, a " happy land," Sukhāvatī, wherein live only

Fig. 39. Dhyāni Bodhisattva
Fresco in the Ajanta Caves. *Photo Goloubev.*

beings destined to salvation. In the time of the Buddha Lokeṣvararāja Amitābha was a monk, Dharmākara. He then vowed to attain to Bodhi. And in a long invocation he described the Land of Buddha over which he would reign. The beings who should people it would all be of marvellous beauty, golden of colour, divine of aspect. They would possess the utmost perfection of supernatural powers. They would remember their previous existences; they would know the most secret thoughts of others. Sin would no more exist for them, and they would be assured of leaving Sukhāvatī only to enter into Nirvāna. At their mere desire treasures of jewels would appear, trees covered with precious stones, which a perfumed breeze would cause to resound with sweet melodies. Innumerable Buddhas would emerge from the rays of gigantic lotuses. Whosoever should concentrate his thought upon the paradise of Amitābha would be assured of rebirth into it.

From Amitābha emanates a heavenly Bodhisattva, Avalokiteṣvara. He dwells near his spiritual father in the " Happy Land." He is the Compassionate, " the Ocean of Pity." He has delayed his entrance into Nirvāna to succour suffering humanity and direct it upon the Path of Emancipation. He protects from shipwreck, from assassins, from robbers, from savage beasts. (He is sometimes represented in the midst of scenes illustrating the " eight perils.") He heals passions, hastens to the aid of whosoever invokes him.

Buddhist iconography knows no less than one hundred and eight shapes of Avalokiteṣvara, from the human form to the shape " with the thousand arms." Various names correspond to these different aspects. The most common are Lokeṣvara (Lord of the World) and Padmapāni. The image of Avalokiteṣvara was placed, in the temples, at the entrance of the sanctuary. Covered with jewels, like all the Dhyāni-Bodhisattvas, he wears in his high headdress a little figure of the Buddha Amitābha. His right hand generally makes the gesture of charity. His principal attributes are the pink lotus (*padma*) and the rosary.

The Bodhisattva Mañjuṣrī is the master of transcendental wisdom. The grammarians place their labours under his ægis.

According to a Nepalese tradition, he was born in China, on the mountain Pañcaṣikha (of the five peaks). Coming to Nepal, he is said to have dried up a lake and erected religious edifices. We are told that he descended to the bottom of the ocean to impart the doctrine to the Nāgas. At once many thousands of serpents became Bodhisattvas. The daughter of Sāgara, King of the Nāgas, though but eight years old, attained the condition of Bodhi.

> At this moment, the venerable Ṣāriputra thus addressed the daughter of Sāgara, King of the Nāgas: "Thou hast but conceived the mere thought of the state of Buddha, O my sister, and thou art incapable of turning back; thou hast boundless knowledge; but the state of Buddha perfectly accomplished is hard to attain. My sister is a woman, and her vigour slackens not; she has done good works for hundreds, for thousands, of kalpas; she is accomplished in the five perfections, and yet even to-day she doth not win Buddhaship. And why? Because a woman cannot even to-day obtain the five places. And what are these five places? The first is that of Brahmā; the second that of Ṣakra; the third that of Mahārāja; the fourth that of Chakravartin; the fifth that of a Bodhisattva incapable of turning back."
>
> . . . Thereupon the daughter of Sāgara, King of the Nāgas, in the sight of all the world, in the sight of Sthavira Ṣāriputra, suppressing in herself the signs that indicated her sex, showed herself endowed with the organs that belong to a man, and transformed into a Bodhisattva, who went in the direction of the South. In this part of space was the universe called Vimala; there, seated near the trunk of a Bodhi-tree made of the seven precious substances, this Bodhisattva showed himself attained to Buddhaship perfectly accomplished, bearing the thirty-two characteristic signs of a great man, having his body adorned with all the secondary signs, illuminating with the splendour that surrounded the ten points of space, and performing the teaching of the Law.[1]

The attributes of Mañjuṣrī are the sword, the book, and the blue lotus. In the shape of Mañjughosha he is seated upon a lion.

[1] *Lotus of the Good Law*, Chapter 11.

Fig. 40. TORANA OF THE STŪPA OF SĀNCHĪ
The miracles of the serpent, and of the fire and the wood.

The Bodhisattva Maitreya belongs to a more ancient tradition, linked to the great stream of Messianic ideas that preceded the Christian era.

He still awaits in the heaven of the Tushitas the period of his last rebirth. He will be of the Brahman caste, the son of Brahmāyus and Brahmāvātī, and his life will be a faithful reproduction of that of Ṣākyamuni, for the last earthly existence of the Buddhas is always the same.

Fig. 41. MAITREYA WITH THE AIGUIÈRE
Foucher Collection, Louvre.

After the Enlightenment he will go to the mountain Kukkutapāda, in the neighbourhood of Gayā. There the venerable Mahākāṣyapa rests in the state of Nirvāna. The Buddha had entrusted to him his own robe, woven of gold, and had charged him to deliver it to Maitreya when he should have attained Buddhaship. When Kāṣyapa " desired to die " he went to the mountain, wrapped himself in the sacred garment, and uttered a prayer. Then the mountain opened and closed again upon him. At Maitreya's arrival the three peaks will move apart, Kāṣyapa will come forth from his retreat and deliver the robe of investiture to Maitreya, and after performing various prodigies will enter into Nirvāna.

The Mahāyāna invokes the authority of Maitreya to prove its superiority over the Hīnayāna school. According to the Indian, Chinese, and Thibetan traditions, the doctrine of the Yogāchāra sect was revealed to the monk Asanga (fifth century A.D.) by this Bodhisattva, in the Tushita heaven.

Like Ṣākyamuni before the Enlightenment, Maitreya wears a rich lay costume. He is recognized by his beaded chignon and *aiguière*, which denote his future condition as a Brahman (Fig. 41).

Vajrapāṇi is a name borne by two members of the Buddhist pantheon. The one is a *yaksha*, the faithful acolyte of the Buddha in Gandhāra art. He appears at the moment of the great departure, to follow the master until his death. He can be recognized only by the thunderbolt in his hand. As a matter of fact, the Græco-Indian artists have given him most varied aspects. At one time he is a Zeus, now he is an Eros, a Herakles, a Pan, or a Dionysus. But he always retains the *vajra* that marks him out from the other assistants of Buddha. A creation of the Hellenistic studios, he disappears with the art of Gandhāra. A new heavenly Bodhisattva, also a bearer of the thunderbolt, then became very popular. Emanating from the Dhyāni-Buddha Akshobhya, Vajrapāṇi wears a figurine of his spiritual father in his tiara, or holds a lotus surmounted by his effigy.

The Bodhisattva Samantabhadra is better known from the texts than from the sculptured monuments. He should be yellow of colour. He makes the gesture of charity and carries the jewel on a lotus. He is cited as the assistant of Avalokiteṣvara represented in the form of Lokanātha.

FEMININE DIVINITIES

These appear late in Buddhist mythology. Only one popular female divinity, the Ogress Hārītī, the Goddess of Smallpox, is found in the Gandhāra sculptures. The pressure of the faithful no doubt forced the monks to incorporate her in their pantheon. A legend explains the worship paid her in the convents.

Hārītī was a Yakshinī, mother of five hundred demons, whom she fed on human flesh. Established near Rājagriha, she carried away from there daily a child to devour. The people came to complain to the Blessed One. He seized the youngest of her sons, Pingala, and hid him under his upturned begging-bowl. The Yakshinī in despair went about the world for seven days seeking for her child. She was advised to betake herself to the "all-knowing" Buddha. Then the Blessed One said to her: "You have five hundred sons. How comes it that for the loss of only one you are afflicted and desolate and seek him everywhere? In this world men have, some an only son, others three or five sons, and yet you cause them to perish."[1] Then the Yakshinī understood the evil she had done to men and was converted. But fearing lest lack of food might lead her back to her former misdeeds, the Buddha promised her that in all monasteries a part of the monks' food would be daily set aside for her and her children.

Hārītī, Goddess of Smallpox, is also the goddess of fecundity. With the genius of riches, Pāñchika, she makes up the tutelary pair. They are generally represented seated side by side. Hārītī carries a child or holds the cornucopia in her hand. The attributes of Pāñchika are the pike—he commands the army of the Yakshas—and the purse.

Tārā is the feminine energy of Avalokiteṣvara. Like him, she is compassionate and succouring. She is the "Saviour," the "Giver of Favours," "She who brings through evil passes." Protectress of navigation and travels, she also guides beings upon the path of Emancipation. Her shapes were multiplied under the influence of the Tantric doctrines which develop the cult of the feminine divinities.

Most frequently she has the appearance of a Bodhisattva. Seated Indian fashion or standing, she makes the gesture of charity. Her tiara is adorned with the image of a Dhyāni-Buddha. She holds the blue lotus (*utpala*) in her left hand. She is frequently found beside Avalokiteṣvara, in the attitude of adoration.

She has many shapes of terror. These are invoked by means of magic rites. The officiator (*sādhaka*), after the customary purifications, betakes himself to a lonely spot,

[1] Chavannes, *Contes*, No. 413.

where he endeavours by meditation to abolish his personality. Then, fixing his thought upon the aspect of the divinity, he causes it to appear by uttering a magic syllable. In this way he obtains complete identification with it. The charms that have power to evoke the principal members of the Buddhist pantheon have been preserved for us in the collections of Sādhanas. The details supplied by these texts have enabled us to identify many medieval statues. Here is the Sādhana for one blue shape of Tārā:

> Next let him contemplate a knife born of the syllable Om and himself adorned with this germ, and let him conceive himself as developed from this knife and identical with the Saver: she stands in the *Pratyāliḍha* attitude, terrifying, letting hang a garland of severed heads, dwarfish and obese, terrible, resplendent (with the colour) of the blue lotus; she has one face and three eyes; supernatural, she gives forth a great terrifying laugh; quivering with delight, she is mounted upon a corpse and arrayed with eight serpents; her eyes are red and round; a tiger-skin clothes her hips; she is in the flower of her youth, arrayed with the five *mudrās*; tongue like a harpoon, all terrible, her teeth inspire affright; in her right hand she holds the sword and knife, in her left the blue lotus and the skull; she has a single chignon, red and wild; Akshobhya adorns her headdress: let her be conceived in this wise, etc.[1]

Among the other Tantric shapes of Tārā we may quote Bhṛikuṭī Tārā "with frowning brow"; Ekajatā, who brandishes the sword, the arrow, the bow, and the skull; Jānguli, who heals the bites of serpents. She plays the *vīnā* and makes the gesture that reassures, and holds a serpent. Parṇaṣavarī, who treads diseases under her feet, is sometimes considered as a form of Tārā.

Another terrible divinity is Mārīchī, emanating from Vairochana. She has usually three faces, one of which is a wild boar's snout. Mounted upon a car drawn by seven pigs, she is accompanied by goddesses with animal muzzles and by Rāhu, the demon of eclipses. Her attributes are the thunderbolt, the hook, the arrow, the needle, the *aṣoka* branch, the bow, and the cord.

Prajñāpāramitā brings us back to the benign goddesses. She personifies transcendental knowledge, and is associated with Mañjuṣrī. The effigy of Akshobhya rests inside her chignon. Seated on a lotus, she makes the gesture of teaching. She holds in her hand the book of the Prajñāpāramitā, or the stem of a pink lotus upon which the book is placed.

The goddess Chundā has a smiling face. Her four arms hold up the lotus, the rosary, and the begging-bowl. A form with sixteen arms is also known.

Ushnīshavijayā sits in the niche of a sacred edifice. She has three faces, eight arms, and carries the image of Vairochana in her headdress. Her principal attributes are the Buddha upon the lotus, the bow, the arrow, the noose, the water-pot. She makes the gestures of absence of fear and of charity.

OTHER DIVINITIES

A very popular god is Jambhala, the God of Riches. He is obese, the colour of gold, generally seated Indian fashion. In his hands he holds a citron and a mongoose. The use of this attribute as an emblem of riches is explained by the attribute of the genius

[1] *Mahāchīna-Krama-Tārā-Sādhana*, translated by A. Foucher, *Iconographie bouddhique*, fasc. II, p. 76.

Pāñchika, the purse made of mongoose-skin. The terrible form of Jambhala treads under his feet a person who vomits up jewels. (See the section entitled "Javanese Mythology.")

Hayagrīva only appears in India as the assistant of Avalokiteṣvara under the shapes of Khasarpana and of Lokanātha. He is clothed in a tiger-skin and holds the stick (*danda*) in his hand. The God of Fever, he flees from the wrath of the goddess Parṇaṣavarī. Hayagrīva the horse-headed is described in the magic texts, but the Indian artists chose rather to represent him under his human aspects, his head surmounted by a horse's head.

Yamāri, or Yamāntaka, is an acolyte of Mañjuṣrī. He carries the stick and the noose. But his terrible shapes are more often invoked. He has three or six faces, brandishes in his multiple hands the sword, the thunderbolt, the axe, the noose, wears a necklace of skulls, and tramples upon a buffalo.

Trailokyavijaya is also a terrible divinity. His four faces express different sentiments. He has eight arms, makes the *Vajrahūnkāra mudrā* with his principal hands, which hold the bell and the *vajra*, brandishes on the right the sword, the hook, and the arrow, on the left the discus, the bow, and the noose. His right foot crushes Pārvatī's bosom; his left foot tramples on the head of Maheṣvara.

The cult of these Tantric divinities spread in the regions of Lamaistic Buddhism. It is chiefly in the Nepalese and Thibetan representations that we can study their iconographic types.

RAYMONDE LINOSSIER

Fig. 42. THE ASSAULT OF MĀRA
Sānchī.

Fig. 1. Avatars of Vishṇu: as a Fish, a Wild Boar, a Tortoise, a Lion, a Child

BRAHMANIC MYTHOLOGY

INVOCATION

An orthodox Hindu, no matter what task he may enter upon, never fails to pay homage to the divinity.

That is the reason for the ritual invocation *Om!* which, followed by one of the sacred names, is found at the beginning of most of the ancient texts. Gaṇeṣa and Sarasvatī are especially invoked, but Ṣiva also very frequently.

Om! Gaṇeṣāya namah!—Homage to Gaṇeṣa, god of initiative and the intellect! God who removes obstacles in the way!

Om! Sarasvatyai namah!—Homage to Sarasvatī, goddess of eloquence!

Om! Ṣivāya namah!—Homage to Ṣiva, dispenser of all gifts!

May we be allowed this triple invocation on the threshold of this inextricable Hindu pantheon, to review which briefly is our formidable task, for the help of these three omnipotencies will be far from too much to ensure a simple and *clear* summary of this mythology—the most tangled and uncertain in existence!

GENERAL SURVEY OF THE HINDU RELIGIONS

Although they are of different origins and different speech, their religious tradition is what unites the scattered peoples throughout the vast territory of Hindustan. Despite the vicissitudes of an eventful history, it was, as a matter of fact, Brahmanism that made the Hindus out of the Aryans, the Dravidians, and the autochthonous Indians; it was Brahmanism that gave India its moral and social unity and in some sort makes a nation of that country.

The Vedic Period. What we know of the ancient period of the Brahman religion is disclosed to us by the *Vedas*, its sacred books: the *Ṛigveda*, or Book of Hymns, the *Sāma-Veda*, or Book of Songs, the *Yajur-Veda*, or Book of Liturgical Formulas, and the *Atharva-Veda*, or Book of Magic Formulas, a kind of poetical treatise on sorcery.

Although the beginning of the Vedic period is lost in a far distant past and its end may be placed about six centuries B.C., the greater part of its traditions still forms part of the religious patrimony of India.

Animism, anthropomorphism, pantheism, and so on to the most abstract symbolism, are met with and interpenetrate it; nevertheless what predominates in the cult is always the adoration of the forces and the phenomena of nature.

The essential part of sacrifice was at first the immolation of animal victims, then later the offering of the *soma*, an intoxicating beverage particularly dear to certain gods. Whey, melted butter, broths, and rice cakes were also offered as burnt-offerings.

Fig. 2. Brahmā on the Lotus
Musée Guimet.

The Brahman Religion. In course of time the priestly caste, having grown powerful, established a very complicated cult, the least details of which they regulated. This cult is minutely described in the prose rituals, known as *Brāhmaṇas*, in which mysticism and rationalism mingle in exposition in the strangest fashion.

If the *Brāhmaṇas* link themselves up with the *Vedas*, the *Upanishads* in their turn touch the *Brāhmaṇas*, which contain several passages strongly impregnated with symbolism.

The *Upanishads*, the most ancient of which—and the most interesting too with regard to the subject before us—go back to the last centuries before the Christian era, reflect all the phases of that slow philosophic evolution that has its source in the *Vedas*, runs through the whole middle age of India, and ends in the kind of pantheistic idealism that brings us down to the threshold of modern times.

It is the present state of these conceptions, in which the Vedic remains and the speculations of the *Upanishads* amalgamate and coalesce with the philosophic systems of Hindustan (Vedānta and Sānkhya) and with the popular superstitions, it is the fusion of all these tendencies, that has been called " Hinduism " by A. Barth, in his *Religions de l'Inde.*

THE VEDIC MYTHOLOGY

Vedic India has left us neither temples nor statues nor paintings of any kind, and only literary monuments remain to bear witness to the majesty and the multitudinousness of its gods.

But while the hymns of the *Ṛigveda*—at least when a certain poetic afflatus gives them life—sometimes can eloquently tell a divine feat, it is no easy task to identify and classify its heroes.

The nature of the written documents that we possess and the character—or rather lack of character—of the deities mentioned in them superabundantly explain this difficulty in reconstructing a Brahmanic Olympus whose hierarchy and iconography should have all the exactness and clarity we could desire.

The *Hymns* were composed in epochs far apart: between one text and another new gods and demigods were born, driving out the old, who sank gradually into oblivion, while the young took possession of the heavens; then the newcomers in turn were dethroned and passed away . . . before they came of age, before their features and their legend had time to take definite clear shape.

" The metal of which they are made is still molten," says M. Bréal. Still, this can only apply to the celestial persons who begin to take on a semblance of consistency; but in the *Hymns* there are a quantity of myths hardly sketched out, the lines of which are so faint that the very eyes of Faith could hardly distinguish them for certain.

India never having had her Hesiod, nor—whatever the Hindus may say—her Homer, and both the soul and the face of her gods being at the same time vague and complex, we believe that it will always be a very risky thing to try to put forward a rational classification of the mythology of the *Vedas.*

The Ancient Cosmic Divinities, Heaven, Earth, Space

Deva, god, comes from the root *div*, ' to be resplendent,' ' to shine.' In primeval India the idea of god was associated with the idea of light. But the most general conception of a Supreme Being was attached to the word *asura*. In the *Vedas* these are neutral beings, neither good nor bad, whose very ancient tradition already begins to become effaced. It will in time be changed so much that in the *Brāhmaṇas asura* will mean demon. This evolution is quite the opposite to what took place in Persia, where *Ahura* (Sanskrit *asura*) means god, while the *devas* are the demons.

An essentially cosmic symbol is the primordial couple Sky-earth. It is not always male and female. Some texts call these conjoined divinities the " first goddesses, mothers of all the gods." Most often, however, the Sky represents the male element; it is Dyaus, " the Day, the Luminous "; " the Vast, the Broad," is Pṛithivī, the Earth.

Aditi, celestial Space, is the mother of the gods, the mother-without-father. It is also the poetic name of the cow as nourisher. We know the place the cow and her milk hold in primitive societies, and the worship paid to the sacred cows in India to-day. The goddess Aditi, then, is a *genitrix*, a cosmic mother.

Divinities of the Sky

Her sons are the Ādityas, the stars of the firmament. They are eight in number. Seven Ādityas dwell in the empyrean with the other gods. The eighth, Mārtaṇḍa, " born from the dead egg " and abandoned by his mother, is condemned to the daily task of crossing the huge sky in his chariot yoked to seven red or white horses. He is called Sūrya (" the Brilliant One "). The arrows he launches are the rays he darts. He is the Sun (Fig. 3).

Fig. 3. Sūrya
From Jouveau-Dubreuil, *Archéologie du sud de l'Inde.*

He bears also the name of Savitā (the Promoter, the Lifegiver), and will be identified later with Vishṇu and Pūshan, or with other sun-gods, good or bad according as they share in the beneficent or maleficent nature of the orb himself.

The myth of the egg dropped by Aditi, which rolls through space, does not appear again outside the *Ṛigveda*, and no representations of it are known.

We must observe, in any case, that the plastic arts of India only developed under the influence of Buddhism. Truly Brahmanic iconography was only able to take shape after the failure of Buddhism and through the resurrection of Brahmanism. That is why these productions of a relatively recent epoch give but a very imperfect rendering of the conceptions of the *Vedas*, and show traces of the successive accretions which in the course of the centuries modified and altered the genuine traditions.

In the *Hymns*, for example, gods with several heads and multiple arms do not exist. They are symbolic creations proper to Hinduism.

Ushas, the Dawn. Ushas, or the Dawn, is the lover, the bride, or, according to others, the daughter of Sūrya, the Sun.

Draped in rose-hued veils, like a young bride her mother has arrayed for her wedding-day, Ushas goes toward the East with light steps. She opens the celestial gates, then upon her car drawn by red cows, bow and arrow in hand, she traverses the sky. As she climbs to the horizon the darkness flees before her. And presently, like a young wife who displays her beauty to the marvelling eyes of her bridegroom, she appears to the eyes of mortals, radiant and unveiled. Ushas makes ready the way for her father and lord. She leads the horses of his car; but, a victim to her double love, she will perish at the hands of him who is both her lover and her father; she will end devoured by the rays of the Sun.

Here we may recognize the theme that forms part of the symbolism of the majority of primitive religions: the father devouring his own children.

Let us here mention that in the *Hymns* Ushas is called the mother of the Sun, a confusion no doubt due to the close relation between Daybreak and the Sunrise, which the Dawn seems to engender. When Ushas bears the name of Sūrya, which is the Sun's name, and is looked on as his daughter, she is then the betrothed of the Star of the Nights. As a matter of fact, Chandra (" the Bright One ")—the Moon—is masculine in Sanskrit.

These betrothed lovers pursue one another, but can never come together. Their attendants are the Aṣvins (from *aṣva*, 'a horse')—that is to say, the Chevaliers, the owners of horses, in the high sense of the word. They are the sons of the Sun and the mare Saraṇyu, the incarnation of the swift cloud driven by the wind.[1]

The nature of the Aṣvins is difficult to divine. They have been likened to the Greek Dioscuri, and it seems they have some connexion with the Shepherd's Star. They are represented as handsome youths. On their golden three-wheeled car, drawn by birds or swift coursers, they go before the chariot of the Sun. They scatter the dew as they shake their whips. In the calm that goes before the dawn it is their voice that rolls like a peal of thunder.

As soon as Rātri, the Goddess of the Night, who protects wolves and brigands, has folded away her veils you must address your prayers to the Aṣvins.

Betake yourself to them in trouble, for the Aṣvins are compassionate. They restore plumpness and good colour to those whom cares have made thin and haggard. They will give back sight to the blind, as they healed the blindness that Utanka, the ardent disciple, contracted through the privations to which his venerated master had subjected him.[2] Despised virgins, forget not that they are the providence of old maids. Warriors, invoke them in battles, for they assist whosoever is slow of foot, whosoever is the last.

Called upon for aid in innumerable contingencies of every kind by poor mortals, it is not surprising that the Aṣvins should have been more often on this lower earth than in their heaven, and that the gods should sometimes have taken exception to this even to the point of threatening to deprive these genii friends of mankind of their due share of sacrificial offerings. It is the Aṣvins who are shown by one legend swarming like moths about the beautiful Sukanyā, the wife of a venerable but hideous and dyspeptic sage, and pressing her to grant them her favours. She promises to gratify them on condition that they will first show her how to rejuvenate her aged husband. " Let him plunge into the

[1] She is the daughter of Tvashṭri, the great Fashioner, the universal Shaper.

[2] *Mahābhārata*, Book I.

sacred lake," said the Aṣvins. And when the old man, thanks to this miraculous immersion, had indeed recovered youth and vigour his faithful wife was free to mock and flout at her would-be gallants!

Varuṇa, the Personification of the Sky. Varuṇa, often compared to the Ouranos of the Greeks, is the master of the Vedic pantheon and the chief of the Ādityas. He belongs to-day to those ancient divinities who had already fallen from the highest rank in the time of the *Hymns*, and who were no longer considered more than secondary gods.

Varuṇa-Sky, Varuṇa-Providence, after having been He-who-had-the-sun-for-an-eye, and who embraced the whole universe, becomes simply Varuṇa, the god of the waters celestial and terrestrial. He is nevertheless still a kind of majestic Jehovah, preserver of eternal order and redresser of wrongs.

The *Hymns* show us Varuṇa brandishing the noose with which he lassoes the wicked. A late representation of the period represents him on his *vāhanam—i.e.*, his mount, an aquatic monster half-bird, half-crocodile, who must originally have been a gavial or a dolphin—in any case, the *makara*, the fabulous animal of the tales (Fig. 4).

Varuṇa has the sky for his garment. He knows not sleep, and nothing escapes his vigilance, for the stars, his eyes, are without number. From his throat distil the seven celestial watercourses, the springs of all the rivers of the earth. God of the waters and of truth, Varuṇa sends dropsy as a punishment for Evil: for Evil is Falsehood, and there is no good but the Good, which is Truth. On this theme we find in the *Aitareya-Brāhmaṇa* a curious legend of the times when human sacrifice was no longer currently practised.

Legend of Ṣunaḥ-ṣepa. In India, more than anywhere else, the father who has no son is looked on as abandoned of the gods. For if we do not leave behind us a son who, in memory of ourselves and our ancestors, offers *ṣraddhas* (funeral cakes) to our manes, if we die without male posterity, who is there on earth and in the heavens to watch over the welfare of our ancestors and ourselves?

Hariṣchandra, king of the solar race, had a hundred wives, but by none of them had he succeeded in having a son. Seeing which, he vowed to Varuṇa that if he would gratify him with a son he would sacrifice the babe to him at his birth.

Now some time thereafter it came to pass that the King found himself the father of a boy. Whereat he showed himself both greatly joyful and greatly grieved: joyful, seeing that at last he had a male scion; grieved when the vow he had made came back to his memory.

And hardly was the new-born bathed when Varuna appeared, saying, "I come for the son you are to sacrifice to me."

"See," said the King, "he is still but a little weak thing; let him live for ten days; he will be more worthy of you."

"Be it so!"

When the ten days had passed: "I come," said Varuṇa, "for the son you are to sacrifice to me."

"Wait, Lord, until his teeth have grown; he will be more worthy of you."

And even so it was each time the god presented himself, the father always finding some new deficiency, and always the indulgent Varuṇa consenting to a fresh delay.

Now the boy having come to an age when he was ripe to bear arms, the father showed no joy of it.

"Father," said the young man, "why do you show no joy?"

"Alas, my son, you were still in your mother's womb when I made a vow to sacrifice you to Varuṇa. . . ."

Then the young warrior fled into the forest.

Protected by Indra, the patron of chevaliers, for three years he lived in freedom, far from the habitations of men, when tidings came to him that a dropsy had been sent upon his father by Varuṇa.

And as he went thinking and devising by what expedient he might appease the wrath of the god he met a poor family of Brahmans: father, mother, and three sons.

"Brahman," said the King's son, "give me your eldest born, and you shall have a herd of cows of me."

But the Brahman would not.

And then, addressing himself to the mother, "Brahmaness, give me your youngest son, and I will give you a herd of cows."

But the Brahmaness would not.

And as he then asked them for Ṣunaḥ-ṣepa, the second of their three sons, they were willing.

Then the young prince gave them a herd of cows, saying to himself that Varuṇa ought to be all the better satisfied, seeing that, thanks to this substitution, instead of a Kshatriya (noble), he would have a Brahman (a religious).[1]

And there were the King's son and the Brahmans in the enclosure of sacrifice. And thither also came King Hariṣchandra, as big as a full cask by reason of his dropsy.

But when Ṣunaḥ-ṣepa was decked with flowers, and the stake set up, and the moment come to bind him to it: "For my part," said his father, "I will not do this."

And neither the mother nor any of those who were there would do it.

"Bind him to the stake," said the King's son to the Brahman then, "and I will give you a thousand cows more."

"Be it so," said the Brahman.

And they sang the hymns. But when the moment came to whet the knife for the sacrifice there was no one willing to do it.

"Unless for another thousand cows," said the Brahman, "I will not."

And when the thousand extra cows had been given, Ṣunaḥ-ṣepa, who saw that for this price his father was resolved to strike him: "O Friend of all!" he cried, speaking to the high priest, "O great sage Viṣva-mitra, have pity upon me!"

Then was heard the voice of Viṣva-mitra: "Address thy prayers to Varuṇa, to Agni and the Aṣvins, not to me!"

And as Ṣunaḥ-ṣepa prayed, one by one his bonds were loosed of themselves from him and fell to the ground.

Whereby the bystanders perceived that the god was propitious to him.

And in that same hour Varuṇa took away the dropsy he had laid upon Hariṣchandra.

[1] The caste of the Brahmans is higher than that of the Kshatriyas.

Fig. 4. COMPASS CARD WITH PICTURES OF GODS CORRESPONDING TO THE CARDINAL POINTS
Jouveau-Dubreuil, *Archéologie du sud de l'Inde*.

And from that day Varuṇa exacted no more human sacrifices.

But when the Brahman would have taken his son away with him, foreseeing that he could derive glory and profit from such an one, Ṣunaḥ-ṣepa said to him, " What is there in common between you and me? "

And the Friend of all adopted him as his son and disciple. Under Viṣva-mitra Ṣunaḥ-ṣepa grew in strength and wisdom: he became a great sage among the sages.

Mitra-Varuṇa. The name of Varuṇa is often joined with that of Mitra, the benevolent god, the god " friend," who is later to become the God of Day.

If the ' conjunctions ' Mitra-Varuṇa, Indra-Agni, and Agni-Soma play the chief part in sacrificial invocations these divinities are nevertheless far from enjoying the exclusive adoration of which the Iranian and Roman Mithra was the object.

Indra, an Anthropomorphic Deity. His Birth, his Feats, and his Adventures. A wholly anthropomorphic god, Indra (Fig. 5) is almost Varuṇa's equal, and his importance was to increase rapidly at the latter's expense. Having the Firmament and the Atmosphere under his jurisdiction, he has his throne in the storm-cloud laden with rain and thunder. The sky is his helmet. The earth lies in the hollow of his hand; he moves it here and there as he wills. As the tire bounds the spokes of a wheel, so Indra embraces the whole universe. His mount is Airāvata, the white elephant sprung from the churning of the sea of milk. The thunderbolt (*vajra*) is his principal weapon; the others are the discus (*chakra*), the elephant goad (*ankuṣa*), and the axe (*tanka*), with which he cleaves the mountains to make rivers and streams flow from them. In the *Hymns* he is represented as the national god of the Aryas. He is formidable and bellicose. He is the patron of the military nobility. He is, in a word, the protector of the Kshatriyas, or Warriors.

His passion for *soma* goes even to intemperance, and when this illimitable drunkard staggers the whole earth staggers with him!

But, like a simple mortal, after repeated libations he is not always exempt from a certain queasy discomfort. Then the Aṣvins, assisted by Sarasvatī, take from the body of a demon a certain specific that restores the body and the wits of the divine drinker.

Good and generous to his faithful followers, he multiplies their herds in peace and aids them with his arms in war.

The struggle of Indra against the Dāsas, or Dasyus, is probably connected with memories of very ancient invasions. When his friend Kutsa is at grips with Ṣushṇa (" the Witherer "), and the darkness threatens to interrupt the combat, it is again Indra who forces the chariot of the sun to slacken in its career, by wrenching away a wheel. He at once places it in the hands of his *protégé*, who uses this wheel as a formidable weapon with which he subdues his foe.

If the name of Ṣushṇa is translated as ' Witherer ' it is because in this mythical combat from which Indra emerges victorious we must see the beneficent thunderstorm and its fertilizing rains, which put an end to the terrible aridity of the dry season.

The morning storm that troubles the calm of daybreak is also symbolically expressed by the intervention of Indra. Having formed the thunderbolt out of the vapours of the waters condensed in clouds, he hurls it upon the Chariot of Dawn and shatters it.

There are few atmospheric phenomena with which Indra is not associated.

The celestial cows—the clouds, in other words—belong to him. He sheds their milk on the earth when he pleases, and this is the rain.

As for the demons who covet the divine cattle and try to steal them, the god speedily overwhelms them with thunderbolts. And this is another occasion of our hearing thunder.

One day, however, Vala had succeeded in getting his herd away from him and had

Fig. 5. INDRA
Chidambaram, thirteenth century.

hidden it in his cave, thinking it beyond all reach there; but he had reckoned without Indra and his avenging thunderbolt. The cave of the thief was pounded to dust, and the herdsman god brought back his parti-coloured herd intact to the celestial pastures.

Not only does Indra watch jealously over his own cattle, but also over that of his allies and his worshippers. When the cunning Paṇis had succeeded in laying hold of the herds of Angiras he at once sent the bitch goddess Sorama to look for them, and, having unceasingly quartered the mountains of earth and the waters of the heavens, Sorama at last one day heard their lowings (the thunder). Then Indra, deriving strength and courage from the sacred songs, took back his own. And thus the rain was restored to the dried-up earth.

One of Indra's many surnames is Vṛitrahan, which is " Slayer of Vṛitra." This demon, whose name means the Enveloper, or the Enemy, had one day turned himself into an enormous serpent whose ninety-nine coils were blocking up many rivers, thus grievously troubling the realm of the waters. So great was the terror he inspired that none of the Immortals dared to go and dislodge him. Indra alone, having fortified his courage with *soma*, went against the monster and slew him.

But at the sight of the horrible corpse of the Enemy, lo, Indra recoils in affright. Leaping over the nine-and-ninety rivers whose course he had restored, he takes to flight; then, like a startled eagle, he finally launches himself through the air.

It was after this famous combat that the gods, full of admiration for Indra, heaped attentions on him, aided and seconded him on all occasions. Henceforth, whatever the importance or triviality of his doings, Agni, Soma, Vishṇu, and the Maruts will never leave him, and the goddesses sing his praises, whether he speeds through space in his car drawn by tawny steeds, or without girders builds up the vault of the sky, or stops the sun upon the slopes of the firmament, or betakes himself, mounted on his white elephant, to his domain, the *svarga*, or third heaven. There it is that in Amarāvatī, the dwelling of the Immortals, he fleets away days of silk and gold by the side of Indrāni his wife. Voluptuous, vigorous, and warlike, as befits the mate of every Hindu god, in whom the chief qualities of her husband should be reflected, Indrāni, although lascivious rather than amorous, does not fail, like Juno, to be jealous. Displeased at the attentions her husband lavishes on his companion, the ape Vṛishakapi, she casts burning glances at the favourite, who takes fire. . . . At this moment Indra appears, is kindled to wrath, and drives away his shameless friend.

It is only fair to say that some time after that Indra was in turn surprised in an amorous *tête-à-tête* with Vṛishakapi's own wife, so that deceived and deceiver found themselves quits, and good friends as before.

But nothing could curb the salaciousness of this god, and every stratagem was good in his eyes. For example, when he cast his desire upon the wife of the sage Gautama it was by employing the hypocritical trick of false likeness that, like Zeus-Amphitryo, he attained his end.

However, it occasionally happened that in the course of his amorous escapades he came badly enough to grief. One day, for instance, he was so well and truly dismembered that the gods were obliged to rebuild him bit by bit, but there was a certain part of his person that they could not find, so that, as time was pressing, and as a last resource, they saw themselves forced to requisition the lacking member from a ram.

The Maruts, Rudra, and Parjanya. The Maruts, gods of the hurricane, are the faithful companions of Indra. They tilt the enormous urn of the rains over the earth. Their strength is titanic. It is a game to them to pile mountain upon mountain (in other words, cloud upon cloud), in front of the Sun's eye, in the midst of the celestial Ocean. Their chariots, with the wheels bristling with gleaming swords (the lightnings), cleave mountains and rocks. The earth shudders at their approach, the sky bellows with fear and shrinks back at their passing. They brandish spears of fire, from their bows they launch dazzling arrows. What we call rain is their horses' incontinency, or else the udder of Praṣni,[1] the dappled cow, which empties itself and sheds upon the earth its beneficent tide.

Their father, Rudra of the red hair, protects the herds and knows all remedies. In the *Vedas* he is generous and helpful, but later, in the *Brāhmaṇas*, becomes a hideous and terrible god, the prototype of Ṣiva, and has for his wife Rudranī, the cruel goddess of bloody sacrifices, she who unchains upon the world, from the depths of the abysses and the forests, Sickness, Terror, and Death. His near relations are Vāyu, or Vāta (the Wind) (see Fig. 4), and Parjanya, who is also a personification of the thunderstorm. As soon as the song of Parjanya rises the tallest trees bow themselves, the earth shivers. Nevertheless, like Rudra, he is a good deity. When he empties his great cask the earth becomes fruitful and everything revives.

Sacrificial Divinities

Agni, Spirit of the Sacrificial Fire. Agni, Fire, is the friend of men. When he is the lightning, to which the rain-laden cloud gives birth, he is regarded as the son of the Celestial Waters. According to other texts, he is their lover.

These variants in affiliation are characteristic of many theogonies, and especially of Hindu mythology, in which, as we have already said elsewhere, the same individual is husband, lover, or father, according to the bias of the document or the whim of the poet.

Fire being considered as the son of the Waters, it will be understood that since they contain it it falls with the rain upon the ground and is incorporated with vegetation. That it should be possible to make it spring forth by the friction of two pieces of wood is, therefore, for a Hindu, in the order of things. Each of the two pieces—the stick and the flat slab—used to obtain fire by rotary motion[2] bears in Sanskrit the same name, *arani.* This word is feminine in gender. That is why Agni, Terrestrial Fire, is sometimes called the " son-of-two-mothers." As soon as he is born he devours them.

The Sun is the celestial fire; Kravyād, the fire of the sacrifice, was lighted by the gods. It is he who wafts them to the offerings when they come down on earth; he it is that bears men's prayer to the heavens.

Kravyād (" Flesh-eater ") has powerful jaws equipped with shining fangs. His hair is red. He is a terrible devourer. The *Mahābhārata* assures us that from time to time he finds himself forced to put himself on a vegetarian diet, and that to cool his maw inflamed by an excessive flesh diet it is not unusual to see him consume a thick forest to the very last leaf.

A fragment of a panel of one of the sculptured chariots that serve on days of solemn festival to carry the gods in procession gives us the image of Agni bestriding the Ram.

[1] The mother of the Maruts.

[2] By means of a string rolled round a pointed stick, the tip of which is placed in a hole made in a slab fixed in the ground. By pulling the string to the right and then to the left a revolving motion is imparted to the stick, and the heat generated by this rapid friction presently sets fire to the wood.

He has four arms and two heads. The fan he uses to blow up the fire is in one hand, another holds the axe, a third the torch, and the last the sacrificial ladle.

His double head is meant to signify that this image symbolizes both the sacrificial fire and the fire of the domestic hearth (Fig. 6).

Fig. 6. AGNI ON THE RAM
Musée Guimet.

Agni is in everything and is everywhere, but he prefers to dwell among men. He knows all their affairs. From him the young man will have his bride. All virgins are under Agni. They are the ones who awake, enkindle, and feed him.

A pretty legend tells how one day the women found it impossible to light a fire in the palace of King Nīla, no matter how much pains they took. The King's daughter having tried in her turn, suddenly, lo, the finest fire in the world sprang up high and bright, leaping to caress, without burning them, the lovely lips whose sweet breath had kindled it. And as the same thing happened every time they wished to light a fire in the King's palace, it was inferred that Agni had fallen in love with Nīla's daughter and wished to take her to wife. Which indeed came to pass.

Soma, the Sacred Beverage. There is another divinity that presides, with Agni, over sacrifice, Soma. Originally an intoxicating plant, the juice of which, mixed with hydromel and milk, was used in the celebration of ritual ceremonies, *soma* was deified at an early date. It was represented as the son of Parjanya. From the inaccessible mountains where he dwells an eagle-falcon bears him to the earth.[1]

Like Agni, Soma has a real existence and a mythical existence, the place of which is the third heaven. There it was that Pūshan discovered it. The gods having drunk of it after Sūrya, the daughter of the Sun, had filtered it, they became immortal.

Jealous of their possession of the *soma*, they had entrusted it to Gandharva, the celestial archer, for safe guarding, but Agni-the-Falcon seized it and brought it to men.

Soma is also the Orb-of-Night.[2] For wives he has the twenty-seven constellations. But Rohinī, the Red One,[3] alone reigned in his heart.

Daksha, offended at the neglect the god showed his other twenty-six daughters, put his curse upon him, and since that time the Moon has intermittent periods of faintness.

Secondary Divinities. The Gandharvas. Viṣvāvasu is the only Gandharva mentioned

[1] Hence he is sometimes called Ṣyenabhrita, eagle-borne.

[2] In order to preserve his sex we shall always call him this. The name of the Moon is masculine in Sanskrit.

[3] The constellation of Taurus, the principal star of which is red.

by the *Hymns*. He is the enemy of Indra. Married to a water-sprite, his son is Yama, the God of Death, whose lover is Yami, his own sister.

In later times the Gandharvas multiplied. They owned a kingdom and a capital city, Gandharvapura, a name that in Sanskrit corresponds to Fata Morgana, Fate, Destiny.

Dancers and singers, they are the minstrels of the empyrean. Unheeding and voluptuous, they spend their time disporting themselves with the Apsarases in the celestial waters; but their desire goes even to mere mortal women, and often on marriage nights the husband is forced to make use of the most powerful exorcisms to drive them away from the bride-chamber.

When any dispute arises between the Gandharvas and the gods the latter do not fail, knowing the weak point of their opponents, to send them the seductive goddess Vāk[1] as envoy; and all the time the Gandharvas remain occupied with her charms the gods put to the best use for their own interests.

The Apsarases, Nymphs of the Lower Heavens. The Apsarases are the recognized courtesans of the sky. Their perfect beauty is accompanied by irresistible seductions, which the gods do not blush to employ upon occasion in order to maintain their power as soon as they feel it threatened. Let some great ascetic, by dint of superhuman constancy, of his penances and meditations, come to the eve of attaining sublime perfection, they will dispatch one of the most alluring of the Apsarases to the imprudent one who has drawn too near to heaven, and the holy man will have nothing left but to start his interminable self-torments all over again. For an appreciable lapse of time the lords of the heavens need have no further fear of him.

But the Apsarases, who are women as much as goddesses, do not always need a command from above to lower their eyes to the earth; they often approach men of their own desire. While accessible to love, their heart is nevertheless without any maternal fibre, and when it pleases them to return to their heaven they simply leave their children behind.

Here is, from the *Ṛigveda* and a tale in the *Brāhmaṇas*, one of those very numerous legends, many of which are, no doubt, lost to us, which remind us of the amorous caprices of some of our own fairies, and which certainly were very popular in their time.

Thus spake, in his love, the King Purūravas to one of the most beautiful of the Apsarases:

" By the Orb-of-Night, the father of my race,[2] O Urvaṣī, daughter of the celestial waters, I conjure thee, tell me all thou wouldst have that I, the great King Purūravas, may become thy bridegroom? "

" This: that thou shouldst embrace me thrice every day, but that thou shouldst respect my freedom, and that I should never see thee naked."

And already the jealous Gandharvas were indignant that their beautiful sweetheart should be sojourning among men longer than was reasonable. But when they saw her carrying in her womb the fruit of her earthly loves they could restrain themselves no longer, and began to fret and fume greatly, saying that at all costs they must find some trick that would constrain the inconstant one to return to the skies.

---

[1] The name signifies " the Voice."

[2] The majority of the kings and heroes of the India of the legends are regarded as descended from the Sun or the Moon.

"I know," said one of the Gandharvas, "that she always ties to one foot of the couch on which she disports herself with the King her pet ewe, which has two lambs: we will slip into the darkened room and . . ."

When Urvaṣī, fumblingly caressing her ewe in the dark, felt that she had only one lamb: "Truly," she said, "I am guarded well! Thieves come in here without fear as if there was no man at my side!"

Stung by these words, the King Purūravas promised himself to keep good watch, fearing lest the thieves might come back to seize the other lamb. And this very thing happened. But as he leaped out of the bed, and was trying in the darkness to cut off the thieves' retreat, lo, the cunning Gandharvas sped a lightning-flash. By its light Purūravas appeared naked to the eyes of Urvaṣī. Now barely had she descried her husband's nakedness when she vanished through the air.

One day when the King was riding over mountains and valleys, looking for his dear and despairing, it came to pass that, having alighted in the plain of Kurukshetra, he saw, in graceful evolutions on the waters of Lake Anyataḥ-plakshā, swans of whitest plumage, the loveliest that might be seen. And as the King could not take his eyes from them, taking who knows what melancholy pleasure in contemplating them, one of the swans in the flock saw him and said, "Daughters of the Waters" —for those beautiful swans were Apsarases—"Daughters of the Waters, here is the King Purūravas whose couch I have shared."

Then the Apsarases, desiring to amuse themselves with the amazement of Purūravas, pressed Urvaṣī to show herself to him in her human shape. . . .

As soon as he recognized his dear Apsaras the King fell into huge excitement, begging her for pity to come back to him—since she was his wife—and claiming his son from her.

"Dost thou not know," said Urvaṣī, "that the heart of a woman and the heart of a hyena are all one? Dost thou verily think that I am thy wife? I passed through thy arms like the first ray of dawn through a transparent wave: what is there left in common between thee and me?"

And as he implored her not to let this be the last time he should see her: "Come back," she said, "to the banks of this lake on the last night of the year."

On the last night of the year Purūravas having therefore come back to the banks of the Lake Anyataḥ-plakshā, he was suddenly transported to a resplendent palace. This was the habitation of the Gandharvas.

And Urvaṣī was there awaiting him.

Then after the night had been spent by the King's side she said to him, "The Gandharvas will ask you what you would have from them as a guesting gift. What will you ask, O King?"

"Whatever you advise me."

"Ask them then for that which will allow you to become like them."

And even so he did.

At this unexpected request the Gandharvas were greatly chapfallen, for it was not possible for them to refuse to grant the desire of a guest, a desire so sacred that the gods themselves could not avoid the obligation.

Will they, nill they, then, they taught Purūravas the method of obtaining the sacrificial fire, which confers immortality on its possessor.

Then, having learned the secret of the fire and received his son from the hands of Urvaṣī, he returned to his kingdom, there to finish out his reign, and thereafter, without dying of mortal death, he mounted straight to the heaven of the Gandharvas.

In the legend of Gangā the union of a mortal with an Apsaras has a much worse ending.

When the goddess of the Ganges consented to wed with the King Sāntanu it was agreed between them that whatever she might do he would never address the smallest reproach to her. This pact he observed strictly until the day when, seeing that she indulged in the bad habit of drowning each of the children born to them in the sacred river, he could not repress a timid remark on this strange conception of motherhood, which resulted in his being abandoned on the spot by his touchy spouse.

Kāma Deva, God of Love. The Indian Eros is armed with a flower-decked bow and a quiver full of arrows that are flowers: virgin flowers of the lotus, the lily and jasmin, gold flowers of the mango-tree, orange-hued flowers of the *aṣoka*.

He rides upon a parrot. His standard-bearer, a Gandharva, follows him. The drawing of a fish figures upon his standard (Fig. 7).

In the South of India Kāma's bow is made with a stave of sugar-cane, and the string is a line of bees. Let us note by the way the importance of the metaphorical part played by the honey bee in the poetical language of Hindustan: the thick, dark hair of a beautiful woman is always compared to a swarm of bees; the manœuvres of a coquette to their wavering, capricious flight; the low, thrilling voice of a lover speaking in his beloved's ear to their deep buzzing in the corolla of the water-lily.

Sent by Pārvatī, the daughter of Himalaya, Kāma one day came to disturb Ṣiva in his meditations. With one single look of his vertical eye the terrible ascetic reduced the God of Love to ashes.

When Rati, the Goddess of Love's Delight, saw Kāma her husband in this plight she filled the heavens with her lamentings. The gods had pity on her. They interceded with Ṣiva, who let himself be moved and resuscitated the guilty one. It was after this misadventure that Kāma bore the name Ananga.[1]

Fig. 7. Kāma, God of Love
Musée Guimet.

Origin of the World. Manu. We have reviewed the cosmic divinities, the Sky, the Earth, the Sun, the Dawn and her Knights, the Aṣvins; the divinities of the Sky and the Atmosphere, Indra, the Maruts and Rudra; those pertaining to sacrifice, Agni and Soma; lastly the secondary divinities, the Gandharvas and the Apsarases. It remains for us to make acquaintance with the semi-divine beings who preside especially at the origin of the world, its birth, its duration, and its end.

[1] Ananga: who has no limbs.

Manu, the First Man. The father of the human race was Manu, the Intelligent. He is the son of the gods. From the offering of whey, cream, and melted butter he made to Vishṇu, after Vishṇu had saved him from the flood, there was born a woman. She was beautiful, and the Aṣvins wanted to have her; but she said to them, "I am his who made me." And she went to Manu. And Manu, full of astonishment, asked her, "Who art thou then?"

Fig. 8. Brahmā on the Peacock
Musée Guimet.

"Dost thou not recognize thy daughter?"

"What meanest thou, O blessed one?"

"I was born of the offering thou madest to the gods."

As Manu desired her, seeing that she was beautiful, she turned herself into a cow, seeking to avoid incest. Then Manu turned himself into a bull. Then, Ida having turned into a she-goat, Manu turned into a he-goat. And so on, the father each time taking the male form corresponding to the female form taken by his daughter. And in this way the animals were born. Here we can recognize the metamorphosis theme that is everywhere found, even in the folklore of France—notably in the lay of Magali.

Manu was the first lawgiver. He is one of the seven mythical sages who shine in the Great Bear.[1]

Yama, King of Hell and Judge of the Dead. Yama, the first man to die, was the son of the Sun (see Fig. 4). He might have lived for ever if he had not had the audacity to venture upon the road by which no man returns. He went down it to the end. It is he who shows men the way they must go.

He reigns over the dwelling-place of the Manes,[2] in the region of light and the celestial waters, near the habitation of Varuṇa, at the farthest edge of the sky.

The dead come to him in crowds, led by Agni, the fire of the funeral-pyre. Two monstrous dogs guard the way and scent out the arrivals. The good, the chosen alone, shall drink the *soma* that will give them immortality. They shall shine, in the night, among the stars. They shall enjoy boundless felicity. They shall have offerings made to them, as to the gods.

Prajāpati, the One God. In the texts brought together under the name of *Brāhmaṇas* the majority of the legends which elsewhere are connected with different divinities are attributed to Prajāpati, regarded as the supreme god, if not the one god, during the whole of the post-Vedic period.

Father of the gods, the demons, and men, after he had constrained himself to great austerities, he created the world by means of a sacrifice. From the sweat of his body was

[1] The name of the Great Bear in Sanskrit is Saptarshi, "the Seven Sages."
[2] Or Fathers; in Sanskrit Pitṛis.

formed an egg. During one year it floated upon the primordial waters, giving birth at length to the world. The upper half of the shell constituted the firmament, the lower half contained the Ocean.

Prajāpati was the god of the enlightened people who leaned in the direction of monotheism, or, at the least, a systematization of the myths.

The tendency to monotheism is equally perceptible in the worship paid to Brahmā, the Creator, father of gods and men. He is a grand and majestic figure, but vague, like all the entities.

The Brahmans came forth from his head, the Kshatriyas[1] from his arms, and from his feet the Sūdras.[2] He never played a very active part. His sovereignty remains abstract, like himself. He hovers, alone, above everything. His epithet is *ekahaṃsa*, the One Swan.

He is shown with four arms. The posterior arms carry insignia. The right hand behind holds an oval disk with beaded rim, called the *brahma-tandram*. " It is averred," M. Jouveau-Dubreuil tells us, " that it is with this instrument he marks men's foreheads with their destiny; but originally it was perhaps a sacrificial ladle."

In his second right hand he holds a rosary made of *rudraksham* seeds.

The left hand behind carries the ablution vase.

But the representations of Brahmā that have come down to us date from the epoch when he was considered as the emanation of the divine energy of Vishnu or Ṣiva, and must be placed in the mythology of Hinduism.

MYTHOLOGY OF HINDUISM

Disdained by the *Brāhmaṇas*, the popular side of the mythology of the *Vedas* reaches its fullest development during the period called that of Hinduism, when Brahmanism was divided into multiple sects, each one placing its privileged god above the other gods and gratifying him with all the legends attributed to the divinities of the old epoch.

The Trimūrti. Brahmā. The conception most closely linked with Vedism and Brahmanism is that of the Hindu Trinity, the Trimūrti. " The Absolute manifests himself in three persons, Brahmā the Creator, Vishṇu the Preserver, and Ṣiva the Destroyer." The syllable we write as *om*, but which is in reality made up of the three sounds, *a*, *u*, *m*, is the symbol of this trinity.

Brahmā, the soul of the universe, source, essence, and end of all things, was too metaphysical, too hieratic, to become wholly popular. His nebulous majesty is unfavourable to his humanization by means of legends, to his plastic portrayal, to the establishment of one of those lively and picturesque cults which have always attracted the belief of the crowds.

The *vāhanam* of Brahmā is the peacock, according to others the swan, the emblem of discernment.

[1] The military caste.

[2] The third caste, lower than the preceding ones.

In the grotto of Trichinopoly (seventh century) the god is seen between two worshippers. One of his four hands holds the discus, the favourite weapon of the Aryas, another the ladle employed in the sacrificial ceremonies.

Fig. 9. SARASVATĪ, KĀRTTIKEYA, LAKSHMĪ
Hindu popular prints. Eighteenth century.

As author of the four *Vedas*, he has four heads. He had five, in earlier times, before he lusted after his own daughter Sandhyā; but as he was pursuing her, and she was cowering down in the hope of escaping his eye, and he was elongating his neck to try to discover her, Ṣiva, scandalized, cut off one of the heads of this unworthy father. That is the head of which he henceforth makes a trophy, wearing it in his own hair.

"The god sitting upon the lotus" is the most frequent designation of Brahmā, because that is the position in which he is almost always shown, upon the sacred water-lily issuing from Vishṇu's navel.

Fig. 10. TRIMŪRTI

Sarasvatī, the Goddess of Eloquence, is his wife. She is mounted on a peacock, and her attributes are the quoit and the warrior conch.

The Only Gods. In this *mélange* of beliefs and traditions that makes up Hinduism Ṣiva and Vishṇu nevertheless predominate. They have absorbed all the myths, whether ancient or new.

Ṣiva. His Emanations. Although in the *Hymns* he is good and beneficent, Ṣiva the Propitious has now become the bloodthirsty and terrible god. He is the chief of the evil spirits, the ghouls, the vampires, the nocturnal phantoms that prowl about the burning-grounds and other impure places. Like Rudra, he is a Paṣupati, a "master of herds," and among his herds we must include the hungry horde of thieves, brigands, beggars, and fakirs who call upon his name.

Fig. 11. ṢIVA DANCING THE TĀNDAVA
Musée Guimet.

According to which one of his multiple aspects is invoked, Śiva is tutelary as Bhava; as Kāla, Time, he destroys all things; as Bhairava he is Dionysiac and raging; or as Mahādeva he is the Lord, the Great God, and the other divinities are but emanations from him.

He is *digambara*, or ' clad in air '; he goes naked, his body smeared with the ashes of cowdung fires. He is the first ascetic. His long hair is done up in a knot on the top of his

Fig. 12. ŚIVA BETWEEN TWO SAIVITE SAINTS, PADANJALI AND VYAGRAPADAR
Musée Guimet.

head; his forehead is marked with three short horizontal stripes[1] and has a vertical eye in the middle.

His headdress is adorned with the crescent moon, a skull, or the fifth head of Brahmā. He wears a necklace of dead men's heads and bracelets of serpents.

It may be remembered how Śiva chastised the temerity of Kāma, who had come to plant love for Pārvatī in his heart. He is the ascetic *par excellence*. Detached from this world's pleasures and all its goods, he remains indifferent to everything but lofty meditations, which alone can open up the path of absolute perfection.

[1] The topknot is the headdress of the Saivite ascetics, who wear the three transversal stripes, the mark of Śiva, on their foreheads.

It is in the posture of this ascetic meditation that he is most frequently represented, as in the temple of Pallava at Kaīlāsanātha (eighth century). The attitude is identical with that of the Buddha teaching the Law. " He had placed upon his right thigh," says the poet, " the lotus of his left foot; upon his left knee his hand sinister, his rosary upon the forepart of his right arm, the hand of which made the gesture called the sign of argumentation " (Fig. 13).

Ṣiva sometimes wears his hair hanging down. The Brahmanic cord, the sign of caste, goes from his left shoulder to his right hip. One of his right arms holds his left leg with a strap.

Self-devotion of Ṣiva. His life is full of instances of self-devotion. Vāsuki, King of the Serpents, is about to vomit forth the venom that covered the surface of the sea. (See the "Churning of the Sea of Milk," p. 135.) The creatures, horrified by this frightful deluge, implore Ṣiva to save them from it. Touched by compassion, he receives the poisonous flood in the hollow of his hand and drinks it. But the venom burned his gullet so severely that the mark remained for ever visible outside upon his throat. Since that time the great ascetic bears among his names that of Nīlakaṇṭha, or " Blue Throat."

One day the gods determined, for the greater good of men, to send down upon earth the goddess Gangā (the river Ganges), who up till then had only dwelt in the celestial precincts. But how prevent the weight of such a cataract from shattering the earth to atoms? Ṣiva once more displayed his unwearying self-sacrifice. Taking the goddess upon his topknot, he was a buffer for her fall. Gangā took a thousand years to reach the ground, and thus the transmission of the sacred river was accomplished without damage, to the greater good of the earth and its inhabitants.

This episode appears frequently in art. In the plate facing page 118 the nymph of the Ganges may be seen on one of Ṣiva's tresses: she has her hands joined in the attitude of prayer.

Fig. 13. A Rishi in Meditation
Musée Guimet.

The vicissitudes of his wandering life, which came after the severing of the fifth head of Brahmā, are also very popular subjects.

We may remember what caused the virtuous ascetic's indignation (see p. 118). Now, as soon as his wrath fell from him, and he perceived the enormity of his act, he was seized with madness. One day as he was going through a forest he found within it certain *ṛishis* (hermits) who were given up to meditation and penance. At the sight of this young beggar, handsome as a god under his rags, the wives of the *ṛishis* were disturbed. . . . Their jealous husbands then set an enormous tiger on him: Ṣiva rent it and clad himself with the skin; a strong antelope: Ṣiva seized it as it leapt and held it motionless; a red-hot axe: Ṣiva caught it in the air.

The Yaksha demons, terrible genii, are Ṣiva's bodyguards. At their head he attacks Tripurā, the city of the air, the home of the Asuras, performing a thousand feats with Pināka, his terrible bow—for the weapons of the Hindu gods have their own names, like the swords of our paladins.

Fig. 14. PĀRVATĪ IN THE GUISE OF KĀLĪ
Musée Guimet.

Victorious over the Asuras, after killing the demon Tripurā, Ṣiva tramples upon his corpse to the rhythm of the Tāndava—that savage, triumphal dance which he will perform at the end of this present Kāli-Yuga, the Age of Iron—that is to say, on the fated day of the great cataclysm, the day of *pralayā*, when in his joy at the universal destruction he will be seized with a monstrous enthusiasm.

Pārvatī, the "Energy" of Ṣiva. When Pārvatī,[1] the daughter of the Himalaya, at length was able to throw herself into the arms of Ṣiva, become her husband, they made the world shake with their embracings!

Pārvatī, the Goddess of the Earth, is the exact counterpart of Ṣiva. She is worshipped under varying names and varying shapes: Umā the Gracious, Ambikā the Mother, Sati the Good Wife, or Gaurī the Shining, the Golden.

But most frequently it is Durgā the Unapproachable, Kālī the Black (Fig. 14), Bhairavī the Terrifying, or Karalā the Horrific. She is then the Goddess of Destruction.

Between her son Skanda, mounted upon a peacock, and her son Gaṇeṣa, who rides on a rat, she is often represented brandishing, at the end of each of her ten arms, harpoon, trident, sabre, arrow, bow, buckler, noose, bell, poignard, and discus.[2] Sitting on her lion, she overthrows the buffalo-giant Mahishāsura, whom she pierces with her trident. Female

[1] The Mountaineer.
[2] The discus, as well as the conch, forms part of her attributes; it had been lent to her by Vishṇu to fight Mahishāsura.

Fig. 15. Ṣiva with the Antelope
Musée Guimet.

worshippers, or Apsarases, playing the *vīnā*,[1] or carrying flowers, complete the group (Fig. 16).

On the Silver Mountain,[2] by the side of Pārvatī, surrounded by his children and his

Fig. 16. DURGĀ OVERTHROWING THE DEMON MAHISHĀSURA
Musée Guimet.

servants, Ṣiva gives audience to the illustrious sages, the famous ascetics who come with adoration to bring the divine pair the inestimable fruits of their ardent piety and their profound meditations (Fig. 17).

For the two spouses are in reality but one and the same person. Pārvatī, whatever the

[1] A kind of lute.   [2] Mount Kailāsa, situated beyond the Himalayas.

name she may bear, is only the *Ṣakti*, the materialized energy of the god himself. Here we have the explanation of his androgynous portraits.

Another wife of Ṣiva mentioned by the texts, is Satī, the daughter of Daksha, the son of Aga.[1]

Daksha had married the daughter of Manu, Prasūti, the goddess genitrix. By her he had "sixteen beautiful-eyed daughters." Thirteen were given to Yama,[2] the King of the other world, one to Agni, one to the Pitṛis,[3] and the sixteenth to Bhava-Ṣiva.

But Daksha was so indignant when he learned that the husband of his sixteenth daughter haunted the cremation grounds that he did not include him among the gods to whom he made a great sacrifice. This offensive exclusion annoyed the beautiful Satī so much that she threw herself into the fire that was to consume the offerings—to the huge wrath of Ṣiva. To disturb the ceremony he sent Vīrabhadra, one of his emanations. Everything was terribly ravaged by him, the bystanders massacred, the gods put to flight, and Daksha decapitated (Fig. 18). Satī, seeing her father in this plight, implored Ṣiva to give him back his life. To which he consented.

And life was restored to him—though not his head, for it had been flung by the "three-eyed giant" into the sacrificial fire, and he had to manage with the head of a ram.[4]

Fig. 17. ṢIVA AND PĀRVATĪ ON THE WHITE BULL
Musée Guimet.

Emanations of Ṣiva and Pārvatī. Among the children of Ṣiva and Pārvatī one in especial is worthy of our attention. This is the chief of the Gaṇas, or acolytes, of Ṣiva. He is called Gaṇeṣa, or Gaṇapati. His attributes are the elephant's tusk and the rosary.

Adventures of Gaṇeṣa. Surprised in the bath by her husband, Pārvatī said to

[1] The name signifies 'not-born,' 'uncreated,'—*i.e.*, primordial.
[2] Or Dharma. The personification of moral law.
[3] The Manes.
[4] *Cf.* the episode of the dismembering of Indra, p. 110.

herself that she must have a servant to guard her door. From the dew of her body mixed with dust she kneaded a handsome young man, who came to life and became her *dvārapāla*—that is to say, the usher who mounts guard on the threshold of the door.

One day when Ṣiva sought to make his way into his wife's apartments he found himself opposed by this stubborn guardian, who forgot himself so far as to strike the god. Ṣiva then called up his *bhūtagaṇas*[1] and bade them slay this rash fellow. As the culprit by his

Fig. 18. Vīrabhadra destroying the Sacrifice of Daksha
Jouveau-Dubreuil, *Archéologie du sud de l'Inde.*

supereminent valiancy held in check not only the demons but also the gods who had come to help them, Vishṇu could not but intervene, as the honour of the celestial troops was at stake. Seeing that it was impossible to overcome Gaṇeṣa by force, he caused the beautiful Māyā[2] to rise up before his eyes. Troubled by the ravishing image, Pārvatī's champion was struck with astonishment for a moment, which was at once taken advantage of by one of his assailants, who cut off his head.

Pārvatī, furious at the death of her own creature, threw herself upon the gods with such frenzied violence that instead of continuing the struggle they judged it prudent to appeal to the mediation of the Sages. Pārvatī consented to make peace provided that his

[1] Troop of demons devoted to Ṣiva. [2] Illusion.

SIVA AND PARVATI
(Musée Guimet.)

life—and his head—were restored to the faithful guardian who had met death in her service.

Then Ṣiva sent the gods to the north, bidding them bring back the head of the first animal they might encounter. This was an elephant. And henceforth Gaṇeṣa *recapitated* and resuscitated, was to bear the name of Gajānana (" Elephant-face ").

Elephant-face, but lion-heart, always! So much so that when he was presented in this state to Ṣiva the latter held no grudge against him. Desiring to see only his valour, he entrusted him with the command of his armies. From this comes the surname of Gaṇeṣa, " chief of the troops." [1]

This god is in any case very rich in surnames. We must add that of Vighneṣvara, " Lord of the Obstacle," by which he is invoked when his aid is sought in difficult undertakings.

The rat that serves him as a mount is a demon he subdued of old and constrained to take this ignominious shape (Fig. 19).

According to other texts, the elephant face of Gaṇeṣa was of much less complicated origin: Ṣiva and Pārvatī had the whim one day to turn themselves into a pair of elephants, and from their amorous play a son was born to them with an elephant head.

But if Gaṇeṣa is the bravest of the brave he is also a transcendent gormandizer.

Fig. 19. GAṆEṢA AND HIS RAT
Jouveau-Dubreuil, *Archéologie du sud de l'Inde.*

One day when the offerings of *modakas* [2] had been particularly copious, and he had stuffed himself to the teeth, he thought that a little night excursion would be good for his digestion. Accordingly he mounted his saddle rat. Now, as they went on their way, one carrying the other, not thinking of any harm, behold, a fine large serpent got in the path of Master Rat. We must not ask how fear gnawed at his legs! Which made him give a sudden jerk and start, not without prejudice to his rider, who tumbled on the ground so unluckily that his belly burst! But the worst thing was that all those excellent cakes escaped and went rolling wildly this way and that. When Gaṇeṣa saw the damage he came to his feet incontinent, and before anything else he picked them all up again, carefully stuffing them back into his paunch, without missing a single one. And to keep them from escaping through the slit that still remained

[1] He is also called Gaṇapati, Chief of the Gaṇas, the little genii of Kailāsa.
[2] Sacrificial cakes.

in his belly he seized the ill-omened serpent and wound it round himself.[1] And in this fashion he who had caused the mischief repaired it.

As Gaṇeṣa was making ready, in this array, to remount his beast and continue his journey, there arose such a riotous clamour in the bosom of the skies that a thousand donkeys might have been braying at once! It was the Orb-of-Night and the Twenty-seven Constellations, his wives, guffawing with laughter at the expense of poor Gaṇeṣa! Whereat he was so angry that, breaking off one of his tusks and pronouncing the great cursing, he flung both straight as a dart at Messire Moon, who was so smartly hit that he turned black as pitch. The poor nights had to wear mourning for the moonlight, to the great satisfaction of thieves, though not of honest folk, who complained to the gods, who thereupon coaxed the touchy son of Pārvatī and entreated his Ventripotence to forgive the mocker. Which he did. But only half, all the same, for he laid upon him—by way of revenge, and to prevent him from laughing, except with proper caution—a certain periodic wasting, which still continues.

Fig. 20. GAṆEṢA
Musée Guimet.

And that is why the god Gaṇeṣa now has only one tusk.

This fairy-tale—to which, in accordance with the expressed wish of our editor, we have given a slightly Western colour and animation[2]—is certainly the most amusing of the explanatory legends that deal with this particular characteristic of the divinity. But there are others.

When Kṛishṇa had gone to Mount Kailāsa to return to Ṣiva the axe the god had lent him to fight against the Kshatriyas, and as he was about to cross the threshold of the divine dwelling, he found the terrible guardian of the door there to forbid his entrance, as Ṣiva was then alone with Pārvatī. Then in an impatient movement Kṛishṇa sped the axe that had conquered the Kshatriyas at Gaṇeṣa's head. He might very well have warded off the blow, but, not wishing to have it said that his father's weapon was ineffective, he contented himself with receiving it on his left tusk, which it broke.

The other version of the same theme has it that one day when Vyāsa, the author of the *Mahābhārata*, was declaiming his work to him Gaṇeṣa pulled out one of his tusks so that he could write down the marvellous poem with this improvised stylus. That is why the elephant-god became the god of the literati (Fig. 20).

[1] Hence certain images of Gaṇeṣa show him with a serpent for girdle.

[2] As we have done to some of the other legends contained in this study.

He is the God of Intelligence too. For the following reason: he and his brother Subrahmanya being of an age to know woman, their father and their mother [1] told them that they would marry the one that went round the world the swifter. At these words Subrahmanya set off at once like an arrow. Instead of dashing after him and trying to outstrip him, Gaṇeṣa first of all saluted his parents most respectfully, then began to go seven times from left to right, around them.[2] "Why do you do this?" they asked him. "Is it not written in the *Vedas* that the son who does seven *pradakshinās* about his parents has as much merit as he who goes seven times about the world?"

Fig. 21. SKANDA KĀRTTIKEYA
Musée Guimet.

This aptness of wit and respectful filial submissiveness brought Gaṇeṣa not one wife, but two, Buddhi and Siddhi, Wisdom and Success.

Kārttikeya, God of War. The circumstances accompanying the creation of Subrahmanya—called also Skanda or Kārttikeya—are at least as strange as those that surround the making of his brother Gaṇeṣa.

The *ṛishis*, being molested by a gigantic Asura, begged Ṣiva to give them a defender. Then, opening his third eye, he plunged its glance into Lake Saravana. At once there rose from the bottom of the waters six infants. The wives of the six *ṛishis* suckled them.[3]

Pārvatī wanted to embrace the six babes all at once, but hugged them so hard that she squeezed them into one! So that they were henceforth one single child, whose body was topped with six heads. And this miraculous infant was to cleave in twain the formidable Asura, the terror of the *ṛishis*. Of the two parts of the giaṇt one became a peacock—the hero took this for his mount—the other a cock, the image of which he put on his standard. Kārttikeya is a warrior-god. He commands Ṣiva's troops. He has four arms, but occasionally only one head. His attributes are the double thunderbolt, the poignard, and the trident; accompanied or not by his two wives, he rides on a peacock holding a serpent in its mouth (Fig. 21).[4]

Among the other emanations of Ṣiva we may further reckon Kuvera, the God of Treasures, who dwells in the bowels of the earth, where he leads a luxurious existence.

[1] Ṣiva and Pārvatī.

[2] This form of reverence is called *pradakshinā*.

[3] These wives were afterward turned into stars; they are the Pleiades (in Sanskrit Kṛittikas). Hence Skanda was at first called Kārttikeya.

[4] According to the *Mahābhārata*, the seed of Ṣiva, cast into the fire, was received by Gangā. That is why Kārttikeya is sometimes given as the son of Agni and Gangā. It was because he was fed by the six stars that make up the Pleiades that he grew six heads.

The Kinnaras, fabulous beings with the body of a man and the head of a horse (or *vice versa*), are his musicians.

Ṣiva-Linga, God of Fecundity. At the same time as he is the destroyer-god Ṣiva is also the God of Fecundity. He is then worshipped in the shape of the *linga* (Fig. 22).

Just as along the roads of Greek and Roman antiquity there might be seen images of Priapus at every field's end, in other words, practically everywhere, so in India to-day we may come upon those little cylindrical boundary-marks, more or less ornamented, which are the *lingas*.

This cult is in no way the same as that of the *ṣaktis*, which often involves orgiastic practices. Even in our day and in spite of the decay of the traditions the *linga* has not lost its esoteric symbolical character.

Fig. 22. ṢIVA IN THE SHAPE OF THE LINGA
Musée Guimet.

VISHṆU AND HIS AVATARS

Vishṇu, the Solar God. As in India the followers of Vishṇu are at least as numerous as those of Ṣiva, it was natural that the myths about Vishṇu in the Vedic epoch should be multiplied by reason of the continually increasing popularity of this god.

Two versions of the legend of the 'three steps'—one in the *Hymṇs*, the other in the *Brāhmaṇas*—show us that the Vishṇu of the *Ṛigvedas* was a god of majesty and power.

Legend of the Three Steps. Gods and giants were battling together. Victory was deserting the celestial cohorts. The Asuras were about to triumph and take possession of the empire of the world.

Vishṇu, a dwarfish Brahman, had taken refuge far from the noise of arms, in the peace of lofty meditations. In dire distress the gods begged for this holy person's intervention.

Tiny, armed with nothing but his intellect, Vishṇu then presented himself before Bali, the giant man-at-arms.

"What do you want?" said the chief of the terrible Asuras.

"Lay down your arms and grant the gods as their refuge nothing but the space enclosed by three steps of mine; the rest of the universe shall be yours."

Stupid Bali, having considered the legs of his tiny interlocutor, hastened to agree to his request.

But, lo! the marvel. Vishṇu takes one step, he clears the Sky; two steps, the Earth; three steps, the Lower World (Fig. 24).

And that is why Vishṇu has been named Trivikrama, which means "Of the three Steps."

This symbolic story probably conceals some solar myth: Vishṇu going through the sky, the air, and the earth, driving away the darkness.

According to a commentator on the *Ṛigveda*, the three fiery manifestations of Vishṇu are flame, lightning, and the sun. The flame spreading on earth, the lightning piercing the air, and the sun travelling across the sky, would accordingly be the three strides of the god

Fig. 23. VISHṆU WITH THE CLUB
Musée Guimet.

Fig. 24. VISHṆU TRIVIKRAMA
Musée Guimet.

Unless we prefer, with another expositor, to see the rise, the apogee, and the setting of the luminary, the three principal phases of the day.

One of Vishṇu's surnames is Nārāyana ("Protector of Men"). He is also, as the Sun, called Sūrya-Nārāyana. He is one of the Ādityas.

Death of Vishṇu. The setting sun is Vishṇu dying. Such, at least, seems to be the esoteric meaning of an episode in the life of the god in which he dies a violent death.

The legend we find on this theme in the *Brāhmaṇas*[1] is a strange one.

By sacrifice all things were created—all things, even the gods—and all things obtained. As the gods were offering a sacrifice in order to obtain Perfection it was Vishṇu who

[1] *Ṣatapatha-Brāhmaṇa*, xiv, I, i, 5 *sq.*

had ended the ritual ceremonies before all the others, whereby he became the most perfect and the most powerful of the gods.

The other gods, who were impatient under his domination, determined to kill him. One day they surprised him asleep. But as he was resting upright on his feet, his head leaning on the horn of his strung bow, they did not dare to attack him. Then the ants intervened. For a great reward they gnawed the string of the bow, which, suddenly released, sprang back and decapitated the divine sleeper.

"We have just slain the most powerful of the gods!" cried the murderers, who seized the *power* of their victim. It was divided into three parts: these are the three principal phases of sacrifice.

Fig. 25. VISHṆU HOLDING THE DISCUS AND CONCH
Musée Guimet.

The memory of the old conception of Vishṇu has only persisted in one of his attributes: the discus, his war-weapon, which recalls the sun's disk (Fig. 25), and in the Garuḍa bird, which serves him as a mount to-day as of yore.

Vishṇu dwells in the Vaikuntha—his paradise—on the top of Mount Meru, all gold and gems, which rises up in the centre of Jambūdvīpa.[1] Lakshmī, the Goddess of Beauty and Good Luck, is by his side. She is one of his wives.

Abode of Felicity, heart of the great lotus which forms the world, Mount Meru sees the nine planets swinging around it and the seven continents spread out at its feet. There the river Ganges takes its rise.

Vishṇu's other wife is Bhūmi-devī, the Goddess of the Earth.

Lakshmī and Bhūmi are always represented with a blue or a pink lotus in their hands.

Vishṇu's colour is blue.

The Avatars of Vishṇu. Vishṇu, whose breath created the world, 'inhales' it at the end of every kalpa, or cycle. After which he will exhale it again, to inhale it once more. The rhythm of these alternate births and rebirths is that of the god's actual breathing. It is determined by the period (kalpa) during which the universe lives and in which its creator opens his eyes on his creation, and the instant when he closes them in the fecund slumber that restores existence to the regenerated universe.

One of the subdivisions of the kalpa is the *yuga*. It is generally at the end of this lapse

[1] The Isle of the Jambu-tree [*Eugenia jambolana*]—*i.e.*, India.

Fig. 26. LAKSHMI
Musée Guimet.

of time that the wicked triumph and the good are in bondage. Then Vishṇu becomes incarnated, battles victoriously against Evil, and inaugurates a new era.

These incarnations are the avatars—that is to say, the god's 'descents' upon the earth.

The *amṣāvatāras* are his partial incarnations, the god being well able to delegate only a part of himself, unless, on the other hand, he invests two or more men at once with his power, though in different degrees.

Thus Rāma, the favourite hero of India, and his brother Lakshmaṇa were both incarnations of Vishṇu, one more complete than the other.

Although the principal avatars of the god are ten in number, it may well be supposed that popular imagination did not stop there; it borrowed a great deal besides from the Vedic legends, among which borrowings we must reckon the avatars of Vishṇu in the form of a fish, a wild boar, or a tortoise. The others are relatively of less ancient origin.

Matsya-Avatāra. The 'descent' of Vishṇu in the shape of a fish forms part of the traditions relating to the deluge. Here is the gist of it.

It was about the end of the kalpa before the great deluge. Manu, son of the Vivasvat-Sun, was engaged in his ablutions, when in the hollow of his hand he captured a tiny fish. The Sage was preparing to return it to its own element, but the fishlet begged him not to do such a thing, so great was its terror of the voracity of the monsters of the sea.

Manu therefore placed his little *protégé* in a bowl, but on the morrow it had grown so big that he was obliged to put it in a jar. Three hours after there was no vase, however large, that could hold it. Manu then threw it into a lake, where it continued to grow so much and so swiftly that the Sage saw himself constrained to give it the sea, so that it might have room to move about. Then the fish said to Manu, "In seven days there will be the deluge. I shall send a great ship for you and the seven *ṛishis*. In it you shall embark a pair of everything that lives upon the earth and in the air, you shall lade it with seeds of every plant, and then you shall go on board. By means of the great serpent Vāsuki you shall moor the ship to my horn, and I will guide you over the waters."

Recognizing Vishṇu in this talking fish, Manu prostrated himself. Hardly had he done all the god had bidden him when, lo! the Ocean rose up out of his bounds, covering the surface of the earth little by little, and Vishṇu appeared in the shape of a giant fish with golden scales, lifting his head, with its single horn, above the waters. He brought the ship to the mountains of the North, and showed the Sage how to let the enormous vessel slide gradually down as the waters subsided. Since this time the northern slope of the mountains of the North have borne the name of "the Descent of Manu."

Saved from the deluge, Manu was the sire of the new human race (see p. 116).

Varāha-Avatāra. The avatar of Vishṇu in shape of a wild boar (in Sanskrit *varāha*) has for its motive the search for and the raising of the earth submerged by the deluge, which the demons were holding in prison. "Going through the sky, tail standing up . . . shaking his mane shaggy with sharp bristles, trampling the clouds under his feet, baring his white tusks, his eye inflamed," Vishṇu-wild-boar plunges into the floods, "follows by smell the track of the Earth . . . lying in the midst of the waters," overthrows the giant Daitya who tries to bar his path, and at last succeeds in snatching up Bhūmi-devī, the

Earth, from the depth of the Ocean. With his terrible tusks the god supported her, and Brahmā was no longer anxious how he might render her capable of enduring the weight of the beings he was preparing to create (Fig. 27).

Kūrma-Avatāra and the Churning of the Sea. The avatar of Vishṇu in the shape of a tortoise forms part of the famous episode of the churning of the sea of milk (Fig. 28).

We know that, the Gods and the Asuras having fought, the Asuras, as happened all too often, were victorious.

Consequently, the supreme gods, Mahendra (Indra), Varuṇa, and the others, having taken counsel together, without coming to any decision, betook themselves to Brahmā, who said to them, "Bow yourselves before the best of the gods and follow his advice." Then all paid adoration to Vishṇu, who counselled them to make peace with the Daityas and the Dānavas,[1] and in conjunction with them to direct their efforts to the possession of the *amṛita*.[2]

FIG. 27. VISHṆU-VARĀHA AND BHŪMI-DEVĪ
Musée Guimet.

Gods and Daityas straightway began to equip themselves for the churning of the sea of milk (see the section entitled "Khmer Mythology," p. 219 *et seq.*), hoping by this operation to bring to the surface everything solid in it, including the cup containing the marvellous liquor. As a staff proportioned to the depth of such a churn was needed, they wrenched Mount Mandara out of the earth. Then they asked the serpent Vāsuki to twine around it and act as a churning-cord. He consented, but on condition that in return he should have his share of the *amṛita*.

The gods on the one side and the demons on the other were about to address themselves to the work and seize the two ends of the monstrous serpent, when the Daityas, who were on the tail side, refused to lay hold of it, averring that this part of the body was ignoble. The gods accordingly changed places with them, and the churners, pulling each their own end alternately and in cadence, began to churn the sea with all their might. But at the first pulls Mount Mandara, which had no fulcrum, dropped into the waters. It was then that Vishṇu turned himself into a giant sea-tortoise, and placed himself under the mountain, and the two crews could effectively go on with their task. Still there was one critical moment, when the serpent Vāsuki vomited up the terrible *hālahala*, whose overflowing would have fatally poisoned all living creatures including the gods and the demons—the latter well placed at the reptile's head to receive the death-dealing flood first

[1] Names of different categories of Asuras.

[2] The beverage of immortality.

of all. Happily Ṣiva was on the watch, and we already know (see p. 121) how he caught the poison in his hand and swallowed it without taking any harm from its virulence, except a scalding in the gullet, the bluish trace of which procured him the surname of Nīlakaṇṭha.

The white elephant Airāvata, which Indra took as his steed; the ruby Kaustubha, with which Vishṇu adorns his breast; the tree Pārijāta, dispenser of good things;[1] the cow Kāmadhenu, the Goddess of Abundance; the moon-coloured horse Uchchaiḥ-ṣravas, the beautiful Apsarases, a quantity of treasures, and a thousand more or less fabulous beings came up first of all out of this churning; then it was the ravishing Lakshmī, a lotus-flower in her hand; then, lastly, the god Dhanvantari, a black youth[2] holding a cup in which the *amṛita* foamed and sparkled.

Fig. 28. Vishṇu assuming the Form of a Tortoise
Modern statuette. Musée Guimet.

The Amṛita, Elixir of Immortality. "At the sight of the god and the vase full of ambrosia the Asuras, eager to possess all good things, hastily seized on the cup." But, seeing that the Asuras were preparing to flee carrying off their precious booty, Vishṇu appeared to their eyes under the lineaments of Māyā (Illusion), whose beauty enchanted them so potently that they abandoned the vase that held eternal life.

This legend is taken from the *Bhāgavata-Purāṇa*. This is a collection of Vaishnavite myths, but as it was only put together about the seventh century A.D. it is not easy to perceive the primitive foundation under the luxuriance of the popular and Brahmanic additions.

The *amṛita* is of the same nature as the celestial *soma*, transported to the moon by an eagle-falcon.[3]

Legend of Kadru and Vinatā. The monstrous reptiles that swarm at the bottom of the ocean also sought to take possession of the philtre of immortality, but they were prevented by Garuḍa, their born enemy, although their brother, as the following legend establishes.

Kāṣyapa had two wives:[4] Kadru ("the Sunburnt") and Vinatā ("the Docile"). The Sage, before renouncing the world, had given them the offspring they desired; the ambitious Sunburnt had asked for a thousand sons, while the Docile had only asked for two, stipulating, however, that they should be more powerful than those of Kadru.

But the motherhood of Kāṣyapa's wives was in no wise to be like that of the other daughters of earth; like the Greek Leda, they gave birth to eggs.

At the end of many centuries—for the Hindu legends delight to count by hundreds of years—there came forth a thousand little serpents from Kadru's eggs. Vinatā's pair showing no sign of hatching, in her eagerness to compare her children with her rival's,

[1] Indra had it planted in his paradise, but, in consequence of feminine intrigues and jealousies, he was obliged to give this tree up to Kṛishṇa.

[2] The physician of the gods.

[3] Struck by an arrow from one of the archers of the Asuras, tradition says that a few feathers of the bird fell to earth, and that it was they that gave birth to the trees.

[4] They were daughters of Prajāpati.

THE CHURNING OF THE SEA
(Musée Guimet.)

she began by breaking one of her two eggs. There came out only an imperfect creature with only one-half its body formed. Aruṇa[1]—for it was he—ashamed to see himself in such a state, cursed his mother. The jealous Kadru, seconded by her thousand sons, reduced poor Vinatā to slavery. This humiliation continued for five ages, at the end of which Garuḍa was at length born from the second egg. To deliver his mother he fought and overcame the children of the Sunburnt. And that is why Garuḍa is the enemy of the Nāgas.

The Nāgas, Dragons or Water-hydras. The cult of these creatures, a kind of hydra or dragon, is still very popular, and certain tribes of India still believe themselves descended from them. Worshippers or protectors of several minor or major deities, the Nāgas[2] with their triple nature—divine, human, and animal—are quite the most curious of all mythical creations.

The *Hymns*, which speak of Ahi, the serpent lying on the waters, the foe of Indra, only mention one serpent-demon, while in the *Mahābhārata* they are legion. It is they who guard hidden wealth, and although they haunt the lakes, the rivers, and the seas, their true habitat is Pātāla, the underground world, the "happy underworld," whose capital is called Bhagavati, which means the Opulent, the Rich. In fact, it is overflowing with treasures.

Fig. 29. THE SERPENT ṢESHA SHELTERING VISHṆU AND LAKSHMĪ
Musée Guimet.

In spite of their venom the Nāgas are not always maleficent. On occasion they can be kind and generous. To human beings who have won their good graces they grant intelligence and invisibility. As for the Nāginis, like the Apsarases, they are most seductive creatures, and, like them, they often come to love men.

When the most powerful of the Nāgas had mortally poisoned King Parikshit, Janamejaya, the king's son, resolved, in order to avenge his father's death, to make a ceremony of incantation that would be effective enough to draw into the flames of the sacrifice every last one of the subjects of Takshaka,[3] and that thus this whole breed of vipers would be consumed.

[1] Aruṇa afterward was the Sun's charioteer.

[2] Nāga means, literally, "those who do not walk, who creep."

[3] King of the Nāgas.

The soothsayer therefore made use of formulas so potent that dragons of the sidereal spaces and hydras from the celestial waters began to fall like flies into the magic fire. But the Genii, who looked on this with no friendly eye, planned to upset the ceremony, so as to save their friends from total extermination. For this purpose they delegated the pious Brahman Astīka, whose intervention put an end to the falling of the serpents.

The Nāginis—the female Nāgas—are more often represented than the Nāgas. They have a woman's shape above, and end in a serpent's tail. Often, like their males, their hands are joined in the posture of prayer. For the serpent-demons seem to have the notion of evil. There are, in fact, kings among them who, to win pardon for some sin, have done penance like the great ascetics.

Fig. 30. Vishṇu lying upon the Serpent Ṣesha
Musée Guimet.

Thus Ṣesha, having declared himself ready to expiate the misdeeds of his race: "Thou art indeed Ṣesha," said Brahmā to him;[1] "henceforth thou shalt live for ever and shalt be called Ananta"—that is to say, eternal—and since that time it is he who by the will of the omnipotent god acts as support to the earth.

It is upon Ṣesha—the seven heads[2] of the fabulous cobra forming a canopy over the head of the Blessed One—that Vishṇu reclines when he sleeps the fecundating sleep that is to re-engender the world (Fig. 30).

The great popularity of the Nāgas has resulted in their figuring in many tales, terrible or simply amusing. Here, for instance, is the one that explains why serpents have forked tongues.

The undersea Nāgas had seized upon the *amṛita*. During the struggle, in the course of which the precious liquor was recaptured from them, a few drops had fallen to the earth. The Nāgas eagerly licked them up. But the ground was covered with *kuṣa*[3] a very sharp, cutting grass: they split their tongues, which thenceforward always remained forked.

We cannot here touch on all the misdeeds and all the prodigies the Indian poems

[1] Ṣesha means "he that remains apart from the rest."

[2] Some authors give him as many as a thousand.

[3] This is the grass used to strew altars.

attribute so generously to the Serpent. The imagination of the various peoples has in Hindustan always been exercised upon this enigmatic figure; traditions come from all points of the East and the Far East have helped to swell the legends about it still more here than anywhere else.

Nara-Siṃha. The lion avatar (Nara-Siṃha) of Vishṇu again had for its object to humiliate the Daityas, or demons.

Hiraṇya-Kaṣipu having desired to cause himself to be worshipped, his own son refused, declaring that worship was due only to Hari (Vishṇu), the omniscient and omnipresent god.

At these words Hiraṇya-Kaṣipu smote upon a pillar, crying, "Let him come forth from this if he is everywhere!" Immediately from the pillar came forth the god in the shape of a man and of a lion, terrible, with his eyes

> red as gold burnished in the fire, his face whose size was increased by a thick and bristling mane. . . . Like a snake seizing a rat, Hari seized his adversary . . . and, laying him back over his thigh, as it were child's play, with his nails he tore that skin the thunderbolt could not pierce. . . . Shooting out looks of insupportable fury, licking the corners of his wide mouth with his tongue . . . Hari, shaking his mane all dripping blood, made a garland for himself with his enemy's entrails [Fig. 31].[1]

Fig. 31. Vishṇu Nara-Siṃha and Hiraṇya-Kaṣipu
Musée Guimet.

Here we have once more an instance of amplification due to popular imagination working on a theme that originally was probably merely the simple dramatization in a symbolical guise of the strife between Light and Darkness—almost equal powers, which for a long time will win only indecisive victories over one another.

For the triumph of the gods to be complete and absolute a strange expedient and a strange hero must be brought into play—in this case Vishṇu.

It must be realized, indeed, that what complicates the task of the mediator is the total

[1] *Bhāgavata-Purāṇa.*

invulnerability conferred of old by Brahmā upon the King of the Demons. Gods, men, or animals, not by day, not by night, no living being could bring him to death. What will Vishṇu do to get the better of all these taboos? He will clothe himself with the omnipotence of a composite personality, neither wholly divine, nor absolutely human, nor altogether animal, and at that hour when it is neither night nor day—that is to say, at twilight—he will have the mastery over Brahmā's *protégé*.

Paraṣurāma. Vishṇu's 'descents' in the shape of a fish, a tortoise, or a wild-boar belong to the epoch of the making of the world; those as dwarf and as lion took place when, the world having at length been created, the gods and the demons were disputing its possession. To this same period (called in Sanskrit, as we have said above, *yuga*, a subdivision of the kalpa) belong the avatars of Paraṣurāma and Rāma-Chandra.

Indra had entrusted the cow Kāmadhenu[1] to the guardianship of the monks: the Kshatriyas having sought to take possession of her, the Brahman Paraṣurāma,[2] an avatar of Vishṇu, cut them all in pieces.

Now, all these dead bodies littering the earth left no place here below for the Brahman, defiled by so many slaughterings. He made his plaint to Varuṇa. "I grant you," said Varuṇa, "for domain the range of your bow." But, learning that under the external guise of the monk with the axe Vishṇu was concealed, he feared that the arrow launched by such a god might be capable of covering in one flight the whole extent of the earth. To correct Varuṇa's imprudence Yama took the shape of an ant and gnawed the bow-string slightly. Paraṣurāma could only draw his weapon half-way. So that his arrow flight merely reached the Malabar coast.

This bowstring gnawed by the ants, which recalls a detail in the episode of the death of Vishṇu (p. 132), allows us to observe once more how traditions change and how popular mythology proceeds: for the most part it is the ancient materials confusedly piled up in its memory that the body of believers makes use of to put together new tales and enrich its repertory of legends without much expenditure of original imagining.

Rāma-Chandra.[3] Vishṇu, incarnated in the person of Rāma (Fig. 32), Prince of Ayodhyā,[4] comes down upon the earth in order to reform morals by preaching through example: this is the theme of the *Rāmāyaṇa*, the most beautiful of the ancient poems of India, and one of the most beautiful in the world.

King Daṣaratha had made a solemn promise to Kaikeyi, the second of his wives, that if she withheld any one of her most cherished desires, on the day she was pleased to disclose it he would fulfil it.

Now, as Daṣaratha, grown old and blind, was preparing to consecrate Rāma, the son of his first wife: "This is my desire," said Kaikeyi: "that my son Bharata may reign, and Rāma be exiled for the space of fourteen years."

Then King Daṣaratha told Rāma, his beloved son, of the promise he had made, that Bharata must reign, and that he, Rāma, must be exiled.

So, with his wife Sītā, Rāma, without further questioning or any reproaches, left the kingdom immediately, never to return until fourteen full years should have passed. And

[1] Kāmadhenu in Sanskrit. Cow of Desires.
[2] Rāma of the Axe.
[3] Rāma-Chandra: Moon-Rāma, Rāma the Bright.
[4] Now Oudh.

his brother Lakshmaṇa was with them. But Sītā having been carried off by the demon Rāvaṇa, King of the island of Lankā,[1] Rāma, aided by the army of the apes, commanded by Hanuman, must needs recapture her. Recalled to his kingdom, Rāma at length ascended the throne of his ancestors. As for Sītā, as soon as the populace learned of her adventure with Rāvaṇa, they murmured against her, declaring that she was defiled; and that although the ordeal of fire, to which she had submitted herself, had shown her innocence. (See the section entitled "Khmer Mythology," p. 218 *et seq.*) Giving way to this popular clamour, Rāma repudiated her, and also his two sons by her.

Fig. 32. Incarnation of Vishṇu as Rāma
Musée Guimet..

Long and long after these events two young minstrels presented themselves before Rāma and began to sing of his feats. As they introduced into their lays circumstances that could be known only to Rāma and Sītā, Rāma questioned them curiously; he recognized in them two of his sons, and presented them to the people as such.

The life of Rāma is from beginning to end nothing but one continual struggle against the *rākshasas*, or demons, of whom he sought to rid the earth. He is rectitude itself, a model of obedience, constancy, humility. He is the noblest figure in the whole Brahmanic mythology, the favourite hero of India.

Lakshmaṇa, his brother, a partial incarnation of Vishṇu, is perfect loyalty.

As for Sītā, who represents conjugal fidelity and female purity, she is an incarnation of Ṣrī, Vishṇu's mate; but, being born of the furrow dug about the altar when Janaka, the King of Mithilā, was preparing to offer a sacrifice, she is also and thereby the daughter of the Earth. And when, driven away by Rāma, she invokes her mother, that mother receives her again into her bosom.

Rāma enlists into the army of Good all nature, both animal and vegetable. The apes will fight the good fight with him at the side of the gods; the very trees, in token of submission and partisanship, will bow themselves as he passes.

[1] Ceylon.

Reminiscences of the Vedas. Although the *Rāmāyaṇa* was recited and known at a very distant epoch, the manifestations of the Rāma cult are comparatively recent, and no trace of it can be found before the seventh century.

No doubt this epic story has been euhemerized under popular influence, but there is certainly a warp of ancient myths in the story of Rāma.

One of the *Vedas* tells us that Sītā, the daughter of Savita (the Sun), was joined in love to Soma, the Moon-god, who is the God of Fecundity as well when in the shape of rain or dew he moistens the earth. Now, we know that at the advent of Rāma-Chandra (the Moon-Rejoicer) the golden age was reigning here below. Might not Sītā, who is the daughter of the Earth, have been originally some rural divinity and Rāma a lunar god?

Fig. 33. KṚISHṆA-AVATĀRA
Modern print, from Jouveau-Dubreuil, *Archéologie du sud de l'Inde.*

The Birth of Kṛishṇa. Mathurā, between Delhi and Agra, in the midst of the tribe of the Yadavas, is where Kṛishṇa was born. These precise geographical and historical indications—for the Yadavas are part of the history of India—did not prevent the hero's life from giving rise to a solar cult.

The legend of the "Black" prince, the King of the Yadavas—who, under the name of Kṛishṇa, is one of the avatars of Vishṇu—is certainly the most graceful, the least superhuman, of the Vishṇu fictions.

Devakī[1] his mother, the wife of Vasudeva,[2] was the sister of the king, Kaṃsa. Kaṃsa, who had been forewarned that he would be assassinated by the eighth of his nephews, slew all his sister's children directly they were born.

When she was pregnant of the babe that was to be Kṛishṇa, directly the child was born she and her husband substituted for him the daughter of a house of poor cowherds, to whom they entrusted the newly born, who grew up in the forest, among the herdsmen, with the shepherd Nanda and his wife Yaṣoda (Fig. 33); so also a half-brother of Kṛishṇa, Balarāma,[3] likewise hidden away privily from the fury of the cruel Kaṃsa.

Kṛishṇa, despite his tender years, was of Herculean strength, and his "infant feats" surpass in prowess those of Hercules and Achilles. Brave and amorous, he kills monsters and demons and wins the love of the ladies.

[1] This name is often given to the Apsarases.

[2] The Vedic name of the celestial genii, which means "the Shining One."

[3] Bala the Strong, also a son of Vasudeva, but by another of his wives, Rohini.

Fig. 34. Kṛishṇa as a Child
Musée Guimet.

Kṛishṇa the Shepherd. The *Gīta Govinda*, the "Song of the Herdsman," celebrates the loves of Kṛishṇa and the herdgirls of the forest of Vrindāvana (Fig. 36). While he wantons with the *gopis* Rādhā,[1] his favourite wife, mourns. Her tears in the end bring back the faithless one, always smiling and always beloved.

The Hindu commentators have given this beautiful poem the same allegorical meaning as Christian mysticism attributes to the *Song of Songs*: they look upon it as symbolizing the trials and tribulations of the Soul that is fain to find union with its God.

It is not surprising that a legend that unites love and 'derring do' in so human and engaging a fashion should have captured a privileged place in popular imagination, and that Agni, Indra, and a score of other celestial great ones have been pillaged of their most remarkable feats and exploits in favour of this plebeian god.

Fig. 35. Kṛishṇa the Herdsman

Representations of the herdsman Kṛishṇa (Fig. 35) abound. Most are very charming. One figurine, rather uncouth in workmanship, and said to have been left unfinished through the death of the artist, is supposed to have been completed by Brahmā himself.

Death of Kṛishṇa. Nevertheless the reign of the carefree friend of the pretty cowgirls was not to be one long, suave eclogue: like the common run of mortals, he was to know adversity. Having done nothing to check the fratricidal struggle of the Kurus and the Pandus,[2] he is cursed by his mother. Bala the Strong, his half-brother, on the point of being vanquished, will call on him for succour, and Kṛishṇa will only arrive at the moment when the soul, in the shape of a white serpent, issues from the mouth of his brother in the death-throes, and goes crawling away to lose itself in the sea, where it will mingle with the Nāgas of the Ocean.

In face of the ruin of everything and everyone Kṛishṇa takes refuge in meditation. A clumsy archer[3] hits him with his arrow in the heel, the only vulnerable spot in his body. He dies. The sun goes out. The world goes back into darkness.

The legend of the herdsman-god allows us to observe yet once more the everlasting permutation of legendary themes. The birth and the death of Kṛishṇa recall in striking fashion those of the eighth Āditya. His mother abandons him at his birth; then he goes away to die in the midst of the Western Sea, exactly like Kṛishṇa, who, after killing Kaṃsa, purging the earth of monsters, and taking part in the great war of the Pandavas against the Kauravas, comes to his end in the City of the Gateways of the Sunset, in the middle of the Western Ocean.

Rustic felicity, warlike glory, fatal human destiny, divide the existence of him who is the most engaging of the incarnations of Vishṇu. If the most pleasing of all the legends

[1] The Goddess of Love.

[2] These are the Kauravas and the Pandavas of the *Mahābhārata*.

[3] Named in the texts Jara, "Old Age."

Fig. 36. Kṛishṇa-Gopāla
Musée Guimet.

of Hindu mythology ends in sadness, is not this because the heart-beats of simple reality are little by little communicated to the artificial life of the fiction? Is it not because we find in this god a human heart?

Vishṇu Kalkin. At the end of our iron age, in the form of the horse-headed giant Kalkin, Vishṇu will once more descend upon earth to exterminate the breed of the wicked. And this will be the day of *pralaya*, the day of total disintegration, the sinister day when Ṣiva will dance upon the ruins of the world. And it is then that Vishṇu will fall on sleep and absorb our universe so that he may create it anew.

We have now surveyed, as rapidly as possible, this fabulous domain of Hindu mythology, so vast and so varied that it can neither be taken in at a single glance nor brought within the bounds of any synthesis.

In the measureless forests of India the immemorial trees are enveloped by luxuriant creepers; their branches, which stretch down to reach the ground, take root where they touch, giving birth in their turn to innumerable scions, to the most unbelievable, the most abundant riot of vegetation.

There we have a true image of Hindu mythology and art: apocalyptic shapes, multiple heads and arms, signs and attributes without number, endeavour to establish a symbolism so extravagant that it is often impossible to say which is the god we catch a glimpse of through this exuberance.

And yet in the midst of this confusion there moves a governing idea that patiently makes its way to the light.

In India, as everywhere else, what legends and their clumsy fictions try to discover and explain is the genesis of our humanity, the knowledge of the phenomena of the universe. If Hindu mythology has a definitely cosmic character when it is interpreted by philosophers and theologians, in its popular versions it denotes a fundamentally human aspiration: to go back to the mystery of our origins in order to discover their first cause, to surprise in His work Him who creates, preserves, or destroys all life.

All is in all. The source of life is one; the multiple comes from the sole. What in short characterizes Hinduism is its definitely monotheistic tendency under the pantheism of its conceptions. Whether he invokes Prajāpati, Brahmā, Vishṇu, or Ṣiva, the thought of the faithful never veers; the names, the epithets, and the attributes of these gods are but the ornaments of the great veil that once lifted will reveal to us the *Īṣvara*, the One God, the Supreme Lord.

H. DE WILMAN-GRABOWSKA

Fig. 1. The Bodhisattva betakes himself to the Pleasure Garden

THE MYTHOLOGY OF LAMAISM

The iconography of Thibetan Buddhism, or Lamaism,[1] contains many narrative elements, illustrations of the life of Buddha and the principal saints. To this strictly traditional collection should be added representations borrowed from Saivistic doctrine (the terrible divinities) and the ancient local cults. Two reformations, one in the eleventh century (Atīṣa), the other in the fourteenth (Tsong Kha-pa), did not succeed in bringing about the disappearance of the magic rites (*tantra* and *sādhana*), which were current in the popular religion from the seventh century of our era, when Buddhism was introduced into Thibet.

In the seventh century Nepal was merely " a dependency of Lha-sa, the capital of Thibet " (Sylvain Lévi). For many centuries Lamaism held sway over Nepal; in the seventeenth century there were still twenty-five sanctuaries in the part of the country that had remained faithful to Buddhism (the kingdom of Patan). To-day Buddhism in Nepal holds only a very diminished place.

It was in the first half of the thirteenth century that the Mongols came into contact with the Buddhist Uigurs; first of all they underwent the religious influence of these tribes. A few years later the Mongols were initiated into Lamaism, which had penetrated into the Chinese province of Kansu. The zeal, the learning, the piety of the lama 'Phags-pa (Matidhvajaṣrībhadra) (1240–80) assured the success of the new doctrine. The Chinese emperors of the Manchu dynasty favoured Lamaism very particularly; on different occasions the Grand Lamas of Pekin (the Changskya Khutuktu) were the object of imperial favours. Many Lamaistic paintings were executed during the reign of the Emperor K'ien-Lung (1736–96).

[1] From the Thibetan *Bla-ma* (pronounced *lama*), 'superior,' 'eminent,' a name given to the members of the Buddhist clergy in Thibet.

"Lamaistic art," remarks M. Jacques Bacot very truly,

> never innovates; the lamas, who are the religious artists of Thibet, are not free to choose their subjects according to their inspiration, nor to interpret them in accordance with their own feelings. Both are imprisoned, stifled by the obligation to observe a rigid and elaborate canon, to change no attitude consecrated by tradition, to forget no single attribute. There is no variety beyond that which comes from the multiplicity of subjects and the richness of the Buddhist pantheon.

Fig. 2. THE LIFE OF PLEASURE IN THE WOMEN'S QUARTERS, AND THE FOUR ENCOUNTERS
Bacot Collection, Musée Guimet.

A study in detail of this superabundant pantheon would inevitably be tedious; we shall therefore confine ourselves to representative types and striking episodes.

Pictured Scenes from the Life of the Buddha Ṣākyamuni. It is a biography taken from the *Vinaya*, or "Disciplinary Rules," that provides the subjects for these illustrations. The artist who translated this history into pictures scrupulously respected the traditional data; our task in identifying them is facilitated besides in many cases by brief inscriptions that narrow and define the field of investigation.

Sometimes the principal scene occupies the centre of the composition. Often, too, scenes done in fine miniature are grouped about an image of the Buddha (Fig. 5). In the first case the central scene is framed about by the episodes that serve as prelude or epilogue to it. Thus the birth of the Buddha is preceded by a representation of the investiture of Maitreya, the Buddha of the future. (See the upper part of the colour plate facing p. 68.) Maitreya, kneeling, is receiving the diadem and the turban. Then the Bodhisattva—we will give this title to him who is to reach Enlightenment so as to become the Buddha Ṣākyamuni—leaves heaven to incarnate himself, in the shape of a white elephant, in his mother's womb. Queen Māyā, the Bodhisattva's chosen mother, is shown in the lower part of the painting lying upon a couch. The elephant, surrounded by divinities, figures in the upper part of the painting. Then comes the central subject, which shows the birth of the Bodhisattva.

The scene takes place in the Lumbinī Garden near Kapilavastu. The Bodhisattva's mother, Queen Māyā, holds with her uplifted right hand a branch of the *aṣoka*-tree; the babe springs forth out of her right hip. The gods Brahmā and Indra receive him in a white cloth. Immediately after his birth the Bodhisattva takes seven paces in each direction in space (to the left in the lower part). The Thibetan artist brings together in a single picture two definitely separate episodes: the scene of the seven steps by the lotus-flowers arranged in the form of a cross, and the scene of the bath by displaying two water divinities above the Bodhisattva, the Nāga Kings Nanda and Upananda, engaged in pouring the contents of two ewers over his body. The god Indra stands to the left of the Bodhisattva; another divinity bears a dish laden with offerings. The episode that follows this (Fig. 2) brings us into the palace King Ṣuddhodana has had built for his son. The Bodhisattva, sumptuously attired, is seated upon a throne piled with cushions. The seven jewels (*ratna*), the attributes of the universal monarch, are arranged in front of him: the councillor, the wife, the general, the white elephant, the jewel that fulfils all desires (*chintāmani*), the wheel (*chakra*), the horse. The Bodhisattva, from whom the sight of human sufferings had been carefully concealed, encounters one after another an old man, a sick man, a dead man; this sudden revelation disturbs him profoundly; a meeting with a monk brings him some comfort. The four excursions are represented on the other side of the balustrade that marks the boundary the Bodhisattva must not pass. In the lower part of the painting is shown the archery scene, farther to the left the hurling of the elephant. Here Devadatta, the Judas of the legend, comes in. Three distinct scenes are shown in the painting: (i) Devadatta,

Fig. 3. THE CUTTING OF THE HAIR: THE AUSTERITIES
Bacot Collection, Musée Guimet.

inspired with treacherous intent, kills the Bodhisattva's elephant; (ii) the young Nanda tries to carry the dead body of the elephant outside the city; (iii) the Bodhisattva, shown facing, finally rids the city of this inconvenient guest. "Having taken this elephant by the tail with his great toe, and passing over seven ramparts and seven moats, he casts him forth beyond the city the space of a *krośa*" (*Lalita-Vistara*). In chronological order this episode takes place before the physical exercises (archery and swimming) and the excursions. Obsessed by the memory of the four encounters, the Bodhisattva comes to the determination to abandon the life of the world; preceded by Brahmā, who represents the gods, the young prince miraculously leaves the royal city of Kapilavastu, without rousing the sleeping women (Fig. 2, upper part, and Fig. 1). Reaching a point at some distance from the city, he abandons his worldly attire and decides to sacrifice his hair to establish the irrevocable nature of his renunciation (Fig. 3). The tresses are received by the divinities. Clothing himself in the garb of a poor hunter, who receives the prince's garments in exchange, the Bodhisattva applies himself to finding a spiritual teacher (*guru*) (Fig. 3, on the left). For six years he gives himself up to austerities, disregarding the gibes of the passers-by; "those who came that way—young men of the village, or young girls of the village, or cowherds, or cattleherds, or herb-gatherers, or wood-gatherers—thought: 'This is a Piṣācha of the dust'; and they jeered at him and covered him with dust" (*Lalita-Vistara*) (Fig. 3, on the right). As the practice of austerities brings him no peace, the Bodhisattva relinquishes his solitude and accepts a plate of sweetened rice and milk offered him by two girls, Nandā and Nandabalā (Fig. 3, lower part, on the left). The other two scenes, which figure in the lower part of Fig. 3, are subsequent to the episode of the Temptation (Fig. 4); they represent, on the one hand, the merchants Trapusha and Bhallika offering the Buddha peeled sugar-canes (lower part, on the right), and, on the

Fig. 4. The Tempting by Māra
Bacot Collection, Musée Guimet.

Fig. 5. SCENES FROM THE LIFE OF BUDDHA
Bacot Collection, Musée Guimet.

other hand, the offering of four bowls by the gods of the four points of the compass (Fig. 4, lower part, in the middle). The Buddha accepts the four vessels, but reduces them to a single one.

The scene of the attack by Māra (the Buddhist Satan) (Fig. 4) follows very closely the details given in the *Lalita-Vistara*. The most monstrous and most hideously grimacing figures are grouped about the Bodhisattva.

> Māra hurled upon the Bodhisattva various missiles and mountains like unto Meru, which, being hurled upon the Bodhisattva, transformed themselves into canopies of flowers and celestial chariots. They threw the poisons of their eyes, the poisons of serpents, the poisons of their breath, and flames of fire. And the ring of fire came to a standstill, like a ring of light for the Bodhisattva.[1]

The Bodhisattva, with right hand outstretched, makes the classic gesture of taking to witness (*bhūmisparṣa mudrā*); for Māra the Tempter, on the point of being vanquished by the Predestined One, calls upon him to produce some conclusive testimony, and the Bodhisattva addresses himself to the Earth: " O Earth! I have realized the thirty perfections, and in my existence in the shape of Vessantara I have made the sacrifice of my wife and my children, and distributed gifts by seven hundreds at a time; but I have neither monk nor Brahman for witness. O Earth, why dost thou not come and bear witness? " (*Pathamasambodhi*). The Earth, thus called upon, bears witness in favour of the Bodhisattva. Māra the Tempter does not confess himself vanquished: he places himself by the throne of the Blessed One (Fig. 5, on the left: he holds a bow and bears the quiver equipped with arrows) and brings his daughters Rati, Arati, and Trishnā, who, the *Lalita-Vistara* tells us, " take the shape of women of different ages " to tempt him who had just attained to Perfect Knowledge. All for nought; the Buddha disdains the Temptresses, and Māra, definitely vanquished, takes himself off.

The last episodes of the Enlightenment cycle are represented in the upper part of Fig. 5. The scenes done in miniature are grouped around a Buddha seated in the Eastern fashion on the pericarp of a lotus; the Blessed One, nimbused and aureoled, makes the gesture of argument (*vitarka mudrā*). The first scene (Fig. 5, No. 1) shows us the Buddha and the Nāga king, Muchilinda, who presents himself in the aspect of a serpent; he at once entwines around the Buddha to protect him. Nāga kings, come from the different points of the compass, present offerings to the Master. The Buddha then betakes himself to the banks of the river Nairañjanā, where he must needs halt, overcome by weariness and illness. Māra the Tempter then approaches the Master, saying: " Bhagavat, the time has come to die "; but the Buddha repels the demon; the times of Nirvāna have not yet come full circle; the Law must be taught to the crowds (Fig. 5, No. 2). Indra, the master of the gods, then draws near to the Buddha and respectfully presents to him the fruits that will hasten his healing (Fig. 5, No. 3). The Buddha can continue his journey; he reaches the banks of the Ganges, crosses the river in miraculous fashion under the eyes of a boatman who had demanded the passage money; then he goes to meet his first five companions (Fig. 5, Nos. 4, 5, and 6). The ascetics remain impassive at the foot of the trees (Fig. 5, No. 7).

[1] *Lalita-Vistara*, Chapter 21.

CEILING OF THE TEMPLE OF LHASA

> But as the Tathāgata (the Buddha) draws near the five high-caste persons these, more and more incapable of sustaining the splendour and majesty of the Tathāgata, uneasy and twitching on their seats, all breaking their pact, go to meet him. One goes forward and takes his wooden bowl and his cloak, this other offers him a seat, this one a rest for his feet, this one brings him water to wash his feet. "You are welcome, Ayushmat Gautama! you are welcome! Sit you down upon this seat made ready for you" [Fig. 5, No. 8].

The five gather round the Buddha, and there in the Deer Park, near Benares, the Master expounds his Law for the first time (Fig. 5, No. 9). This is the beginning of his public life; fresh conversions increase the circle of the first hearers. Here is Yaṣas, the son of a rich banker of Benares, joining the blessed troop of the Five. Young Yaṣas wakes in the middle of the night; impelled by an unseen force, he goes toward the river Vāraṇa, sees the Buddha, and addresses him. "Monk, I am tormented; monk, I am lost!" Bhagavat makes answer, "Young man, come hither! This place shall be free of torment for thee, it will nowise be for thee a cause of perdition." Then Yasas lays down on the brink of the stream his shoes all adorned with jewels (Fig. 5, No. 10) worth a hundred thousand pieces, passes across the stream of the Vārana, and comes where Bhagavat is; then, having paid homage to Bhagavat, he takes up his place not far off (Fig. 5, No. 11).[1]

The conversion of three famous hermits, the brothers Kāṣyapa (Uruvilvā Kāṣyapa, Gayā Kāṣyapa, and Nadī Kāṣyapa), follows close upon that of Yaṣas. The Buddha first of all goes to the eldest of the brothers and asks permission to spend the night in his temple of the fire (*agni-charana*). The Buddha finds there a venomous serpent, which he subdues, and which takes refuge in his begging-bowl (Fig. 5, No. 12). Kāṣyapa refuses to recognize the superiority of the Master (Fig 5, No. 13), who performs a whole series of miracles, Kāṣyapa's disciples are unable to light the sacrificial pyre. The proud hermit then addresses himself to the Buddha, and the pyre lights at once of itself, and is only quenched after the Master's intervention (Fig 5, No. 14). The four great kings then come to pay homage to him (Fig. 5, No. 15). At length the Buddha disappears at the moment when a flood in the river Nairañjanā threatens to submerge the hermitage. Kāṣyapa is anxious, jumps into a boat, sets out in search of the Blessed One: the latter miraculously crosses the river walking on the waves. "Kāṣyapa! thou art not saved, and thou knowest not the path that leads to salvation." Overcome by this prodigy, profoundly humiliated, Kāṣyapa recognizes the Master's superiority and is converted (Fig. 5, No. 16). Following his example, Gayā Kāṣyapa and Nadī Kāṣyapa are converted too (Fig. 5, No. 17).

Bimbisāra, King of Magadha, hears that the Buddha is sojourning, with his disciples, in the neighbourhood of his capital Rājagṛiha; at once he sends an envoy to beg the Master to pay him a visit (Fig. 5, No. 18). Seeing the Buddha accompanied by Kāṣyapa, the people of Magadha begin to wonder: "Is Kāṣyapa the disciple of the Buddha, or is the Buddha the disciple of Kāṣyapa? Kāṣyapa performs a whole series of prodigies the better to establish his Master's superiority (Fig. 5, No. 19). King Bimbisāra then offers the community his bamboo park; the Master takes up his residence in it with his disciples (Fig. 5, No. 20); he then goes to Ṣrāvastī, where he is received by the rich merchant Anāthapiṇdada, who acquires the park of Prince Jeta; this magnificent residence is offered to the

[1] *Lalita-Vistara.*

Buddha, who receives King Prasenajit there (Fig. 5, No. 21). The heretics take offence at these generosities. The disciple Ṣāriputra then invites them to a kind of tourney. The heretic master Agnidatta turns himself into a monstrous, many-headed serpent, which is immediately overcome by a giant *garuḍa*, a magic shape of Ṣāriputra (Fig. 5, No. 22).

Fig. 6. THE GREAT MIRACLE OF ṢRĀVASTĪ
Bacot Collection, Musée Guimet.

The King Prasenajit, constantly harried by the heretics, calls upon the Buddha to perform a decisive miracle. The Master then executes a whole series of prodigies, a detailed description of which is found in the *Divyāvadāna*. The Thibetan picture-maker reproduces the well-known episode of the multiplication of the images (Fig. 6); magic Buddhas, surrounded by divinities and by monks, are shown in medallions set against the many-coloured aureole surrounding the principal representation of the Blessed One. The Buddhas are invariably seated upon the lotus. Divinities, among whom we recognize many-headed Brahmā and Indra, and monks are grouped about the throne of the Master. The lower part of the composition (Fig. 6) represents the rout of the heretics.

> At this time there was in this assembly Pāñchika, the great general of the genii. There came into his mind this reflection: "These folk are impostors who will torment Bhagavat and the Assembly of the Religious for a long time still." Full of this idea, he raises a great thunderstorm, accompanied with wind and rain, which demolishes and causes to disappear the edifice destined for the heretics. The latter, caught in the thunder and the rain, begin to flee in all directions.[1]

The Buddha next ascends into the heaven of the three-and-thirty gods to teach the Law there to his mother. This scene is represented in the upper part of Fig. 7, on the right. Queen Māyā is kneeling at her son's feet. A little to the left may be seen a monk hovering in the air. This is doubtless the disciple Maudgalyāyana, who is making for the heaven of the three-and-thirty gods to invite his Master to descend upon earth again. It will be observed that the heaven of the thirty-three gods rests upon a kind of stepped pyramid.

[1] *Divyāvadāna.*

The painter has been led, by the exigencies of his composition, to alter the rank assigned to the heaven of the three-and-thirty gods, which ought to occupy the second plane of Kāmadhātu (domain of desire). The miraculous descent of the Master took place near Saṅkāṣya. Viṣvakarma, the architect of the gods, builds a triple ladder for the purpose. The Master, escorted by Brahmā and Indra, arrives at the foot of the ladder. (See also Fig. 9, No. 1.) The nun Utpalavarnā employs a subterfuge so as to be the first to see the Blessed One again; she appears in the guise of a universal monarch (*chakravartin*), an ingenious plan, which enables her to push without trouble into the first row of the spectators.

Fig. 7. THE DESCENT FROM THE HEAVEN OF THE THREE-AND-THIRTY GODS
Bacot Collection, Musée Guimet.

Grave dissensions spring up in the Community, fomented by Devadatta, the treacherous cousin of the Buddha. The scenes about to be described represent the traitor's misdeeds. After several fruitless attempts Devadatta obtains magic powers (Fig. 8, No. 2). In order to profit immediately by this enviable privilege he gives a demonstration to Prince Ajātaṣatru, the son of Bimbisāra, King of Magadha (Fig. 8, No. 3). The white elephant, the horse, the monk, the child on the king's knees, are all magic transformations of Devadatta. The prince offers him five bowls full of food, as a token of his veneration. This generous gift is repeated every morning. Intoxicated by his successes, Devadatta goes to the Buddha and asks him to hand over the rule of the Community to him. The Master uncompromisingly refuses, and at once Devadatta sees himself stripped of his magic powers (Fig. 8, No. 4). Devadatta then takes away the five hundred monks he has won over to his teaching and withdraws—while a famine is ravaging the country—into Kukkuṭārāma, where he receives the gifts of Prince Ajātaṣatru. The two good disciples Ṣāriputra and Maudgalyāyana go to Devadatta, who invites the newcomers to take their place beside him (Fig. 8, No. 5). Despite his efforts to remain awake, he is overcome by slumber and sleeps (Fig. 8, No. 6). While Ṣāriputra exhorts his renegades to be converted Maudgalyāyana performs miracles. They finally succeed in convincing the guilty ones, who abandon Devadatta. Waking up, Devadatta rushes in pursuit of the fugitives; but he is brought to a stand by a ditch that Ṣāriputra causes to appear before him (Fig. 8, No. 7). The Buddha finally decides to excommunicate the traitor. Ananda, the Master's favourite disciple, assembles the inhabitants of Rājagṛiha and makes this announcement to them. " The Community proclaim that the character of Devadatta has become different from what it was, and that everything he does and says must be imputed only to himself, and not to the Buddha, the Law, and the Church." Far from inducing Devadatta to repent, this condemnation merely aggravates his resentment. The King Bimbisāra remains faithful to the Buddha; but the heir to the throne, egged on by Devadatta, has his father imprisoned (Fig. 8, No. 8). The old king patiently endures vexations and torments, and succumbs at the very instant when Ajātaṣatru, touched by tardy repentance, is about to restore his freedom. Devadatta does not fail to profit by the old king's disappearance by pointing out to Ajātaṣatru that it is to his advice he owes his elevation to the throne, and in return for his services asks him to recognize him as the Buddha. "But," says Ajātaṣatru, "thou hast not the characteristic signs of the perfect Buddha: the golden hue, the wheel." " I will provide for that," replies Devadatta. He summons a goldsmith; his body is smeared with castor-oil and gold leaf laid upon it (Fig. 8, No. 9). And on the sole of his feet the print of the symbolical wheel (*chakra*) is marked with a red-hot iron (Fig. 8, No. 10).

Devadatta has a catapult built. Five hundred men are employed on this task. But they refuse to work the machine; the Blessed One causes a magic ladder to appear, the workmen thereupon descend and gather round the Master, who converts them (Fig. 8, No. 11). Devadatta then has the catapult brought into action and succeeds in hurling a huge stone at the Buddha. Vajrapāṇi, armed with his thunderbolt, breaks the missile up into fragments (Fig. 8, No. 12); one of these fragments hits the Buddha's foot. The blood begins to flow. The disciple Daṣabala Kāṣyapa pronounces these words: " Blessed One, if it be true that thou hast in thy heart thy children and thine enemies alike, let the blood cease to flow! " The hemorrhage stops at once (Fig. 8, No. 13).

Later, the Ṣākyas send Devadatta to the Master to entreat his forgiveness. The villainous wretch smears his nails with poison and tries to scratch the feet of the Lord; but he changes his feet to crystal, upon which the nails are broken [Fig. 9, No. 1]. Living, Devadatta feels himself tortured by infernal fires, and when, by the advice of his brother Ananda, he seeks to take refuge with the Buddha he is cast into hell [Fig. 9, No. 2]. The two disciples Ṣāriputra and Maudgalyāyana visit the nether regions; they see Kokalika, one of Devadatta's adepts, who shares his master's sad fate. He is enduring, with another damned soul, a horrible torture. Upon the prodigiously hypertrophied tongue of the heretics a pair of oxen drag a plough the share of which opens a long bloody furrow [Fig. 9, No. 3].

Māra the Tempter now comes upon the stage again; the Buddha, growing old, desires to free himself from formal ties and enter into Nirvāna, and Māra rejoices. "Let Bhagavat enter into complete annihilation; now has the time of complete annihilation come for the Sugata." . . . " Not so much haste, O sinner, thou hast but a short time longer to wait. In three months, this very year, will take place the annihilation of the Tathāgata in the

Fig. 8. SCENES FROM THE LIFE OF BUDDHA
Bacot Collection, Musée Guimet.

element of Nirvāna where nothing remains of that which constitutes existence." And the sinner Māra reflects thus: "He will enter then into the complete annihilation of Ṣramaṇa Gautama!" And, having learned this, content, satisfied, glad, transported, full of pleasure and satisfaction, he disappears in that very spot (*Divyāvadāna*).

The Buddha then goes on his way toward Kuṣinagara; he halts in the wood of the two *ṣāla*-trees. Knowing that his hour is come, he requests Ananda to "place the couch of the Tathāgata between the two *ṣāla*-trees, with the head to the North"; disciples and genii arrange the funeral couch (Fig. 11). When the preparations are complete the Master

Fig. 9. SCENES FROM THE LIFE OF BUDDHA
Bacot Collection, Musée Guimet.

lies down on his right side, both feet together, and gives up his spirit to meditation, to the thought of enlightenment, to the thought of Nirvāna.

Various divinities stand behind the couch of the Blessed One. To the disciple Ananda he gives his last instructions.

> "The body of the Tathāgata is to be treated like that of a sovereign of the world. His body shall first be wrapped about in a new linen cloth, then in a piece of cotton, and this repeated five hundred times; it shall then be placed in a metal sarcophagus containing oil; it shall be covered again with another metal sarcophagus; then shall a funeral-pyre be raised of all kinds of sweet-smelling materials; thereon shall the sovereign's body be burned, and, lastly, at a crossroad a vaulted tumulus shall be builded. This is the way in which the funeral of the Tathāgata is to be celebrated." [1]

The Master subsequently gives his disciples a last commandment: "Monks, forget not this, that all component things perish!" and he enters into Nirvāna (Fig. 11).

On the seventh day, after the funeral ceremonies, the body is borne to the place where it is to be cremated; the pyre lights of itself miraculously at the moment of the arrival of the venerable Mahākāṣyapa (Fig. 11, upper part, on the right). The gods and the monks

[1] See Rockhill, *Life of Buddha*.

Fig. 10. THE PARADISE OF AMITĀBHA: DESCENT OF AVALOKITEŚVARA
Bacot Collection, Musée Guimet.

are grouped in front of the pyre, divinities appear to the waist in luminous rays, singing in concert. The ashes are taken up and subsequently placed in urns (Fig. 11, upper part, on the left) and distributed among the representations of the faithful peoples by the Brahman Drona.

Failing a complete translation of the biography of the *Dulva*, we have pieced together the texts edited and translated by Burnouf, Foucaux, Rockhill, and Schiefner, and commented upon the principal Thibetan illustrations of the life of the founder of Buddhism.

Fig. 11. The Entry into Nirvāna and the Cremation
Bacot Collection, Musée Guimet.

The correspondence of the pictures and the texts mentioned in the course of our description shows that the Thibetan artist drew his inspiration exclusively from the *Lalita-Vistara* and the *Dulva*. With rare exceptions we have only had generally to refer to the extracts from the original Sanskrit that are incorporated in the *Divyāvadāna* (partly translated by Burnouf in his *Introduction à l'histoire du Bouddhisme indien*), or to the summary of the biographical passages given by Rockhill (*Life of Buddha*), or to the systematic biography derived from the *Dulva*, which has been analysed by Schiefner (*Leben*). We have here kept only these fundamental references.

Amitābha and the Sukhāvatī Paradise. Amitāyus and Vajradhara. Amitābha ("Endless Light") (in Thibetan, Od-dpag-med), the metaphysical Buddha, forms with Ṣākyamuni and the great tender-hearted Avalokiteṣvara a kind of triad. Amitābha is throned in the paradise of the West, "that pure universe which is a mine of happiness." In pictures he is represented seated; his joined hands, brought together on his bosom, make the gesture of meditation (*dhyāna mudrā*) and often hold the begging-bowl (*pātra*). He is red in colour, his halo is green, his favourite animal is the peacock. Representations of the Sukhāvatī heaven, which are so widespread in Central Asia, are, on the contrary, very rare in Thibetan iconography (Fig. 10). "Amitābha, the guide of men, is seated on a throne formed in the centre of a pure and graceful lotus" (*Lotus of the Good Law*, Chapter 24). The Bodhisattva

Avalokiteṣvara stands at his right, Mahāsthāmaprāpta at his left. Divinities, faithful followers, and monks surround the throne, and the purified souls of the faithful come forth from the lotus. Avalokiteṣvara, who is to carry out his mission as the great consoler, delegated by the Buddha Endless Light, leaves the Sukhāvatī heaven; escorted by the gods, he lets precious jewels fall upon the earth (Fig. 10, No. 1). The compassionate Bodhisattva visits first of all the ogres of Ceylon, and converts them (Fig. 10, No. 2), then he teaches the Law to the Asuras (Fig. 10, No. 3) and the Yakshas; lastly "he shows himself in a supernatural fashion to the assembly of Ṣākyamuni at Jetavana"; he is then surrounded by the seven jewels (Fig. 10, No. 4).

Fig. 12. AMITĀYUS
Bacot Collection, Musée Guimet.

Amitāyus (in Thibetan Tshe-dpag-med, "Infinite Life") is a form of Amitābha that wears the adornments, necklaces, bracelets, ear-pendants, and diadem of the Bodhisattvas. The two hands joined in meditation hold the vase of ambrosia (*amṛita*) surmounted by a flower. This Buddha is generally seated in the Eastern fashion; sometimes he is represented standing (Fig. 12). In the paintings he is gold in colour.

Vajradhara (in Thibetan Rdo-rje-chang) also wears the characteristic adornments of the Bodhisattvas: his attributes are the bell and the thunderbolt (in Sanskrit *vajra*; in Thibetan *rdo-rje*). Vajradhara is considered as the Adi-Buddha (in Thibetan Mchog-gi dang po'i Sangs rgyas)—that is to say, the supreme Buddha (Fig. 13). As a matter of fact, he occupies only a second-rate place in the pantheon of Lamaism. The most popular divinity is unquestionably the Bodhisattva Avalokiteṣvara.

Fig. 13. VAJRADHARA
From a fifteenth-century Lamaiṣtic album.
C.-E. Bonin Collection, Musée Guimet.

Avalokiteṣvara (in Thibetan Spyan-ras gzigs). Avalokiteṣvara is the spiritual son of the Buddha Amitābha. He is the compassionate and succouring being *par excellence*, the consoler of the afflicted or the famishing damned souls (*pretas*). Avalokiteṣvara assumes multiple aspects; but it is the eleven-headed shape that is especially revered in Thibet. The eleven heads of the Bodhisattva are arranged pyramidally; nine heads are peaceful of look; the tenth is a scowling head, with a forehead eye; the last is the head of the Buddha Amitābha (Fig. 14). The Endless Light Buddha had delegated his powers to the All-Compassionate. Going about the world, he saw with anguish the hells full of contemptible creatures and the earth covered with sinners, and so great was his emotion that his head broke. Rudely drawn from his beatified calm, Amitābha endeavoured, though in vain, to restore his son's head; however, he managed, after several fruitless attempts, to endow him with eleven heads, the last being made in his own image (Fig. 14).

Avalokiteṣvara's shoulders are generally covered with a gazelle-skin, the head of which hangs over the left shoulder, and his ordinary attributes are the rosary, the lotus, the ewer, the bow, and the conch. The Grand Lama of Lha-sa, the spiritual master and temporal sovereign of Thibet, is looked upon as an incarnation of the Bodhisattva Avalokiteṣvara, while the Tashi-lama of Tashilhunpo (Bkra-ṣis lhun-po) claims to be the incarnation of Amitābha.

Avalokiteṣvara sometimes borrows the shape of a white horse to go to the help of those in perdition. This is the horse Balaha, who saves merchants fallen into the power of the ogresses (*rākshasīs*). He furthermore accomplishes, at the request of his devotees, a long series of miracles, which are enumerated in the *Lotus of the Good Law* (Chapter 25).

Maitreya (in Thibetan Byams-pa). Before leaving the heaven of the Tushitas Ṣākyamuni invests Maitreya with the turban and the diadem. Thus solemnly and ceremoniously invested, Maitreya is regarded as a Buddha; and so he figures in this aspect in the iconography of Lamaism; he makes the gesture of instruction (*Dharmachakra mudrā*), and is seated in European fashion. Most frequently Maitreya is represented in the guise of a Bodhisattva, sometimes sitting in European fashion (Fig. 15). A *stūpa* (monument, either funerary or commemorative) figures in his diadem; he makes the gesture of instruction, and holds two blossomed branches which support the wheel (*chakra*) on the right, on the left a ewer (*mangalakalāṣa*). In pictures he is painted white, yellow, or ochre; his garments are green or red.

Fig. 14. AVALOKIṬEṢVARA WITH THIRTEEN HEADS
Musée Guimet.

Fig. 15. MAITREYA
Bacot Collection, Musée Guimet.

Fig. 16. THE FIVE UPPERMOST HEADS OF A COLOSSAL STATUE OF AVALOKITEṢVARA
Musée Guimet (presented by Dr Péralté).

Mañjuṣrī (in Thibetan Jam-dpal). The worship of Mañjuṣrī was particularly widespread in Central Asia in the tenth century. This Bodhisattva, who is the incarnation of

Fig. 17. THE WHITE TĀRĀ
Musée Guimet.

transcendental Wisdom victorious over Error, is the object of a special veneration in the eastern part of Thibet. The sword is the principal attribute of Mañjuṣrī; to it is added the book which very happily completes the pious symbolism which makes Mañjuṣrī the supreme incarnation of Wisdom (Fig. 18). His favourite animal is the lion.

Tārā. Born of a tear of the All-Compassionate Avalokiteṣvara, Tārā symbolizes sublimated compassion; she is especially venerated in Thibet, where she is regarded as a Bodhisattva. The two queens, wives of the first Buddhist King of Thibet, Srong-btsan Sgam-po, are held to have been incarnations of Tārā. The king married first of all the daughter of Aṃṣuvarman, the King of Nepal; then he obtained the hand of a well-endowed princess, a relative of the powerful T'ang Emperor T'ai tsung; the two prin-

Fig. 18. MAÑJUṢRĪ
Bacot Collection, Musée Guimet.

Fig. 19. THE GREEN TĀRĀ
Musée Guimet.

Fig. 20. MARĪCHĪ
Musée Guimet.

cesses were fervent Buddhists; they were very speedily promoted to the rank of incarnations of Tārā; the Nepalese princess became a green Tārā (in Thibetan Sgrol-ljang) (Fig. 19). The green Tārā is seated on a throne; her left foot hangs carelessly down; the lowered right hand makes the gesture of charity (*vara mudrā*) and holds a branch of lotus; the left hand also holds a lotus, but the gesture is that of argumentation (*vitarka mudrā*). Of the Chinese princess, lighter in complexion, is made a white Tārā (in Thibetan Sgrol-dkar) equipped with the same attributes (lotus) as the green Tārā. The white Tārā is seated in the Oriental fashion; she has the forehead eye. The Lamaistic iconography possesses a further series of one-and-twenty Tārās. Ten statuettes belonging to this series figure in the Musée Guimet. These twenty-one Tārās are very frequently represented in the paintings, and usually surround a gold-coloured Tārā of somewhat languid beauty.

Marīchī, Sitatāpatrāparājitā, Ushnīshavijayā. Marīchī (in Thibetan 'Od-zer can-ma) is habitually represented with three heads (Fig. 20); the middle face, peaceful of aspect, has the forehead eye; the right-hand face is red in colour and grimacing. On the left is a sow's head. Under the shape called Vajravarāhī ("diamond wild sow") (Fig. 21) Marīchī is incarnated in the abbesses of the convent of Semding (Bsam-lding).

The most celebrated of these incarnations (Khubilghan) is in the convent of Bsam-lding, near the lake of Yam-dok (in Thibetan Yarbrog rgya mthso). In this convent, which belongs to the un-reformed sect of Kar-ma-pa (and therefore to a school of the Red Church), the Mother Superior is venerated as an incarnation of the goddess. She lives according to the severest of rules; she is forbidden ever to lie down; she must spend her nights in meditation; but by day she is permitted to doze a little in an armchair. Once during her existence, in a sealed room in the convent where rest the mummies of her previous incarnations, she must pay a visit to her predecessors in order to present her homage to them. She must besides go to Lha-sa in solemn procession, and she is received there with high honours. It is told how in 1716 a Mongol conqueror came to Bsam-lding to pillage the convent and how he sent orders to the Mother Superior to come to meet him, that he might see for himself whether she had a sow's head (Vajravarāhī dākinī is represented with a sow's head, and her incarnation (Khubilghan) is shown with a mark in the shape of a pig's face on the nape). The Mother Superior sent a refusal in reply, and when the exasperated Mongol came to the convent and had the external walls demolished he found a desert place where pigs were grazing under the ward of a great sow. When the danger had passed the desert changed back to the convent, the pigs into monks and nuns under the rule of the honourable Mother Superior. The Mongol was converted and offered rich gifts to the convent.[1]

Fig. 21. VAJRAVARĀHĪ
From a fifteenth-century Lamaistic album.
C.-E. Bonin Collection, Musée Guimet.

Fig. 22. THE GODDESS SITATĀPATRĀPARĀJITĀ
Musée Guimet.

Sitatāpatrāparājitā (in Thibetan Gdugs-dkar-chan-ma) is regarded as a form of Tārā; she is also akin to Avalokiteșvara; her name figures in the list of the titles borne by the compassionate Bodhisattva. She is usually provided with three heads, and may even have four. She has eight arms; her hands hold the parasol, the wheel (*chakra*), the bow, the arrow, the book, the noose, sometimes even the thunderbolt (*vajra*) or the bell (*ghanta*) (Fig. 22).

Ushnīshavijayā (in Thibetan Gtsug-gtor rnam-par rgyal-ma) also has three heads; one of his eight hands holds the double *vajra*; the other hands make various gestures: *vitarka mudrā* (argumentation), *vara mudrā* (charity), *añjali* (salutation, sometimes the gesture of reassuring). The attributes are an image of the Buddha Amitābha: the arrow, the bow, the vase of fortune.

[1] Grünwedel, *Mythologie des Buddhismus in Tibet und der Mongolei*, pp. 155–156.

The Terrible Divinities (in Thibetan Drag-gṣed). This group includes eight divinities: Lha-mo (Ṣrīdevī), Hayagrīva, Lcham-Sring, Yamāntaka, Mahākāla of the six arms, Brahmā, Kuvera, Yama.

Fig. 23. LHA-MO
Bacot Collection, Musée Guimet.

1. *Ṣrīdevī* (in Thibetan Lha-mo, or Dpal-ldan Lha-mo). This goddess is regarded as the protectress of the two great lamas of Lha-sa and Tashilhunpo.

> Being of all the goddesses the one who most ardently defends the doctrine of the Buddha, she was armed by all the gods: Hevajra gave her two dice to determine the life of men; Brahmā a fan of peacock feathers; from Vishṇu she received two bodies luminous like the sun and the moon; she wears one on her navel, the other in her hair. Kuvera, God of Wealth, made her a present of a lion, which she carries in her right ear. Naṅda (in Thibetan Dgah-bo), the Nāga king, gave her a serpent, which she hung in her left ear. From Vajrapāṇi she had a club; other gods gave her a mule. Venomous serpents serve for the bridle of her steed, etc.[1]

Fig. 24. LHA-MO
Owned by Commandant Vautravers.

Lha-mo had married a king of the ogres (Rākshasarāja), whom she hoped to convert; failing to achieve this, the goddess seized the king's son and flayed him alive; from his skin she made a saddle, which she placed upon a swift steed and took to flight. Wounded in his affection and in his dynastic hopes, the king of the ogres fell into a fearful anger; he launched at the fugitive a poisoned arrow that hit the rump of her mount; Lha-mo immediately healed the wound and pronounced a terrible anathema (Fig. 23).

[1] Grünwedel, *op. cit.*, p. 175.

A painting, executed in 1777 at the command of K'ien-lung, the Emperor of China, represents Lha-mo surrounded by numerous divinities (Fig. 24). The satellites of the goddess and the divinities are enumerated in an inscription, drawn up in Chinese, Mongolian, Manchu, and Thibetan, which figures at the top of the painting.[1] The goddess, with her body painted dark blue, wears a garland of severed heads; she holds the skull, and in her hair appear the goddesses of the four seasons. The serpent-harnessed mule is led by a goddess with the head of a sea-monster (Makara) and followed by the lion-headed Dākinī (Fig. 25). Yamāntaka figures in the upper part of the painting, between two divinities accompanied by their chosen mates (*ṣakti*). The painting is framed round with a double representation of the eight precious emblems and the seven jewels. On the back an inscription, also in four languages, gives the date and furnishes details with regard to the execution of this painting.

Fig. 25. DĀKINĪ, THE LION-HEADED GODDESS
Musée Guimet.

In the two-and-fortieth year of K'ien-lung an imperial decree was published, ordering the lchang-skya-hu-tog-thu (Grand Lama of Pekin) to draw holy images (following the text of the *Sūtras* in order to pay homage to the goddess Ṣrīmatī, of good omen), the image in the shape of a quadruped and that in the shape of a lion, protectors of the Law, the goddesses of the four seasons of good omen, the goddess that increaseth happiness, the five goddesses of great longevity, the twelve goddesses that eternally protect the origin of the Law. And this with the fulness of their marvellous virtue and their good augury for making all things succeed, all these images [are to be executed] on a roll [Fig. 26].

2. *Hayagrīva* (in Thibetan Rta-mgrin). This divinity, the protectress of horses, scares away demons with her neighings. A horse's head may be seen in her bristling hair. Hayagrīva was very especially venerated by King Khri-srong-lde-btsan, the protector of

[1] This inscription, vertically reproduced in Fig. 26, should be read horizontally.

Padmasambhava (see p. 176 *et seq.*). Her attributes are the sceptre, the noose, the wheel, the sword, and the lotus.

3. *Lcham-Sring* is the God of War; he is customarily assisted by two divinities: Srog-bdag (the master of Life), who bestrides a wolf, and Rigs-Kyi-bu-mo (the high-born

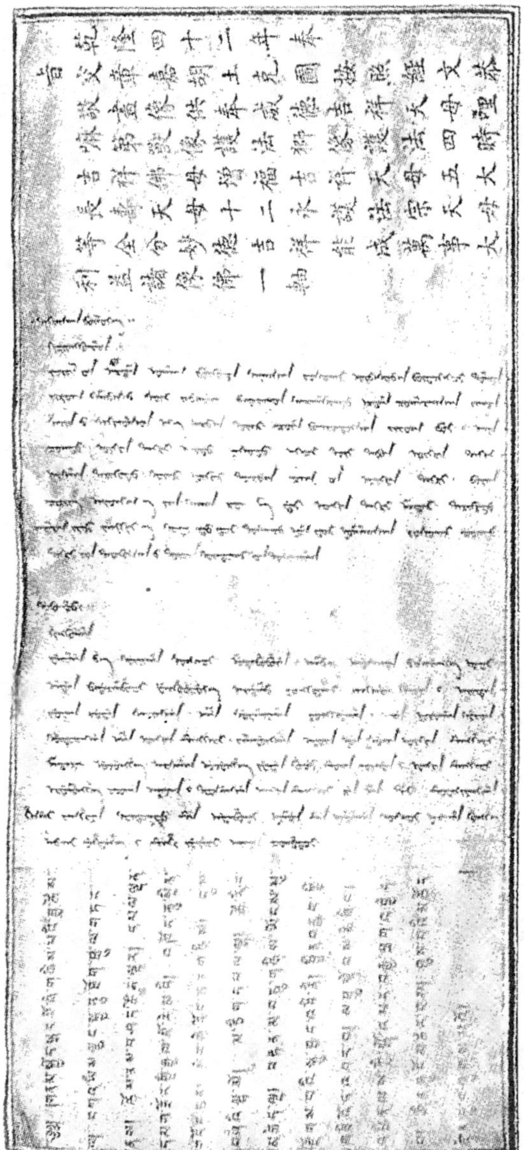

Fig. 26. Inscription on the Back of the Picture representing Lha-mo

Fig. 27. Yamāntaka
Musée Guimet.

Fig. 28. The White Mahākāla, Wearer of the Jewel that fulfils all Desires
Musée Guimet.

maiden), who rides on a lion. He presents himself in the habitual aspect of the terrible divinities, with grimacing face and bristled hair, and he brandishes a glaive.

4. *Yamāntaka* (in Thibetan Gṣin-rje gṣed) is a terrible manifestation of the Bodhisattva Mañjuṣrī; he is one of the most complex divinities of the Lamaistic pantheon; it was by adopting this form that Mañjuṣrī succeeded in subduing the King of Hell, the ferocious Yama. Yamāntaka is represented with nine heads (the principal one is that of a bull), sixteen feet, and thirty-four hands, which hold a considerable number of attributes, such

as the knife (*gri-gug*), the arrow, the wheel, the thunderbolt, the axe, the conch, a man impaled; two hands hold an elephant-skin, etc., etc. (From a text in the *Bkah-gyur* (*Kāng-gyur*) Buddhist encyclopedia, the *Ṣrīmahāvajra-Bhairavatantra.*) Very frequently Yamāntaka is represented embracing his chosen mate (*ṣakti*; in Thibetan *yum*) (Fig. 27).

Fig. 29. Mahākāla with Six Arms
Musée Guimet.

5. *Mahākāla* (in Thibetan Mgon-po, which answers to the Sanskrit *nātha*, 'protector') is a form of Ṣiva. This divinity is presented in several guises. Now it is a variant of the God of Riches known under the name of the "Tutelary God, wearer of the jewel that fulfils all desires" (Fig. 28), now the "Protector with four arms, or with six arms" (Fig. 29).

Fig. 30. Vaiṣravaṇa
Musée de l'École Française d'Extrême-Orient.

6. *Brahmā* (in Thibetan Tshangs-pa), or White Brahmā (in Thibetan Tshangs-pa dkar-po), carries a white bull and brandishes a glaive; he is customarily represented on horseback.

7. *Kuvera*, or *Vaiṣravaṇa* (in Thibetan Rnam-thos-sras), belongs also to the group of the genii who are the guardians of the four points of the compass; he is the God of Riches; his emblem is a banner and his attribute a mongoose (*nakula*) vomiting pearls. He is the guardian of the North (Fig. 30).

8. *Yama* (in Thibetan Gṣin-rje), the God of the Dead, also bears the title of King of the Law (in Thibetan chos-kyi-rgyal-po). King of the Law exercising his authority upon internal affairs, those relating to the infernal realms (*chos-rgyal-snang-sgrub*), and King of the Law ruling over external affairs, those relating to the world (*chos-rgyal-phyi-sgrub*). In this shape he is often accompanied by his sister Yamī, who strips off the garments of the damned. Yama is represented standing on a bull; he brandishes a sceptre in the shape of a child's skeleton (in Thibetan *Dbyug-gu*) and holds a noose; he has a bull's head (Fig. 31).

Fig. 31. Yama, the God of Death
Musée Guimet.

The Tutelary Divinities (in Thibetan *Yi-dam*). The most efficacious of the tutelary deities are, in the opinion of Grünwedel, those that act conjoined with their feminine energy (*ṣakti*; in Thibetan *nus-ma* and *yum*); they are ordinarily called *vajra* (in Thibetan *rdorje*). These last divinities, generally known as *yi-dam*, are composed of two groups, one of which includes the meditative Buddhas, while the other includes divinities that are manifestations of Buddhas and Bodhisattvas acting with a view to some determinate act of salvation.

Fig. 32. SAMVARA
Musée de l'École Française d'Extrême-Orient.

The most important *yi-dams* are Samvara (in Thibetan Bde-mchog) and Hevajra (in Thibetan Kye-rdor, or Kye-ba-rdorje).

Samvara is a divinity of definitely Saivite origin, who is incarnated in a special form (Dpal-'Khor-lo Sdom-pa) in the Lchang-skya Khutuktu, the Grand Lama of Pekin. Here is a detailed description, after Grünwedel (*Mythologie des Buddhismus in Tibet und der Mongolei*, p. 106), of Dpal-'Khor-lo Sdom-pa (Fig. 32):

> The god, with twelve arms and four heads, moves onward to the left, embraced by his *ṣakti.* On his fourfold head he wears a crown made of skulls (in Thibetan *thod-pan*) and a tall headdress on the front of which is seen a fourfold thunderbolt (in Thibetan *Sna-tshogs rdo-rje*), which shows a white half-moon on the left side. The forward face is blue; the two on the left green and red; in the bronzes the fourth face forms the back, the one on the right is white. The hands hold the following attributes: to the right a fragment of elephant-hide (in Thibetan *glanglpags*), which covers the back, the drum (*damaru*; in Thibetan *changte*), an axe (*paraṣu*; in Thibetan *dgra-sta*), a trident (*triṣūla*; in Thibetan *kha-tvang-rtse-gsum*) with a flag, the knife (*gri-gug*), and, lastly, a thunderbolt (*vajra*; in Thibetan *rdo-rje*); on the left, from the top down, the rest of the elephant-skin, a *khaṭvānga*, then a cup made of a skull (*kapāla*; in Thibetan *thod-pa*, *thod-khrag*), the lasso (*pāṣa*; in Thibetan *sags-pa*), the four-faced head of the god Brahmā (Tsangs-pa' i-sgo), and, lastly, behind the back of the *ṣakti*, a thunderbolt. The god is blue; the *ṣakti* is cherry-red; the trappings white; under the left foot lies the corpse of a naked woman with four hands and white trappings and the *khaṭvānga* in one of her hands. Under the right foot we may see a male corpse, blue in colour, girt with a tiger-skin, and with four hands also.

Fig. 33. THE YI-DAM KĀLACHAKRA
Owned by M. Ed. Chauvet.

The *yi-dam* Hevajra is even more laden with attributes than Samvara; he is described with great luxuriance of details in the *Hevajra tantra*; he is customarily represented with eight heads, sixteen arms, and four legs. The *ṣakti* that embraces the *yi-dam* very closely holds a knife (*gri-gug*).

A Tantric form of the Bodhisattva Kālachakra (in Thibetan Dus-kyi 'Khor-lo; literally " wheel of time ") is also known; it symbolizes a system of mystical philosophy that took its rise in the country of Zambhala, and was expounded by Kulika Mañjuṣrī kīrti (see p. 172), who is regarded as one of the previous existences of the Grand Lama of Tashilhunpo (Bkra-ṣis lhun-po). In his *yi-dam* shape (Fig. 33) Kālachakra has four heads and twenty-four arms. His principal attributes are the *chakra*, the knife, the skull, the mirror, the jewel, the conch, the lotus flower, the bell, and the thunderbolt. He tramples under his feet: (i) on the left a crowned figure with four arms holding the trident, the *damaru*, the skull, and the knife; (ii) on the right a figure with a monstrous face, entirely crushed and bent double at the thorax; this figure holds a bow and an arrow. Two squatted female figures contemplate the two trampled ones. The *ṣakti*, who has four heads, carries the knife, the *damaru*, the jewel, and the mirror. The *yi-dam* are legion; they are always differentiated one from the other by some detail, sometimes in the attributes, sometimes in the number of heads or arms. They are reproduced in the iconographic collections issued by the different monasteries of Thibet. The best known is that of the *Five Hundred Gods of the Monastery of Snar-thang*.

Fig. 34. Subhūti
Bacot Collection, Musée Guimet.

The Guardian Kings of the Four Points of the Compass (Lokapāla; in Thibetan Jig-rten skyong). We mention these guardian kings only as a matter of form, as they are studied in detail under other headings. They are: (i) Vaiṣravaṇa (in Thibetan Rnam-thos-sras), the guardian King of the North, King of the Yakshas (in Thibetan Gnod-sbyin); (ii) Virūpāksha (in Thibetan Mig-mi-bzang), guardian King of the West, King of the Nāgas (in Thibetan Klu); (iii) Dhṛitarāshṭra (in Thibetan Yul-'khor-srung), guardian King of the East and King of the Gandharvas (in Thibetan Dri-za); (iv) Virūḍhaka (in Thibetan 'phags-skyes-po), guardian King of the South and King of the Kumbhāṇḍas (in Thibetan Sgrul-'bum).

The Saints. 1. The group of the sixteen *Arhats* is studied in the section on Chinese Buddhism.

2. The previous existences of the Grand Lamas of Tashilhunpo (Bkra-ṣis lhun-po) and the Grand Lamas of Lha-sa. The monastery of Tashilhunpo (at Shigatse) appears to have been founded by a disciple of the reformer Tsong Kha-pa (fourteenth century); the superior of the monastery is known as the Tashi-lama, and he is regarded by the Lamaists as an incarnation of the Buddha Amitābha (Endless Light).

Subhūti (in Thibetan Rab-'byor) is regarded as the first incarnation of the Grand Lamas of Tashilhunpo. Subhūti, garbed as a monk, receives the homage of the genii of the waters (Nāgas), whom he is protecting against the attacks of the fantastic birds (the Garuḍas), their hereditary enemies (Fig. 34). The interest of Subhūti in the Nāgas derives from the fact that he had himself been a Nāga in a previous existence. The guardian Kings of the four cardinal points always figure in the lower part of the pictures representing Subhūti. A little above are seen Nāgas fighting against Garuḍas. In the upper part on the right is the disciple Maudgalyāyana; on the left Subhūti paying a visit to the Buddha, accompanied by his mother.

Kulika Mañjuṣrī kīrti (in Thibetan Rigs-ldan-'jam-dby-angs-grags-pa), King of the country of Zambhala. This philosopher-king, a fervent adept of the Kālachakra system (wheel of time), is similarly supposed to have reigned over heretics who worshipped the

Fig. 35. Kulika Mañjuṣrī kīrti
Bacot Collection, Musée Guimet.

Fig. 36. The Āchārya Bhavaviveka
Bacot Collection, Musée Guimet.

chariot of the sun; he banished them from his states after having invited them to expound their doctrines; not long after these same heretics, repentant and converted, came to implore for pardon. This appears to be the scene depicted in the painting seen in Fig. 35. Kulika, sumptuously clad and adorned, surrounded by councillors and servants, receives the heretics. In the lower part may be observed a guardian king who carries the attributes of Virūdhaka (the sword), of Vaiṣravaṇa (the mongoose), of Virūpāksha (*stūpa*-jewel). In the upper part is a representation of the supreme Buddha Vajradhara.

The *āchārya Bhavaviveka* (in Thibetan Slob-dpon-legs-ldan-byed), founder of the Madhyamika Svatantra school.

Bhavaviveka, in the course of his apostleship, converted a great number of heretics belonging to the famous sect of the Digambaras (naked heretics). Our painting (Fig. 36) represents a scene of conversion. A heretic is humbly abjuring his error and submitting to having his hair cut by two disciples of the Master.

Abhayakara (in Thibetan 'Jigs-med 'byung-gnas). This patriarch was born in the ninth century, in Bengal; he opposed the progress of Islam desperately, and wrote numerous treatises and commentaries on the *Vinaya* (in Thibetan *Dulva*), or disciplinary rules. He performed a miracle to save certain of the faithful whom a king of low caste (Chandāla) was holding arbitrarily in his gaols. To force the king to free his prisoners he caused a

Fig. 37. ABHAYAKARA
Bacot Collection, Musée Guimet.

Fig. 38. THE SA-SKYA PANDITA
Bacot Collection, Musée Guimet.

monstrous serpent to appear (Fig. 37). The king, thrown into a state of terror, immediately had the prisoners released. In the lower part of the painting is a form of Mahākāla that is a subject of especial veneration among the Moṇgols—the *gur-gyi-mgon-po* (" protector of the tent "). In the upper part, on the right, the blood-drinking ogress (*na-ro-mkhah-spyod-ma*) and a great sorcerer.

Rta-nag-'gos-lo-tsa-va-khug-pa Lhas-rtis. A scholar and translator of high repute, pupil of the great master Atīṣa (eleventh century), head of a school of copyists. In a painting in the Bacot Collection he is depicted with the reformer Atīṣa (Dīpangkara Ṣrījñāna) on his right; on the left Vajrasattva embracing his *ṣakti*; then to the right again Yama, the King of the Hells.

The *Sa-skya pandita* (1181–1251). This great monk was ordained by the reverend Yaṣodhvaja (in Thibetan Ggras-pa rgyal mtshan), and became eminent in all the branches of learning then in honour: medicine, grammar, sacred literature; to him we owe a great number of translations of theological works. Bonds of kinship linked the Sa-skya pandita and the lama 'Phags-pa, the chief engineer of the conversion of the Mongols to Lamaism.

In the course of a voyage to Nepal he succeeded in converting a famous heretic: our picture undoubtedly enshrines this episode. The Sa-skya pandita is seated on a gilded throne covered with a yellow material (Fig. 38). Behind him is a temple consecrated to the Bodhisattva Avalokiteṣvara. In the upper part may be seen a representation of the

Fig. 39. MKHAS-GRUB DGE LEGS DPAL-BZANG
Bacot Collection, Musée Guimet.

Fig. 40. BSOD-NAMS PHYOGS-GLANG
Bacot Collection, Musée Guimet.

Bodhisattva Mañjuṣrī. On the left is the reverend Yaṣodhvaja. Below the god Achala (Mi-gyo-ba).

Gyun-ston rdo-rje dpal. This monk was one of the most accredited representatives of the Kālachakra system; he also gave himself to the study of sorcery; thanks to his knowledge of the *Sādhanas*, he caused the terrible Mahākāla to appear. The divinities present are Bhairava (in Thibetan 'Jigs-byed) (upper part, right, of the colour plate opposite) and Mahākāla (lower part, to the left).

Mkhas-grub dge legs dpal-bzang (1385–1439). Pupil of the celebrated reformer Tsong Kha-pa, whose teaching he followed for thirteen years. At the age of forty-six he was raised to the dignity of Abbot of Dgah-ldan (Fig. 39). Tsong Kha-pa, seated on the white elephant, is shown in the upper part of the picture.

Diṅnāga (in Thibetan Bsod-nams phyogs-glang) (1439–1505) also frequented the monastery of Dgah-ldan, and subsequently withdrew into solitude, where he pursued his meditations and his labours. Diṅnāga is represented in his hermitage (Fig. 40). In the foreground celestial damsels, standing upon clouds, hold the ends of a cloth upon which our aureoled child passes along: a portraying of a prophetic dream supposed to have decided Diṅnāga's religious vocation. In the upper part of the painting the child Diṅnāga is shown kneeling before his Master, who is cutting his hair. On the right appears a form of Mañjuvajra; on the left Ṣrīdevī (Lha-mo).

Sumatijñanaṣrī bhadra (in Thibetan Pan-chen Blo-bzang Ye-ṣes dpal bzang-po) (1663–1737). This Tashi-lama was eight years old when he was solemnly recognized as an incarnation of Mahāpandita Sumatidharma dhvaja (1569–1662). He received in 1713 an envoy from the Emperor of China, who conveyed to him an imperial message.

The *pan-chen* is represented seated on a richly decorated throne; he holds the begging-bowl in his left hand, and with his right makes the gesture of argumentation (*vitarka mudrā*). In the lower part appear Lha-mo, the God of War, and a white Brahmā.

Fig. 41. TSONG KHA-PA
Bacot Collection, Musée Guimet.

Tsong Kha-pa (1355–1417) and his disciples. Tsong Kha-pa is in reality merely the surname of Arya mahāratna sumatikīrti (in Thibetan Rje-rin-po-tche-blo-bzang grags-pa). This surname means "the man of Btsong-Kha." Tsong Kha-pa was, in fact, a native of the little valley of Btsong-Kha (the Valley of the Onions), situated in the country of Amdo, to the south-east of the Blue Lake, where stands to-day the celebrated convent of Sku-'bum (the Hundred Thousand Images). He is said to have been taught by a monk from the country of the West (India?), who helped him to gain access to the oldest Buddhist texts; the reading of these texts allowed him to realize very rapidly the need for reforming Lamaism. In spite of Atīṣa's efforts (in the eleventh century) the discipline of the clergy was extremely lax, and not only was magic currently practised, but it was the essence of all religious exercises. These were the tendencies against which Tsong Kha-pa set himself to work; he studied first at Sa-skya, then at 'Bri-gung, then at Devachan; he went to Lha-sa and founded

upon the metaphysical dogma of transmigration a hierarchical constitution for the clergy, which combined in a harmonious compromise the contradictory advantages of election and the hereditary principle: two Popes, one at Lha-sa, the other at Tashilhunpo (Bkra-ṣis lhun-po), shared under different titles the supreme authority over the whole body of the clergy.[1]

[1] Sylvain Lévi.

The sect of the Dge-lugs-pa (virtuous), founded by Tsong Kha-pa, became the official church; its members wear a yellow headdress and yellow robes to distinguish them from the un-reformed red sects.

Tsong Kha-pa (Fig. 41) carries the book and the sword that are the attributes of the great Bodhisattva Mañjuṣrī who inspired him; on his left there stands as a rule the disciple Mkhas-grub dge legs dpal-bzang, who was raised to the dignity of Abbot of the monastery of Dgah-ldan (see Fig. 39). The successor of the reforming saint Rgyal Thsab-rje is usually shown at his right.

Fig. 42. THE GRAND LAMA NGAG-DBANG BLO-BZANG RGYA-MTHSO (1617–80)
Owned by M. R. Pfister.

From 1439 the Grand Lama of Lha-sa (Dalai Lama) was officially regarded as a reincarnation of the Bodhisattva Avalokiteṣvara.

> As soon as a Grand Lama dies the soul of the Bodhisattva passes into the body of an unknown babe, which must be born at least forty-nine days after the soul of the saint has left his body. Under the guidance of certain oracles the place where the Sprul-ba (' magic body ') is communicated to the infant is sought out. It is the Ḍharma-pāla (in Thibetan chos-skyong) of Gnas-chung, near Lha-sa, an incarnation of the god Dpe-dkar, who devotes himself to the search. The child that is recognized to be the incarnation of the Bodhisattva and its parents are brought to Lha-sa. As soon as he is four years old he is taken in solemn procession to the Potala, and entered as a novice in the monastery of Rnam-rgyal. At seven or eight years old he is invested as a monk (*dge-slong*), and he is regarded as the head of the two monasteries of Rnam-rgyal chos-sde and Hbras-spungs. Henceforward he gives himself up to study and asceticism.[1]

Mkhas-grub-bsod-nams-rgya-mthso received the title of Dalai Lama (*dalai* is a Mongolian word meaning 'ocean'; in Thibetan *rgya-mthso*).

The fifth Dalai Lama Ngag-dbang Blo-bzang rgya-mthso (1617–80) (Fig. 42) was a politician and a diplomat. The Jesuit Father Grueber, who stayed at Lha-sa in 1661, judges him with great severity. In 1650 Ngag-dbang Blo-bzang solemnly recognized the Grand Lama of Tashilhunpo as an incarnation of the Buddha Amitābha. It is a print of the feet and the hands of the Grand Lama of Tashilhunpo that appears in the painting (Fig. 42) representing the fifth Dalai Lama.

Padmasambhava. The Great Sorcerers. Padmasambhava (in Thibetan Padma 'byung-gnas), a native of Udyāna (north-west of India, Swāt), was called to Thibet by the Dharmarāja (King of the Law) Khri-srong-lde-btsan (A.D. 755–797). The Buddhism of

[1] Grünwedel, *op. cit.*, pp. 76, 78.

Padmasambhava was a strange mixture of magical practices, and of mystic religiosity strongly influenced by the old Iranian beliefs. This somewhat opportunist conglomeration was admirably suited to the "ultra-montane barbarians," but Padmasambhava had to reckon with the partisans of the ancient Thibetan religion, the Bon-pos; he succeeded in overcoming their opposition, and it appears that the royal environment was progressively won over to the new doctrines. The reforms undertaken by Atīṣa (eleventh century) and by Tsong Kha-pa seem to have resulted in modifying the teachings of this enigmatical person in the direction of orthodoxy. The books of the Reformed Church only mention him with regret, and the official chroniclers are particularly sober of detail when they find themselves obliged to bring him on the stage. The story of Padmasambhava, the *Padma thang yig*, has never been able to break through the rigours of official censorship. Let us hasten to add that this ostracism has in no way marred the prestige of the great saint of the Red Sects, who is the object of special veneration in the tiny Himalayan state of Sikkim.

The complete account of the existences of Padmasambhava the *guru* of Oddiyāna (Udyāna) (partly translated by G.-C. Toussaint) represents an enormous accumulation of legendary elements. The editors of the *Padma thang yig* set down to their hero's credit a great number of miraculous feats drawn from the legend of the Buddha or of the Blessed Avalokiteṣvara. Like the Buddha Ṣākyamuni, Padmasambhava can boast of princely origin as the son of the blind king Indrabhūti; he imitates the Buddha in his laudable desire to abandon the world, but we must admit that to attain his ends he adopts an attitude that is not strictly inspired by the feeling of benevolence for all living creatures that characterizes the true Buddhist.

> And he (Padmasambhava), to forgo reigning, gave himself to austerities.
> Then, naked, with the sixfold trapping of bones,
> Having in his hand *vajra*, bell, and three-pointed *khaṭvānga*,
> He began to dance upon the terrace of the palace.
> To behold this sight came a great concourse of folk,
> Whom he affrighted, feigning pursuit with the *vajra* and the *khaṭvānga*,
> And a powerful heretical minister remonstrated with him.
> There in that place were the dame Katamā and the son of Upata,
> Pratakara. He aimed full at the head of mother and child.
> The *vajra* pierced to the brain of the child, who perished.
> The *khaṭvānga* smote to the heart the mother, who expired.
> Then the ministers addressed themselves to the King.
> "Marked out for a sovereign, he has done injustice.
> Already he has killed the son of the feudatory lord, pretending reprisal,
> And now, behold, he has slain the wife and the son of the minister.
> If his crime be not punished in accordance with the law,
> Later, when once he is king, he will do still more wrong:
> We ask for the penalty of impalement."
> Such was the request, which made the King anxious and unhappy.
> Now, to comply with the severe law and the ministers,
> The King said, adopting the views of the world,
> "Is he the son of a Being—non-human, or what?
> Is he a celestial being incarnated? I know not.
> He shall not be slain, but he shall be banished beyond the frontiers." [1]

[1] *Padma thang yig*, Chapter 21. From the translation by G.-C. Toussaint.

In this wise began the wandering life of the necromancer Padmasambhava. The iconography of the Red Sects has a representation of Padmasambhava repentant, " naked, with the sixfold trapping of bones, having in his hand *vajra*, bell, and three-pointed *khaṭvānga*." That is the classic type of the great sorcerer (*mahāsiddha*; in Thibetan *grub-chen*). The most widely popular image shows us a Padmasambhava of less fierce aspect, seated upon the lotus (Fig. 43), holding the thunderbolt (*vajra*), the skull, the trident (*khaṭvānga*), wearing a headdress with turned-up brims surmounted by a half-*vajra*. His two wives are sometimes represented at each side of him.

Fig. 43. PADMASAMBHAVA
Bacot Collection, Musée Guimet.

The Great Sorcerers (Mahāsiddha; in Thibetan grub-chen). The group of the eighty-four sorcerers has a place apart in the iconography of Lamaism; it is not a question of official saints, but of personages whose activity is solely manifested in the domain of magic; they affect the propitious setting of cremation-grounds (*śmaśāna*), strewn with corpses. All classes of society, all ethnic types, are represented in this group: the King and the *śūdra*, the Aryan and the Dravidian. The biography of the eighty-four great sorcerers has been translated by A. Grünwedel (*Die Geschichten der vier und achtzig grossen Zauberer*). From this source we have derived the details that follow.

The great sorcerers are grouped around a central image representing a Buddha or a holy Lama; the complete series includes seven paintings. Sometimes the eighty-four great sorcerers figure in a single painting. We give reproductions here of only two out of the series of seven.

The central subject of Fig. 44 represents the lama Rje-btsun-thams chad-mkhyen-pa kun-dgah-sñing-po. The lama has on his head a characteristic yellow bonnet (in Thibetan *zva gser*), which stands out against a red aureole. His right hand makes the gesture of argumentation (*vitarka mudrā*). In his left hand, which rests on the sole of his feet, he holds a book and a veil.

1. *Udhili*, scion of a noble family of Devīkota, took delight in studying the flight of birds; he was initiated by the sage Karnari, in such fashion that he could fly about in air.

2. *Darika* first of all attached himself to the famous necromancer Lūipā, who sold him for a hundred pieces of gold to a woman responsible for the upkeep of five hundred *bayadères*; he spent twelve years in this woman's service. Like Udhili, he could fly freely in the air.

3. *Putali* received a picture and the teachings of the *yi-dam* Hevajra (in Thibetan Kye rdor, or Kye-ba rdo-rje). Putali attained at length, after twelve years' study, to the state of *mahāsiddha*; he was journeying, carrying the picture, when he met with a king. The king, considering the picture of the god, who was trampling under his feet the body of a demon, said to Putali: " It is unseemly that my god should be a footstool for thine."

He then had a painting executed showing the god trampled underfoot by the demon. Putali then put forth his magic power, and the god resumed his rightful place. This prodigy hastened the king's conversion.

4. *Panaha*. This *mahāsiddha*, a native of Sandhonagara, belonged to a family of *ṣūdras*; he had received magic shoes, which allowed him to go swiftly from place to place.

5. *Kokilī* was King of Champarna; he received the surname of Kokilī on account of the particular pleasure he felt in listening to the song of the cuckoo. The scene represented in the picture is the king's conversion: a Buddhist monk stands before the king and addresses an exhortation to him.

6. *Anangopa* stands inside a hut of green branches.

7. *Lakshmīkarā*. Sister of King Indrabhūti, who was himself a great sorcerer; she had married the son of Jalendra, King of Lankapura.

8. *Samudra*. This *mahāsiddha* is seated on a little rocky islet; he is simply clad with a loincloth, and his hair is drawn up into a knot on top of his head. In his hand he holds a kind of pestle. A disciple, completely naked, is seated near him.

Fig. 44. THE GREAT SORCERERS (MAHĀSIDDHA)
Bacot Collection, Musée Guimet.

9. *Vyāli*, the pupil of Chārpāti, makes the gesture of argumentation. A sorceress, placed by him, seems to be helping him.

10. *Nāgabodhi* figures among the disciples of the great patriarch Nāgārjuna; after his master's death he withdrew into a deep cavern on the side of Ṣrīparvata. He obtained the supreme *siddhi* of the Mahāmudrā.

11. *Sarvabhaksha*.

12. *Sakara.* This *mahāsiddha* wears the garb of the Buddhist monks. In front of him is an image of Padmapāni.

13. *Kapālika.* Master of a house originally belonging to Rājapurī. His five sons and his wife dying the same day, he betook himself to the place of cremation (*ṣmasāna*), where he met with Krishnacharī, who converted him. During nine years he studied the magic rites, wearing ornaments made out of his son's bones, and using his wife's skull as a cup.

Fig. 45. THE GREAT SORCERERS (MAHĀSIDDHA)
Bacot Collection, Musée Guimet.

14. *Kirava.* King of the city of Grahara; he holds a short sword and a round buckler.

The central part of the second painting (Fig. 45) is occupied by a representation of the lama Rje-grags-rtod-pa-lha-dbang grags-pa.

15. *Pachari.* A native of Champaka.

16. *Mekhalā.* This sorceress, a native of Devi-Kota, was the eldest sister of the sorceress Kanakhalā, who was converted by Krishṇacharī.

17. *Manibhadrā* (other name *Bahurī*), from Agrapurī, was converted by the sage Kukkuri. She is represented flying in the air.

18. *Kanakhā*, sister of the sorceress Mekhalā.

19. *Kalakala* made himself conspicuous by his turbulency, so much so that his neighbours, inconvenienced and infuriated by the hubbub he made, forced him to live in a cemetery. There he met an adept in Tantrism, who initiated him.

20. *Kanta*, or *Kantali.* This magician, a native of Manidhara, begged for his food among the streets of his birthplace; he was always clad in rags patched up as best he could. He was initiated by the *dākinī* Vetālī.

21. *Dhahuli.* This *mahāsiddha* was a ropemaker by trade. He was converted by an ascetic.

22. *Chārpāti.* This great magician was above all an alchemist; he taught Nāgārjuna the recipe for turning metals into gold. The latter is said to have given him in exchange a magic footgear, made of leaves, that enabled him to fly in air.

23. *Kumari* the potter was a native of Yomanasrī.

24. *Teli.* This great magician is seated upon a rocky platform; various vessels are ranged before him. In the background appears a person wearing a red bonnet and the costume of the monks.

25. *Champaka.* This sage, son of the King of Champaka, was converted by a *yogi.*

26. *Bhikshana.* This great magician is seated on a bearskin; he has a nimbus, and near him is a red *dākinī.*

Milaraspa (pronounced Milarepa; Mila, 'clad in cotton').

Milaraspa was a magician, a poet, and a hermit; all in turn, and so completely that the Thibetans find it difficult to refrain from separating the three personages, and according to whether they are necromantics, lay, or religious, Milaraspa is their greatest magician, their poet, or their saint. [See the colour plate facing p. 182.]

This strange being lived in the eleventh century (1038–1122) of our era. His memory is still living in Thibet like that of a recent personality. His present adherents are the heirs to his word orally transmitted by spiritual heredity uninterrupted for a thousand years. Certain of them meditate on the slopes of Mount Everest, where the first Milaraspa meditated in solitude.[1]

Padmasambhava, Milaraspa, and Tsong Kha-pa reflect three very different tendencies of Thibetan Buddhism. Padmasambhava reminds us of the favour enjoyed, at the beginning of Lamaism, by magical practices. As M. Jacques Bacot very justly observes, the conversion of Milaraspa "marks the appearance of mysticism in Thibetan Buddhism."

To begin with, Milaraspa is a magician. By his incantations he brings about the death of thirty-five members of the family of his uncle, who had cheated him of his paternal inheritance; later he annihilates the harvest belonging to the inhabitants of his native village, by letting loose violent hail-showers. Abandoning the study of magic, he goes to the school of Mar-pa, the pupil of the famous Naropa; this sudden change expresses the new tendencies of Buddhism.

It is the first attempt it makes to break away from the old magical religion with which it had intermingled four centuries earlier. The position of Buddhism in Thibet had been very precarious up to the ninth century. The primitive religion (Bon-po) had for the moment regained the upper hand. The grand sorcerer was in the ninth century the first personage next after the king, and represented the official religion. The history of Milaraspa already shows a reaction. The reform of Tsong Kha-pa is to be no more than the crystallization and codifying of the slow work of several centuries. . . .

After he has expiated his magic practices Mila plunges himself into mystic contemplation. Three centuries later Tsong Kha-pa will make an indirect attack upon mysticism itself, by means of a stringent liturgy: he will found the Thibetan theocracy and adapt Buddhism to the temporal government.[2]

[1] Jacques Bacot, *Le Poète tibétain Milaraspa*, p. 10.
[2] *Ibid.*, pp. 30–31.

In his pictures Milaraspa appears clad in white; his long ringlets fall down upon his shoulders; his left hand holds a flower; the right hand is placed near his ear, as though to catch the murmurs and echoes of the forest.

Set forth in the lower part of the painting we see the first episodes of the legend of Milaraspa: the destruction of his uncle's house by a scorpion "big as a yak"; the fall of hail; a little above, to the right, the arrival of the sorcerers from India, the meeting of Mar-pa and Milaraspa. The whole accompanied by inscriptions which are commentaries on the scenes illustrated.

Fig. 46. THE LEGEND OF GESAR
Saint-Victor Collection, Musée Guimet.

The Legend of Gesar. The hero Kesar, whose high exploits are recounted in a series of texts for the most part coming from Ladakh, is distinguished from the King Gesar, whose legendary origins, according to H. Francke, may be considered as going back to a very remote epoch and linked with the pre-Buddhist mythology of Mongolia. In our opinion the two legends have a common origin. The Ladakh version is laden with seasonal myths: Kesar has the power to make himself invisible up to the celebration of his marriage; at this moment he resumes his real shape (summer), but he is none the less endowed with the faculty of making himself invisible (belated fall of snow in springtime). The hero then battles against a giant of the North and delivers a girl who had been imprisoned in an iron cage. This version differs appreciably from the one shown in the illustrations in our possession. Although representing a legend from outside India, our picture documents have the Buddhist hallmark. The painting here reproduced (Fig. 46) gives us a central theme borrowed from Buddhist mythology, a representation of a handmaid of the goddess Lha-mo, named Mthing-gi zal bzang-ma, who bestrides a mule and holds an arrow (sometimes a fly-whisk) and a mirror. At the top there is a Tantric

MILARASPA (MILAREPA)
(Musée Guimet.)

representation of Ratnasambhava, flanked by two sorcerers. The episodes of the legend of Gesar are grouped about the central picture. Gesar appears entirely clad in white and with a four-cornered hat surmounted by a feather. To begin with, in a space of time not exceeding seven days, he destroys two demons (first and second days) (Fig. 46, Nos. 1 and 2); on the third day the three black birds of evil omen (Fig. 46, No. 3); on the fourth and the fifth days a yak and a black horse, shapes of demons (Fig. 46, No. 4); on the sixth a black she-goat (Fig. 46, No. 5); and finally, on the seventh day, he subdues a

Fig. 47. HOMAGE OF THE EIGHT GREAT NĀGAS AND OF THE ANIMALS
Part of Fig. 49.

heretical master (Fig. 46, No. 5). He makes two naked men drag a plough (Fig. 46, No. 6). The hero is sometimes facetious; the tale of his encounter with 'Brug-ma, the girl who is to be his wife, begins with a jest.

When Joro (Gesar) was one day a-hunting, Aralgho Goa ('Brug-ma), the daughter of Ma-Bajan, killed a sheep; with the flesh of this sheep she made a pie, which she put in a bag she carried on her back. Joro met her and asked whose daughter she was and whence she was coming. She replied, "I am the daughter of Ma-Bajan, my name is Aralgho Goa; my father has sent me to ask you for a camping-ground." "Remain here!" answered Joro, who took the meats she had prepared and gave them to his mother. When Joro came back he found the girl asleep; then Joro went to his father's herd of horses, took a new-born foal, brought it, and wrapped it up in the maiden's robe, then woke her up suddenly with the cry, "Arise! Arise!" The maiden awoke and sat upright. "What a sinner of a girl," cried Joro, " what a shameless piece has come my way! Is it from your dealings with your father that you give birth to a babe with a horse's head? Or were you in league with your eldest brother, whence doubtless the horse's mane of your child, or with your youngest brother, which would explain this horse's tail? Or did you give yourself up to a troop of slaves, to have your infant furnished with four horse's hoofs like this? Arise, shameless girl!" "What is this man saying, what does he want of me?" And the maiden rose up hastily, letting the little foal fall out of her lap [Fig. 46, No. 7].[1]

Gesar marries the maiden, then continues his life of adventures; he destroys the enchanted rabbits (Fig. 46, No. 8), kills the seven (or nine) evil spirits (*alvin*) (Fig. 46, No. 9), and reascends to heaven, where he finds once more the three Kings of the Law, among whom we recognize Srong-btsam-sgam-po, the first Buddhist King of Thibet, who wears in his headdress a little representation of Amitābha (Fig. 46, No. 10).

Fig. 48. (1) GṢEN-RABS-MI-BO AND HIS MAGIC BODY. (2) THE DESCENT OF THE BIRD. (3) THE BIRTH OF GṢEN-RABS-MI-BO. (4) HOMAGE OF THE ANIMALS.
Parts of Fig. 49.

Iconography of the Bon-pa. Legend of Gsen-rabs-mi-bo. The pre-Buddhist religion of Thibet is called Bon, and its adepts Bon-pa; the Bon communities are particularly numerous in Eastern Thibet; the priests live in monasteries where numerous pictures and statues of divinities that display a very strong Buddhist influence are found. This contemporary aspect of the Bon religion (*bsgyur bon*) is very different from the primitive form, a coarse Shamanism that gave a very large place to the cult of natural forces and demons and bloody sacrifices. In order to fight more effectively against Buddhism the Bon-po religion turned opportunist, adapting the iconography of the Buddhists to its own legends (Fig. 49). The story of the life of the great prophet of the Bonpos, Gṣen-rabs-mi-bo, is manifestly a copy of the legend of the Buddha Ṣākyamuni. Gsen-rabs-mi-bo leaves the Tushita heaven (in Thibetan *dgah ldan*) in the shape of a beautiful blue bird

[1] J. Schmidt, *Die Thaten Bogda Gesser Chan's*, pp. 48–49.

Fig. 49. THE LIFE OF GṢEN-RABS-MI-BO
Owned by Général Comte d'Ollone.

(*gyu-bya-khu-byug*), and becomes incarnated in his mother's womb. Section 1 of Fig. 48 represents at the same time Gṣen-rabs in his natural shape, and at his feet the blue bird, his magic body. The magic bird descends from heaven at the spot where in later days there will stand the *stūpa* marking the descent of the Master from the home of the Gods (Fig. 48, No. 2) (Ston-pa Lha-las babs-pa'i mchod-rten). Gṣen-rabs is born on the fifteenth day of the first month of spring, at dawn, in a garden of delicious flowers. He issues from his mother's right armpit (Fig. 48, No. 3); his colour is that of the snowy summits lit up by the sun. A slight ablution of *amṛita* gives him the fine golden colour he preserves until his Nirvāna. The first years of Gṣen-rabs recall the *Child-deeds of the Buddha*. He is instructed by a learned tutor, and becomes skilled in the arts of magic, to the point of being able to transform one body into several and to unite several bodies into one. He receives the homage of the eight great Nāgas and the animals (apes, gazelles, etc.) (Figs. 47 and 48). In this same painting are seen the principal divinities of the Bon-pa; the *khyung* with outspread wings (Fig. 47) and the *gsang-ba*, or a form very much akin to this divinity (Fig. 50) (Musée Guimet, *Guide-Catalogue des collections bouddhiques*, p. 116).

J. HACKIN

Fig. 50. Gsang-ba
Part of Fig. 49.

Fig. 1. SUDHANA DROPS THE RING BY WHICH THE KING'S DAUGHTER WILL RECOGNIZE HIM
Borobudur.

THE MYTHOLOGY OF INDO-CHINA AND JAVA

THE following pages will not be in any way concerned with the Annamite peoples, whose beliefs and traditions are attached to the civilization of China. I shall deal only with the regions which have been more or less strongly marked with the imprint of Hindu civilization, namely, the Khmer empire, which in the first centuries of the Christian era comprised almost the whole of the Indo-China peninsula, including a great part of the present Siam and Laos, and the kingdom of Champa, which corresponded very closely with the modern Annam. The heart of Indo-China, between the two zones of civilization—Chinese in the north and Hindu in the south—has always been barbarian and hostile to any foreign penetration, and is still not too well known. Here are aboriginal peoples, Jaraï, Sedang, Bahnar, Stieng, often described by Europeans under the general name of Moïs, among whom customs and traditions of a far distant past are still perpetuated. To the two rival and neighbouring peoples, the Khmers and Chams, I will add the inhabitants of the islands of the Dutch archipelago, the civilizing element in which came also from India, and whose centre is in Java and Sumatra.

These three peoples, whose monuments and sculpture are generally treated in histories of art as deriving direct from India, do as a matter of fact present an outward appearance of very close relationship. But it would be to some extent an exaggeration to represent them as Hindu colonies in which artistic forms only repeat prototypes from elsewhere, with some slight variations.

As a matter of fact, the word *India*, in the period when Java, Champa, and the Khmer territory saw the beginning of the full development of their civilization, did not denote a definite political unit; it was merely an assembly of little states, more or less independent, and history has not preserved for us the memory of any direct incursion of one of these small states into one of the three countries of Southern Indo-China.

The word *colony*, as we generally interpret it, supposes the incursion of a people into the territory of another by armed force, or at the least a governmental violence imposing its power and its laws upon the subdued nation, which is not the case with the countries under consideration.

The relations of these countries with India, as shown in the annals, the inscriptions, or the travellers' narratives that have come down to us, have evidently left a deep influence among the peoples who with the waves of Hindu immigration received new cults and new trends of ideas; but it does not follow that these peoples were barbarians or savages merely because we do not know what they were before the Hindu civilization was introduced to them.

With regard to Cambodia, for instance, M. Groslier has succeeded in showing that Funan, the country that immediately preceded the Khmer kingdom between the first and the sixth centuries of our era, already had an advanced civilization and a well-developed art, although it has left no traces except in relations with China. This civilization was strongly impregnated with Hinduism, and the first Khmer temples still show a very marked touch of this Hindu-ized art of Funan; but from the Angkor period—*i.e.*, about the ninth century—a reaction set in, and the Khmer builders and decorators changed the original elements to such an extent that the moment when Khmer art attained its culmination was the moment when the Hindu memories, still vividly active in literature and religion, almost entirely disappeared from architecture and decoration.

The same phenomenon may be observed in Cham art, but much less marked; nevertheless M. Parmentier, the best authority on this art, could say that "there are in it qualities of simplicity and distinctness that are not to be found in purely Hindu art."

With regard to Java and Sumatra, Mr Krom recognizes that the peoples of the great western islands of the Indian archipelago, Malayo-Polynesian by race, had at the beginning of our era, when the Hindus arrived, a certain degree of culture and civilization; they had an organized administration, "but," he adds, "we have no works of art and can form only a vague idea of the true character of the culture of that time."

To sum up, we may say that the Hindu contribution to these different countries was of a spiritual, religious, and intellectual nature. It was not that a new civilization or a new cult was substituted for others, but that they grafted themselves upon already existing forms of art and beliefs. To be convinced of this it suffices to note the very obvious differences between the architectures of these three countries and those of India in the same epoch. We can observe that local craftsmen did not copy servilely a type imported from elsewhere, but, on the contrary, placed at the service of a new religion or new cult an already formed artistic mentality, which only accepted the myths and legends to interpret them in a new fashion.

I shall quote a typical example of this native mentality applied to Hindu iconography: the scenes of violence, of brutality, of obscenity even, so frequent in India, and especially so in Thibet, are carefully expurgated from Khmer, Cham, and Javanese art, in which an

Fig. 2. HEAD OF BUDDHA
Angkor Vat.

instinctive repugnance for the horrible and gruesome turns away from these monstrosities. Sweetness and serenity seem to reign over the majority of the Khmer or Javanese bas-reliefs; if in the sculptures of Angkor Vat scenes of murder and carnage necessitated by the themes depicted are to be found, it seems as though the artist had taken pains to soften, or rather to transpose, the ferocious and cruel side of these scenes by a decorative convention, a highly sophisticated theatricality or a jolly kind of comic treatment. These battles of heroes, these hand-to-hand combats, often terrible and bloody, turn to circus games or theatrical displays.

Similarly with regard to the statues of divinities, M. Delaporte had already noted, in his *Voyage au Cambodge*, that

> while their neighbours, in some sort possessed by their art more than they possessed it, allowed themselves to be dominated by the tyrannical preoccupations of a mythology that was often monstrous, the Khmers for the most part did not hesitate either to suppress the hideous deformities of the idols, or, when they were obliged to reproduce them, to disguise them cleverly enough to derive very successful decorative effects from them.

Finally we may conclude by saying that if Java, Champa, and Cambodia had about the same period received similar architectural forms and artistic technique, the art of each of the three countries would have no reason to be different from the others; only differences of workmanship and skill could remove them from the imported prototype. The facts are quite otherwise, and M. Parmentier declares in the *Études asiatiques* that "if sprung from a common origin [these arts] would necessarily resemble one another and differ little from the model; but the reality is very different."

The iconography of these countries carries the proof of a native reaction in the very choice of the subjects they borrowed from India; thus the Nāga and the Garuḍa had in Cambodia a popularity and a success they never met with either in India or in the neighbouring countries. On the other hand, the lion's head (Banaspati, or head of Kala) assumed in Java an importance and a vogue that is not found elsewhere.

If the life of the Buddha is faithfully reproduced at Borobudur after the actual text of the *Lalita-Vistara*, M. Foucher, who devoted a long time to the study of these bas-reliefs, concludes that "we are dealing not with a slavish reproduction of Græco-Buddhist models, but with an individual Javanese adaptation of the Indian adaptation of the art of Gandhāra." And, again, he declares that this Græco-Buddhist art "went through a far-reaching transformation in Insulinde," and that "the local artists succeeded in adapting in their own fashion the pictorial legend of the Saviour that had come to them out of India."

It is to be observed that in the three countries of whose beliefs and divinities I am about to give a summarized account no written literature exists, no ancient document has come down to us. The sacred legends of India which were interpreted by the artists of Java, of Champa, or Cambodia probably came to these countries in an oral guise, either direct or by gradual stages through the intervening countries; it is easy to understand that these oral traditions may have altered and been burdened with elements foreign to the country of their origins.

The mythology of these countries will then be mainly the interpretation of the works of art found in them.

As for Cambodia, it will be the art of the glorious epoch that stretches from the sixth century to the fourteenth, which many people erroneously call the art of Angkor (Angkor being a centre of glorious monuments, and only representing a momentary localization of the Khmer civilization), that we shall take as a basis for the exposition of the Cambodian mythology.

From the fourteenth century sculptural and monumental art suffers an interruption, and the ancient Khmer traditions are preserved in the form of statuettes, paintings, decorative panels of carved wood.

Cham art, which may be taken as a transition between Khmer and Javanese art, less fortunate, stops with the decay of the kingdom of Champa brought about by the repeated invasions of the Annamites.

Lastly, for the mythology of the Sunda Isles, certain temples, the bas-reliefs of which can be reckoned, from the purity of their lines and their supple workmanship, in the first rank of Asiatic sculpture, are veritable illustrations of the texts they represent, and give the literature a living form.

Islam, which in the fifteenth and sixteenth centuries took possession of the whole archipelago by degrees, arrested Hindu culture, except, however, in the island of Bali, which never allowed itself to be penetrated, but kept its Hinduism almost intact, with traces of earlier cults still remaining alive among the people.

Fig. 3. BUDDHA
Drawing by Mlle Sappho Marchal.

Fig. 4. SCENE OF COMBAT INSPIRED BY THE "MAHĀBHĀRATA"
From the Bapuon.

MYTHOLOGY OF INDO-CHINA

KHMER MYTHOLOGY

THE oldest traditions recall a legend that attributes the origin of the first Khmer dynasty to the marriage of a Hindu prince with the daughter of a Nāga king. We know that the Nāga, a symbolical personification of the cobra de capello, the heads of which are multiplied and spread out fanwise, assumed a great importance in Cambodia. The Nāgas were supposed to have been the first occupants of the Khmer territory, called in native tradition Kuk Thlok (land of the Thlok-tree), almost the whole area of which was covered with water. The Nāgas were demi-gods, and played a fairly important part in Buddhism, but are also found in certain Brahman myths. They lived in subterranean waters, and are symbolical of the moist element. M. Finot thus tells the legend of the first pair who reigned over Cambodia.

> Adityavamṣa, King of Indraprastha (Delhi), being displeased with Prah Thong, one of his sons, drives him out of his states. The prince arrives in the country of Kuk Thlok; he makes haste to seize the throne. One evening he is surprised on a sandbank by the rising tide, and forced to spend the night there. A Nāgī of marvellous beauty comes to disport herself on the sand. Immediately the King falls in love and becomes her accepted bridegroom. The Nāgarāja (King of the Nāgas), the bride's father, increases his son-in-law's possessions by drinking up the water that covered the country, builds him a capital city, and changes the name of the kingdom to Kambuja.

This legend, which is also found in the neighbouring countries, recalls the historic fact of a Hindu immigration. It is even met with in India, and M. Coedès has noted a striking parallel between the Hindu version linked with the mythical origin of the Pallavas and the Cambodian version. The aboriginal religion being taken to have the serpent cult as its basis, we see that the Nāgī (Fig. 7) would represent the autochthonous element and

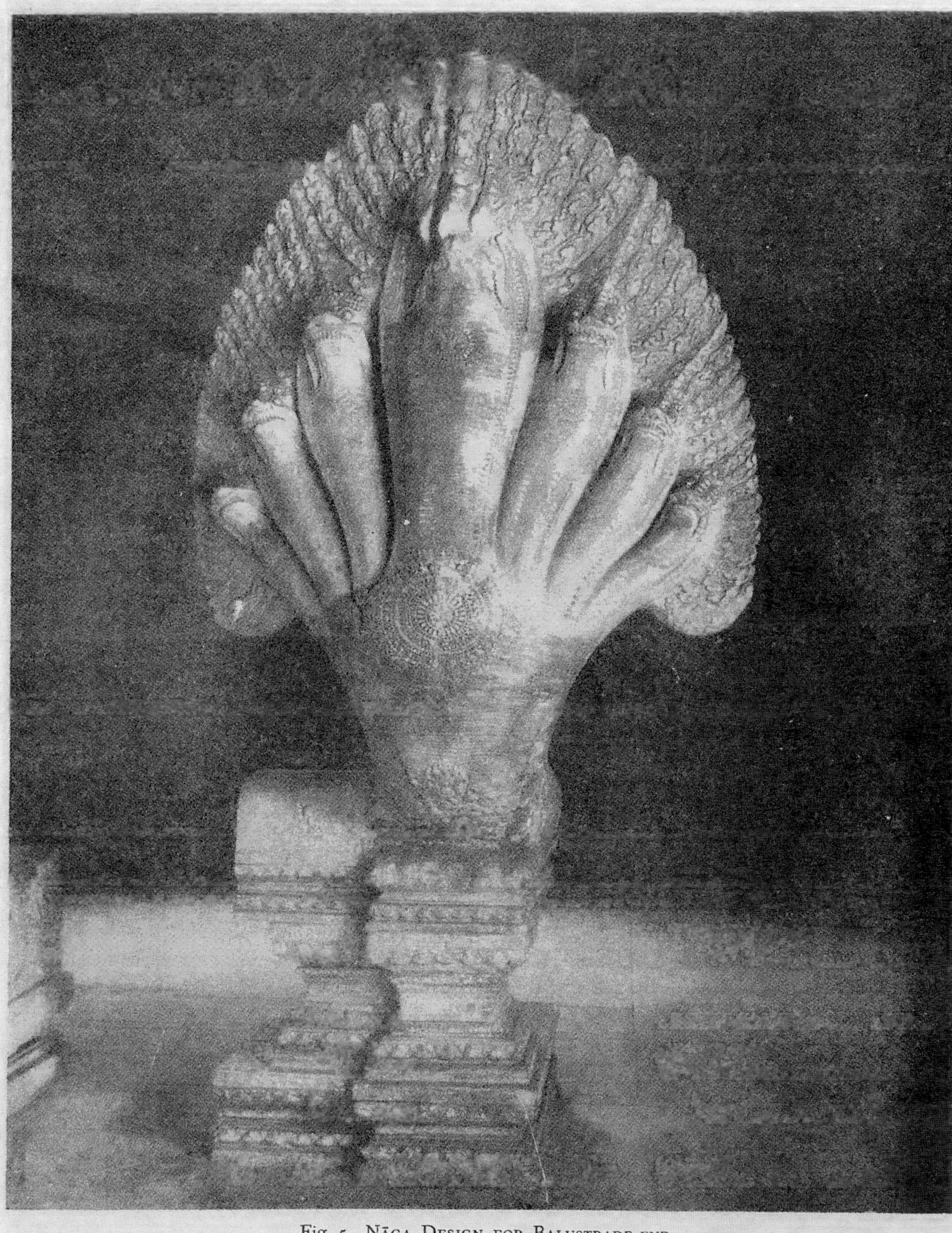

Fig. 5. Nāga Design for Balustrade-end
Musée Delaporte.

the Hindu prince the stream of immigration. This legend of a serpent presiding over the destinies of the kingdom persisted for centuries, and the Chinese traveller Chou-Ta-Kuan, who visited Angkor in the thirteenth century, relates the tradition he found in the capital of the Khmer country.

> In the palace there is a golden tower on top of which the King sleeps. All the natives pretend that in this tower there is the spirit of a serpent with nine heads, the master of the land of the whole realm. He appears every night in the shape of a woman. With him the sovereign first lies and unites himself. . . . If the spirit of this serpent fails to appear one night the moment of the death of the King has arrived. If the King omits to go there for a single night some misfortune befalls.

M. Finot concludes from this that, according to this popular belief,

> the King every night re-enacted the union of his first ancestor with the spirit of the Nāga folk who had founded the kingdom and consequently remained its master. The numerous many-headed Nāgas sculptured on the terraces, the stairways, the tympanums of temples and palaces, proclaimed to the eye this sovereignty of the Nāgī, the mother of the nation [Fig. 7, No. 1].

With regard to native beliefs before the arrival of the Hindus, we know very few details: but a part of these beliefs has survived and is preserved in our times in certain superstitions foreign to the two cults, the Buddhist and the Brahman, that took their place. We shall find traces of them in the brief summary of modern Buddhist beliefs that follows. For this summary I have made use of the volume by M. Adhémard Leclère on Buddhism in Cambodia (1899). These beliefs were partly brought together in a Cambodian book, the *Trai Phum*, which served the author just cited as the basis for his work.

We know that Buddhism forms two great groups, often called Northern Buddhism (*mahāyāna*) and Southern Buddhism (*hīnayāna*). The latter is still observed in Ceylon, Burma, Siam, and Cambodia; but in the first centuries of our era, in the Angkor period, the Northern Church, whose texts are in Sanskrit, prevailed.

A purely Cambodian legend makes the Buddha, a short time before his death, journey to Cambodia in company with his faithful disciple Ananda; they arrive, according to this legend, in the place called Kuk Thlok, a name we have already observed as denoting ancient Cambodia.

Other legends mention the arrival of sacred texts brought from Ceylon in a junk and intended for the King of Vieng-Shan about the year A.D. 638. The junk having run ashore in Cambodia, the inhabitants took possession of these texts and deposited them in Angkor Vat. Purely legendary tales that recall the memory of the introduction of a religion coming from India, probably brought by Buddhist missionaries. We may, however, note that in A.D. 638 Buddhism was already known in Cambodia, and the temple of Angkor Vat was not yet built. This merely to show that too great historic accuracy must not be looked for in native tales and traditions.[1]

Buddhistic Cosmogony. According to the Cambodian texts called *Satras*, preserved in the monasteries of the bonzes, two creatures existed before all things, a man and a woman, the male principle and the female principle, whence there issued the world of animate beings and inanimate things. The gods themselves, Brahmā, Ṣiva, Vishṇu, with

[1] According to the Cambodian legend, Angkor Vat was built at the orders of the god Indra to serve as a palace for his son the young prince Precha Ket Mealea.

Fig. 6. PRAH PEAN: THE THOUSAND BUDDHAS
Angkor Vat. *Photo École Française d'Extrême-Orient.*

all the demi-gods and secondary divinities, were descended from this primeval couple. Then the *Satra Khmer* reveals the birth of dragons or serpents from which came in their turn the sun, the moon, and the planets.

Another Cambodian work, the *Kampi prah Thomma Chhean*, teaches that in the beginning a form, *rupa*, existed in itself from all eternity, before the birth of all things: the book calls this form "the holy state of nothing and the void," which is not greatly enlightening.

Then the *Prah Keo*—the holy jewel—(perhaps a personification of the sun) was born and in turn begat the earth, water, fire, the wind, space, human beings, and animals. This text makes man come from the dirt of the body of Prah Thorni (the Earth), while woman was born from the shadow of man. This Cambodian genesis is known, it seems, only to the clergy, and the general belief of the laity is as follows.

Before all things was Prah Prohm, the uncreated, being and non-being at one and the same time, in whom all things were enfolded in a latent state. Without Prah Prohm's expressing any desire, for he is incapable of desire, what was within him became manifest, and thus was born the world of sense phenomena. The worlds thus created are very numerous and distributed in unlimited space in groups of three; in turn each of these triads is reabsorbed and disappears to melt again into Prah Prohm, the essence and principle of things, while other worlds are reborn. At no moment can reabsorption in Prah Prohm affect all the worlds at the same time, otherwise he would become other than what he is, which is impossible, since he is immutable. We can see in this myth a symbol of everlasting evolution, the eternal rebeginning of all things.

In the native beliefs, M. Adhémard Leclère tells us, there arises a confusion between Prah Prohm, the uncreated in whom all things are reabsorbed, and Nirpean (Nirvāna), in which all existences dissolve and disappear.

We must remember that the two religions, Brahmanism and Buddhism, have never been wholly dissociated in the mind of the Cambodian, and that the Buddhist legend can hardly be separated from the Vedic and Brahmanic myths.

It can be understood that with so indefinite a shape, so confused a significance, Prah Prohm never had any cult in Cambodia, and that the popular mind has retained only a weak memory of him.

We have seen that in the immensity of the universes the worlds are joined in groups of three: these triads float upon a mass of water, itself resting upon a layer of air, and are isolated within the infinite ether. These three units are bound up with one another and devoted to the same periodic destruction and rebirth. Each of these three worlds is composed of a flat disk; the diameter of the disk we inhabit, according to Cambodian texts, is 1,348,064 yuch, or more than 10,000,000 miles. All round it is a long ring of mountains more than 500,000 miles high, and in the middle is the Prah Sumer, or Mount Meru, on the summit of which is Indra's paradise. This monarch of mountains is enclosed within a sevenfold girdle of concentric mountains separated from one another by seas. In the ocean that surrounds the mountain-chain farthest away from Mount Meru there are four great continents situated at the four cardinal points.

We live in the southern continent (Jambūdvīpa); it is here life is shortest and hardest.

Fig. 7. (1) NĀGI. (2) BUDDHA CUTTING OFF HIS HAIR. (3) VIRADHA BETWEEN LAKSHMAṆA AND RĀMA

From bas-reliefs in Angkor Vat. Drawings by Mlle Sappho Marchal.

In this continent we find a mountain, Prah Hembopean, peopled with more or less fantastic animals living in the forest; in this forest the ascetics who flee from the world to devote themselves to meditation take refuge. Cambodian tales often make mention of this place: here is where King Vesandar (Vessantara), the charitable king, the penultimate incarnation of the Buddha, retires with his wife and his children. This is the forest that Sanselchey, another legendary hero, traverses mounted upon the king of lions and armed with the marvellous bow, to rescue his aunt, whom a Yeak, or king of the giants, has carried off. The mountains are, in short, the abode of supernatural and fantastic creatures: ogres, half-human birds, spectres, etc., which will be enumerated presently. Here also are found trees bearing flowers in the shape of women, a fabulous country that folklore adorns with a thousand fairy charms.

Under the Earth's surface are placed the hells, and above are the paradises, one over the other. These are the Moon and the Sun, which give the Earth light as they turn round about it; the circles they describe have Mount Meru for their centre, the path of the Moon being a little lower than the orbit of the Sun. Besides this daily path, the Sun travels another path in the space of a year—the path of the constellations, which are twelve in number.

The Cambodian calendar is fixed by periods of sixty years, comprising five cycles of twelve years, each of which bears the name of an animal.

There are nine planets:

Prah Atit (the Sun), whose sign is the Reachea-Sey (lion), of precious substance covered with gold (Sunday).
Prah Shan (the Moon). Sign, the tiger, of crystal covered with silver (Monday).
Prah Angkea (Mars). Sign, the pig, blue-coloured (Tuesday).
Prah Put (Mercury). Sign, the donkey, light-coloured (Wednesday).
Prah Prahas (Jupiter). Sign, the elephant, red-coloured (Thursday).
Prah Sok (Venus). Sign, the peacock, green-coloured (Friday).
Prah Sau (Saturn). Sign, the buffalo, blue-coloured (Saturday).

The two other planets, under the guardianship of the Asuras, the enemies of the gods, correspond to no known planets. They are

Prah Rahu. Sign, the Kruthreach (King of the Garudas), yellow-coloured.
Prah Ket. Sign, the Yeak Kompeant, gold-coloured.

Eclipses are interpreted by the Cambodians as caused by a voracious monster, Rahu, who hurls himself upon the Sun and Moon to devour them, but, being interrupted in this attempt, is obliged to let go his hold.

According to a legend of Brahman origin, Rahu is a sort of monster who, having succeeded in stealing the *amrita*, the liquor of immortality, which the gods brought up from the churned ocean, was denounced to Vishṇu by the Sun and the Moon. That indignant god flung his discus at the thief and cut his body into two parts: these two parts, being immortal by reason of the *amṛita*, wander among the signs of the Zodiac, unable to join again; but when one of them finds the Sun or the Moon in its path it hurls itself on them and tries to devour them.

In the Buddhist legend if Rahu hates the Sun and the Moon and seeks to devour them

PRIEST-KING
(ANGKOR-VAT.)

it is because their rays quench his; but Buddha intervenes, commanding Rahu to relinquish his prey, and the obedient monster takes flight.

Rahu occupies a place in Cambodian mythology that is above everything decorative, without any very definite religious character; no worship is paid to him, and his legend has more or less disappeared from memory. He remains an ornamental motive very often used in the modern decoration of the pediments of pagodas.

The grinning, conventionalized mask of Rahu is also believed to be seen in the central motive of the lintels of Khmer temples.

According to M. Adhémard Leclère, pregnant women invoke Rahu seizing the Sun or the Moon to beg him for an easy delivery and strong boys.

The duration of the life of a world and the whole planetary system composing it, including its hells and its paradises, depends upon the conduct of its inhabitants. The more the good exceeds the evil, the longer will that world endure; its destruction involves the whole triad.

The three agents of destruction are fire, water, and wind. First of all a terrific conflagration burns and devours all the regions of the world, with all the beings that dwell in it. The last burning that took place lasted, it seems, for " a space of time only to be represented by a unit followed by a hundred and forty zeroes."

This period of burning is followed by a period of rains and floods that submerge everything, which lasts as long as the burning. Lastly, the winds begin to blow, the waters subside, and the worlds are reconstituted as before.

Norok (Hell). There are eight great hells placed one below the other under the surface of the earth: we must observe that this term hell (*Norok* in Cambodian) does not absolutely correspond to the Roman Catholic meaning generally given to it: the word purgatory would be more accurate, for the Norok is a place of suffering where the damned expiate their sins and crimes, but their torments are not eternal. When they have made an end of expiating their sins the damned are born again to begin a new life.

The hells are more and more terrible according as they are deeper below the earth; the periods of suffering in these hells are longer in proportion to their depth.

To the eight great hells thus superimposed there correspond eight degrees of torments; but in each there are included sixteen little hells, which brings the total number to a hundred and twenty-eight; thus in Avichey (Avichi), the lowest of these hells, the suffering is a hundred and twenty-eight times as intense as in the first.

But the damned are granted a lightening of their pains by fleeting visits to paradise. "There are damned," says the *Trai Phum*, "who are damned by day and blessed by night; others who are damned under the waning moon and blessed under the waxing moon, or *vice versa*." One detail of these hells may be noted, that the tormentors of the victims, the executioners, are souls likewise damned, who in this way expiate their own sins, and who suffer all the pangs they inflict upon their victims.

" The picture of the Cambodian hell in the *Trai Phum*," says M. Roeské, who has translated a section from that work, " is not the mere description of a Gehenna, it is a real moral code. In each article of the code is stated the crime, the condemnation, the penalty." We find this enumeration of torments in the temple of Angkor Vat, on the southern front, in the gallery of the bas-reliefs. Each one of the scenes represented has, carved in the stone, the name of a hell, and the sin, the punishment of which is seen, is explained.

Of the thirty-two hells of Angkor Vat a certain number are described in the *Trai Phum*. Lastly, independently of the hells quoted above, there is a hell only peopléd with phantoms, spirits, wandering souls, and situated between the three worlds that form the triad. " It is the hell of deep night, intense cold, absolute silence, and continuing hunger." The rays of the Sun never penetrate here. Ghosts or spirits (*pretas* or *khmoch* in Cambodian) in popular belief are beings moderately tall, always famished, with enormous bellies, but all the rest of their frames incredibly emaciated; they feed only on filth or excrement, without ever being satisfied. Some have pigs' masks for faces, others vomit fire that burns them away, others cut and slash their flesh with their own nails.

The *kmoch pray* are ghosts of women dead in childbirth and of stillborn babes. To protect themselves against these wandering maleficent spirits, the natives make offerings to them. Sometimes these spirits glide into the body of one of their relatives and make him sick or bring him to die; ceremonies of exorcism accompanied with offerings made through a village sorcerer, who sings and dances before the sick man, in the end drive away the spirit. It is pleasant to add that the bonzes, or Buddhist priests, are silent on these gross superstitions and never take part in ceremonies of this kind.

The *pretas* sometimes affect shapes of animals (*daerechhan*) or formidable giants (Yeaks). The *daerechhan* are beings that have been condemned to be born again in the shape of beasts without reason. Every animal species has a king that dwells in a determinate place (Himalaya or Hembopean for the majority of the large terrestrial animals or large birds). The kings of the fishes dwell in the concentric seas around Mount Meru.

Beside these animals there are a great number of a fantastic character, which figure very frequently in the tales and legends of the country: their reproduction in Cambodian drawings, sculptures, paintings, and jewels is often the basis of superb decorative motives. Among them I will cite the Reachea-Sey, a lion that has the power of leaping and flying through the air. The architecture of Angkor multiplied the representations of this animal (*Seng*) on the projections of the temple stairways.

The Kruth (Garuḍa) is a bird with a human bust, with monstrous clawed feet, which in ancient as well as modern Cambodian art is more extensively found than in any other country. The Garuḍa, or Kruth in Cambodian, appears everywhere, more or less conventionalized, from the walls of Angkor, where it draws itself up threateningly, squeezing in its two uplifted hands the tails of serpents whose heads curl up at its feet (Fig. 8), to the pagoda roofs, where in the shape of wooden brackets it upholds the ends of the timbers.

This is the mythical bird, the serpents' foe, which in the Brahman religion is the god Vishṇu's mount. If we remember that the Nāga represents the watery element, and set this alongside the fact that Garuḍa, Vishṇu's mount, is a solar divinity; we can interpret the myth of Garuḍa devouring the Nāgas as representing the sun drying up the marshes and the stagnant pools.

Then come other creatures, Kenor, or Kenarey, akin to the Gandharvas of India through their musical talents, with bird's wings and feet and a human bust. Modern Cambodian drawings often give very graceful conventionalizations of these strange creatures (Fig. 9).

Fig. 8. Garuḍa at the Corner of a Door at Bantei Kedei
Photo École Française d'Extrême-Orient.

Beside the foregoing animals that dwell in the hells between the three worlds, there are the Yeaks (Yakshas), a kind of ogre both ferocious and simple-witted who can fly in the air. They are the servants of the god Indra, and form part of the pompous train that accompanies him. They can change shape as they please, and they shoot arrows that turn in the air to serpents, flames, or showers. A Cambodian Jātaka, *Prah Sanselchey*, shows a Yeak king carrying off a princess to make her his bride.

Another kind of Yeak lives under the earth and is guardian to the wealth buried in the ground; they come somewhere near the Asuras (non-deities) of the Brahman religion. The Asuras are, for the Cambodians of to-day, giants, of old powerful enough to battle against the gods, but, having been vanquished, they are now forbidden to leave the subterranean kingdom situated beneath Mount Meru.

According to M. Adhémard Leclère, the social position of these Yeaks is not well defined, they are half-way between men and the *tevodas* (*devata*); it is admitted that they are expiating sins and that their punishment consists of being placed in the ranks of the monsters of the Cambodian pantheon; nevertheless they have a magical power that makes them superior to men.

The Paradises. Above the earth, one over the other, are the six-and-twenty paradises; above the last one is Nirvāna, or Nirpean. The duration of life in these paradises increases with the height of each.

The earth to the Cambodians is a neutral place, a place of trial where men, it is true, enjoy and suffer; but their enjoyments are far below those of paradise and their sufferings far below those of hell.

There men have the position and status their previous works entitled them to.

In Cambodia the Brahman and the Buddhist religions have not only lived side by side, but have even in the end mingled intimately with each other. If it may seem, at first sight, that Buddhism has got the upper hand and occupies the first place, it is none the less true that a Brahmanic foundation has remained very much alive and still holds a large place in native beliefs. In all royal ceremonies at Pnom-Penh the two cults are associated, and a corps of *bakus*, or Brahman priests, is maintained in the king's palace.

The cult of Ṣiva appears to have left few traces in the beliefs of to-day, and that of the *linga* has lost all meaning to the modern Cambodian. Ṣiva is called Prah Eysor (Īṣvara) by the Cambodians. On the other hand, the god Vishṇu (Prah Noreai-Nārāyaṇa) still figures on the sculptured pediments of the pagodas, and his two avatars, Rāma and Kṛishṇa, still furnish subjects for painters and decorators.

But the Brahman god that has remained the most popular in Cambodia is Indra (Prah En), the God of the Sky, who hurls the thunderbolt and governs the world of the stars. He dwells in a palace of gold upon Mount Meru and lives surrounded by *tevodas*, servitors, *bayadères*, etc. He is regarded as the lord of the blessed.

The Cambodian Jātakas frequently show Indra intervening with the Bodhisattva, the hero of these tales, either directly or through his angels or *tevodas*

In Cambodia the *tevodas* are no longer divinities, but the blessed who reap in Indra's paradise the reward of the merit previously acquired in their last existences. Certain of these *tevodas* do not live in paradise, but in the forests, and there they keep watch on mankind, noting sins and good actions. In the popular tales and the modern Cambodian theatre the *tevodas* play an important part: it is they who intervene to bring aid to the hero or the heroine as soon as danger threatens.

They are sometimes confused, in the native mind, with the Neak Tas, the genii who protect the villages, the roads, and frequented places; they are doubtless a survival of autochthonous traditions. The Cambodians often pay worship to fragments of more or less sculptured stones, which they call Neak Ta and place under shelters in the shape of little houses.

Prah En, or Indra, seems, in the modern popular folklore, to have shed a part of his divine attributes in order to play the most varied parts and to intervene among mankind under the most fantastic aspects.

Lastly we must note the *tevodas*, guardians of the world, or *lukabals* (*lokapāla*), who watch over the earth and its inhabitants. The earth is divided into four regions, of each of which a *lukabal* is king.

The kingdom of the East is under the ward of the *tevoda* Tossarot, who has under his orders white *tevodas*, Khandas (Gandharvas).

The kingdom of the South is under the ward of Virulak, who has under his orders blue *tevodas*, Kampean (Kumbhāṇḍas).

The kingdom of the West is under the ward of Virulappak, who has under his orders Kruths (Garuḍas) and Nāgas clad in red.

Fig. 9. KENAREY
From a modern document.
Drawing by Mlle Sappho Marchal.

The kingdom of the North is under the ward of Kōverō, or Peysrap (Kuvera, or Vaisravana); his subjects are the Yeaks clad in gold.

These *tevodas* are the "four hundred millions of eyes of Indra and the witnesses to all our actions before the tribunal of Yama, the great supreme judge."

Yama is one of the great Brahmanic deities whose cult, with that of Indra, remained very popular. He is the god of the nether world, who judges the dead and decides their fate: the just after judgment ascend to heaven and the wicked go down to hell. The bas-reliefs of Angkor Vat present the Hindu Pluto in the shape of a god with multiple arms carrying clubs, mounted on a bull; he is seconded by two assessors sitting on either side.

Buddhism. Avalokiteṣvara. The miraculous legendary life of the Buddha has naturally provided the Cambodian artists with a repertory from which they derived frequent inspiration, whether to decorate the temples of the glorious period of Angkor or to instruct the devout by means of the mural paintings of the pagodas.

Among the Buddhist representations of the Angkor period, while Mahayanism, or the Northern School, was at the height of its prosperity in Cambodia, we must begin by giving first place to the Bodhisattva Avalokiteṣvara, the compassionate and pitying divinity so popular in Japan and in China under his feminine shape Kwannon, or Kuan-yin. We owe to M. Finot the discovery of the important part played by this Bodhisattva, known especially by the name of Lokeṣvara, "Lord of the World," in ancient Cambodia.

Fig. 10. LOKEṢVARA
Drawing by Mlle Sappho Marchal.

It is now recognized that all the great temples of the period of the Bayon and this monument itself were dedicated to Lokeṣvara; it was only later that these temples became Saivite and the new cult modified or effaced the sculptured representations of the Bodhisattva.

Avalokiteṣvara is recognizable in Cambodia by his attributes—rosary, book, flask, and lotus—and above all by the presence of a little figurine, his spiritual father, the Dhyāni-Buddha Amitābha on the front of his hair-knot. Besides the attributes mentioned above, there are often seen in the eight hands with which the Khmer sculptor endows him the *vajra* (thunderbolt), the *ankus*, or elephant-goad, the conch, the discus, and the glaive (Fig. 10).

A peculiarity of certain of these statues of Avalokiteṣvara lies in the multitude of little figures, sometimes not very clear owing to the weathering of the stone, which cover all the upper part of the body and even the lower part of the legs. Here iconography is translating in plastic fashion the sacred texts which speak of thousands of beings, divinities, demigods, *ṛishis*, emanating from the body of the Padmapani (Avalokiteṣvara); the Buddhas themselves come forth from the pores of his skin. In the shape of Siṃhanada Lokeṣvara he "irradiates the five Buddhas." Hence this series of statues with multiple figurines is known by the general name of irradiating Bodhisattvas.

Among the temples of Angkor a little chapel isolated in the middle of a great pool is especially dedicated to Avalokiteṣvara. MM. Finot and Goloubev succeeded in interpreting the symbolism of this shrine known as Neak Pean (the coiled serpent), which was a place of pilgrimage where the sick used to come and dip in the water of the pools, invoking Lokeṣvara the healer.

A very fine sculptured group, unhappily very incomplete and fragmentary, stands before the main entrance to the shrine of Neak Pean; it represents a horse prancing and about to take flight through the air; on his chest and his tail hang a cluster of human beings. In this we recognize an episode of the *Valahassa-Jātaka*, in which Lokeṣvara turns himself into a horse and bears away the merchant Siṃhala and his companions, to save them from the wrath of the *rākshasīs* on the island where they had been shipwrecked.

Among the other narratives of previous lives of the Buddha that have provided illustrations for the Khmer bas-reliefs we may also quote the *Vessantara-Jātaka*. We see the charitable king relinquishing his wife and his children to the Brahmans who come and ask him for them represented on several sculptured pediments.

Buddha. The Buddha Ṣākyamuni himself has been very often depicted either in full or low relief by the Khmer sculptors. He is most often clad in the monastic robe that

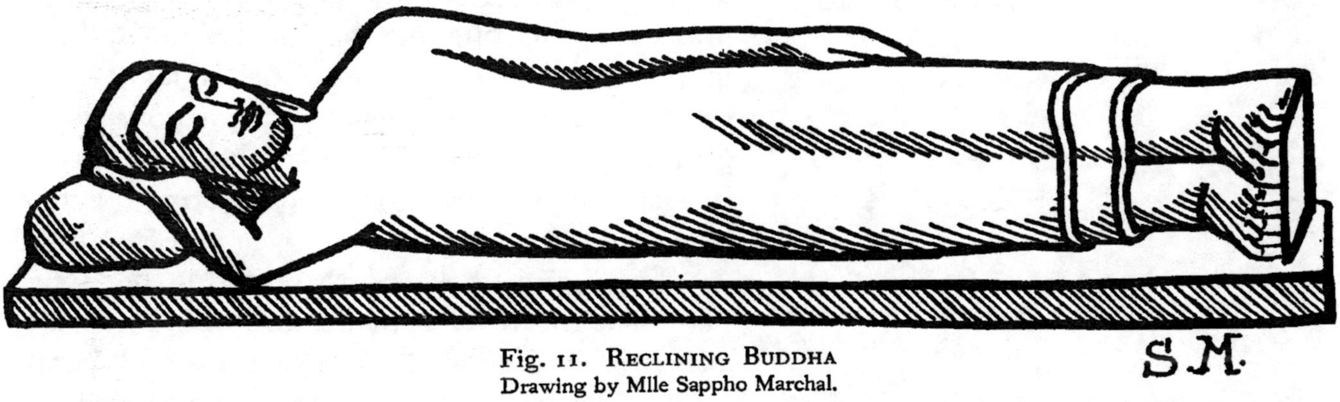

Fig. 11. Reclining Buddha
Drawing by Mlle Sappho Marchal.

leaves the right shoulder bare; in certain statues the robe is only indicated by a simple incised line, and the bust seems naked. The Buddha's head is always surmounted by the *ushṇīsha*, or protuberance of the skull adorned with hair. The presence of the *ūrṇā* (sign in the middle of the forehead) is somewhat rare in Cambodia. The Khmer sculptors sometimes executed in full relief an image of the meditating sage of a serenity that attains a high perfection of artistry; I cannot but endorse the following judgment of M. Groslier (*Sculpture khmère*, p. 44):

> My impression is that in no country his worship reached, nor even in his own native land, has any image of Gautama embodied the idea of Buddhism more intelligently. Not one has so perfectly epitomized his doctrine, his meditation, his renunciation, his profound benevolence.

The most widely spread among the Buddhist statues of Cambodia is that of the Buddha meditating upon his future mission and protected from the thunderstorm by the piety of a Nāga king, Muchilinda, who shelters him with his heads forming a hood above him.

He is also seen seated, or less frequently standing (see Fig. 25), making the various gestures of instruction, of the absence of fear, or of charity. Sometimes the Buddha is depicted lying on his right side, one hand folded under his head, the other lying along his body: this is the moment of the death of the Buddha, his entry into Nirpean (Fig. 11).

A scene frequently reproduced in bas-relief is the assault of the demon Māra and his army upon the Bodhisattva (at this moment Gautama has not yet reached the state of Buddha, not having attained supreme enlightenment). While the great sage meditates under the *bodhi*-tree (the sacred fig-tree) Māra comes to harass him, and, followed by his grinning army of demons, disputes his right to reign over the world (Fig. 12). Then the future Buddha recalls his merit acquired in previous existences; on Māra requiring proof of this affirmation, the Goddess of Earth, Prah Thorni (*dharani*), appears and certifies the word of the Bodhisattva. In witness thereof she seizes her hair and wrings it, to bring gushing from it a flood of water that drowns the army of Māra. M. Coedès says on this subject: "The drowning of Māra in the floods that pour from the hair of the Earth, which is not to be found in the canonical texts, seems to be a legend peculiar to Siam and Cambodia." M. Duroiselle also notes this legend as enjoying great popularity in Burma. The water gushing from the hair of the goddess comes from the ablutions poured out as offerings by the future Buddha in previous existences. M. Coedès lays stress on this iconographic device, which consists in giving shape to the charity of the Bodhisattva in testimony to the good works done by him in past lives.

Fig. 12. THE ASSAULT OF MĀRA
A stele at Angkor Vat.

The figure of the Earth wringing her long hair brought in front of her breast is a motive very widely used in modern Siamese and Cambodian decoration: it is often seen carved on the pedestal supporting the statue of the Buddha in the pagodas.

We sometimes see also the attempt at seduction made by the daughters of Māra upon Gautama.

The gesture of the Buddha putting down his right hand to touch the Earth, which evokes the scene of the temptation of Māra, is very often reproduced in Khmer statuary (Fig. 13).

Another scene often represented in the bas-reliefs of the temples is that of the Great Departure, where the Bodhisattva is seen leaving his father's palace in order to follow the ascetic life: he is mounted on his horse Kaṇṭhaka, whose feet are upborne by the four *lokapālas*, the wardens of the world, so as to prevent the sound of hoof-beats on the ground, which might have given the alarm. His faithful squire Chhandaka follows him.

A pediment of Prah Pithu in the enclosure of the royal city of Angkor Thom shows the episode in which the Bodhisattva, having cast aside his princely garments, himself cuts off his hair, which a divinity hovering in the air gathers up, and bids farewell to his groom and to his horse (Fig. 7).

In other bas-reliefs we see the offering of food to the Buddha by the animals in the forest; and a bas-relief recently discovered has for its theme the four *lokapālas* each offering a begging-bowl to the great Sage; the latter amalgamates the four bowls into one, so as not to make any distinction between the gifts of his worshippers.

Before leaving the subject of Buddhist iconography we must mention a trinity that frequently appears in Khmer sculpture, whether in isolation against a stele, or on the walls of the temples. The central personage is the Buddha between an Avalokiteṣvara standing and Prajñāpāramitā, the corresponding feminine form, "the purest manifestation of femine perfection, supreme wisdom."

In this trinity M. Georges Maspero sees a tendency of Mahayanist Buddhism to become a disguised Saivism, and he invokes the authority of Professor Kern to identify Prajñāpāramitā with Bhagavatī, the *ṣakti* of Ṣiva, " with whom Lokeṣvara, the revealed form of Jina Amitābha, is frequently confounded in ancient Khmer epigraphic documents."

Fig. 13. Buddhist Stele

It must be added that the Buddha, especially in Siamese art, sometimes shows himself clad in princely garments, with jewels and a diadem, which is in contradiction to the primitive Buddhist legend that makes him strip off adornments and rich attire as soon as he devotes himself to the life of meditation; but according to M. Coedès " the Buddha with the crown and the insignia of royalty is quite in the tradition of the Mahāyāna."

M. Finot takes the legend of Jambūpati, one of the most powerful sovereigns of Jambūdvīpa, as the origin of the adorned statues. This most arrogant king refuses to do homage to the Buddha, looking upon him as an inferior. The great ascetic, in order to convert him, appears to him magnificently clad, gleaming with gold and flashing with precious stones, and thus overwhelms him with his splendour.

We find a memory of Tantric Buddhism in Cambodia in the person of Hevajra, of whom, however, there are only very rare examples; but one of them, a bronze, is of such remarkable workmanship that it is one of the finest pieces of Khmer sculpture. This is a divinity with eight heads and multiple arms in a very elegant dancing pose (Fig. 14), the chaste mind natural to the artists of Cambodia has suppressed the conjunction with his *sakti* so common in Thibet.

Among the Buddhist attributes and signs still venerated in Cambodia we must note the *prah bat*, or sacred feet, representing the footprints of the Buddha. These are flat stones, shaped like the sole of a foot, with eleven parallel lines crossed by other lines forming compartments that contain representations of a great variety of signs, the whole grouped around the *chakra*, or central wheel.

Fig. 14. HEVAJRA
Khmer bronze in the Musée Albert Sarraut at Pnom-Penh.
Photo Direction des Arts Cambodgiens.

Brahmanism. Brahman mythology has furnished abundant themes for the Khmer iconography of the Angkor period; we shall review the representations of the principal divinities before coming to allegorical scenes and illustrations of the great Hindu poems.

The god Brahmā (Prah Prohm in Cambodian) has a somewhat subordinate place in art: in any case his cult was never very widespread. He is recognizable by his four faces set two and two back to back (Fig. 15); that is why for a long time the four faces of the towers of the Bayon were taken to be those of Brahmā. Considerations that cannot be dealt with in the limits of this rapid survey proved that this interpretation was erroneous.

Fig. 15. BRAHMĀ
Photo Direction des Arts Cambodgiens.

In the bas-reliefs Brahmā is seen bestriding his mount, the *hamsa* (sacred goose). His *ṣakti*, or feminine energy, is Sarasvatī, equally infrequent among the Khmers.

On the other hand, the god Vishṇu, whose multiple avatars lend themselves to varied and decorative combinations, appears very often in sculpture. The most common form is that of Vishṇu-Chaturbhuja (four-armed), holding in his hands discus, conch, sword, and club. Standing on the shoulders of his mount, the Garuḍa bird, he makes a decorative motive very much employed on the lintels of the ancient temples, as well as on the pediments of the modern pagodas (Fig. 16). One of the legends that most frequently inspired the Khmer artist is the god resting on the serpent Ananta, motionless in the midst of the waters surrounding the world. Vishṇu, or Nārāyaṇa (Prah Noreay in Cambodian), is plunged in a deep sleep,

Fig. 16. VISHṆU MOUNTED ON GARUḌA

Photo Direction des Arts Cambodgiens.

and from his navel there emerges a lotus stem, upon which the god Brahmā is seated; his wife Lakshmī holds his feet, and divinities pay homage to him.

Fig. 17. Ṣiva and his Ṣakti, Bantei Sréi
Photo Direction des Arts Cambodgiens.

The tortoise avatar of Vishṇu figures in representations of the churning of the sea of milk, an episode that will be described later.

The wild-boar form that Vishnu assumed to uphold the world above the waters of chaos and prevent its annihilation is not very common at Angkor.

On the other hand, he appears several times as Nara-Siṃha (lion-man), a form Vishṇu assumed to devour Hiraṇya-Kaṣipu, the King of the Asuras. This king had desired to be paid the same honours as the god, but his son refused to pander to this sacrilegious caprice, and was brutally illtreated by him. Then Vishṇu intervened, coming out of a pillar and rending the King of the Asuras in pieces.

But the two avatars of Vishṇu that still remain an inexhaustible source of inspiration for the Khmer artists are those of Rāma and Kṛishṇa, and to these we shall presently return.

Vishṇu's *ṣakti* is Lakshmī, the Goddess of Beauty and Youth; she is sometimes seen in bas-reliefs standing upon a lotus bloom between two elephants on their hind legs pouring water on her head or waving lotus stems: in Cambodian sculpture water, which is difficult to represent, is often replaced by the lotus, the symbol of that element.

In the shape of an isolated statue we see her standing adorned, tiaraed, and usually holding a lotus bud in her hand.

The god Ṣiva, less often shown alone, figures especially in scenes in the bas-reliefs. His principal attribute is the trident, and he is recognized by his frontal eye and the Brahman cord he wears over his shoulder.

We see him also in Angkor art represented as an ascetic, meditating on a mountain among hermits or *ṛishis* in grottos and in the midst of animals grazing at liberty.

Fig. 18. The Bull Nandin
Musée Guimet.

It should be observed that in Cambodia this god never has the terrible and ferocious aspect of the destroyer of the worlds; never does this god wear necklaces of skulls, nor the crescent, nor the tiger-skin with which he is seen in India.

He sometimes holds his *ṣakti* Pārvatī on one knee (Fig. 17), and often rides upon the bull Nandin. Durgā, his *sakti* in his destroying and bellicose form, is far from popular. Ṣiva is sometimes symbolized simply by his bull Nandin, but it is especially the *linga* motive that serves to represent this god.

This *linga*, in Cambodia, does not exclusively carry the phallic meaning sometimes assigned to it. It sums up the creative energy of the powers of nature; the sexual idea that may be attributed to it is incorrect if we halt on this particular concept alone; in Oriental symbolism it is one of the expressions of the intense life that ends in absorption into the godhead. We must remember these words of Sir Monier Monier-Williams in everything that concerns the sexual question in the religions of India: "In India the relation between the sexes is regarded as a sacred mystery, and is never held to be suggestive of improper or indecent ideas," and we must not look upon this symbol with our Western Latin traditions.

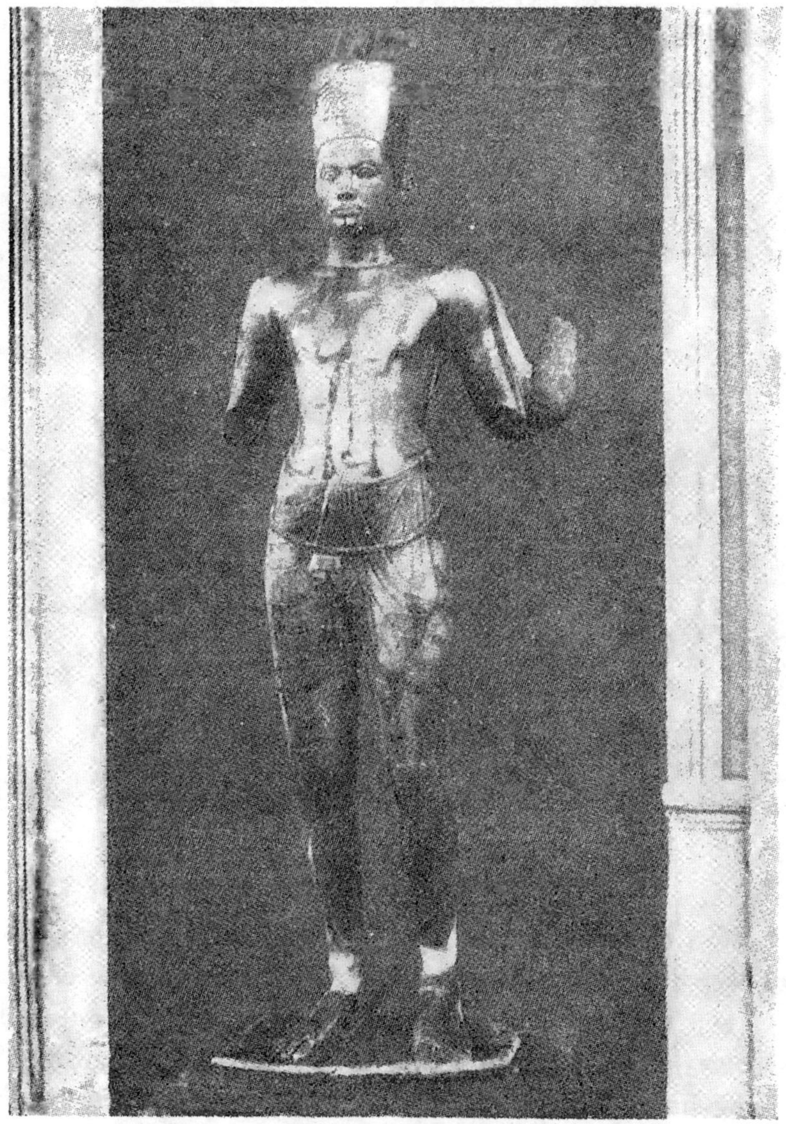

Fig. 19. HARI-HARA
Musée Albert Sarraut. *Photo Direction des Arts Cambodgiens.*

The form in which this emblem is given concrete embodiment in Cambodia is that of a vertical pillar divided into three equal parts: a lower part square in section, an octagonal middle part, and a top part cylindrical and rounded off at the end. This emblem was always set in a pedestal with a slightly hollowed-out flat stone carrying a runnel on one side to empty away the waters of ablution. A slight fillet is engraved on the rounded end.

The Ṣiva natarāja, or the dancing Ṣiva, so popular in India, is, if not unknown, at any rate fairly uncommon in Khmer iconography.

A religious manifestation that attained great artistic beauty between the fifth and the eighth centuries is that of Hari-Hara, a combination of the two divinities Ṣiva and Vishṇu in the same person (Fig. 19). This double god, with the head wearing on one side a tiara and on the other a plaited chignon, holds the attributes of both Ṣiva and Vishṇu.

Ṣiva is often accompanied in the bas-reliefs by the gods Brahmā and Vishnu (Fig. 20).

Ṣiva's son Gaṇeṣa enjoys very great popularity in Cambodia, and his statues are numerous. This god, who symbolizes wisdom and intelligence, has a massive human body and an elephant's head; the obese and shapeless aspect of this divinity is less emphasized than in certain neighbouring countries. He has only one tusk, and holds a fragment of the other in his hand; he carries the Brahmanic cord that denotes his Saivite origin, and often holds in his hand a begging-bowl into which he dips the tip of his trunk.

Another son of Siva, who sometimes appears in the bas-reliefs, is Skanda, or Kārttikeya,

Fig. 20. Brahmanic Trinity
From the Bayon. *Photo École Française d'Extrême-Orient.*

the God of War, who embodies the destructive power of his father; he rides on the peacock, the emblem of the pomp and the pride of combats.

Among the other Brahman gods we have already had occasion to cite Indra and to show the important place he holds in Cambodia. He is recognized by his mount, the three-headed elephant Airāvata. This mount has taken the chief place in certain decorative motives, such as the angles of the gates of the wall of Angkor Thom.

We have also seen the god Yama, who presides over the nether world and judges the dead.

Among secondary divinities we must first of all cite the Apsarases, graceful feminine creatures, born of the churning of the ocean for the pleasure of the gods; their effigies are found in profusion on the walls of the temples, frequently in a very deeply cut ornamental framing, and they enliven with their smiles the architecture of the Angkor monuments. They are the ballerinas of the heavens, and they are seen sometimes motionless, in long skirt, holding flowers (Fig. 21), sometimes dancing with knees apart.

Then come the Yakshas (Yeaks), Cambodian ogres with red eyes, with ferocious set grin, with threatening fangs, often conventionalized in a curious fashion in modern Cambodian decoration (Fig. 22).

Among the last-named must be ranked the *dvārapālas*, or door-wardens, standing at the entrance of shrines and generally leaning upon a club.

Fig. 21. APSARAS
From the Bayon. *Photo E.F.E.O.*

I have already more than once had occasion to show the fairly intimate connexion that was at work in Cambodia between Brahmanism and Buddhism: I shall find a fresh proof of it in the fact that in the royal palace of Pnom-Penh a sacred sword is preserved which is the palladium of the kingdom. This sword, which is displayed in certain ceremonies, is entrusted to the keeping of the *bakus*, the Brahmans maintained by the king, for the cult of Ṣiva and Vishṇu has survived in the etiquette of the court as in the traditions of the people. A legend tells how this sword, the least spot of rust on the blade of which would be a presage of disaster for Cambodia, was forged in the celestial abode by Indra according to the directions of Brahmā.

In the year 93 of the Christian era, according to this legend, a Khmer king, endeavouring to capture some wild elephants, notched the sacred sword in correcting the elephant he was riding; this was the signal for a gradual decadence that fell upon the country from that moment. In actual fact M. Groslier supposes that the weapon preserved in the royal palace dates from the fourteenth century.

Hindu Legends and Epic Tales. It remains for me to point out one of the most fruitful sources upon which the Cambodian artists draw very frequently for their mural decorations in the modern pagodas, or to execute vast frescoes in bas-relief on certain temples in the ancient land of Khmer, or to find subjects for items in the *répertoire* of the king's dancing-women.

These are poems such as the *Mahābhārata*, the *Rāmāyaṇa*, and other legends connected with the gods Vishṇu and Ṣiva, which became as popular in Cambodia as in India. But these poems, in leaving the country of their origin, became more or less transformed and overladen with new episodes. I shall very briefly glance at some of these legends. From the *Mahābhārata* the Khmers especially adopted the famous battle that brought the army of the Pandavas and the army of the Kauravas to grips in the plains to the north of Delhi; at Angkor Vat may be seen the death of Bhīshma, the general who was in command of the army of the Kauravas, his body riddled with arrows, while he dictates his will to his attendants (Fig. 23). Another episode in the same poem represented in the same temple is that of the Sun and the Moon denouncing to Vishṇu the demon Rahu, who stole the *amrita*, the liquor of immortality.

The *Rāmāyana* had among the Khmers a success that is not yet exhausted; furthermore there are a Cambodian version and a Siamese version of this epic in which important variants are found. Mlle Suzanne Karpelès, who has studied these versions, finds a great deal of charm and delicacy in these added episodes.

Fig. 22. HEAD OF A YEAK

The sequence of the innumerable tales that make up this poem, the subject of which is Rāma's war, with the help of the army of the apes, to recover his wife who had fallen into the hands of the King of the Yeaks, contains prolixities and repetitions. I shall give a summary of the principal episodes most frequently met with both in the modern iconography and on the old Khmer temples.

The hero of the *Rāmāyaṇa* is an incarnation of the god Vishṇu; it was the gods themselves who went to find him as he lay sleeping at full length upon the serpent, and beg him to reincarnate himself once again and purge the world of the demon Rāvaṇa.

This request of the gods to Vishṇu, as the result of which the god was reborn as the son of King Ayodhya Daṣaratha, is the prelude to the series of the adventures of Rāma.

Rāma and his brother Lakshmaṇa first of all go to be taught in the hermitage of the ascetic Viṣvamitra, who becomes their *guru*: they deliver him from harrying birds, monsters akin to Rāvaṇa, the King of Lanka (Ceylon), who reigns over the Yeaks or Rākshasas. It is easy to recognize in these Yeaks the negroid races of Dravidians living in the south of India, and in Rāma and his companions the Aryan races that peopled the north of India.

When their studies are over Rāma and his brother return to Ayodhya. The King of Mithila has promised his adopted daughter Sītā to the victor in an archery contest; the target is a bird placed behind a rotating wheel. (In the Hindu version there is a bow exceedingly stiff to bend.) Of all the competitors Rāma is the only one to accomplish the feat, and he weds Sītā. Daṣaratha, now grown old, is fain to hand over the throne to his first-born son, Rāma; but to keep the word he had rashly given in bygone days he yields to the remonstrances of his second wife, who insists that the power shall be given to his second son, Bharata: his favourite son Rāma is therefore banished from the kingdom and condemned to exile. In this exile Rāma is followed by his wife, Sita, and his brother, Lakshmana, who in their devotion to him wish to share the perils of his adventurous life. The three go into the forest to lead the life of ascetics, and a thousand strange adventures befall them. Like the knights-errant of the medieval romances, Rāma and his brother protect the unfortunate and slay the evildoers who cross their path.

One day a *rākshasa* called Virādha seizes Sītā and is preparing to devour her, but Rāma and Lakshmaṇa arrive in time to deliver her, and slay the monster (Fig. 7); in the Hindu version they merely cut off both his arms.

Rāvaṇa, the King of the *rākshasas*, whom the artists make very imposing with his

Fig. 23. DEATH OF BHĪSHMA
From the Bapuon. *Photo Musée Guimet.*

ten heads and his twenty arms, having heard the beauty of Sītā lauded, decides to seize her. He secures the help of a demon called Maricha, who at his command turns himself into a gilded stag and roams close by Rāma's hermitage. Sītā, seeing this marvellous animal, begs her husband to slay it, that she may have the skin. Rāma pursues the stag and strikes it with his arrow (Fig. 24); but in the moment of death the demon imitates Rāma's voice and calls to Lakshmana for help. Lakshmaṇa, believing his brother to be in danger, dashes to the rescue and leaves Sītā alone. At this moment Rāvaṇa appears before Sītā, and in spite of her protests and her distress seizes her forcibly and carries her away through the air. A vulture, Jatayus, a friend of Rāma, tries to make the King of the *rākshasas* relinquish his prey, but the fray is fatal to the bird, which falls wounded to death, while Rāvaṇa carries Sītā off to his palace in Lanka (Fig. 25).

When the brothers return to the hermitage they learn from the dying vulture the sad tidings of the rape; before it expires the bird is able to point out to Rāma the direction taken by the ravisher.

Rāma and Lakshmana are disconsolate and give themselves up to grief.

A monster, Kabandha, a "*rākshasa* with a huge body, a broad breast, headless, but with a face in his belly," meets the two men and tries to devour them. Rāma and Lakshmaṇa cut off Kabandha's arms; he relates his story and indicates to Rāma the way to recover Sītā.

Some time after the two brothers make the acquaintance of the white ape Hanuman, the son of the Wind, who brings them to Sugrīva (Sukrip), King of the apes, dispossessed by his brother Valin (Bali) of all his property and of his kingdom. Sugrīva is living in solitude in the forest, when Rāma and Lakshmaṇa come to find him and conclude a treaty of alliance with him (Fig. 26); Rāma will help Sugrīva to reconquer his throne, and the army of the apes will be placed at his disposal to help him to fight the *rakshasas* who are keeping Sītā prisoner.

Fig. 24. RĀMA AND THE STAG MARICHA
From a bas-relief at Angkor. Drawing by Mlle Sappho Marchal.

Sugrīva goes off and challenges his brother Valin, and a terrible fray takes place between the apes; Rāma secures victory for his ally by slaying Valin with an arrow that ends the battle. The death of Valin, like the two previous scenes, is an episode very often reproduced; in a famous bas-relief of Angkor Vat there is seen Dara (Tara), the widow of Valin, and the army of the apes surrounding the body and lamenting (Fig. 25). Sugrīva, nominated king of the apes, prepares an army to go and deliver Sītā; to discover the exact spot where she is kept a prisoner Rāma sends Hanuman to Lanka to reconnoitre, and after various adventures Hanuman reaches the grove of Aṣoka, where Rāvaṇa has his captive guarded by *rākshasīs* (female demons). Hanuman discloses himself, reassures Sītā, and receives a ring from her to bring to Rāma as a proof of his success. This scene is frequently found in the bas-reliefs of Angkor (Fig. 27). Before leaving Lanka the ape Hanuman sets fire to Rāvana's palace, and then returns to give Rāma tidings of his beloved wife; then the army of the apes makes ready to march against Rāvana. But the arm of the sea that separates India from Lanka must be crossed: a dike is constructed, and the army is enabled to get over the strait. Rāvana makes ready to withstand the assault, assembles generals and soldiers, and the encounter takes place. The battle is rich in incident of every kind. Rāvana multiplies tricks and ruses, endeavours to dishearten Rāma and his brother Lakshmana. The bas-reliefs of Angkor Vat retrace the episodes of this Hindu Iliad:

Fig. 25. (1) VALIN AND SUGRĪVA, FROM A PEDIMENT AT ANGKOR VAT. (2) THE RAPE OF SITĀ (MODERN). (3) STANDING BUDDHA

Drawings by Mlle Sappho Marchal.

there we behold Rāvaṇa, terrible with his multiple arms brandishing a thousand weapons, standing on his chariot drawn by human-headed horses. Over against him, upright in his car or sometimes mounted on the ape Hanuman, Rāma hails arrows upon his adversary in the thick of the inextricable *mêlée*, where apes and giants confront one another, and bite, a. ¹ claw, and slay each other.

Of course, prodigy plays an important part in these fights; one episode that has often beguiled the chisel of the Khmer sculptors is that of Indrajit, one of the sons of Rāvaṇa, which M. Finot describes as follows, after a bas-relief of the Bapuon:

Fig. 26. The Alliance of Rāma and Sugriva
From the Bapuon. *Photo Musée Guimet.*

> Indrajit, skilled in magic, hurls upon Rāma and Lakshmana arrows that turn to serpents, coil about the two princes, and fling them to the ground. . . . It is in mind to send apes to find in the sea of milk miraculous plants of reviving. But at that moment there appears in the sky as it were a thunder-cloud: it is Garuḍa arriving with all the speed of his wings. The serpents flee in terror, leaving the two heroes at liberty, and Garuḍa heals them in a moment by touching their wounds.

Enchantments and apparitions raised by Rāvana or his sons in vain endeavour to conquer the army of the apes and overthrow Rāma and his brother. At length, after numberless combats in which victory remains long uncertain, the advantage is with Rāma,

Fig. 27. Sītā and Hanuman in the Grove of Aṣoka
Angkor Vat. Drawing by Mlle Sappho Marchal.

who recovers his dear wife Sītā, but her trials are not yet ended. Her stay with the giant Rāvana leaves a suspicion of her purity: that suspicion must be destroyed, and now comes the episode of the ordeal of Sītā, so frequently figuring in Khmer sculpture. A pyre is made ready: the queen takes her place on the fire in the midst of a huge concourse, and comes forth untouched, the flame having spared her. Agni the fire-god solemnly hands her back to her husband, certifying her purity.

The triumph of Rāma concludes with his entry in his chariot Pusspaka into the city of Ayodhya, where he is to reign.

Fig. 28. The Churning of the Sea of Milk
Angkor Vat.

A myth particularly dear to the Khmer decorators must be told: it is that of the churning of the sea of milk, which at Angkor Vat extends over a length of some fifty yards.

At Vishṇu's suggestion the gods make a pact with the Asuras (demons) with the object of bringing out the *amṛita*, the liquor of immortality, by churning the ocean of milk. The churn-staff is Mount Mandara, around which is coiled the serpent Ananta, to serve as a rope; Vishṇu in the shape of a tortoise supports the mountain used as churn-staff. This god takes an active part in the churning in other ways: after seeing him as a resting-point for the churn-staff we see him half-way up in human shape brandishing discus and sword, and on the top of the mountain animating and superintending the action; Devas and Asuras pull alternately. The gods have been placed at the tail end of the serpent to leave the disadvantage with the demons, when the reptile's jaws belch out poisonous

Fig. 29. KṚISHṆA LIFTING THE MOUNTAIN GOVARDHANA
Angkor Vat. Drawing by Mlle Sappho Marchal.

flames, while the clouds, driven away from the opposite side, refresh the gods with beneficent rains (Fig. 28).

The sea of milk is churned in this way for more than a thousand years, and from it there start up in succession all kinds of fantastic creatures, until the moment when the poison let loose threatens to overwhelm the world and cause it to perish under sulphurous vapours; at Brahmā's request the god Ṣiva swallows the poison, which stays in his throat, whence he has his surname of Nīlakaṇṭha (blue throat). At length appears the goblet of *amṛita*, the liquor so greatly desired; from the tossing waves emerges likewise the Goddess of Beauty, Lakshmī: at sight of her the whole world is charmed. The sages sing her praises, the celestial musicians play their sweetest melodies for her, and the Apsarases, also

Fig. 30. Rāvaṇa in his Chariot
Bas-relief from the temple of Angkor Vat.

born from the sea of milk, dance for her. Two elephants dip up water from a golden vase, to pour it over the head of the goddess. Before this charming welcome Lakshmī smiles at the gods and throws herself on Vishṇu's breast; the Asuras, jealous at this preference, seize the cup of *amṛita*, but Vishṇu, in a female shape, distracts their attention, cheating them, so that he is able to restore the liquor to the gods. The vexed demons flee away and return to the nether realms of Patala.

Of the life of Kṛishṇa, another avatar of Vishṇu, Khmer iconography has especially retained some boyhood scenes: we often see the young god represented uprooting the two *arjuna*-trees, dragging an enormous mortar, to which his adoptive mother had tied him to make him keep quiet.

The episode most frequently reproduced is that of Kṛishṇa lifting Mount Govardhana " as a little boy lifts a mushroom," to shelter his companions the herdsmen and their cattle from the storm (Fig. 29).

The bas-reliefs of Angkor Vat show some scenes of the fight against the Asura Bana; the latter may be recognized by his multiple arms and by the lions that draw his chariot. Kṛishṇa, mounted upon Garuḍa, conqueror of the flames surrounding the city of Ṣoṇitapura, fights with Kārttikeya, Bana's ally, and then, continuing his onward march, ends by triumphing, after several vicissitudes, over his enemy. As he is just about to be slain Bana is saved by the interposition of Ṣiva, who says to Kṛishṇa, " I know that thou art the Supreme Being. In all nature there is not one that can vanquish thee. Let thyself, then, be moved. I have promised Bana my protection: let not my word be in vain." And Kṛishna, appeased, replied, "Let him live, since thou didst promise him life, for we are not distinct one from the other: what thou art that I am also." " This scene," says M. Challaye, " expresses the most lofty ethical idea of the ancient Hindu religion: the kinship, the identity, of all the gods, of all men, of all creatures."

Among Saivite episodes we may mention the well-known story of the god Ṣiva harassed in his retreat by Kāma, the God of Love, who launches against him his arrow of sugar-cane; his assailant is reduced to ashes by the indignant god, and his wife Rati comes and laments over the body.

A scene from the *Rāmāyaṇa* that is fairly often reproduced is the following: The demon Rāvaṇa, arriving in front of the mountain Kailāsa, upon which Ṣiva sits with his wife, conceives the bold plan of overturning it and smashing up paradise. To that end he places himself underneath the mountain and endeavours to shake it loose. Pārvatī, affrighted by the shock, embraces her husband, but the god puts his foot on the mountain and crushes the demon, who is caught under it.

M. Coedès observes that the sculptors of Angkor, who executed many replicas of the scenes referred to above, " knew by heart the *Rāmāyaṇa* and the most salient episodes of the *Mahābhārata* and the *Harivamṣa*." At the same time the Hindu texts were not always the only source from which they drew, for the following episode, which is frequently reproduced, is of unknown origin: it is when Rāvaṇa, having hit upon the spot where Indra's women's house is situated, turns himself into a chameleon in order to slip into the palace directly the god has gone and seduce the women.

Fig. 31. Rāvaṇa shaking Mount Kailāsa
Bauseai Srei.

Fig. 32. APSARASES
Cham art.

CHAM MYTHOLOGY

CHAM art has more than one link with Khmer art, and we shall have occasion to meet with the same gods and with similar cults. I shall glance rapidly over the mythology of Champa, in the first place because to-day the Cham people belongs, so to speak, to the past, and the pale gleams of its ancient civilization are fading out more and more before the neighbouring civilizations; next because, as M. Finot declares:

> Champa, pressed upon by the Annamites to the north, by the Cambodians to the west and the south, exposed by sea to the incursions of pirates, had a troublous and precarious life. It never had leisure to develop, like Cambodia, its architecture, the first monuments of which are nevertheless remarkable works. Its culture little by little decreased, while it wore away its strength in a desperate resistance against the Annamite pressure. In the end it succumbed, and except for a few enclaves of Cham population in the south of Annam, apart from one or two temples in which priests more like Polynesian sorcerers than Hindu Brahmans celebrate disfigured rites, Chinese manners and customs have spread over the whole of Annam, and even over Cochin-China, whence the Cambodians were thrust back at the end of the eighteenth century.

The last Chams to-day form two groups: a group that is Muhammadan in religion, and another that has remained Brahman, which vegetates in Southern Annam.

The artistic and religious history of this country is a reflection of its political history: it was, says M. Parmentier, a long drawn-out decay, which, " slow at first, subsequently became accentuated in a rapid fall that ended in veritable barbarism."

Saivism. In the days of its splendour the Cham kingdom was predominantly Saivite, and in the temples that have been preserved to the present time the form under which the Hindu god was most frequently worshipped was the *linga*. In Champa the *linga* is a monolith, as in Cambodia, but the shapes are more various: it is sometimes cylindrical, sometimes polygonal and cylindrical, sometimes shaped like a club, and even emphatically realistic in treatment. M. Parmentier notes a tendency to give a very definite personality to the *linga* by the addition of figures (*mukha-linga*). At other times the *linga* is enclosed in a sheath (*koṣa*), often of great value, adorned with faces and inlaid with precious stones.

Idols of Ṣiva in human shape are less common: he is then seen sometimes calm in his ascetic guise, sometimes terrifying in his warrior guise. The anthropomorphic Ṣiva displays two or four arms; he is either standing or seated; he has the frontal eye, that eye which can reduce to ashes those who come under its gaze, and he wears the Brahman cord, sometimes replaced by a serpent (Fig. 33). For attributes he has the trident, the rosary, and the sword; his mount, the sacred bull Nandin, often accompanies him. This bull is bedecked with necklaces, with jewels, with bells, and in our day, according to Mme Jeanne Leuba, the Chams still go and place offerings before him.

Fig. 33. ṢIVA
Photo École Française d'Extrême-Orient.

The monstrous and terrifying form of the god Ṣiva is not common, and mainly consists of the multiplying of arms and heads.

In the guise of an ascetic Ṣiva tells his rosary and wears the chignon; sometimes he has a cylindrical bonnet, as is seen on the pre-Angkor statues of Cambodia.

Ṣiva also appears in his more or less threatening guise as the *dvarapāla*, or door-warden, leaning upon a club or gesticulating terribly: in the latter case he often holds in his hand the *vajra*. "Sometimes he is snapping his fingers," says M. Parmentier, "a classic gesture still repeated by the Cham priests."

In Ṣiva's train comes his *ṣakti*, Umā, or Pārvatī, his feminine energy, who like him has the frontal eye, the emblematic attributes, and the discus and the conch. She frequently has several arms, and shows herself sometimes cruel and sometimes benevolent. To her, in her Cham name of Lady Pō Nagar, the temple of Nhatrang is dedicated. Here follows a condensation, after Mme Jeanne Leuba, of the legend attached to it.

A pair of woodcutters who had no children, finding a little girl, adopted her and brought her up, cherishing her in the best way they could. When this child was seven years old she found as she roamed about a piece of eagle-wood, which she took back to her old parents, and which they carefully kept put by. When she was old enough to marry, she told her adoptive parents that she must leave them and go to China, there to marry the Emperor's son. This was, she said, a command from Heaven, for she was the daughter of a divinity who had sent her upon the earth solely that she might become the wife of the Chinese Emperor's son.

Poignant were the feelings of the parents, who had grown greatly attached to the child, and were in despair at this departure. They dared not, however, oppose this divine mission, and the girl, promising to come back to see them, cast the piece of eagle-wood into the sea, and immediately disappeared.

A fisherman found the piece of wood in his nets, and, recognizing it as of a very precious nature, deemed it worthy to be offered to the Emperor of China. The latter wished to sacrifice it to the gods, but his son begged the piece of wood from him so urgently that the Emperor gave way to his wish.

The son took it and carefully preserved it in his bedchamber; one day a beautiful girl presented herself in front of him, and he fell in love with her. The Emperor having given his consent, the marriage took place, and from this union was born an adorable little girl.

But the young wife had it in mind to keep her promise, and asked leave to go back and see her parents at Nhatrang; her husband refused and wished to keep her at home. She wept and entreated, but all her prayers were in vain; then the eagle-wood was once more cast into the sea, and the young woman disappeared. The old woodcutters were overjoyed to see her back again, but the husband in a fit of jealousy made ready a fleet and sped to Nhatrang.

Then the princess, infuriated at this lack of trust, called upon her father, who destroyed the fleet, and the royal bark was turned into a rock. It is the very rock that may still be seen in the middle of the lagoon, and which the Chams have marked with an inscription.

The princess remained at Nhatrang, lavishing care upon its people, and healing the sick. So when she died they raised to her the temple that bears her name. The Chams continued to make Lady Pō Nagar the object of a cult, and her statue became an idol still popular in our own days among the Annamites.

Umā is sometimes represented like Ṣiva with several arms, seated on the head of an elephant and armed with the hook. In sum she presents the same characteristics as Ṣiva.

After Umā, in the hierarchical order, comes Gaṇeṣa, the son of Ṣiva, presented in the shape of an obese man with an elephant's head and four arms; unlike the Javanese images, he always displays human feet. One of his tusks is broken, and his left hand holds a ladle in which he dips the tip of his trunk. His forehead often has the eye of Ṣiva; he has the Brahman cord worn *en sautoir*, and his jewels are treated as live serpents (Fig. 34).

Skanda appears to have had a special cult in Champa: this warrior-god has the peacock for his mount, sometimes the rhinoceros. He always has a chignon in four divisions, and is depicted in the guise of a man fully arrayed, holding sometimes the sword, sometimes the *vajra* (Fig. 35).

Vishnuism. The cult of Vishnu and his *ṣakti* Lakshmī holds a lesser place in the Cham religion than that of Ṣiva and Umā. Vishṇu appears more frequently in architectural decoration than as an idol: the bas-reliefs show this god in the scene of the birth of Brahmā, lying upon the serpent Ananta, whose heads form a canopy over him; a lotus comes out of his navel to support the four-faced god.

As attributes Vishnu holds the hollowed discus, the conch, the lotus, and the club; his *vāhana* (mount) is the Garuḍa bird, the devourer of serpents.

Lakshmī likewise holds the lotus bud, the conch, and the quoit, and is always represented seated.

Garuda appears as half bird, half man. M. Parmentier observes that he resembles rather a lion equipped with wings than a bird, and he notes certain fantastic forms of the beak that come something near the face of an ape.

Brahmā occupies a rather inconspicuous place in Cham iconography; he is characterized by his mount, the sacred goose, and his four faces.

By the side of these persons of the Brahman pantheon we may also place Indra in the second rank, the God of Thunder mounted on an elephant, and Sūrya, the God of the Sun, mounted on a galloping horse and brandishing a sword.

Among the genii we meet with the *rākshasas*, a kind of ogre represented sometimes as demons flying and gnashing their teeth. Their king, carved in a bas-relief, displays ten heads, ten arms, and four legs.

The Apsarases often find a place in decorations, notably in the motive in which they

Fig. 34. GAṆEṢA
Photo École Française d'Extrême-Orient.

Fig. 35. SKANDA
Photo École Française d'Extrême-Orient.

are represented to the waist, as though they were coming out of the wall and holding a lotus bud.

Among the fantastic animals in Cham iconography we must cite the following:

The lion, sometimes treated in the Indian manner, with eyebrows like horns.

The *gaja-siṃha*, the lion-elephant, but more of the lion than the elephant; from his jaws a new creature is often seen emerging.

The *makara*, often employed as a *pièce d'accent* or as a decorative motive, a kind of lion's head, the nose of which changes into a trunk, and which shows jutting fangs; from its open jaws there usually emerges a creature seen to the waist.

The obese and hunchbacked dwarf found in classical Khmer art, which has not yet been identified, is likewise seen in Cham art.

Buddhism. Buddhism has not had many adepts, and this religion is far from having had among the Chams the popularity we saw it enjoyed among the Khmers, as Saivism was always the predominant religion. Images of Buddha are rare: he is clad in a tunic, which leaves the right arm uncovered, and has no *ūrnā*. The *ushṇīsha* is only indicated by a little ball-shaped chignon on top of the head.

A mingled religion made up of Saivism and Buddhism is recognized in a few statues: the inscriptions also bear witness to the fusion of the Buddhist and Brahman religions, " a fusion less surprising," says M. Parmentier, "than the curious final mingling of Brahmanism and Islam."

Statues of Avalokiteṣvara, the only distinguishing characteristic of which appears to be the figurine of Amitābha on the chignon, are exceedingly uncommon in Champa.

Modern Cults and Beliefs. The decadence that brought the Cham people to its almost complete downfall caused the primeval beliefs to lose their purity; the divinities were confounded in an ill-defined cult, and ended by disappearing more or less completely before the rising power of Islam and the local superstitions.

Among the surviving Chams those in Cambodia, the Bani Chams, are Muslims, and the Kaphir Chams, remaining in Annam, are Brahmans. But the ceremonies practised by the latter are adulterated with sorcery and Islam; the Brahmanism they observe is merely a bastard and deformed religion.

" Just as shellfish fasten upon and incrust a piece of wreckage," says Madame Jeanne Leuba,

> so all the beliefs, all the superstitions of the neighbouring peoples, tacked themselves on to a Saivite foundation, to make up by degrees a shapeless mass of heterogeneous elements. The principal divinities of the Brahman pantheon, Ṣiva and Umā, Vishṇu, Lakshmī, and Brahmā, were replaced by a legion of modern divinities, the chief of which are Pō Nagar, Pō Klong Garaï, Pō Romé, Pō Binh Thuor, Pō Dam, Pō Sah, or Pō Ovlah, who is no other than the Ovlah of the Islamists, Allah. These are not only fictitious personages, but for the most part effigies of ancient kings deified by the Chams, of whose befogged minds the most absolute confusion in the whole matter has taken firm possession.

This writer also notes that the Chams of to-day, having lost the exact significance of the religious statues of their fathers, make use of a stone, of any casual round boulder, of a very coarse graven image, to represent their divinities. The least things, even the most ordinary and commonplace, become the object of a cult, and these idols are often endowed with a maleficent power that makes them feared and dreaded.

Other idols are compassionate and kind. Mme Jeanne Leuba mentions a little triangular stone set in the ground under a tree on the road to Langbian, with wooden weapons planted all round its altar, which receives gifts of the humblest kind: " quids " of betelnut, tobacco, matches, cash, etc. Certain very poor worshippers are not, it appears, afraid to appropriate some of these tiny offerings, but first asking permission of the stone to do so.

In ritual sacrifices eagle-wood ranks as a precious thing; the legend recounted above shows that this superstition is a very ancient one.

The Chams encumber their ordinary life with superstitious customs, which entail rites, offerings, feasts, or sacrifices. Some of these practices are not always harmless—for example, the belief in the virtues of human gall, which is not peculiar to the Chams, but is found among all the peoples of Indo-China. Human gall passes for a marvellous stimulant to bravery. And so, until last century, Cambodians and Chams did not shrink from crime in order to obtain the secretion endowed with such potent virtue.

Fig. 36. THE BATH OF THE BODHISATTVA
Bas-relief at Borobodur.

Fig. 37. Scene from the Life of the Buddha
Borobodur.

JAVANESE MYTHOLOGY

We know practically nothing of Java before its Hindu-ization. The Malayo-Polynesian population, which had come perhaps from Indo-China, could not have been altogether savage when the first Hindu elements made their way into the archipelago. These immigrants, merchants, seamen, etc., came, it is believed, from the southern part of the east coast of India.

The oldest traces of Hindu civilization have been found in the west of Java, and date from the fourth and fifth centuries of our era: these are inscriptions in the Sanskrit language. The two centuries that followed show a movement toward the centre of Java, which was then under the shadow of the predominance of the great Sumatran kingdom of Ṣrīvijaya. As the Hindu culture was not addressing itself to an uncivilized population, from its fusion with the native element there sprang up an Indo-Javanese culture forming a quite homogeneous whole; it is sometimes difficult enough to assign certain qualities to a Hindu origin rather than to the autochthonous foundation. This may be observed in the language that was newly born in this period, Kavi, a compromise between Sanskrit and Malayo-Polynesian, which shows the mingling of the two races.

The same evolution is found in art during this period: Javanese elements mingle more and more with the Hindu forms, in sculpture as well as in architecture.

About the middle of the eighth century the kingdom of Ṣrīvijaya established its influence over the Strait of Malacca. This was the kingdom of Palembang, whose supremacy was extended by the Sailendra dynasty as far as Central Java: Mahāyāna Buddhism ousted the Hīnayāna form, which till then was flourishing.

With the Ṣailendra period coincide Mahayanism and Saivism, the latter being especially prevalent among the common people, while the former had its votaries at the Court and among the governing classes. This explains the construction in this epoch of numerous Buddhist monuments. Borobodur belongs to this period (ninth century). Presently the Ṣailendra dynasty was turned out of Java, and the native sovereigns regained their power; Sumatran art, after having been Buddhist, then became Saivite. However, the opposition between Mahayanist Buddhism and Saivism was never very deep, and in the mind of the common people the two religions had a tendency to coalesce. Mr Krom puts forward as characteristic of the art of this period the majestic temple of Lara Jonggrang at Prambanan, which is the apotheosis of Saivism, in contradistinction to Borobodur, which had been the apotheosis of Buddhism.

In the tenth century civilization emigrates from Central Java to the eastern region of the island, and a change then took place: the autochthonous Javanese foundation reacted against the Hindu element. Javanese society was in process of driving out the old Hindu foundation, to return to the native-born element; this was the evolution that, modified by Islam, was to end in modern Java.

The dynasty that in the thirteenth century rivalled the kingdom of Ṣrīvijaya and coincided with this reaction against Hindu influence had its capital at Singasari. At the end of the thirteenth century the capital was changed from Singasari to Majapahit, and in 1377 the kingdom of Ṣrīvijaya was reduced to impotence. The most important temple of the art of the period of Majapahit's sovereignty over the island empire is the temple of Panataran, dedicated to Ṣiva and situated in Eastern Java. This temple, like that of Borobodur, is interesting for its iconography and the numerous illustrations of legends that adorn its walls.

The abandonment of the Hindu tradition becomes more and more marked: the Hindu art of Central Java became the Javanese art of Eastern Java. Buddhism and Saivism tend more and more to join with one another, " a tendency," says Mr Krom, " which led, in the Majapahit period, to the construction of a Ṣiva-Buddhist temple, and to the aphorism ' Ṣiva and Buddha are but one.' "

In the fifteenth century came the decline of the Javanese Empire and of Javanese art: Islam, which had made its way by degrees through the northern coast of Sumatra, became predominant in the archipelago.

In 1526 the last Hindu king disappeared; Hinduism nevertheless continued to maintain itself in certain mountainous regions of Java, and has persisted still in our days in the island of Bali; in reality this island was never "Javanized," and received its Hinduism direct, hence it has an essentially Indo-Balinesian civilization, which gives it a slightly individual character in the archipelago.

Toward the end of the sixteenth century the art of Java was completely Islamized, and in the seventeenth the Dutch East India Company definitely established itself in the island.

Saivism. We have seen that Java received Brahmanism from India in a shape in which Saivism was predominant; accordingly we shall find the image of Ṣiva, the supreme deity whom all things obey, the Mahādeva, in the guise of an all-powerful majestic god with four arms, with a serpent for girdle, his third eye in his forehead, the skull and half-moon in his diadem: in his hands he holds the rosary and the fly-whisk.

Under the aspect known in Java by the name of Nandi-Keṣvara he is generally seen placed near the entrance of the temples, holding a lotus bud and a jar with the trident at his side.

Terrifying and destroying, he becomes the Mahākāla. And, lastly, as Bharata-Guru, he is the dispenser of divine wisdom: he is then represented in the guise of a corpulent, bearded ascetic, and his hair is plaited. He holds the jar and sometimes the rosary.

Ṣiva's wife, Pārvatī, is especially popular in the form of Durgā with eight arms; she represents light and good, and fights against the bull-demon representing darkness and evil. Stricken to the death by the goddess brandishing her weapons, the Asura Mahisha, who had turned himself into a bull, is seen emerging from the beast's neck to resume his demon shape (Fig. 38).

In Javanese art monuments are called Chandis: the word originally meant a commemorative building. It may have been derived from one of the surnames of Durgā, for that goddess is closely linked with the cult of the dead.

Fig. 38. Durgā slaying the Asura Mahisha

The Lara Jonggrang group of temples derives its name from a statue of Durgā-Mahishasuramardini, situated in the great temple of Ṣiva, and believed by the natives to be the image of the princess, the chief heroine of the legends of the group.

Pārvatī, or Umā, has four arms, and in two of her hands, brought round upon her breast, she holds a lotus flower, and in the others the rosary and the fly-whisk, which are the attributes of Ṣiva-Mahādeva.

Their elephant-headed son Gaṇeṣa is the God of Wisdom, who helps men in trouble or with distressing tasks to perform. In classical Indo-Javanese art, the most ancient form, he does not present the fierce and macabre character he displays in the East Javanese school of Singasari, where he appears rather terrible, though richly arrayed, hung about with a great quantity of skulls, and often with jewels carved with human skulls. He holds the axe and the rosary or the fly-whisk with his posterior hands, and in his anterior hands the little ladle and a fragment of a tusk.

Ṣiva's mount, the bull Nandin, as a rule has no part of an animal but the head; we may note on this point that the mounts of the Javanese deities often affect human shapes, and only the head denotes their animal nature.

In the evolution of Indo-Javanese art the *vāhanas* of the gods lose more and more their human aspect to approximate to the animal shape.

The *linga*, Ṣiva's emblem, the symbol of fecundity, is made in Java, as in Cambodia, with three sections, square, octagonal, and cylindrical. It is often set upon a richly ornamented pedestal with a stone hollowed out to receive the waters of ablution; the waste runnel is sometimes a very handsome decorative motive with a serpent's head.

We should mention the combination of the male and female elements in the person of

Ṣiva, a mixed being who unites the characteristics of the god and of his *ṣakti* Umā under the name of Ardhanari.

Vishnuism. Vishṇu was much less popular than Ṣiva; nevertheless several Javanese monarchs have been regarded as his incarnation.

He is depicted with four arms or under the guise of one of his avatars: wild boars, dwarf, or *narasiṃha* (lion-man). The Garuḍa that is his mount approaches the Hindu model rather than the Cambodian; in Java this fantastic creature often assumes in iconography great importance at the expense of the god he carries. His face sometimes displays something bestial and a ferocious grin in which practically nothing of the bird remains. In the admirable group of Vishṇu on Garuḍa, in the museum of Mojokerto, may be seen an example of the so-called consecration-statues, in which a prince was supposed to receive divine honours after death and assumed the aspect of a god. "The wrathful, powerful, bellicose figure of the Garuḍa trampling on the serpents," says Mr Krom, "is dominated by the god in his calm majesty. This happy attempt to create a harmony in contrast is peculiar to the artists of Eastern Java."

Fig. 39. VISHṆU-KUVERA
Bronze in the Musée Guimet.

Ṣri, or Lakshmī, Vishṇu's *ṣakti*, is much more popular; her cult is, besides, independent of that of the god. Originally the Goddess of Glory and Prosperity, in Java she speedily became the special divinity of the rice, which forms the staple food of the natives. Ṣri, the Javanese Ceres, holds in her left hand an ear of rice, and with the right makes the gesture of charity.

We sometimes see Lakshmī receiving a sprinkling from two kneeling elephants.

Brahmā is very rarely met with in the Dutch Indies; still we must cite a fine statue of this god with four faces now in the Leyden Museum, dating from the Brahman period between A.D. 900 and 1500. He wears the little beard of the ascetics, and his hands, joined in front of his breast, hold a vase in the shape of a lotus bud, which holds the elixir of life; his mount is of human aspect, and its animal character is denoted only by the goose's head.

The form of Hari-Hara, uniting Ṣiva and Vishṇu, which we have seen in Cambodia, has not in Java the mixed character it presents among the Khmers; the Saivite character has the upper hand. A very fine specimen of this deity is the so-called statue of King Kritarajasa, the founder of the kingdom of Majapahit, who died in 1399, and was apotheosized in the guise of Hari-Hara. Richly arrayed, he leans with one hand upon a club and holds a rosary in the other; his upraised posterior hands hold the shell out of which emerges a snail, "the symbol of liberation," and an object from which there escapes a flame. To right and left are two little female figures, Rukmini and Satya-bhama, his wives (Fig. 40).

Fig. 40. KING KRITARAJASA IN THE GUISE OF HARI-HARA

Among the minor gods we must mention Kuvera, the God of Riches, obese and equally popular with Saivites and Buddhists; his most frequent attributes are the mongoose and the lemon (Fig. 41).

The *rākshasas* are demigods common to both religions; they have a ferocious and cruel aspect, and, armed with a club, they guard the entrance of sanctuaries. Their round eye, their threatening fangs, their frizzled knot of hair, are their distinguishing characteristics. "The rings with which they adorn their ears," says Mr Krom, "are alike the attributes of the *rākshasas* and of their kin the *yakshas*."

The Kinnaras and the Nāgas only appear as a decorative element in architecture. The Kinnaras with outspread wings sometimes hold in their hands a flower and another object in their bird's claws.

Superb winged Nāgas, placed like Atlases or cariatides, adorn the base of the temple of Panataran. The *makara*, a marine monster, a kind of crocodile with tremendous jaw, whose snout is elongated into a trunk, is an ornamental element that was largely employed in Java.

The *makara* is employed with the *kala* head to serve as a framing for the entrance of temples, a decorative composition both curious and strange.

The *kala* head is a motive imported from India, but marked by Javanese art with undeniable originality; it is a conventionalized head of a monster seen full face, with bulging eyes, enormous nose, thick eyebrows, very conspicuous fangs, and no lower jaw. This head is sometimes given the name of Kīrtimukha, or Banaspati, "master of the forests." It is Saivite in origin, but as the keystones of arches where it is to be seen on the façades of temples it has lost its character as a religious symbol, to develop into a purely decorative motive; it seems to express an ideal beauty revealed under a terrible aspect.

Hindu Legends. The *Mahābhārata* and above all the *Rāmāyaṇa* were an inexhaustible quarry that the artists of Java exploited very frequently.

At Prambanan, the ancient capital of the island, the decorators represented sequences of scenes drawn from the *Rāmāyaṇa* on the walls before which the pilgrims used to parade. We shall recall some of these episodes treated in bas-relief, asking the reader to refer to the brief summary of Vālmīki's epic given above in the section on Khmer mythology.

First of all we shall cite the scene in which the gods, with Brahmā at their head, come and find Vishṇu sleeping on the serpent Ananta, to beg him to reincarnate himself in the hero Rāma. Among the gods M. Przyluski thinks he can identify the *lokapālas*, the five divinities who are the guardians of the world.

Beside Vishṇu is seen his *vāhana* Garuḍa in the special aspect he is given in Java, described above. Then we see Daṣaratha, King of Ayodhya, who, childless heretofore, by sacrifice obtains a divine elixir, by means of which his three wives bring into the world four boys, Rāma, Lakshmaṇa, Satrughna, and Bharata. This last scene has also been identified by Mr Havell as representing the hero Rāma between his three brothers brought before the deity by the *rishi* who is Daṣaratha's spiritual director. The rest of the panel shows the Court of King Daṣaratha.

Fig. 41. KUVERA
Bronze in the Musée Guimet.

Next we have the Svayamvara of Sītā, the trial of the bow by which Rāma wins his wife, an episode we have already seen at Angkor. This scene in Cambodia is encumbered with spectators and many supernumerary persons, while at Prambanan clearness and conciseness are given by a reduction in the number of persons represented.

In another bas-relief we see Rāma and his devoted brother Lakshmaṇa in the forest after the fatal decree that exiles them from the kingdom; in a grotto is a hermit who is supposed to be a friend of the hero. On the right of this panel is represented the meeting of Rāma with Jatayus, the King of the vultures, who warns him of the dangers run by the lovely Sītā when the two brothers leave her to go hunting.

The death of the monster Kabandha, who bears a face on his bosom, is found in Java, as in Cambodia; but here the monster is slain by Rāma with an arrow, and not with the sword. Following the advice given by Kabandha, Rāma betakes himself to the country of the apes and makes an alliance with the dethroned King Sugrīva, who will help him to recover the imprisoned Sītā. In this theme M. Przyluski, comparing the Javanese bas-relief with the one at Angkor Vat, notes that the ceremony of the pact of alliance upon which neither Vālmīki's poem nor the Khmer sculpture is very explicit, is given in more detail at Prambanan. There may be seen in particular the person who acts as go-between, the offerings, and the victim, a doe sacrificed on this occasion, which are found in alliance ceremonies among many primitive peoples.

Fig. 42. Bas-relief inspired by the Wayang
Drawing by Mlle Sappho Marchal.

Other scenes from the *Rāmāyaṇa* are found in the Panataran group, sculptured on panels in the main temple. A detailed study of these bas-reliefs was published by Brandes.[1] Mlle Lulius van Goor remarks that "its sculptures are executed in a way that distinguishes them clearly from those of the centre of the island; the figures recall the puppets of the Wayang theatre peculiar to Java."

Among the legendary figures that have remained popular we must set apart Hanuman, the ape ally of Rāma. According to Mr Krom, he is "the being of supernatural strength placed by the epic and the Wayang almost in the ranks of the gods."

The Wayang shadow theatre goes back, it is believed, to primitive Indonesian rites; but its present repertory is especially taken from the *Mahābhārata*: the Pandavas represent the sympathetic element, and their adversaries, the Kauravas, the maleficent powers. Scenes from the *Mahābhārata* have likewise inspired certain bas-reliefs in the temples; at Chandi Kedaton there have been identified sculptured panels the subject of which is taken from the *Garudeya*, a tale in old Javanese inspired by a fragment of the *Mahābhārata*.

Buddhism. The arrival of the Hindus in Java has been attributed to the downfall of the Ṣaka power at the beginning of the fifth century; the Buddhists, driven out of India after Brahmanism had supplanted their religion, took refuge with the Ṣaka immigrants in Java, and brought thither the cult of the great Sage Ṣākyamuni. The Buddhist sculptures of the Dutch Indies are reputed to be among the finest known.

Buddha in Java is always represented clad in monastic garb, with the *ūrṇā* and the

[1] *Wolkentooneelen van Panataran* (The Hague and Batavia, 1909).

Fig. 43. EPISODE FROM THE "SUDHANA KINNARAVADANA"
Fragment from a bas-relief at Borobodur.

ushṇīsha, and seated on the lotus throne in the posture called *padmāsana*, making either the gesture of charity, or the gesture of absence of fear, or that of instruction, or that of calling the earth to witness.

Beside the Buddha is found the series of the six, and, later, five, Dhyāni-Buddhas, or transcendental Buddhas, called in Java Jinas; they resemble the terrestrial Buddha, and display the same expression of countenance. They differ only in the position of the hands.

Fig. 44. Avalokiteṣvara at Chandi Mendut, Java
In a niche on his headdress is his spiritual father Amitābha. *Photo A. Diemont.*

In Mahayanism the veneration of the Bodhisattvas is very widespread, and among them Avalokiteṣvara enjoys especial favour; he is recognized by his spiritual father Amitābha, represented in a niche on his headdress. With one hand he makes the gesture of dispensing divine favours, and in the other he holds a lotus stem: he is found either standing in a graceful posture on one hip, or seated in the posture of meditation and royal ease—*i.e.*, with one leg bent and the other upright. His torso is covered with gems, and the serene expression of his face sometimes attains a profound beauty, as is the case with the Avalokiteṣvara at Chandi Mendut, in the centre of Java, which can vie sculpturally with the finest European works; with one hand he makes the gesture of charity and with the other that of argumentation (Fig. 44).

The same verdict may be passed upon the admirable statue of Prajñāpāramitā, in the Leyden Museum, which puts into concrete shape the loftiest possible elevation of thought: the face, says Mr Havell, has that ineffable expression of purity and grace that is found in certain Italian primitives.

It is seated upon the symbolic lotus, in the posture of meditation; the book, the

Fig. 45. BUDDHIST SCENE. SUJĀTA'S OFFERING
Bas-relief at Borobodur.

emblem of wisdom, is placed on a lotus bud, and the stem of the flower is coiled around its left arm (Fig. 46).

> In the Buddhism of Eastern Java the figure of the Buddha is overshadowed by a supreme being who may be identified with Vairochana, the most lofty of the Dhyāni-Buddhas. . . . Elsewhere he may be found in the person of Amoghapāṣa, a manifestation of Avalokiteṣvara with eight arms, which might equally pass for Jina.[1]

In Java we meet with figures of Tārā; she is associated with Avalokiteṣvara in popular imagination, and shares in her charitable virtues; sumptuously clad, she holds flowers in her hands and a very rich tiara upon her head.

Fig. 46. PRAJÑĀPĀRAMITĀ
Leyden Museum.

In the bas-reliefs of the temple of Chandi Mendut we may see a representation of Kuvera, the God of Riches (who belongs to Buddhism as well as to Saivism), surrounded by *yaksha* children, and alongside a scene the central personage of which is the child-devouring ogress Hārītī, who, being converted, became the beneficent Goddess of Health and Abundance. M. J.-Ph. Vogel sees in these bas-reliefs a memory of the Græco-Buddhist iconography of Gandhāra.

Lastly we must once more mention in the Buddhist pantheon Mañjusrī, the symbol of knowledge trampling upon ignorance, recognizable by his book resting on a lotus and making the gesture of scattering divine favours; and next the guardians of the law, personifications in terrible form of the Buddha defender of the faith, trampling under their feet the enemies of religion: among them is Vajrapāṇi, who in his capacity as *dharmapāla* is marked with ferocious energy.

The episodes of the life of the Buddha were the theme of a long sequence of bas-reliefs on the walls of the terraces of Borobodur, the great Buddhist monument of Java (A.D. 750 to 800). These bas-reliefs form admirable decorative panels which trace the life of the great Sage through his previous existences and in his last life from the Tushita heaven, where he decides upon his last reincarnation, to his entering into Nirvāna. These pictures are directly inspired by the Jātakas and the *Lalita-Vistara*. M. Foucher, who in his work on the Græco-Buddhist art of Gandhāra has studied certain of these pictures, recognizes that the Javanese were perfectly acquainted with the texts of the Buddhist scriptures, and that they followed them very faithfully in their sculptures (Fig. 45). I shall not attempt any description, for how is any choice to be made among the sixteen hundred sculptured panels that adorn the walls of Borobodur? It would be necessary to recount the multiple episodes of the life of the Buddha, which would be outside

[1] N. J. Krom.

the scope of this study. The beauty of these sculptures and the masterly composition of certain scenes give a very vivid artistic commentary on the texts, and one fairly easy to interpret.

Toward the decline of Majapahit art certain bas-reliefs are visibly inspired by the types of the Wayang marionettes (Fig. 47). In this way on certain individual figures there may be noted a considerable development of headdress ornaments and jewels around the ears (see Fig. 42). This is the period when Javanese art was already beginning to escape from Hindu leading-strings and draw near to the Indonesian popular beliefs. In the island of Bali, where these beliefs still impregnate every act of native life, very marked differences from Java can be observed.

A proof of the originality of the Bali superstitions will be seen in the fact that merits and sins have no effect on the rebirths of the soul after death, death to the natives representing the total liberation of the soul delivered from the body, which goes to heaven to live among the gods until its next reincarnation upon earth.

Lastly, among the traces of a pre-Hindu civilization may be cited a legend current in a tribe now reduced to a few individuals living far scattered in the forests of Sumatra; this legend recounts the exploits of a hero called " Bitter-tongue," who, by magic words, is said to have petrified certain individuals on the plateau of Pasemah. As a matter of fact, we find in this place a series of blocks sculptured with rather crude images. These sculptures, which display an art strange and naïve at the same time, remind us of the extraordinary giants of Easter Island, whose origin is still a mystery. (See the headpiece on p. 57.)

C.-H. MARCHAL

Fig. 47. WAYANG PUPPET
In the collection of M. L. D. Petit. From *Oost en West*, Amsterdam.

Fig. 1. THE ASSAULT OF MĀRA
Fragment in the Musée Guimet.

BUDDHIST MYTHOLOGY IN CENTRAL ASIA

THOUGH heavily breached from the eighth century of our era by the thunderbolt advance of Islam, Buddhism none the less held, until the eleventh century, the lines of oases lying north and south of the desert of Takla-Makan. From that period deserted Buddhist monasteries and sanctuaries were covered by the sands; the remarkable dryness of the climate ensured the preservation of the documents that had escaped the iconoclastic zeal of the Muslim conquerors.

In 1893 the French travellers Dutreuil de Rhins and Fernand Grenard collected, in the Khotan region, manuscripts and fragments of statuettes. The Russian savants, set on the alert by the remarkable finds of their compatriot Petrovsky, Consul-General at Kashgar, set on foot the first methodical researches (Klementz, 1898); they were followed closely by other missions: British, Dr (later Sir) M. Aurel Stein (1900–1); German, Grünwedel-Huth (1902–3), A. von Le Coq (1904–5), Grünwedel-A. von Le Coq (1905–7), A. von Le Coq, (1913–14); French, Paul Pelliot-Louis Vaillant (1906–8). The illustrated documents collected by these different missions carry the mark of the numerous and varied influences that were exerted upon this Asiatic Macedonia.

Indo-Hellenistic art, an instrument of Buddhist propaganda, had become loaded, from contact with Sasanian Persia, with Iranian elements that we will find in Bāmiyān (Afghanistan), as well as in Kizil (Chinese Turkestan). At Turfan (von Le Coq's mission) the influence of China was already active; from the sixth century the Chinese were there taking the place of the Avar princes (Juan-Juan), who had themselves succeeded occupants of Iranian race. We have similarly to reckon with Thibetan influences, particularly strong in the Tun-Huang region (Chinese province of Kansu). "Advanced sentinel of Chinese civilization to the west, Tun-Huang brought all the civilizations of Nearer Asia into touch with the Far East." [1]

The documents collected by the Pelliot mission at Tun-Huang are to be found in part in the Musée Guimet; the paintings and the statues that come from the western sites of Chinese Turkestan are shown in the Louvre.

The Dhyāni-Buddhas. The group of the five Dhyāni-Buddhas, rarely represented in Central Asia, figures in a painting brought back from Tun-Huang by M. Paul Pelliot (Fig. 2), now in the Musée Guimet. Vairochana appears in the middle of the composition; golden-coloured, he is seated in the Oriental fashion upon the pericarp of a lotus placed on a pedestal stamped with eight lions grouped in fours and back to back (the lion is Vairochana's favourite animal). A backpiece adorned with two winged rams on their hind legs, definitely Iranian in style, surmounted by two dragons with *makara* heads, is contained inside the aureole. Vairochana carries in his joined hands a *chakra* (wheel) placed upon a small pedestal. A conical diadem, adorned with four spikes and five tiny Buddhas, forms the uniform headdress of the holy persons. In our opinion this is the first time we meet with a representation of the group of the Dhyāni-Buddhas, arrayed as Bodhisattvas, in Central Asia. The Buddha companions of Vairochana are, above and on the left, Ratnasambhava, bearer of the Jewel-that-fulfils-desires (*chintāmani*), with winged horses on the pedestal, and on the right Amitābha, with the lotus, swans being on the pedestal. Below, on the right, is Amoghasiddhi, green of hue, holding the *vajra*, and on the left Akshobhya of the *vajra*, identified by his elephants. The companion Buddhas are themselves attended by little genii who are musicians or offering-bearers. Flowers and torch-holders appear in various places, as well as emblems belonging to the well-known series of the seven jewels and the eight precious objects—conch, fish, vase, *vajra*, parasol, standard, jewel.

The donor and various deceased members of his family are represented in the lower part of the painting; they are accompanied by two attendants and a servant. These persons are grouped to right and left of a green square upon which a votive inscription should have been traced.

The document we have just described is distinguished by the exceptional quality of its decorative composition. The very harmonious colour of the emblems, the aureoles, and the nimbuses stands out strongly against the neutral background of the canvas. The treatment of anatomical details, the broad faces, the sloping shoulders, the slender waists, calls for comparison with the Khotan paintings (Hārītī of Domoko, Sir Aurel Stein's mission) and the well-known frescoes of Horyūji, in Japan, these two examples representing the application of æsthetic formulas whose kinship has already been noticed.[2]

Lastly let us add that this document presents a real iconographic interest: we see in it, already perfectly established, in a composition in which the five Dhyāni-Buddhas figure, the pre-eminence of Vairochana, whom certain sects of Japanese Buddhism regard as the

[1] Paul Pelliot.

[2] De Visser, in a lecture to the India Society.

Ādi-Buddha, the Supreme Buddha (see under the heading Dainichi-nyorai, in the section entitled "Japanese Buddhism").

The Paradises. The sites of Central Asia have similarly provided a great number of representations of Paradise. These compositions, complex and sumptuous, reproduce a rigidly fixed iconographic schema; they range themselves about a central personage, the Master of Paradise. In the stereotyped setting of a palace built upon piles is shown the assembly of the gods presided over by a Buddha, the master of this Paradise, whether this is Amitābha, the ruler of the Happy Land of the West (Sukhāvatī), Ṣākyamuni, the future Buddha Maitreya, or even the Master of Medicine (Bhaishajyaguru). Change in the central personage and his assistants does not alter the general arrangement of the composition in any way. Everywhere we see identical trains of musicians and dancers. The souls of the elect appear in the guise of small children, the purity of this new state implying a birth without spot or stain. The bodies of the elect are represented springing out of the lotuses that adorn the garden plots of the 'Happy Lands.'

This doctrine of Amidism still counts very faithful adherents in Japan; the iconographic traditions of Central Asia survive in it, deriving, to-day as much as in old times, the best of their inspiration in a particularly sacred text, the *Amitayur dhyāna sūtra.* It is this text that serves as the basis for the illustrations that figure in the margin of the representations of the paradises. There we see episodes of a well-known legend that introduces King Bimbisāra, Queen Vaidehī, and their son Ajātaṣatru (see the legend of the Buddha in the section entitled " The Mythology of Lamaism ").

The Life of the Buddha. The Tun-Huang site, so rich in figured monuments, has revealed to us some illustrations of memorable incidents in the life of the Buddha. But while at Khotan and at Kizil the traditional data are respected, at Tun-Huang, farther away from the Indian sources, the persons of the legend wear Chinese costume: in the birth scene the Bodhisattva comes out of the wide sleeve of a garment of Chinese pattern. Other scenes are treated with such luxury of new details that the interpretation of the traditional themes is made new by them. The painting of Māra's attack, from Tun-Huang (Pelliot mission), illustrates with awkward and touching application a characteristic passage of Chapter 21 of the *Lalita-Vistara.* Māra's imps are there described as " having heads, feet, and hands contorted about; heads, eyes, and visages aflame; bellies, feet, and hands deformed . . . tongues wrinkled like straw mats; eyes red and sparkling like those of the black serpent full of venom." (See the headpiece on p. 242.) " Some vomited forth serpents' venom, and some took serpents' venom in their hands and swallowed it. The Bodhisattva is tranquilly seated on the sheaf of grass offered by the peasant Svastika. The aureole and the nimbus hide the trunk of the tree of Bodhi, whose conventionalized foliage may be seen. The painting has two borders in which figure, in varied postures, numerous Buddhas. These are most probably the principal forms venerated in Central Asia. In the lower part is a representation of the seven jewels (*sapta ratnāni*), the box of seals, representing the counsellor, the elephant, the woman, the jewel, the general, the horse, the wheel (*chakra*).

Avalokiteṣvara. The artists of Central Asia very often represented the miracles wrought by the All-Compassionate Avalokitesvara to save the faithful in danger. The

Fig. 2. THE DHYĀNI-BUDDHAS
Tenth-century painting from Tun-Huang. Pelliot Collection, Musée Guimet

pious craftsmen were inspired by the twenty-fifth chapter of a well-known Buddhist text, the " Lotus of the Good Law " (Saddharmapuṇḍarīka); the inscriptions (in Chinese characters) that figure on the cartouches opposite the four episodes shown have also been

Fig. 3. AVALOKITEṢVARA WITH THE THOUSAND ARMS
Tenth-century painting from Tun-Huang. Pelliot Collection, Musée Guimet.

borrowed from that text. The first, placed on the left hand in the upper part, is very explicit. " If when pursued by brigands who overturn thee and cast thee at the foot of the mountain Kin-Kang thou dost invoke the power of Kuan-Yin (Avalokiteṣvara) they shall have no power to hurt so much as one of thy hairs." The second episode is shown below on the left; a man is seen surrounded by flames; the inscription furnishes a precise

Fig. 4. The Miracles of Avalokiteṣvara
Tenth-century painting from Tun-Huang. Pelliot Collection, Musée Guimet.

commentary on the scene: "If anyone has a mind to injure thee and throws thee into a pit of fire, if thou dost invoke the power of Kuan-Yin the pit of fire shall turn into a pool of water." On the right, above, are seen two men hurling a third from the top of a rock; but thanks to the miraculous intervention of Avalokiteṣvara a cloud interposes, and the brutal fall is changed to a gentle descent. "If, being on the peak of the peak of Sü-mi (Sumeru) a man overturns thee, if thou dost invoke the power of Kuan-Yin thou shalt remain suspended in space like the sun." The last scene represents a man surrounded by a serpent, a scorpion, and a tiger. "If, being threatened by the poisoned breath, like unto smoky fire, of reptiles, of venomous serpents, or of scorpions, thou dost invoke the power of Kuan-Yin, at once at the sound of thy voice they shall take to flight."

The iconography of Avalokiteṣvara is not limited to these illustrations of the *Saddharmapuṇḍarīka-sūtra*; a representation of Avalokiteṣvara with the thousand arms, surrounded by a train of divinities, seems to have enjoyed particular favour in the whole of Central Asia (Fig. 3). The thousand arms arranged in the form of an aureole around the Bodhisattva symbolize his ever-active compassion; the hands hold numerous attributes, and among these attributes a water-jar from which escape drops of dew which are gathered up by a famishing damned soul; a poor man on the left of the Bodhisattva receives pieces of money. The divinities that surround Avalokiteṣvara seem to correspond with one another two by two; two forms may be noted of Ṣiva, Maheṣvara, and Mahākāla, who holds up with his third hand the drapery with which he is to extinguish the sun. Two terrible divinities appear in the lower part; these are, beyond any doubt, two forms of Vajrapāṇi. Two small genii, one with an elephant head, the other with a wild boar's head, raise suppliant arms to Vajrapāni; these are representations of "popular divinities subdued by universal religion and become *Yakshas* (genii). They are the personifications of maleficent genii crushed and converted by the bearers of the thunderbolt." [1]

Kshitigarbha. Although belonging to the group of the eight great Bodhisattvas, Kshitigarbha never figured among the stars of Indian Buddhism and Lamaism. On the other hand, he enjoyed throughout the whole of Central Asia a popularity attested by the extraordinarily wide diffusion of his image. The votive paintings of Tun-Huang (mission of M. Paul Pelliot and Sir Aurel Stein) show him to us in the guise of a particularly benevolent divinity devoting himself untiringly to alleviating the severity of the sentences pronounced by the ten Kings of Hell. Kshitigarbha is the master of the six paths (*gati*)—that is to say, the six good and bad states which souls experience after judgment. Representations of these six paths commonly enframe the upper part of votive pictures consecrated to Kshitigarbha. To the right appear the human beings, the Asuras, the demons; to the left the gods, the animals, the famished damned. Kshitigarbha, wearing the travellers' shawl on his head, holds the ringed stick (*Khakkara*) that tells the faithful of the coming of the mendicant monk; the Bodhisattva makes use of this stick to "shake the doors of Hell."

The Kings of Hell, to the number of ten, are customarily grouped all around the central figure.

The first king is called Ts'ên-kuang; it is he who undertakes the first division, setting on one side the elect, on the other the reprobate. The second king, Chu-kiang, places the

[1] E. Chavannes.

KUANYIN
(PELLIOT COLLECTION.)

souls in front of the mirror that reflects evil actions. The third, Sung Ti, puts the guilty to the torment of fire and hot water. The fourth, Wu Kuan, presides over the punishments administered by the *Yakshas*. The fifth, Yen-lo (Yama), judges those who have com-

Fig. 5. THE BODHISATTVA KSHITIGARBHA
Tenth-century painting from Tun-Huang. Pelliot Collection, Musée Guimet.

mitted the ten deadly sins. The sixth, Pien-ch'êng, sees to the beating of the guilty weighed under the supervision of the eighth king, named P'ing-têng Tu-shï; the ninth king is only a duplicate of Ts'ên-kuang. Lastly the tenth, Chuan-lun, is no other than the king with the wheel (*chakravartin*), the holder of the seven jewels; it is he who pronounces the last sentence and who assigns the souls to one of the six states.

Lastly there are the four satellites—Sung, Wang, Ts'ui, Chao—and the two assistants—unknown to later iconography—the monk Tao-ming and the Lion with the golden mane. Kshitigarbha is likewise venerated in Japan (see Jizô). In Japanese Buddhism he is shown in the shape of a monk holding the *khakkara* and the Jewel-that-fulfils-desires (*chintāmani*). This very form was borrowed from Central Asia (Fig. 5). The Chinese and

Fig. 6. THE BODHISATTVA MAITREYA
Tenth-century painting from Tun-Huang. Pelliot Collection, Musée Guimet.

Fig. 7. BODHISATTVA
Tenth-century painting from Tun-Huang. Pelliot Collection, Musée Guimet.

Fig. 8. THE BODHISATTVA SAMANTABHADRA
Tenth-century painting from Tun-Huang. Pelliot Collection, Musée Guimet.

Japanese Buddhists have not been satisfied with a single Jizô (in Chinese, Ti-tsang); they venerate six, "each of them undertaking the task of saving beings from one of the states."[1]

Maitreya. Samantabhadra. Other Bodhisattvas are also represented, some very nearly like the Indian models, like the Maitreya (Fig. 6) and the Samantabhadra in the Musée Guimet (Fig. 8) (Pelliot Collection), others treated in the Chinese manner (Fig. 7). However, if the treatment of the face is definitely Chinese, the elegant line of the arms, the slender suppleness of the hands, remain within the Indian tradition.

[1] De Visser, *The Bodhisattva Ti-tsang in China and Japan.*

The Guardian Kings of the Four Points of Space (Lokapāla). In Gandhāran India these personages were represented "under the commonplace and neutral guise of secondary divinities."[1] In Central Asia we see a complete transformation: to the divinities of debonair aspect succeed warriors clad in armour, breastplate, backpiece, and bellypiece (Fig. 9). The first two pieces are fastened by means of cords that are tied to a girdle. Leather corselets were the defensive armour of the Chinese from the Han period down to the T'ang period (from the second century B.C. to the tenth century A.D.). The Japanese Shitennô (see the section entitled "Japanese Buddhism") are near relations to the *Lokapāla* of Central Asia.

J. HACKIN

[1] A. Foucher.

Fig. 9. LOKAPĀLA
Tenth-century painting from Tun-Huang.
Pelliot Collection, Musée Guimet.

Fig. 1. Maitreya and the Eighteen Arhats
Fourteenth-century rock-carving from Hangkow.

THE MYTHOLOGY OF MODERN CHINA

THE POPULAR RELIGION AND THE THREE RELIGIONS

The mythology of modern China was formed in the course of the ages by the juxtaposition of elements of varied origin: we find in it, all pell-mell, alongside of old native divinities, certain great figures of Buddhist origin, who sometimes, indeed, play in it a strange and unexpected part: historical heroes deified in a recent epoch, Taoist personages, etc. And as there never was any body specially in charge of religion, to direct, or at any rate to codify, its development, doctrine and mythology shaped themselves without co-ordination, accepting the ideas and the personages that struck the popular imagination at different times, not without contradictions and duplications.

It is often said that the Chinese have three religions, Confucianism, Buddhism, and Taoism; and by this it is not meant that some are Taoists, others Buddhists, and others Confucianists, but that each Chinese is individually an adherent of the three religions at the same time. That is one of the false notions so prevalent about China. The reality is quite different. The Chinese are no more capable than ourselves of believing in three distinct religious systems at once—of believing, for example, as Buddhists that there is no supreme god governing the universe, the gods being mediocre beings of limited power, subject to birth and death, inferior to the Buddhas who have attained complete enlightenment; as Taoists that the world is governed by a trinity of supreme gods, personal, all-powerful, and eternal, the Three Pure Ones; and again as Confucianists that the supreme power that rules the world is the impersonal Heaven, impersonal though endowed with consciousness. The three religions, as definite systems, have now for several centuries had only historical interest: the people neither practise all three together, nor each of the three separately. Little by little throughout the ages a popular religion has taken shape, which borrowed various features from all three, but which is definitely distinct from them all, and must be regarded as a system apart.

But if none of the three religions has to-day adherents in the true sense of the word they all three have their proper clergy: Buddhist bonzes, Taoist monks and sorcerers, and for the official religion—ordinarily quite wrongly called Confucianism—functionaries of all ranks. The members of these clergies are regarded as enjoying special powers. Until the Revolution the mandarins (not particular officials charged with religious matters, but ministers, prefects, sub-prefects, etc.), by virtue of their official rank, not only conducted ceremonies to the official divinities of their districts, but furthermore commanded those of these divinities whose hierarchical rank in the celestial organization was lower than their own rank in the terrestrial administration. The bonzes have marvellous powers in everything that concerns the souls of the dead; they deliver them from the torments of hell, redeem their sins, etc. The Taoist monks have the power to drive away demons and to protect the living against them; besides these monks there are lay Taoist devotees who have various recipes against evil spirits and diseases. Their respective domains are not, however, clearly defined, and it must not be believed that there are exact boundaries; on the contrary, there are undecided zones where bonzes and *tao-shï* obtain similar results by different methods; but in many cases their parts are absolutely distinct. It would nevertheless be incorrect to define them as different categories of sorcerers, which would imply a somewhat pejorative sense: they fill the *rôle* of the specialist priests known in all antique religions, sacrificers, evokers of the dead, exorcists, prophets, physicians, etc. They are themselves, as a general rule, in a similar condition of mind to that of the laity around them. There are, indeed, to-day here and there a few bonzes who are almost strictly Buddhists, or a few literati who hold exclusively to the official ritual and dogma; but these are comparatively rare. Ordinarily the Buddhist or Taoist literati and monks believe in the popular religion like everybody else, and even in their ceremonies, when their ritual is exclusively Buddhist, or Taoist, or Confucian, their personal interpretation often approximates far more nearly to that of the popular religion than to that of the religious system to which the ritual belongs. There are to-day, from this point of view, considerable personal variations: the most intelligent of the bonzes or the *tao-shï*, or, indeed, those who have marked tendencies to mystical meditation, and, among the literati, even allowing for a certain external agnosticism, those who have the philosophic mind, arrive at creating a personal system almost in conformity with the label they give themselves (Buddhist, Taoist, Confucianist); and as the popular religion is very malleable and very elastic, and allows all individual interpretations, they do not appear to belong to a different religion from the laity, and do not lose touch with them.

These personages lead very different kinds of lives. The officials were not bound to any particular observances on account of their religious functions, except a fast in the few days immediately before a sacrifice, long or short according to the importance of the occasion; they had no special costume for religious ceremonies, and merely put on their official robe and bonnet, with the insignia of their rank, exactly as for civil ceremonies.

The Buddhist monks live communally in great temples, or are detached in little isolated chapels; these outliers are recalled to their mother house for three months, from the fourth to the seventh months of every year. They may be known by their shaven heads and their distinctive dress (Fig. 2). We know that the rule prescribes three superimposed garments: an undergarment, a kind of drawers from the navel to the knee, a

Fig. 2. Group of Bonzes

robe from the shoulders to the knees, and a cloak called *sanghati*, a kind of great sleeveless toga draped above. The place of this is taken in China by a tunic with long sleeves; it seems also that originally the Chinese bonzes wore the ordinary lay garb, distinguished only by their shaven heads; a conservative tendency, like that which gave birth to the sacerdotal robes of the Roman Catholic priests, is the origin of their modern costume.

They have kept the robe in the antique fashion, crossed on the breast, while the laity adopted, about the ninth and tenth centuries of our era, the garment cut round at the neck, without a collar, and buttoned very high on the side, which persists to the present day. The ceremonial robe, the *k'ie-sha* (*kashāya*), is a robe stitched with gold, pretty closely in conformity with the rule: the piece of stuff, as is ordained, is cut into pieces that are then sewn together again, and the seams are marked with gold braid, hence the popular name of gold-braided dress. It is worn over the ordinary dress, by putting it on the left shoulder and the neck, and bringing it round on the breast in front by passing it under the right arm, which is left free; the upper piece is fastened through a metal ring on the left side of the breast. A red lacquer crown in the shape of a conventionalized lotus flower serves as headdress in certain ceremonies.

Definite entry upon the religious life is preceded by a kind of novitiate, longer or shorter as the case may be. The candidate, after having his head solemnly shaved before the assembled chapter, receives the Three Refuges: " I take refuge in Buddha; I take refuge in the Law; I take refuge in the Community! " Then he engages to practise the Ten Prohibitions: not to kill living beings, not to steal, not to commit acts of immodesty, not to lie, not to drink wine, not to perfume himself, not to sing or dance, not to sit on a high seat, not to eat after midday, not to touch gold or silver. He thus becomes *sha-mi* (*śrāmaṇera*). The final ceremony of entering the order takes place some years later. The characteristic part of this in almost all the sects is the burnings the novices inflict upon themselves: each one kneels before the abbot; upon his shaven head there are stuck, with fruit paste, a varying number of little disks of incense, which are lighted and allowed to burn while he recites prayers. The hair never grows upon the scars, which remain very apparent always.[1] The monks have many regular ceremonies: in the first place, the meeting of the *uposatha*, on the fifteenth and the last day of every month, with recitation of the rule and public confession, then others at various times of the year—that of the *avalambana*, *yü-lan-p'ên*, to feed the hungry demons, on the fifteenth day of the seventh month, the moment of the separation of the monks after the ninety days of summer communal life, etc.

From these points of view they differ hardly at all from the Buddhist monks of other countries than China. But the rule is far from being strictly followed. The prohibition against eating anything after midday is hardly ever observed, even on the *uposatha* days, except here and there from individual devoutness: the Chinese bonzes have an evening meal like the laity. On the other hand, mendicancy, which is one of the twelve rules for the monks, is as much reduced as possible, and in general they live on the income of the temple lands; as these lands have been given and not bought, they consider that they are living on alms and conforming to the rule. A few only, out of personal piety, or sometimes in order to obtain the wherewithal for small repairs to their temple (for important repairs subscription-lists are sent round), go along the highways begging, taking with them a small

[1] They are clearly to be seen in Fig. 2, on the skulls of the four bonzes in the front rank, to the left, especially the third one, who is short and badly shaved. This photograph, with a great number of those illustrating this article, was communicated to me by M. R. des Rotours, whom I must thank for most obligingly placing at my disposal his fine collection of negatives of the temples of Pekin and its surrounding country.

portable shrine or simply a statuette. We know that the Buddha forbade his monks to call or to knock at house-doors, and that he ordered them to announce their presence by shaking a staff loaded with rings on the upper part, the *khakkara*, or, as the Chinese call it, the sounding rod, *shêng-chang*, or the tin rod, *si-chang*; but to-day this instrument is no longer employed save in certain religious ceremonies, and the mendicant monks announce themselves by prayers recited in loud tones, or by a bell, which they shake as they walk.

The Taoist clergy is made up not only of monks, *tao-shï*, and even of nuns, *tao-ku*, but of lay masters, *shï-kung*, as well; the first, however, are far from having the importance

Fig. 3. Lao-tsï setting out for the West
Musée Guimet.

they have in Buddhism. Entry into the religious life is not one of the conditions of salvation, it is merely a convenient way of putting into practice the minutely elaborate rules of the Taoist life. The monks usually live in temples or communities like those of the Buddhist monks. Their temples are called by a special name, *kuan*, a word which properly means 'to look.' The origin of this term is said to go back to antiquity. Several centuries before our era (the Taoists do not fix the time precisely), in the time when the Primordial Heaven-honoured One, one of the members of the Taoist supreme Triad, came down into this world to teach men the Way, and lived at the royal court in the form of the great master Lao-tsï; there was in the West a fervent adept, the Warden of the Pass, Yin Hi, who built himself a grass hut to 'look.' Authorities are not agreed as to what he 'looked' at. According to some, warned of the coming of a saint by a supernatural light in the East, he had built this hut on the wayside to 'look' at all who passed by, and in this way he recognized Lao-tsï; according to others, he occupied himself with astrology, and it was while 'looking' at the stars in the sky that he saw the supernatural light announcing the coming of the saint, and could thus go to meet him. It is known that Lao-tsï had at that time determined to leave the world, and was departing to the West, riding upon a green ox (Fig. 3); Yin Hi became his disciple, and before his final departure the master entrusted to him the *Book of the First Principle and its Virtue*, the *Tao tê king*, in which he had put together some aphorisms on the True Doctrine. It was seemingly from this hut meant to 'look' from that the Taoist temples derived their name.

In their temples the *tao-shï* are subjected to rules that are very similar to those of the bonzes. There are five fundamental prohibitions, the Five Prohibitions of the Very High Lord Lao, which are almost the same as those imposed by the Buddhists on the lay faithful—to kill no living creature, not to eat meat, not to drink wine, not to lie, not to steal, to commit no act of immodesty, not to marry—and from these come a very great number of less important rules. Ordination demands the presence of a certain number of fully ordained monks, and therefore can only be performed in a few great temples: for the whole of Chihli and Shantung the temple of the White Cloud, Po-yün-kuan, near Pekin, is where the ceremony takes place. The rites are not well known. The newly made brother receives the Three Refuges, which are the Principle, *Tao*, the Holy Books, *King*, and the Masters, *Shï*, and the abbot pulls him by the arm to symbolize by a gesture his entry into religion. There are three degrees: that of Master of Marvellous Behaviour, that of Master of Marvellous Virtue, and, lastly, that of Master of the Marvellous Principle, the highest of all; the disciples ought to pass them in succession, but it seems that to-day they are all three passed successively on the same day, the day of ordination. The ordinary costume is a long grey robe with wide sleeves (these are sometimes white), and they let their hair grow and knot it on top of the head, instead of shaving it off like the bonzes. As for the ritual costume, it consists of a robe made out of two hundred and forty pieces sewn together, divided by ten ribbons, symbolizing the three San-t'ai stars of the Great Bear, with a girdle made of two bands decorated with clouds; upon their heads they place the "crown of the Five Sacred Peaks," and on their feet sandals of straw.

They have numerous fast days throughout the year: the three days called *hui-jï*, when the Three Agents (Sky, Earth, Water), *San kuan*, examine the merits and demerits of men—the seventh day of the first month, the seventh of the seventh month, and the fifth of the tenth month—and the eight dates of the solstices, the equinoxes, and the beginning of each of the four seasons, which are the days on which the eight gods record good and bad actions. For one of these eight occasions they must make an unbroken retreat of a hundred days, without budging even for religious ceremonies, with meditation and recitations of the Holy Books. They have besides ten fast days every month: the 1st and the 8th, in honour of the Great Bear; the 14th, in honour of the Envoy of the Great One and the Three Agents; the 23rd, in honour of the eight gods, etc.; lastly the last three days of the month, in honour of the Great One. On these days they must abstain from wine, from the "five sharpnesses"—leek, garlic, onion, mustard, shallot—as well as from milk, fermented milk, and cheese; they must wash with infusions of peach-tree and bamboo; the night before, at the fifth watch, just before sunrise, they purify their garments by a fumigation.

The majority of the members of the Taoist clergy is made up of the lay masters who live in the world and are married. These are veritable sorcerers, who from father to son have knowledge of certain formulas and practise certain rites. Each one has his specialty: there are mediums, exorcists, healers, etc. The neophyte enters the community by an initiation the ritual of which changes with the locality: at Fukien, where de Groot saw and described the ceremony, the most essential part consists of ascending and descending several times a ladder the rungs of which are replaced by twelve sabres. The most celebrated of these lay masters is the head of a certain Chang family, who bears the official title of Celestial Master, T'ien-shï. He claims descent from Chang Tao-ling, a person supposed to have lived in the second century of our era, and after receiving a revelation of books and formulas upon Mount Ho-ming, in Szechwan, to have succeeded in making the elixir of immortality; then, having spent a few years longer upon earth to protect mankind, delivering the country of Shu (Szechwan) from the demons that infested it, going to the summit of Mount K'un-lun to seek for two swords that drive away evil spirits, etc., he at last drank the elixir of immortality and ascended into heaven in broad daylight, upon a five-hued dragon, taking with him his wife and two of his disciples.

Chang Tao-ling had, we are told, a great number of disciples, from whom he exacted as fees five bushels of rice. His grandson Chang Lu, who succeeded about A.D. 190 in organizing a little independent principality around Han-chung (Shensi), set up there a veritable Church with a hierarchy possessing both spiritual and temporal powers: the faithful called themselves demon-soldiers; instructors called libationers, *tsi-tsiu*, explained the holy books and administered a department; above them there were great libationers; lastly Chang Lu himself had assumed the title of Prince Celestial Master. All these persons were equipped with charms and talismans of every kind. To heal the sick they made them confess their sins, which were written upon three leaves of paper, burned, buried, and thrown into water, in honour of Sky, Earth, and Water; those who were not cured were looked upon as unbelievers. On the other hand, there was demoniac possession to punish certain crimes. The conquest of the country by General Ts'ao Ts'ao, in 215, ruined the administrative side of the work, but Chang Lu was carried off to the capital, where he received titles and lived for several years longer (at least until A.D. 220), continuing to devote himself to alchemical studies. These are the persons to whom, in spite of a good many gaps in the genealogical tree, the Chang family of Celestial Masters to-day claims to be akin, and it is in memory of his ancestor that its head has his residence in T'ien-mu shan (Chekiang), the native country of Chang Tao-ling. It was only in 748 that his official title of Celestial Master was definitely recognized. He is said to have great authority over gods and demons; according to some he presides over the advancement or abasement of the local gods. His charms and amulets are peculiarly powerful; his seal is printed on children's garments or on paper hung round their neck; in certain regions it is believed that only he or talismans specially made by him are able to deliver from the haunting of foxes.

BONZE AND DRAGON
(Musée Guimet.)

The mandarins of old days in their function as priests of the official religion, the Buddhist monks, the Taoist monks and lay masters, each in the ceremonies he conducts, address themselves not only to different persons, but also to categories of beings which, if we hold strictly to the doctrine of each religion, are in reality of completely different nature. The sections devoted to Buddhist mythology clearly show what is meant in that religion by a Buddha, a Bodhisattva, or an Arhat, so that I need not deal with it here. The Heaven-honoured Ones of Taoism were modelled on the Buddhas, and these Immortals (although they were known long before the introduction of Buddhism) on the Arhats, and there are only shades of difference between them. Between these personages and the divinities of the official religion in pure doctrine there is no single point in common, and even between the nature of the latter and the secondary gods of Taoism there is an almost insurmountable difference.

But these diverse notions, in mingling to make the popular mythology, became simplified and in some fashion standardized: what was most subtle in them disappeared, and there survived only what was understood or seemed to be understood at first glance, which will tell how many of them lost their individual shape. All the supernatural beings, whether they have the titles of Fo (Buddha), P'u-sa (Bodhisattva), Lo-han (Arhat), T'ien-tsun (Heaven-honoured Ones), Sien (Immortal), Ti (Emperor), Hou (Empress), Wang (King), etc., or even the least exalted of all, Shên (god, or goddess), are of the same nature and are hardly distinguished from one another, except by the more or less extensive power they enjoy. There is not, it is true, any term in the language to denote them collectively, but that is almost the only thing that remains of their original diversity of nature and origin. On the other hand, there is a word to denote their supernatural power; this is currently known as *ling-yen*, in statelier language *ling*, and this word is uniformly used for all of them, from the great Bodhisattvas down to the simplest little gods; but naturally only the greatest Buddhas, Bodhisattvas, Heaven-honoured Ones, Emperors, Immortals, etc., have it complete with all powers (the Buddhist system reckons exactly ten): eye and ear that see and hear all things, knowledge of the past and the future as of the present, the faculty of taking every shape, the power to be in any place instantaneously, etc. It is by virtue of their degree of supernatural power that they are differentiated from one another, but they all rank in one and the same class. The different titles they are given simply mark the degrees of a hierarchy, a little nebulous indeed, and when one of them goes up in favour he goes up in status to some extent, and from a simple spirit, *shên*, he is raised to the rank of Bodhisattva, P'u-sa. The Emperor Kuan, one of the most popular gods of the official religion, is often commonly called the P'u-sa Kuan, though he has no right to the title; all that Buddhism was able to do for him was to give him a position as God of the Place, K'ie-lan-shên (*saṅghārāma-deva*), protector of the temple and the monks; the little Hearth-god is often known as the P'u-sa of the Hearth; the Sun and the Moon receive the title of Buddha in the prayers of their fervent devotees. But that does not mean that they are made true Buddhas or Bodhisattvas; there is no attempt at assimilating certain native gods to different forms of the great Bodhisattvas; this syncretism, which existed in former times (certain persons tried to make Confucius himself a transformation body of one of the Buddha's disciples), had disappeared by the eighth century of our era. There is merely the use of these titles themselves as simple indices of supernatural power, discarding every other inherent idea, and hence we find them attributed to the most unexpected personages. Besides, titles of Buddhist and Taoist origin, equivalent in degree, are constantly interchanged, and it is not uncommon, in current talk, to hear the Buddhas and Bodhisattvas of a Buddhist temple spoken of as Immortals (the Taoist term), and to hear, for example, by way of explaining the popularity of pilgrimages to a particular one among them, that "the Immortals of this pagoda are endowed with considerable supernatural power." Perhaps to avoid confusion they ought to be given as a collective name an expression like "the Beings endowed with supernatural power": it is simpler to call them gods. Yet this idea of a god is very different from that to which ancient mythologies have accustomed us.

Fig. 4. A Soul examined by the God of Walls and Moats before Kuan-ti

Every god, great or small, is a man who after his death was promoted, for various reasons, to the dignity of godhead (Fig. 4). The Buddhist legends gave successive biographies through countless ages of the Buddhas and the great Bodhisattvas; similar Taoist collections contained the lives of the Heaven-honoured Ones; modelled on these there were collections for the various gods. The important gods had spent several existences in acquiring the merits that had procured their promotion; for the secondary gods one single life was enough. The patron gods of towns have their human biographies: their names are known, their birthplaces, and the reasons for their promotion. The god of the Yellow River is a man who, about the third or fourth century of our era, was drowned crossing it. The god of the bar of the Chekiang is Wu Tsï-sü, an ancient Minister of a local prince, who, being put to death unjustly, revenged himself by trying every year to destroy the country, and especially its capital Hangchow, by hurling the waves against it. The judges of the underworld are ancient officials of integrity whose names are given and the exact date of whose death is known. In the house the privies have for divinity a young woman who was assassinated there among familiar objects; the Goddess of the Carrying Chair is a girl who died in her chair during the wedding ceremony

Fig. 5. The Jade Emperor (Yü-Huang)

while she was being solemnly carried from the home of her parents to that of her husband. One of the greatest gods, the Emperor Kuan, is a general who died at the beginning of the third century of our era.

And these are not just legends, made up once for all and transmitted with casual belief in them. People become gods every day in China. In 1915, in a village near Ju-nan (Honan), a young man of a family called Wang, renowned for his filial piety and his good behaviour, declared one day to his brother: "Last night I saw a God of Walls and Moats; he told me he was recalled to the Jade Emperor and that I was appointed to take his place. I shall die in ten days." His family made fun of him, but on the morning of the tenth day he took a bath, summoned his whole family, gave good counsel to each one, dictated his last wishes, forbade them to mourn him with funeral ceremonies after his death, and at noon precisely stretched himself at full length, heaved a sigh, and died. The relatives, according to his instructions, did not wear mourning, the neighbours were astonished, and the rumour came to the ears of the sub-prefect, who held an inquiry and sent a report to the President of the Republic. Yüan Shï-k'ai interested himself in the matter, and ordered the prefect to conduct a fresh inquiry, and, upon receiving a favourable report, decreed a posthumous title to the deceased. The dead man appeared to various persons in dream, and thus it was known that he had in reality become God of Walls and Moats. This story was told me in 1919, by the nephew of the deified himself, who had been present at his uncle's death.

Divinity is a charge just like public office: the title endures, but the holders vary and succeed one another. When the God of Thunder, or the god of a city, is spoken of it is a title that is uttered; the holder of that title has changed frequently in the course of the ages. They are official gods, who receive an office, lose it, receive promotion, are degraded, and finally die to be born again as men on earth; only the highest in rank, like the Heaven-honoured Ones or the Bodhisattvas, have ceased to be subjected to birth and death, so that they hold their offices in perpetuity. For thanks to their merits they have been rewarded by the gift of the Elixir of Immortality; or else one of the Peaches of Immortality of the Lady queen of the West, Si-wang-mu. The Taoist ideas have filled the popular mind on this point, and the legend of Kuan-yin shows that even a Bodhisattva does not owe his beneficent everlastingness to his merits alone, but that his body, after apparent death, must also be immortalized by ingesting the Peaches of Immortality.

To such an extent is divinity an office that certain individuals delegate it. The great gods, who have many temples and statues, cannot dwell in all their images at once. The power to be in several places at the same time is so unintelligible that, while it is granted traditionally to the Bodhisattvas, they are only shown as using it accidentally, to come to the succour of living beings. To animate each of their statues and portraits they select souls of just persons: these are charged to represent them, have the right to take the whole or part of the offerings, and must make a report of everything that takes place in their temple. Sometimes when a temple is abandoned an evil spirit takes possession of a statue left derelict, and if he succeeds in bringing worshippers back he seizes on the offerings until the god whose place he has usurped punishes him.

The popular religion is far from being one and the same; if certain fundamental ideas are found from one end of China to the other, the details vary infinitely from one place to another. The mixture of the three systems is not everywhere composed in the same fashion, and according to the region one or other takes the predominant part: the great Buddhist temples of Chekiang preserve a centre of Buddhist influence in this district; the presence of the great official ceremonies of the capital on the one hand and the tomb of Confucius on the other has given a preponderant influence to the ideas of the literati in the North; Szechwan, in the West, and Fukien, in the East, are especially Taoist, and so on. These divergencies are most of all perceptible in what concerns beliefs and the externals of feasts; less so in mythology, and although the relative importance of each of the gods is not always the same in different provinces, the pantheon is very nearly the same, at least in its main lines, throughout the whole empire. It is an unheard-of swarm of gods and spirits of every kind, an innumerable rabble. Naturally it would be impossible to describe them all; the space at my disposal would barely suffice to give a list of them, as will be seen if the reader merely glances at the fourteen volumes of Père Doré's *Recherches sur les superstitions en Chine*. I have selected those, both great and small, which seemed to me most alive in the religious feeling and in the worship of the people of to-day, and I have tried to describe them as the mass of people most commonly represents them to itself. It must be remembered also that we are here dealing only with mythology, but that if we wished to make a picture of popular religion in its entirety we should still have to make a place for those obscure powers, vaguely characterized, and generally impersonal, which frequently, more than the more representative personages of the visible pantheon, have played the principal part in the religious life of the Chinese of all times.

THE SUPREME GODS

Yü-Huang, the Jade Emperor. The world is governed by a supreme deity, the sovereign master of all the others, the Jade Emperor, Yü-Huang, or the Supreme August Jade Emperor, Yü-Huang Shang-ti, or, as he is popularly called, Mr Heaven, Lao-t'ien ye; and these two names clearly show the hybrid character of the popular religion, for the first is borrowed from Taoism and the second from the official religion. The title Jade Emperor is, in fact, that of the second of the Three Pure Ones, the supreme triad of Taoism that dwells in the highest of the thirty-six heavens, Ta-lo. The three persons of this triad (in which a trace of some remote influence of the Christian ideas on the Trinity has been erroneously suggested) are not three sovereigns ruling together. The first, the Primordial Heaven-honoured One, Yüan-shï T'ien-tsun, governed in the beginning, but long since resigned his charge to his disciple, the Heaven-honoured Jade Emperor, who is thus the supreme deity of the present time, and who in due course will hand over to the Heaven-honoured One of the Dawn of Jade of the Golden Gate, Kin-k'üe Yü-chên T'ien-tsun, the third person of the triad. But the god of the popular religion is not the Taoist deity, the teacher rather than the sovereign of the world: his two acolytes are forgotten, and he himself, the inheritor of the old Emperor on High of the antique mythology, who gave kings their investiture, is very far from practising the Taoist Inaction, and on the contrary guides directly and in person the affairs of heaven and earth. To know how this divine figure was given shape, why the ancient Lord on High survived (in a changed form) the disappearance of almost all the religion and mythology of antiquity, we should have to know much more of the history of the popular religion during the first ten centuries of our era. In the tenth century the modern figure was completely established.

It is in this guise of supreme deity ruling the universe, as the emperor rules China, sovereign of both gods and men, that the curious visions of two emperors of the eleventh and twelfth centuries present him. The Emperor Shên-tsung, of the Sung dynasty, himself narrated his. On the first occasion, "on the twenty-seventh day of the eleventh month of last year [December 11, 1007], as it was near midnight and I was about to go to my bed, suddenly the room was lit up and I beheld gods with starry bonnets and silken robes, who said to me: 'On the third day of next month you must set up for the space of a month in the audience-chamber of the palace a Taoist shrine, awaiting the descent of a celestial writing, the noble charm of great success, in three paragraphs.' I arose, but they disappeared immediately." He had a whole series of other visions in the following years, and his ministers took care that they should be materialized immediately. In 1012 the gods brought him a letter from heaven. "In the tenth month I saw in a dream a god who brought to me a letter from the Jade Emperor, which said: 'Before this I had ordered your ancestor Chao to transmit to you a celestial letter, now I have just ordered him to visit you again.' Next day I dreamed anew that the following words of the Heaven-honoured One were communicated to me: 'Let my throne be to the West, and let six thrones be prepared for my suite!' On that same day in the hall of the Extending of Grace there was established a Taoist shrine. In the first quarter of the fifth watch I felt in the first place a strange perfume, after a moment a light filled the hall, paling the lamps and torches, and I saw that the Transcendent Immortal Heaven-honoured One had arrived. I bowed before him; suddenly a yellow mist rose up; in a moment the mist dispersing ascended the steps of the West, and I saw his train on the steps of the East. The Heaven-honoured One sat down; there were six persons who accompanied him and sat down after him. I would have saluted the six persons; the Heaven-honoured One stayed me and, giving me the order [of the Jade Emperor], said in the first place: 'I am the Human August One, Jên-Huang, one of the Nine August Ones [who in Taoist mythical history were the first sovereigns of the world at its origin]. I am the first Ancestor of the Chao family [to which the emperors of the Sung dynasty belonged]. I came down into this world again to be the Yellow Emperor Huang-ti. All men declare him the son of Shao-tien. This is false: his mother, startled by the thunder, dreamed of a celestial man and bore him. In the time of the Later T'angs [923–935], having received the command of the Jade Emperor, I descended once more on the first day of the seventh month [August 1, 927] to govern this lower world entire, and to be the head of the Chao family [*i.e.*, the founder of the Sung dynasty, 960–976]; from that time it is now a hundred years.' With these words, leaving his throne, he mounted upon a cloud and departed."

After these singular favours accorded him by the Jade Emperor, the Emperor Shên-tsung erected a statue to him in one of the palace buildings (1014), and decreed him the title of Most High, Creator of the Heavens, Bearer of the Sceptre, Regulator of the

Calendar, Incarnation of the Tao, Jade Emperor, Great Emperor of Heaven. A century later, in 1115, one of his successors, the Emperor Hui-tsung, changed the last two titles to that of Supreme Emperor, Jade Emperor of the Exalted Heaven, thus confounding him with the Supreme Emperor of the official religion; but this innovation was not retained. Chinese literati generally attribute the 'invention' of the Jade Emperor to Shên-tsung; but it is evident that, for the Emperor to have so definite a vision of his ancestor bringing him the order from the god, that god must already have ranked as supreme god in popular belief. And this is still more necessarily the case if, as they believe (though for no conclusive reason), the emperor was in reality a deceiver and had purely and simply invented his visions in order to hoodwink the people, for with false visions even more than genuine ones it is essential to base them upon a well-established belief; the revelations would have had no interest whatever if they had emanated from an unknown god.

Fig. 6. The Jade Emperor and his Court
Popular print.

The Jade Emperor is represented seated on a throne, in full ceremonial imperial costume; he is clad in the long dragon-embroidered robe; on his head he wears the *mien*, the imperial bonnet, formed of a flat shape from which hang before and behind thirteen tassels of coloured pearls strung on red cords, and in his two folded hands he holds the imperial ceremonial tablet (*kuei*). He is given the expressionless face by which the Taoists endeavour to express calm and majesty; long whiskers and drooping moustaches, with a chin-tuft, enframe his visage.

The Family and the Court of the Jade Emperor. The Jade Emperor has a whole family. One of his younger sisters is the mother of Yang Tsien, a god highly popular under the title of Second Lord of Quality, Êr-lang, who drives away evil spirits by setting the Celestial Dog, T'ien K'ou, to chase them. The goddess Horse's Head, who takes care of the silkworms, is one of his second-rank wives. One of his daughters, Miss Seventh, Ts'i-ku-niang, is invoked by girls who desire to know their future husbands. After prostrating herself and burning incense the inquirer sits down with her head enveloped in a veil, while her companions continue to burn incense and pray, and either her husband's face, or scenes from his life, as the case may be, pass swiftly before her eyes.

The Jade Emperor's palace is in heaven (Fig. 6). Popular imagination has not endeavoured to locate it more precisely; those who desire to be more exact in these matters admit with the Taoists that he dwells in the highest of all the heavens, Ta-lo, whence he dominates the entire universe, the lower heavens, the earth, and the stages of the infernal regions. There is his palace. And this palace has a porter, Wang the Transcendent Official, Ling-Kuan, who, long lost among the crowd of the innumerable undistinguished Taoist deities (he was merely one of the twenty-six generals of the Celestial Court), suddenly became very popular at the close of the fifteenth century (Fig. 7). The *tao-shï*, Chou Sï-tê, who claimed to derive all his magic powers from Wang and his revelations, had taken advantage of his prestige with the Emperor Yung-lo (1403–25) to have an official temple erected to him west of Pekin, the Temple of the Celestial General, where sacrifices were to be offered on the day of the winter solstice. In the middle of the temple had been set up a statue of the god, which had been miraculously discovered on the sea-shore; every three months his embroidered silk garments were changed, and every ten years his whole wardrobe was burned and renewed. It is told how when he was alive Wang, a man of prodigious strength, applied himself to protecting the people from the exactions of the mandarins and from evil spirits: as a recompense he received a seal from the Jade Emperor. He stands at the door of the celestial palace, his knotty staff in his hand; he thrusts away the unwelcome, and at the same time is always ready to go and fulfil the errands on which the Jade Emperor sends him forth to right wrongs by slaying the guilty persons indicated by the latter. This is why his statue is placed at the entrance of the temples of Yü-Huang and of many Taoist temples in general; he is represented standing, covered with his armour and staff in hand.

Fig. 7. The Transcendent Official pursuing a Fox-demon

Celestial Administration and Ministries. And above all there is a whole court, ministers, generals, guards, an army of officials and functionaries; just as upon earth the Emperor conferred duties upon terrestrial mandarins, in the same way he assigns duties to the gods, who are mandarins entrusted by him with definite functions. And they must come and render account of their stewardship every year on a fixed date, generally New Year's Day.

They ascend to his Court to pay him homage, and present their reports on their administration, and he gives them preferment or punishes them, according to their deserts. It is a complete celestial administration.

The Taoists have drawn up a whole system for this on the pattern of that of the empire, and have invented the series of celestial ministries. There is a whole long roll of them: the Ministry of Thunder and Wind, the Ministry of the Waters, of Fire, of Time, of the Five Peaks, of Literature, of War, of Riches, of Works, of Epidemics, of Smallpox, of Exorcism, of Medicine, and so on. Each one has its president, like the earth ministries in the days of the Empire, with his assistants and his army of subordinate officials.

But this organization is far from having been accepted in all its details by popular religious feeling. If certain of these ministries, that of Thunder, for example, or that of Riches, seem to be accepted, at any rate in certain regions, for the most part certain gods alone were admitted, to the exclusion of others. We have too little knowledge of the relations of popular religion with Taoism throughout the centuries to see clearly in what cases the *tao-shï* created around the popular gods new divinities that failed to win favour, or in what cases, on the contrary, popular religion arbitrarily chose or rejected among the *tao-shï* creations. But whatever the circumstances governing each individual case, the result is that the Taoist catalogue of deities hardly at all represents the living religion of to-day, which is less regular, but also less heavy in organization; it too is, however, highly disciplined, and the gods have their places in it like men in the human social order.

All the gods have one object, and only one, man and his material and moral welfare, which is one of the conditions necessary for the proper working of the world. But their functions bring them more or less directly in touch with human society; and thus without much trouble we can divide them into three classes: nature gods (rain, wind, thunder, mountains, waters, etc.), gods in charge of living beings, either social groupings or individuals, and lastly, gods in charge of the dead.

The Heaven and the Supreme Emperor in the Imperial Religion. When the common people speak of Mr Heaven it is always under the shape of Yü-Huang that they figure him, as a personal divinity, a most powerful celestial emperor who governs the world as the terrestrial emperor until lately governed the Empire, and whose officials are the gods. But in certain lettered circles, under the influence of the philosophy of the great Confucian masters of the Sung period, the 'Five Masters,' in whose theories every generation of literates has been brought up for the last seven centuries, first place is given to an impersonal power called simply Heaven, T'ien, in which is absorbed the Supreme Emperor of Antiquity, a personal celestial sovereign, and prototype of the Jade Emperor.

This Heaven is not the material and visible sky, but its essence. It is a concrete expression for the Active Principle, Li, who moves all things. Thus he produces all. "There are persons who ask with hesitation: 'What does Heaven signify?' The four seasons succeed one another, and all things are produced. That is clear and evident!" We must not conclude from this that he is a creator. There are two principles—the Active Principle, Li, the first mover, and the Passive Principle, K'i, subtle and tenuous matter—which have existed from all time; their union constitutes what is called the Great Unity, T'ai-yi, or the Great Summit, T'ai-ki; it is by virtue of this union that subtle matter, K'i, transformed according to two modes, the mode of rest, *yin*, and the mode of movement, *yang*, which alternate *ad infinitum*, produced the Five Elements—Metal, Wood, Water, Fire, Earth—and all things in general.

It is clear that in this system there is no need for any personal deity. And, in fact, the latest of the Five Masters, the man who had the most considerable influence on the formation of the modern Chinese spirit, Chu Hi, formally declares that there is none. "Certain persons ask for an exposition of the phrase of the Shï king, 'The Supreme Emperor causes intelligence to descend to the people.' The Heaven gives birth to beings and they develop according to their nature (thus given by it); upon those who are well made descend the hundred felicities, upon those who are ill made descend the hundred calamities; in these

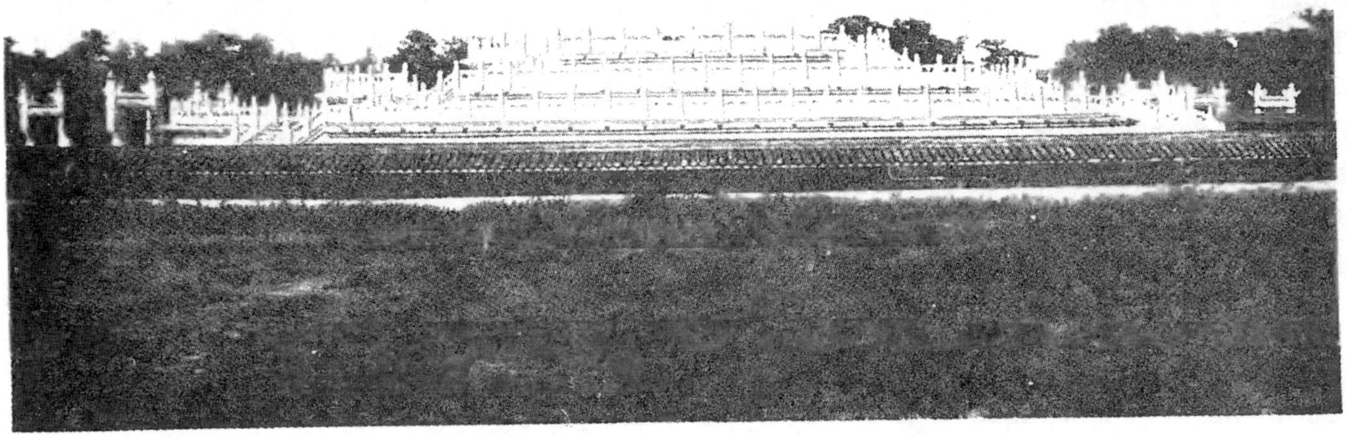

Fig. 8. THE ALTAR OF HEAVEN, AT PEKIN

conditions how could there in deed and in truth be a lord and master in the azure above?" Nevertheless the Heaven still retained, if not something anthropomorphic, at least a certain consciousness in virtue of which it rules not only the physical but also the moral world; certain terms of the Classic Books, which cannot be refuted since they are the work of the saints of antiquity, oblige us to admit that it knows all things. But in a fashion peculiar to itself. "Heaven knows things without ears, without eyes, without heart, without reflection. . . . It sees and hears through the people; it manifests its majesty through the people."

It is this knowledge that, in spite of its quite special character, justifies the sacrifices the emperor had to make every year before the Temple of Heaven, a great enclosure planted with trees, situated in the southern suburbs of the capital, *nan-kiao*. In the midst of this enclosure there stood on the one side the Altar of Heaven (Fig. 8), a circular mound in three terraces, adorned with marble balustrades, and, on the other side, the temple in which prayers were made for the harvest, *K'i-nien miao*, situated a little to the north of the Altar of Heaven and joined to it by a paved causeway (Figs. 9 and 10). The winter solstice sacrifice on the Altar of Heaven, called simply the sacrifice of the suburb, *Kiao*, was one of the most important ceremonies of the official religion. All who took part in it, the emperor included, were obliged to prepare beforehand by fasting, which meant that for three days (in ancient times the fast lasted ten days) they withdrew into the Palace of

Fig. 9. The Temple where Prayers are made for the Harvest

Fig. 10. Interior of the Temple where Prayers are made for the Harvest

Fasting (Fig. 11) away from the women, and abstained from certain dishes, from music, etc. When the day arrived a magnificent procession went to fetch the emperor two hours before sunrise, and brought him to the Temple of Heaven: at its head the elephants, next the troop of musicians, singers, and players of instruments, then the flag-bearers, banners of the twenty-eight Zodiacal constellations and the Five Planets, the Five Peaks, and the Four Rivers, etc.; behind these the teams of dancers with peacock feathers, dancers armed, dancers with fans and parasols; and behind these the princes and the high officials, each group being separated from the one in front by a company of soldiers. The emperor, clad

Fig. 11. The Pavilion of Fasting in the Temple of Heaven

in his dragon-embroidered robes and wearing his bonnet with pearl tassels, then mounted a monumental chair carried by thirty-six bearers, and, preceded by exorcists, went from the palace to the Temple. The victims had been slaughtered and cooked whole in huge cauldrons the night before, and all had been made ready: the throne of the Supreme Lord of the August Heaven, Huang-t'ien Shang-ti, upon the highest terrace of the mound, with those of the Imperial Ancestors to right and left, also the tablets of the Sun, the Moon, the Wind, the Rain, the Peaks, the Rivers, etc. On arriving the emperor ascended the mound, and lighted a pyre in front of the Supreme Emperor, the smoke of which invited him to descend and be present at the ceremony. Then the emperor, prostrating himself, presented the incense, the rolls of silk, the disks of blue jade; after which, prostrating himself three times, he made a libation kneeling to the Supreme Emperor, then to each of his Ancestors; lastly he was given a piece of roasted flesh, which he offered in like manner. During this time at the foot of the mound the singers sang to the accompaniment of the flutes the official hymns composed by the Office of Music, and the dancers wove their evolutions to the sound of the gongs and musical stones, first the armed soldier dancers and last the civilian dancers wearing peacocks' feathers. The ceremony completed, the emperor prostrated himself nine times in farewell, and came down from the altar; under his eyes were burned, on a pyre placed in a corner of the enclosure, one of the victims with the rolls of silk and the jade disks; then the procession formed up again to escort him back to the palace. After the Revolution the sacrifice was for some time performed by a deputy of the President of the Republic; but Yüan Shï-k'ai, who was, perhaps, influenced by his secret thoughts of a restoration of monarchy in his favour, was the last head of the State to celebrate it; since his death in 1916 it has been in abeyance, perhaps for the first time since the origin of Chinese civilization.

The spring sacrifice, which was held in the temple where prayer is made for the harvest, was less solemn, but the offerings, practically identical, were similarly accompanied with music and songs, as well as military and civilian dances; the throne of the Supreme Emperor was placed in the midst of the temple, with the same tablets to right and left as for the *kiao* sacrifice; in the prayer, which was burned, the emperor proclaimed the approaching beginning of the work of the fields, and asked that rain and sunshine should come in their season in such wise that the harvest might be good. Like everything else relating to the cult of Heaven, this ceremony has not taken place for some years.

The official religion, always inclined to symmetry, also had sacrifices to the Earth, *ti*, as representing the *yin* principle in opposition to the Heaven, representing the *yang* principle, and distinct from the God of the Soil, *shê*, who was a territorial deity inferior to this supreme pair. Earth had a square altar, in two stages, in the northern suburb of the capital (even numbers and the North are *yin*), and her great festival was at the summer solstice, with ceremonies similar to those of the winter solstice sacrifice to Heaven, except that the victims were buried instead of burned. The dates chosen had themselves a symbolic meaning: the summer solstice is the time when the *yang* principle attains its apogee, and similarly with the winter solstice for the *yin* principle; but these are also the moments when the contrary principle, annihilated for a moment, is about to begin to increase day by day, to the detriment of the one that is triumphant on this day. The sacrifices were intended to help on this growth, and accordingly to help on that regular alternation of the two principles which is the prime cause of the orderly movement of the universe.

THE GODS OF NATURE

The Sun and the Moon. The nature gods play only a very unimportant part in Chinese religion. It is true that the emperor paid official worship to the Sun and the Moon; each has an open-air altar like that dedicated to Heaven, but of one stage only, in a suburb of the city, the Sun in the east side and the Moon in the west. The sacrifices were held biennially, in the odd years of the sixty-year cycle for the Sun, which is the quintessence of *yang*, the Active Principle, to which the odd numbers belong, and in the even years for the Moon, the quintessence of the Passive Principle, *yin*, to which the even numbers belong. They took place one in the morning at sunrise in mid-spring, the other at sunset in mid-autumn. The offerings consisted of a group of three victims, an ox, a sheep, and a pig, with wine, pieces of silk, and jade, red for the Sun or white for the Moon. Music and military and civilian dances accompanied the ceremonies. But like much belonging to the official religion this was a dead worship that was continued through habit, but to which no importance now attached. On the other hand, the Sun and the Moon have also their Buddhist and Taoist divinities, but these are mere catalogue divinities to whom nobody addresses himself. It is true that we find fairly commonly images or statuettes of the Woman in the Moon, Ch'ang-o or Hêng-o, seated on the three-legged toad, but these are merely *bibelots* or drawings, which are hardly ever regarded as of religious significance to-day (Fig. 12).

Fig. 12. THE GODDESS OF THE MOON
Musée Guimet.

She was the wife of a hero of the mythological times, Yi the Excellent Archer; one of his most celebrated feats was when one day the ten brother Suns, ascending all together into the sky, threatened to set the earth on fire; he shot down nine of them with his arrows. Si-wang-mu, the Queen of the Immortals, had one day given him the drug of immortality; but his wife stole it in his absence and began to drink it. She had not quite finished when he returned; she fled in terror. Thanks to the potion she could soar in the direction of heaven, but as she had not swallowed the whole dose she was forced to stop half-way and remain in the Moon. Yi himself soon after mounted to the abode of the Immortals and became the regent of the Sun.

The worship of the Sun and the Moon nevertheless exists, though somewhat rare, as a personal cult. Their devotees put up a red lacquer tablet to them, or simply paste against a wall a strip of red paper with their names side by side. They prostrate themselves before this tablet and burn incense on the three feast-days of the Sun, which are the 1st of the second month, the 19th of the third month (his birthday), and the 19th of the eleventh, according to the *Book of the Holy Prince Sun*. For the rest of the year they content themselves with reciting a prayer in verse.

The Lady who Sweeps the Sky Clear. The Lady who Sweeps the Sky Clear, Sao-ts'ing-niang, is, as her name shows, charged with the task of clearing the sky after rain,

Fig. 13. The God of Thunder and the Goddess of Lightning smite a Guilty Person
Popular print.

by driving away the clouds with her broom. She is represented as a woman with sleeves rolled up and a broom in her hand. She is a simple leaf of paper cut out into the silhouette of a sweeper, and is commonly kept in the women's quarters and brought out after rain to be hung up under the roof so that the least breath of wind shaking her makes her actually sweep the air. Her broom not merely sweeps the clouds away, it gathers them as well, at least in certain regions where she is hung up in the same way, when dry weather has lasted too long, to bring the rain.

My Lord the Thunder and the Mother of the Lightnings. The Thunder god, My Lord the Thunder, Lei-kung, is one of the ancient deities retained in the modern religion almost

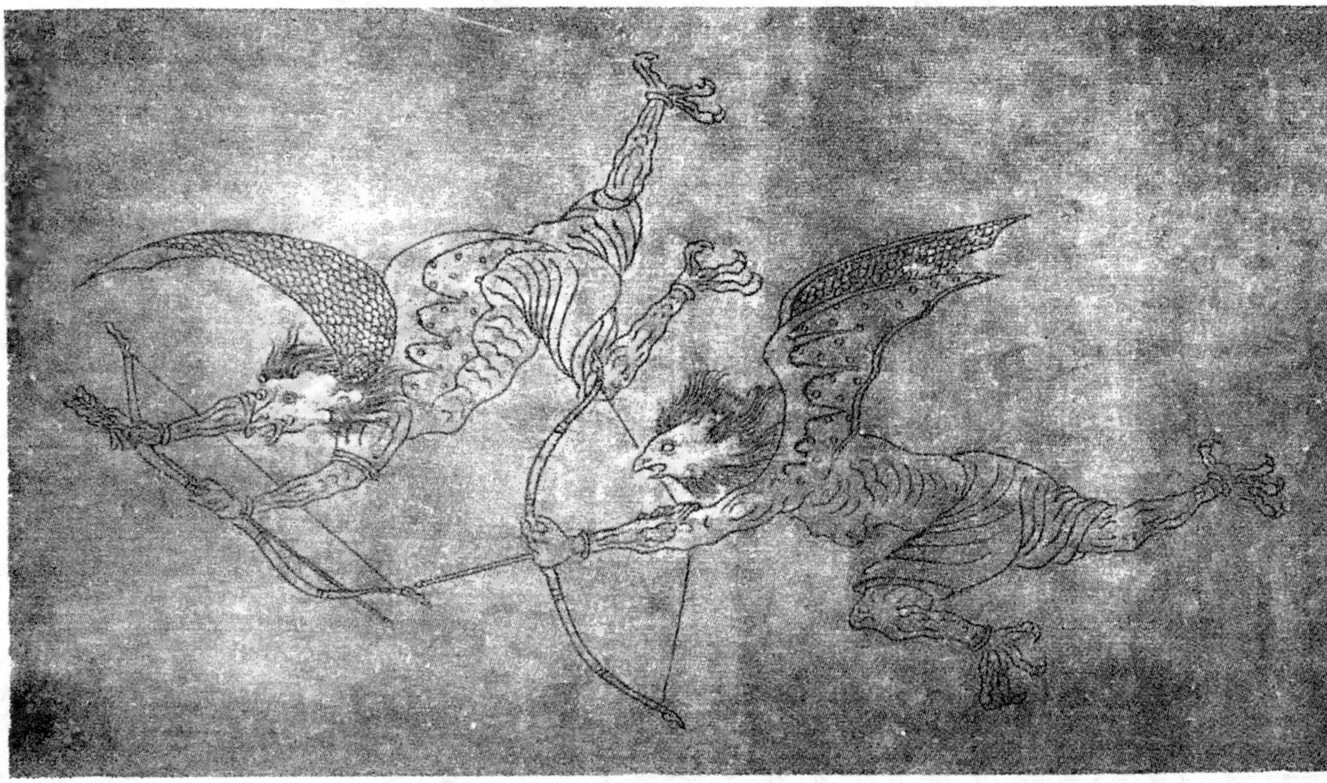

Fig. 14. TWO THUNDERS
After the painter Li Lung-mien. Eleventh century.

without modification. Originally he was, perhaps, an owl; he has retained the beak, the wings, and the talons (Fig. 13), but he has assumed a man's body, blue all over; his hideousness is proverbial. He is clad only in drawers, wears a chaplet of drums, and holds in his right hand a wooden mallet with which he beats them to make the roll of the thunder, and in his left hand the dagger, with which he smites the guilty persons he has been ordered to chastise (Fig. 13, top). The Taoists have split him up into a whole collection of deities that form the department of the Thunder. The president is the Thunder Ancestor, Lei-tsu, who is given the place of honour in the temples and chapels of the Thunder, and in whose name printed pardons are drawn up; my Lord the Thunder is one of his subordinates, with several others. But the popular religion has not ratified this distinction, and to-day, as in ancient times, knows only one God of Thunder, who is called sometimes Thunder Ancestor and sometimes the Bodhisattva My Lord the Thunder. He has a whole family, and there are many tales about the misadventures of the inexperienced little Thunders—the one who was caught in a cloven tree and could not get free by himself, and owed his safety to a passing woodcutter; the one who was still clumsy and could not manage to take flight, and ended by getting beaten to death by a peasant who was sick of the noise of his brattlings while he made his unsuccessful attempts; and so on.

My Lord the Thunder makes the peal, but not the lightnings; these are produced by the Mother of the Lightnings, Tien-mu, by means of two mirrors. It is told how the Lord King of the Orient missed his shot as he played in his palace with a Jade Maiden at a game that consists of throwing wands in such a way that after they touch the ground with one tip they jump back and fall into a great vase with a narrow mouth. The Heaven began to laugh, and from his open mouth came forth the Lightning. The goddess is represented standing upon a cloud, raising her two mirrors above her head (Figs. 13 and 15). At Pekin she is commonly regarded as the wife of the God of Thunder.

Fig. 15. The Goddess of Lightning and the Gods of Rain and Wind
Popular print.

The Rain. The Gods of the Rain and the Wind (Fig. 15) are also made by the *tao-shï* subordinate to the Thunder Ancestor in the departments in which they are ranked. These are divinities of very ancient origin and have retained their old titles of Master of the Rain and Count of the Wind, which were given them in antiquity; they are represented standing on clouds, the first as a warrior covered with yellow armour, carrying a vase filled with water, the second as an old man with a white beard clad in a yellow mantle with a blue and red bonnet, and holding in his hand a waving fan or a bag full of wind. But these spirits, which have their place not only in the Taoist cult, but also in the official religion, have almost disappeared from the popular religion. At Pekin, for instance, the Master of the Rain is still known; popular pictures show him holding in his hand a cup out of which he makes the water spurt with the point of his sabre. But the Count of the Wind is forgotten, and the divinity that produces the wind is an old woman, Madame Wind, Fêng p'o-p'o, who travels over the clouds seated upon a tiger, carrying in her arms the bag containing the winds.

In any case, when the dry weather has gone on too long and rain is needed it is not to these deities that application is made as a rule. The ceremonies to bring rain vary according to the different regions. In many places the statue of the local God of Walls and Moats is brought from his temple and installed full in the sun until the rain falls, which they say is seldom very long; and almost everywhere there is told the story of the prefect or sub-prefect who in a long drought went to the god and said to him, " We are both of us entrusted with the government of this district; let us both expose ourselves to the sun, and let the head of the one responsible for this drought burst open! " Then he had the statue carried out on to the market-place and stood by its side; after a little while the head of the statue split open. Here we have the last trace of a more barbarous rite of antiquity, in which rain-maker witches were made to dance in the sun until either rain came or their death. This custom, which originally was intended to bring down the rain through the witches' own powers, was understood from the first century of our era as a torture applied to the spirit that possessed the witches. With the softening of general customs it was a simple matter to come to torturing the god not by means of an intermediary, but directly in his own statue. In any case this is only one process among a great many. One of the strangest is known as " laughing at a dog"; this is practised in the southern part of Szechwan; for according to a very widely spread proverb when any one laughs at a dog the weather cannot remain fine. A dog is rigged out in a complete bridal dress, is seated in a palanquin decorated with embroideries and flowers, and carried in slow and stately procession through every street in the city, while everybody looks on and laughs at him.

The Dragon Kings, Lung-Wang. But above all throughout China very different beings are invoked to obtain rain—the dragons, monsters with bodies covered with scales, with four feet, which can mount up to the sky and walk over the clouds, and which produce the rain. In the centre and the south a great procession is generally made. A dragon, constructed of a wooden framework covered with paper or cloth, is carried by men or young people, who go along dancing behind a child dancing backwards and carrying the dragon's pearl; or an earthenware dragon is carried on a litter around which young people dance; sometimes it is only a banner with a dragon on it borne behind banners of every kind with inscriptions asking for rain, and a water-carrier follows and dips a willow-branch from time to time in one of his buckets and sprinkles the street and the passers-by, crying, " Here comes the rain!" In Szechwan there is a similar procession, but it is the dragon that is sprinkled with water: every house has a tub in front of the door, and the children splash it as it goes by. Dragon dances and processions are very ancient rain-producing ceremonies. Already in the time of Confucius the people of Lu, his birthplace, performed in the fourth month of the year a representation of the dragon that comes forth from the river: two troops of six or seven men, one of adults, the other adolescents, executed a ceremonial dance in the middle of the river Yi, crossing over by a ford, and then came up out of the river to sing on the rain altar. In other places, in the third century B.C., the picture of a winged dragon was drawn in order to avert drought.

In the beliefs of to-day, strongly tinged with Buddhist ideas, the dragons compose a vast people governed by the Dragon-king Lung-Wang. They have scaly bodies and four feet armed with claws; their heads are topped with horns, and the middle part of their skulls forms a mountain-shaped boss; they have power to rise to the skies as well as to dive beneath the waters, and to make their bodies large or small as they please. Like the Nāgas of Hindu folklore, to which, since the first days of Buddhist preaching, they have been likened by missionaries and believers, they possess a marvellous pearl which the pictures seldom fail to show in front of them in the shape of a large ball; when, as often, they are shown in pairs facing each other the pearl is placed between the two opposing heads. From the Nāgas they have borrowed also the power to assume human shape when they wish, and they take advantage of this to move about among mankind, most frequently in order to marry or to carry away girls.

Their sovereign, the Dragon-king, is of enormous size; he is a *li* in length—more than five hundred yards. This was clearly seen when the First Emperor of Ts'in, who had himself gone voyaging over the seas to seek the Islands of the Immortals, which his envoys had seen, but could not reach, tried by his magicians' advice to frighten the Dragon-king by bidding his soldiers beat drums on his ships. The noise attracted the Dragon-king, who appeared on the surface, five hundred yards long; the emperor had him riddled with arrows, so that his blood reddened the entire ocean. But on the following night he dreamed that he wrestled with the Dragon-king and was beaten; the next day he fell ill, and died in seven days.

But the Dragon-kings are very rarely represented except in human shape, which, according to the legends, they commonly prefer, and it is only when slain or vanquished that they resume their monstrous aspect. It would seem that the theatre had the greatest share in creating the habitual type seen in popular pictures; fat, with long beard, heavy moustaches, and enormous eyebrows, face painted all over with many colours, spots and stripes in which all semblance of a human face disappears. The statues simply give them the aspect of a bearded heavy mandarin, comfortably seated, and it is mainly by mottoes and inscriptions that they can be distinguished from many other divinities of similar iconographic type.

The Buddhist books translated into Chinese reckoned some eight, the others ten, Dragon-kings (Nāgas). But from the moment that the Dragon-kings became to the Chinese the kings of the seas their number had to be fixed at four, for to the Chinese the earth is surrounded by Four Seas, one on each side, at each of the cardinal points, and these Four Seas surround it with a continuous girdle like the river Oceanus of the Homeric mythology. The Taoists adopted this system of popular folklore; they have four Dragon-kings for the Four Seas: the Dragon-king who Increases Virtue, Kuang-tê, for the Eastern Sea; the Dragon-king who Enlarges Good, Kuang-li, for the Southern Sea; the Dragon-king who Enlarges Favour, Kuang-jun, for the Western Sea; the Dragon-king who Increases Generosity, Kuang-shê, for the Northern Sea. But these names are hardly more known to the common people than those of the ten Buddhist Nāgarājas. The only really popular names are those which were given them in the tale of the *Voyage to the West*, and which, though akin to the Taoist names, differ from them considerably. The Dragon-kings are brothers, and have the same family name, Ao. They are called Ao Kuang (Eastern Sea), Ao K'in (Southern Sea), Ao Jun (Western Sea), and Ao Shun (Northern Sea). Each governs one of the Four Seas, the ruler of the Eastern Sea being the chief over the other three, under the orders of the Jade Emperor, to whom they must go to pay homage once a year, like all the gods. It is in the third month that they ascend to the Celestial Court, and that is why the third month is a month of great rains.

The great Dragon-kings have very little place in the popular religion of China. At the very most the local dragons, each in his lake or his river or his whirlpool, have slightly more standing in their own district. What interests the Chinese peasants is not these mythological creations, but the beast endowed with supernatural might, which lives in the water, but which is able to ascend into the sky by piling the clouds together—the dragon rain-maker.

The Gods in Charge of Administrative Groups

To assist him in governing the earth the Jade Emperor has appointed celestial officials of every kind. There is a complete hierarchy of gods, just as there is a complete hierarchy of terrestrial functionaries; there are celestial ministers, there are celestial administrative districts. The holders of the various celestial offices, appointed by the Jade Emperor, go every year to give account to him of their administration, and on this occasion he distributes to them rewards and punishments, promotion or reduction in rank.

Fig. 16. The Great Emperor of the Eastern Peak
Popular print.

The Great Emperor of the Eastern Peak. The greatest of the terrestrial gods is the Great Emperor of the Eastern Peak, T'ai-yo ta-ti, god of T'ai-shan, the great mountain of Shantung (Fig. 16). In the official catalogues, as in the Taoist books, he is not alone: he belongs to a group of mountain divinities, the Gods of the Five Peaks, who since the beginning of the eleventh century all bear the title of Holy Emperor, Shêng-ti (Fig. 17). Of these he is the chief, and the others are the God of the Southern Peak—that is to say, of Hêng-shan (in Hêng-chou fu, Hunan); the God of the Western Peak — *i.e.*, Hua-shan (in T'ung-chou fu, Shensi); the God of the Northern Peak—*i.e.*, Hêng-shan (although this name seems identical with that of the Southern Peak, it is written in Chinese with a totally different character, and this is another mountain, situated in the prefecture of Ta-t'ung, Shansi); and the God of the Central Peak—*i.e.*, Sung-shan (in Ho-nan fu, Honan).

But these are devices of the scholars and the priests bent on symmetry: in ancient days the only cult really reverenced was that of the Eastern Peak, just as in our own time it has remained the only really popular one.

The Great Emperor of the Eastern Peak is generally considered as a kind of regent over the earth and over man under the authority of the Jade Emperor. But his chief *rôle* is to preside over human life; it is he who appoints birth and death, and he has scribes who keep the registers of both. In the temples consecrated to him many inscriptions recall this *rôle*: "For all creatures he procures life." "His authority presides over the mechanism of life."

Fig. 17. THE GREAT EMPERORS OF THE FIVE PEAKS (BELOW) ACCOMPANYING THE GREAT EMPEROR OF LITERATURE (ABOVE) AND HIS ASSISTANTS (CENTRE)

In the first centuries of our era he had even become the god of the dead: it was from his mountain the souls of men set forth to be born; to his mountain they returned after death. The very spot where they returned had been localized, the hill Hao-li, to the south-west of T'ai-an; according to others, they set forth from this hill, where they were assigned their destiny at birth, and returned after death to the hill Shê-shên. And these ideas have left a trace in the present-day beliefs with regard to the nether world: one of the ten kings who govern its divisions still bears the title of Lord of the Department of the Eastern Peak, T'ai-shan fu-kün; but this title, which in the twelfth century appears to have really denoted the God of T'ai-shan, is no longer attributed to him in our times, and no one to-day dreams of considering this little nether-world god and the Great Emperor of the Eastern Peak as one and the same personage. Only among the poets is he still spoken of as presiding over the dead: the popular faith has made a much more important divinity of him. All earthly affairs are entrusted to him by the Jade Emperor, who places complete confidence in him; the nether regions accordingly are in his charge, but they are no more than a part of his vast jurisdiction.

He has also an enormous administration under his orders. A thirteenth-century inscription enumerates seventy-five offices controlled by him; his temple at Pekin, Tung-yo-miao, now contains more than eighty. Going through the list of them, we can take note of the variety of the matters assigned to this god. He watches over everything that concerns life on earth, both human and animal (impossible, indeed, that it should be otherwise, since birth as an animal is one of the punishments of guilty souls, and since if these births were not under his control the god could not follow the whole career of the souls through their successive existences), not merely birth and death, but also destiny, fortune, honours, posterity, etc. There is also an office of the registry of births, and one of the registry of deaths, an office of the four kinds of birth (or, at Pekin, four departments, one for human births, one for births among quadrupeds, one for births from an egg, one for births by transformation), an office to assign a high or low social position at birth, another to distribute fortune, another to determine the number of children. Men's good or ill deeds also engage the attention of a series of offices: offices of thieves, of those who unjustly appropriate others' goods, of abortions, of poisonings, of acts of injustice, of merits, of filial piety, of loyalty, of the setting free of living creatures, of the slaying of living creatures, of the reading of holy books, of the acts that we hide from our own consciences, etc. There are other offices whose task is to adjust the fate assigned at the moment of birth in accordance with the merits and demerits acquired in the course of existence, an office of retribution for good actions, of retribution for bad actions, of swift retribution (Fig. 18), of lengthening of life (Fig. 19), of shortening of life, of the registering of good fortune, of misfortunes, of the diminution of happiness, etc. Five or six offices are specially devoted to human officials; others have charge of divine officials, Gods of Walls and Moats, Gods of the Soil, Gods of the Mountains, etc.; others, again, have charge of the priests and monks, bonzes or *tao-shï*. There are offices for neglected souls who have no sacrifices; there are others for the demons, for those unjustly brought to death, for vengeance claimed, for the nether regions; certain offices have the task of dispensing various diseases. And, lastly, there are departments for natural phenomena, a department of the Waters, of Rain and Wind, of the Five Cereals, and so on.

Fig. 18. The Office of Immediate Retribution, in the Temple of the Eastern Peak, at Pekin

For the colossal labour of keeping all these registers an enormous staff is needed: this is recruited from among the souls of the departed. The thirteenth-century inscriptions already mentioned give the name and the origin (in their last earthly existence) of all the directors of these offices. These directors themselves have in their service subordinate employees, scribes, keepers of books, etc. Sometimes the dead are not enough, and the living must be taken as well. Such was the position of Shên Sêng-chao, a Taoist devotee of the fifth century of our era. For the most part he lived like everybody else, engaged in ordinary occupations; but every thirty days precisely, when evening fell, he donned a yellow bonnet, put on a coarse robe, and, after performing certain ceremonies in his room, he carried out the duties of a secretary in one of the offices under the Eastern Peak, and when there was anything to record in this administration he had to set his seal to it. In this way he became acquainted with many supernatural matters, and he now and then had occasion to predict fortunate or unfortunate events to various persons; his prognostications always came true. On the other hand, the dead chosen out for a post do not always possess the necessary experience, and they must sometimes be sent back among the living for a kind of probationary course. A certain Li Hüan-chï once upon a time explained this to his younger brother as follows: "I am a spectre, and this is my history. I was appointed a keeper of the books to the Eastern Peak. My predecessor having been promoted to a higher rank, the King of the Eastern Peak wished to appoint some one to take his place, but as no one was sufficiently qualified he summoned me and said: 'Your capacities render you worthy of this post, but you have not studied enough. Go among men and study with Pien Hiao-sien; when your studies are finished you will return and I shall appoint you.' It was for fear lest people might be terrified at the sight of a spectre that I assumed the shape of a living man. My education was completed in less than a year, and for two years I have held the post of keeper of books to the Eastern Peak."

Fig. 19. THE OFFICE OF LONG LIFE, UNDER THE CONTROL OF THE EASTERN PEAK, IN HIS TEMPLE AT PEKIN

The Great Emperor of the Eastern Peak is ordinarily shown seated, in imperial costume; his statues are as impersonal as possible, and he is barely distinguished from the Jade Emperor. In fact, among the common people there are in their houses few pictures and still fewer statues of so great a personage; they are satisfied with setting his seal or amulets bearing his name on the walls, which is sufficient to keep off the evil spirits.

Like almost all the gods, he has a family; but only his daughter, the Princess of the Motley Clouds, Pi-hia yüan-kün, is really known and worshipped. She is often simply called the Lady of T'ai-shan, T'ai-shan niang-niang, and is the protectress of women, alongside of her Buddhist rival Kuan-yin (Avalokiteṣvara), and also the patroness of foxes, animals endowed with supernatural faculties, capable in certain conditions of assuming human shape and mingling with men. I shall presently come back to her *rôle* as protectress of women.

The Gods of the Administrative Districts

Every administrative district has its protecting deity whose office it is to look to the welfare of the inhabitants. Certain gods, who bear various names to-day, are the heirs of the ancient Gods of the Soil in the ancient religion, whose hierarchy, like the line of the princes, descended from the God of the Soil royal down to the Gods of the Soil of the villages, *via* those of the principalities, of the districts, and so on. The official religion pays veneration to these under their old name of *shê*, on fixed dates. In the popular religion the Gods of the Soil are called *ch'êng-huang shên*, literally, ' Gods of Walls and Moats '; in administrative districts of every degree, or in an inferior rank, those whose jurisdiction, great or small, does not extend to an administrative district, are called simply *t'u-ti shên*, literally, ' Gods of the Place.'

The Gods of Walls and Moats (Ch'êng-huang). The God of Walls and Moats is the god who plays the most important part in the religious life of the Chinese cities and towns, whose official protector he is. He is not their founder; the founder is often paid special worship under names that vary in different places (one of the most common is simply the Ancestor of the Village, *shê-tsu*). He is the deity entrusted by the Jade Emperor with the government of a district; he is the modern substitute for the ancient God of the Soil, *shê*, whose place he has taken and who has almost wholly disappeared from the popular religion, to figure only in the official religion. Originally he was the most important of the feudal deities, the personification not of the harvest-giving earth, but of the fief itself as delimited territory with its own separate existence under the suzerainty of the Son of Heaven; and as such he protected the people of the territory and the lords of the manor. Thus there was a whole divine hierarchy of Gods of the Soil called *shê*, corresponding to the human hierarchy of the princes. When the feudal world disappeared in the course of the third century before our era, the hierarchy of the princes being replaced by a hierarchy of officials, the princely Gods of the Soil became provincial Gods of the Soil, regularly venerated by the governors, prefects, and sub-prefects. But all living reality little by little dropped out of this wholly administrative cult: the *shê* have, indeed, survived in the schedule of official sacrifices, and from the highest down, from the Emperor (or in our time the President of the Republic) to the village notables, there are offerings made to them at stated periods; but it is a lapsed and out-of-date cult that is only maintained from force of habit, and now interests hardly anybody except literati devotedly attached to archaic ritualism. In the living religion the *ch'êng-huang*, newcomers of uncertain origin, have entirely taken their place from every point of view: it is they that now protect the town and the district where they have a temple; it is they who are prayed to to give peace, happiness, riches, a good harvest, and the like, to the whole people. As the Viceroy Wu Yung-kuang of the Two-Hu (Hupeh and Hunan) said at the beginning of last century, "The God of Walls and Moats truly presides over the administration of a region; he gives happiness to the good and misfortune to the wicked" (Fig. 20).

The God of Walls and Moats is not the old god under a new name: even although to-day he comes very near the other, he is in reality something quite different, and the influence of Buddhist and Taoist ideas was very powerfully at work in his evolution. Like all the gods of the present-day pantheon, the *ch'êng-huang* are considered as officials of the Celestial Court, men who by their merits have deserved to be entrusted with this charge after death for the period of one existence; but that is the common recent interpretation of this worship in the religious system of to-day. In reality their origin goes much further back. They seem to be the longest-lived of those spirits to whom the people have in all times paid an "irregular worship," or one not recognized by the public authorities, and who from the Han period, in the first centuries of our era, were already banned by the mandarins, who had their temples pulled down and prohibited sacrifice to them. Local heroes, great persons whose tomb or votive temple was near by, officials who had left favourable memories behind, little by little became the protectors, the patrons, of the common folk. The temple of the *ch'êng-huang* of Wu-hu, in T'ai-p'ing fu (Anhwei), claims to date back to the year 240 of our era. In A.D. 555 there is for the first time noted that a God of Walls and Moats received a sacrifice from a mandarin, when the general of the northern Ts'i, Mu-jung Yen, entrusted with the defence of the city of Ying (to-day Wu-ch'ang, in Hupeh), added to various mundane devices official prayers to the local *ch'êng-huang*. About the same period Siao Ki, King of Wu-ling (a prince of the imperial family of the Liang, who reigned over the south of China), also made offerings in the temple of a God of Walls and Moats. His sacrifice has always been famous on account of a portent that occurred on this occasion: a red serpent suddenly came forth and twined about the victim's head. It is probable that at this period the temples of the *ch'êng-huang* were already widely scattered about the empire, for the author of the *History of the Southern*

Fig. 20. A God of Walls and Moats
Musée Guimet.

Ts'i, who wrote half a century later, relates the fact without finding it necessary to give any explanation. Three great writers of the eighth century, Chang Yüe in 717, Chang Kiu-ling in 727, and Tu Mu in 842, all made sacrifices, when they were provincial mandarins, to the God of Walls and Moats of their respective cities, King-Chou for the first, Hung-chou for the second, and Huang-chou for the third. The prayers they composed on these occasions have been preserved in the collections of their literary works: Chang Yüe asked generally for happiness for the people of his jurisdiction, that wild beasts should not devour his subordinates, nor insects ravage the crops; Chang Kiu-ling, more directly importunate, besought that a flood might subside and that the torrential rains might stop so that the harvests might not be lost; Tu Mu prayed for rain, asking for an end to a three years' drought that was ruining his prefecture. In 751 Chao Kiu-chêng, governor of Soochow (Kiangsu), rebuilt the temple of the local *ch'êng-huang* and composed an inscription for it. His contemporary, Tuan Ts'üan-wei, similarly restored that of Ch'êng-tu (Szechwan) and erected a stele; and the governor Li Tê-yü offered a sacrifice to him about 830. Although according to Li Yang p'ing, a writer of this epoch, these gods were not then inscribed in the register of official sacrifices, the foundation or removal of an administrative centre was almost immediately followed by the erection of a temple of the God of Walls and Moats; that of Siang-shan (Chekiang) was built in 706, the same year as the sub-prefecture was created; that of Fêng-hua (Chekiang) was founded, by imperial orders, in 865, by the Government of the department of Ming, Li Tsung-shên: it was rather more than a century since the seat of the departmental administration had been fixed in this sub-prefecture (738); that of Ting-hai (in the Chusan Islands, Chekiang) was built in 916, seven years after the creation of the sub-prefecture (909); and so on. Elsewhere the cult, going further and further, was soon to achieve still greater heights: about 934-936, the king of Wu-yüe, a little kingdom occupying the north of Chekiang, conferred the title of king upon three Gods of Walls and Moats in his dominions, those of

Fig. 21. AN INQUIRY PRESIDED OVER BY THE GOD OF WALLS AND MOATS
Popular print.

Hangchow, his capital, of Yüe-chou (Shao-hing fu, Chekiang), and of Hu-chou. The emperors of the Sung dynasty accepted this cult and confirmed these gods in their titles, sometimes even enhancing them; thus that of Hangchow, their capital, received promotion in 1172. Under the Mongol dynasty the title of king was conferred on the God of Walls and Moats of the new capital, the Pekin of to-day. The Ming dynasty began by following the example of its predecessors; its founder T'ai-tsu conferred the title of emperor on the *ch'êng-huang* of the capital (then Nankin); the title of king on those of K'ai-fêng fu and some other localities; the titles of marquis and count on the gods of the prefectures (*fu*) and the sub-prefectures (*hien*); but in 1370 all these titles were suppressed, and the designation of God of Walls and Moats of such and such prefecture or sub-prefecture was considered sufficient. From time to time various erudites, out of regard for orthodoxy and religious purism, warred against these cults as modern corruptions of the true doctrine that had no existence in ancient times, and endeavoured to have them excluded from the official religion, but in vain; it needed the Revolution and the coming of the Republic to make them lose their place in the State ritual. But official recognition, however important, is not essential for the worship of these deities; they are above everything popular deities, and their worship is deeply implanted in the religious feeling of the common people.

Fig. 22. THE GOD OF WALLS AND MOATS OF THE CAPITAL
Popular print.

Each district has its God of Walls and Moats, whose title varies: the old titles conferred in times past have been preserved in current use in spite of decrees and edicts to the contrary. Frequently they are ancient or modern historic persons, but alongside of them there are a number of local heroes, real or imaginary. Pekin has Yang Ki-shêng, a Ming official, executed in 1556 at forty years of age; Nankin's is Yü K'ien, President of the War Office under T'ai-tsu of the Ming dynasty, who repulsed the Mongols after the capture of the Emperor Ying-tsung (1449), but, having refused to take measures for freeing the imperial prisoner, he was executed on the return of his master in 1457. The patron of Soochow (Kiangsu) was for a long time the Prince of Ch'un-shên, a minister of the kingdom of Ch'u in the third century before our era, and protector of the philosopher Sün-tsï, who is, with Mencius, the most celebrated of the Confucian masters of that period: the capital of this prince's fief is supposed to have been at Soochow; to-day he is no longer God of Walls and Moats for the whole city, he is merely God of the Place, *t'u-ti*, for the Eastern quarter. The deity of the prefecture of Ning-po (Chekiang) is Ki Sin, who was a general of the party of Liu P'ang, King of Han, the founder of the Han dynasty, in the days when he was still struggling for supremacy with Hiang Yü, the King of Ch'u, and who gave his life for his master in 203 B.C. Liu P'ang, who had long been besieging the city of Yung-yang (near K'ai-fêng fu), had found himself in turn invested by the troops of his rival, and, being cut off from all provisions, was about to be reduced to surrender; Ki Sin offered to pass himself off as his master. Mounting upon the royal chariot, and drawing the curtains round him, he went out to the enemy's camp proclaiming that the King of Han was giving himself up, and while the whole enemy army, with loud cheering, had its attention solely concentrated upon him, his master was able to escape unobserved with a score or two of horsemen. When Ki Sin came to the presence of Hiang Yü and alighted from the chariot and was recognized, the other, in a rage at being tricked, had him burned alive. In this case there is no link between the hero and Ning-po; his selection as *ch'êng-huang* was in any case inevitably long delayed, since Ning-po is a recent city: the beginning of the ninth century saw the establishment of the sub-prefecture of Yin on the site of the present city, with a very modest extent; it developed quickly enough, and three-quarters of a century later a local chief named Huang Ch'êng, who had been brought into prominence by the dissolution of the T'ang empire, protected it with a long earthen wall. Only in 916 was the temple of the God of Walls and Moats built, some fifty paces south-west of the circumvallation, by the governor Ch'ên Ch'êng-ye. The God of Kuei-lin is Chang Tung-ch'ang, an officer of the Ming Emperor Yung-ming (1648–62), who was put to death by the Manchus in 1659. And, again, if the office is immutable the holders often change: the god of Hangchow, the capital of Chekiang, is to-day Chou Sin, a mandarin of the early days of the Ming period, who was put to death in 1412, and was officially raised to this dignity a few years later. Before him the city already had a *ch'êng-huang* who had under the Sung dynasty received the title of King of Eternal Firmness, Yung-ku wang, but whose name, or when he lived, is not known. His temple had originally been on the mountain of Fêng-huang, but the Sung emperors, having built their palace on this hill when the city became their capital, transferred it to the mountain Pao-yüe (1139), and then again to Wu-shan, where it remains to-day, serving both for the prefecture and the two sub-prefectures into which the city was divided down to 1914.

The reasons governing the choice of the holders of these divine posts are very various and sometimes hard to see: if Chou Sin justly became the protector of the inhabitants of Hangchow, inasmuch as it was in an effort to protect them from the exactions of a dishonest official that he exposed himself to the calumnies that caused his death, if Su Kien justly became the protector of Nan-ning (Kwangsi), which he defended against the barbarians in 1075, and under the ruins of which he was buried, no conceivable link binds Ki Sin to Ning-po. Sometimes the bond is exceedingly slight: the God of Walls and

Fig. 23. THE GOD OF WALLS AND MOATS JUDGING A WRONGDOER
Popular print.

Moats of the sub-prefecture of Lin-an (Chekiang) in the tenth century (I do not know if he is the same to-day) was a ten-year-old boy, the fan-bearer to Ts'ien Liu, King of Wu-yüe (907–932): his master put him to death in a moment of anger because as he fanned him he had struck him on the shoulder with the long handle of the fan. Soon after this the child appeared to him, and the prince, terrified, exclaimed, "I have killed men innumerable, and this little boy appears to me!" And so, to appease the ghost, he named him god of this sub-prefecture.

Frequently official adoption must have been no more than recognition of a popular cult more or less ancient. Thus in 908 Ts'ien Liu, King of Wu-yüe, recognized as god of Yüe-chou (Shao-hing), conferring on him the title of marquis, the former governor P'ang Yü, who died some three centuries before, to whom the people had long before erected a temple.

The feast of the God of Walls and Moats is one of the principal popular feasts. It includes great processions in which the whole population of the city takes part. At the head, behind heralds whose office is to clear the streets through which the god is to pass, go gongs and drums, then groups of children and men carrying incense-sticks, followed by banner-bearers and parasol-bearers; then comes the statue of the God of the Place, borne on its palanquin, going first to make sure that everything is in proper order; sometimes instead of the statue it is a grandee got up like the God of the Place, with a long white beard and a knotty staff; behind the God of the Place is carried in a kind of big pot the vinegar with which the streets are sprinkled to purify them, and then the great perfume-burner. Then comes the train of the god, his servants represented by men or boys in disguises, his horse, his two attendants Ox-head and Horse-face, his executioners, and, lastly, the god himself—*i.e.*, his statue—in a great palanquin. To the procession are joined various troops, troops of penitents like the Red-clothed (red being the colour of the garments of those condemned to death), who move slowly on, cangue on neck, chains on hands, with gongs and banners, or groups of men disguised as demons. Some join in fulfilment of a vow: boys or young men in costumes like those of the ancient imperial couriers, a little flag in their hand, who will burn a letter of thanks for the healing of some disease, some enclosed in a little cage, like criminals, in expiation of some unknown transgression, in order to obtain health.

The God of Walls and Moats has a whole administrative staff under his orders. His most celebrated subordinates are Mr White, Po lao-ye, and Mr Black, Hei lao-ye, who see everything that goes on in the district, the first during the day, the second during the night. They are represented as two long, thin individuals, with high conical bonnets, clad one in white, the other all in black. There are also Ox-head and Horse-face, but these are more strictly infernal satellites. And furthermore all the Gods of the Place and of the District are in his dependence.

The Gods of the Place (T'u-ti). Below the Gods of Walls and Moats, and subordinate to them, are the Gods of the Place, *t'u-ti*. These are little local gods, each in charge of a larger or smaller territory. Nearly every quarter, every street of the towns or villages, and every hamlet has at least one, and sometimes several; every temple, every public building, has its own. That belonging to the officials' *ya-mên* is in Szechwan, buried in the middle of the first building of the lawcourts: he is called the Inquisitor God of the Place, and he listens to and registers evidence and judgments, to enable him to make his annual report on the official conduct of the mandarins. There is one for every bridge, there are others for the fields, etc., etc. The most important are those of the villages; but in many places, although officially their only title is God of the Place, *t'u-ti*, they are currently referred to by the title of God of Walls and Moats, *ch'êng-huang*, and although etymologically this title is unjustifiable, it responds exactly to the *rôle* of the patron-god of the village, which is the same as that of the patron-gods of the administrative cities.

The Gods of the Place are sometimes celebrated persons: in the thirteenth century, when the capital of the Sung dynasty was at Hangchow, the official Great school having been installed in the house that had once been lived in by General Yo Fei, it was he who was adored in it as God of the Place; for the same reason a great Buddhist temple of Hu-chou had Shên Yo, a great writer of the sixth century, as God of the Place. To-day (or at least a few years before the downfall of the Manchu dynasty) the God of the Place of the Academy, Han-lin yüan, at Pekin, was the celebrated Han Yü, one of the greatest poets of the T'ang dynasty, who lived between the eighth and ninth centuries.

Fig. 24. THE GOD OF WALLS AND MOATS AND THE GOD OF THE PLACE

Popular print.

The part played by these gods is analogous to that of the Gods of Walls and Moats, but they are subordinate to the latter. They keep the register of all the persons belonging to their district; that is why all deaths are announced to them. A group of women of the family, on the evening after the death of the sufferer, go weeping, preceded by a man carrying a lantern, to the pagoda of the god and burn incense and silver paper, returning home again still weeping.

THE HOUSEHOLD GODS

Of a still lower grade, every house has its gods, who are charged with the protection of the buildings and their inhabitants. As has already been indicated, there is not only a God of the Place, but also gods of the various parts of the dwelling. Antiquity knew only five, who were called the "Five Sacrifices," and who quite recently were still the only ones admitted by the official religion. The Outer Door (with two leaves), *mên*; the Inner Doors (with one leaf), *hu*; the Passages of the house, *hing*; the Impluvium, *chung-liu*, commonly known as the God of the Place, *t'u-ti*; the Hearth, *tsao*. It cannot be definitely said that popular religion accepts or repudiates this list: everybody, or nearly everybody, knows who are the Gods of the "Five Sacrifices," but the God of the Inner Doors and the God of the Passages have no longer any place in religious observances, and although when the list is repeated their names are still given they are practically forgotten and as though they did not exist. On the other hand, if certain gods have thus disappeared from the popular religious consciousness there are others that did not exist, or, more accurately speaking, have left no trace in the written rituals of antiquity, divinities of certain parts of the house, the Bed, the Latrines, as well as others in general charge of the house and the family living in it, Gods of Riches, etc., etc. Lastly, to complete the survey of all the protectors of the family, we must add the Ancestors, whose cult goes back to the remotest antiquity. It is not merely the number and the functions of the household gods that have changed with time, it is their respective rank as well. To-day the most important of them is the God of the Hearth, My Lord Hearth, as he is ordinarily called, while in the ancient days he was a little looked down upon and considered as "an old wives' cult," according to a saying attributed to Confucius himself. Then it was the God of the Impluvium that held first rank in noble houses and princes' palaces; his place was in the runnel of the door that occupied the centre of the dwelling, leading from the second to the third court of the palace (the palaces of the princes were made up of three successive halls of reception and audience, each one at the end of a great court, and it was behind the back-door of the third court that the actual living quarters of the prince and his wives were found); and so great was the fear of offending him by breaking down his runnel that it was forbidden to pass this door in a chariot, under penalty of seeing the driver beheaded, the horses slaughtered, and the pole of the chariot cut off on the spot. The ruin of feudalism was fatal to this aristocratic god; he lost his precedence when, about the third and second centuries before our era, the patrician rites, which were complicated and costly, had to give place to the simpler plebeian customs, and the God of the Hearth, a more popular god, gradually outstripped him in prestige; he has recovered a certain amount of importance only in those regions where, by complete transformation, he is confused with the God of Riches.

The God of the Hearth. The God of the Hearth and his wife have their image in every house; this is not a statue, but simply a crudely coloured drawing in which the god is generally portrayed as an old man with a white beard, in mandarin costume, sitting in an armchair; beside him is his wife, standing, and feeding six domestic animals: a horse, an ox, a pig, a sheep, a dog, a hen; or else she is simply sitting by him in ceremonial dress, and the six domestic animals, when they are shown, are either lying down at her feet, or arranged round the central group made up by her and her husband. Sometimes they have two assistants beside them, the Youthful Wood-gatherer and the Water-carrier. This drawing, printed in extremely bright crude colours, is pasted in the niche that serves him for a temple above the kitchen stove, a little construction of a few bricks with a roof imitating enamelled tiles (the whole about a foot high and a foot wide), and open to the south, because, as the God of the Hearth is the chief of the household gods, he who governs the house must be placed in the same way as the Emperor in his audience-chamber and in general, as every master of a house in his reception-room. Throughout the whole year an empty wine-cup is placed before this little shrine, with a pair of chopsticks; on the 1st and the 15th of the month, about six in the morning, before the first breakfast, the head of the family burns two red tapers and some incense-sticks, but without presenting either rice or wine. The offering is in any case not very ceremonious, for, after all, this is only a little god: the father of the family prostrates himself once, lights the tapers and the incense-sticks, most frequently without making any prayer, then he goes off to his affairs, and only comes back when they are all but burnt out; he then prostrates himself afresh and waits on his knees until they are completely extinguished of themselves; then he rises, and, the ceremony being thus finished, the family takes the morning meal.

Fig. 25. THE GOD OF THE HEARTH, DIRECTOR OF DESTINY
Popular print.

Only three times in the year is he offered a repast: on the anniversary of his birth, which is the third day of the eighth month; on the twenty-fourth of the twelfth month, and the twentieth of the first month, at his setting out for and his return from his yearly journey to heaven, when he goes to the Court of the Jade Emperor to give an account of all that has taken place during the year in the house entrusted to his charge; in almost all families it is the twenty-fourth of the twelfth month that is the most important feast, for this is the day of his departure, and it is deemed important to give him a pleasant memory, so that he may make a favourable report.

The God of the Hearth and his wife each keep a register in which they enter all the actions of the household; he concerns himself with the men and she with the women: everything that is done, whether it be good or whether it be evil, must be noted in it with complete impartiality. Every month, on the last day, he takes his registers and goes to give an account to the God of Walls and Moats; annually, on the first day of the year, he goes to give an account to the Jade Emperor, or, as is commonly said, to Mr Heaven (Lao-t'ien-ye), the sovereign of the gods, while his wife does the same to the Holy Jade Empress, Yü-huang shêng-mu. He is, in fact, an official of the Celestial Court, which gives him the title of Household Steward, and, like every official, he must go every year to pay homage to the sovereign; the Jade Emperor examines his report, and according as he finds good or evil predominating he increases or diminishes the family's portion of good luck and happiness for the ensuing year. The belief in the God of the Hearth's journey to heaven is an ancient one: a Taoist author of the fringes of the third and fourth centuries of our era (Ko Hung, who was born about A.D. 250 and died between 328 and 331, being eighty-one years old) quotes still earlier works in which it is mentioned, adding besides that, " for his own part, he has not been able to verify whether it was true or false "; the only difference from modern ideas is that, since in the days when these ancient works were composed the cult of the Gods of Walls and Moats had not yet been established, there was no intermediary between the God of the Hearth and Heaven, so that he went up to heaven every month, and not merely at the end of the year, as he does to-day. " In the night of the last day of each month the God of the Hearth ascends to heaven to present his report upon the transgressions of men."

On the evening of his annual departure, on the 24th of the twelfth month, the god is regaled with a full dinner of six dishes; there is, besides, a special cake, a round ball of rice flour, without sugar, filled inside with a paste of red haricot beans. After his dinner everything is made ready for his journey: before his niche is placed a little paper palanquin, carried by two little statues of men, also made of paper; the father of the family prostrates himself, then he detaches the image of the god from the niche and lays it in the palanquin; after which he places the palanquin on a tray, which he carries from the kitchen outside the main door of the house, which is wide open, and through which he must go out to do honour to the god. During all the time he is carrying the god he must take pains to keep his head always turned to the south, which is often very difficult and obliges him at some moments to walk backwards. As soon as the father has gone outside the house a few handfuls of straw are cast to the ground before him: on these he sets the palanquin, still turned to the south, also some silver paper representing silver ingots, destined to defray the expenses of the journey to heaven. He then says: " God of the Hearth, when you ascend to heaven, keep our faults to yourself! If we have been lacking in due respect in serving you, be a little lenient! " And he burns the palanquin while the children let off crackers, and then goes back into the house. The kitchen stove is next extinguished, and must remain unlit during the absence of the God of the Hearth, which continues for a month; during this time all cooking is done on little portable stoves, which are moved every day and put out every evening. The God of the Hearth does not come back for a whole month, returning on the twentieth day of the first month. On that day a new print is purchased, and a meal similar to that for his departure is prepared, for he comes back in the evening precisely in time for dinner; he is welcomed with crackers, the new print is placed in the shrine, then the tapers are lit and offerings are presented; these the family eats the next day.

While the God of the Hearth is absent no one takes his place, for his wife ascends with him and goes to pay homage to the wife of the Jade Emperor; there is no one to take down the transgressions committed during this time, which is very lucky, for at the new year's feasting many people gamble and drink more than they ought; but thanks to the absence of the god, sins committed at this time of the year are not recorded against them. To set alongside this advantage there are drawbacks, if not in the departure of the God of the Hearth himself, at any rate in that of the other gods. For he is not the only one to go at the year's end to pay homage to Mr Heaven: all the gods who have an official charge and are mandarins of the Celestial Court, like the God of Walls and Moats, and so on, have the same duty to fulfil at the same period. During this absence of the gods the evil spirits are free, and do as they please. The demons of sickness also are loosed during these days. In his youth, while still a student, Kuan Shï-jên, who died Minister of the Imperial Household in A.D. 1109, at sixty-five, one New Year's Day morning met a troop of most ugly demons of ferocious aspect, who were passing through the street just in front of the door of his family's house. He asked them who they were. "We are the demons of the plague: on the first day of the year we spread diseases among men." "Will you be going into my home?" "No. When for three successive generations a family amasses virtue, or when that family is about to be elevated, or when its members eat no beef, any single one of these three things is enough to prevent us from entering there!" And suddenly they disappeared.

The Gods of the Doors. The outer door of the house is a door with two leaves: accordingly it has two gods, so that each leaf may bear an image of its own, for if there was only one god, whose image occupied the middle of the door, he would be represented half on each leaf, and would be cleft in two the moment the door was opened. To-day it is generally Ts'in Shu-pao and Hu King-tê, two generals of the T'ang Emperor T'ai-tsung, who fulfil this *rôle*: they took the place of Shên-t'u and Yü-lü, who were the two Gods of the Doors in antiquity and down to about the thirteenth and fourteenth century. These were, properly speaking, the keepers of the door through which ghosts come away from the world of the dead to go wandering on earth among men, situated at the north-east corner of the world; according to the *Book of Mountains and Seas* (*Shan hai king*), a little collection of works on mythological geography composed about the fourth and third centuries before our era, they dwelt there upon a mountain, at the foot of the mighty peach-tree, whose trunk is three thousand *li* (a thousand miles) round, and in the branches of which opens the Door of the Ghosts, and they seize with rush-ropes the maleficent ghosts and fling them to tigers to devour; it was the mythical Yellow Emperor Huang-ti who thought of hanging their effigy carved in peachwood on the doors, as well as images of tigers, to drive away the evil spirits. At that epoch the images of these gods were placed on the inner doors, while the image of the tigers was placed on the outer doors of the houses, and this custom continued into the century that followed the Christian era; but later, approaching the twelfth century of our era, in the time of the Sung dynasty, their image was placed on each of the leaves of the great outer door. And, indeed, they have not altogether disappeared, in Szechwan they are specially the Gods of the Door in time of mourning; as soon as any member of a household is dead the images of the gods are carefully scraped off the ordinary doors, and the four characters of their names are pasted on the two leaves of the outside entrance-door. Their modern substitutes are historical personages who held high military posts at the court of the T'ang dynasty, in the beginning of the seventh century. The story is told how the Emperor T'ai-tsung, having one night heard a demon making a noise at the door of his apartments in the palace by hurling bricks and tiles about, fell seriously ill. The two generals Ts'in Shu-pao and Hu King-tê proposed to him that they should mount guard at his door: this they did for several nights in succession, and the demon now did not venture to appear, so that the Emperor recovered. He then had the portrait of each of the generals painted in full panoply, and one pasted on each leaf of the entrance-door; the demon still did not dare to come, and the Emperor was able to sleep in peace. But some time after the din broke out again at the little back-door, a door with one leaf. This time it was Wei Chêng who mounted guard and drove the ghost away.

To-day representations of the two generals are everywhere in abundance: they are painted at full length on the doors of public buildings, of temples (except Buddhist temples,

Fig. 26. The God of the Right Door-leaf

Fig. 27. The God of the Left Door-leaf

which have their own door-gods), of palaces, of private houses. The common people content themselves with sticking on to each leaf of the main door of their houses a coarse coloured print. They are almost always shown in military costume, helmeted and in complete armour, with the little flags on the shoulders that were the insignia of rank before the Manchu dynasty, armed with sabre and halberd, and the better to strike terror into the demons they are given fierce faces with great beards (Figs. 26 and 27); at other times, though more rarely, they are in the dress of civilian mandarins. Sometimes the image of Wei Chêng is also stuck on the single-leafed back-door, but this is much less common. Ordinarily no worship is paid to the Gods of the Doors; their image is put up, and that is all. All the same they are watchful deities, and it is thanks to them that evil spirits do not enter the houses. Many tales show them in their *rôle* as guardians. Once upon a time, in Hangchow, a slave in a wealthy family was in the habit of going out at night to get drunk. One night his master heard a great noise before the door, and, coming out, found the slave unconscious. He had him picked up and brought in to his bed, but the man died almost at once. Before he died he had time to tell how he had been attacked by the ghost of his sister-in-law, long since dead. She was carrying her head in her hand, and had attacked him in revenge, for long ago, when he was very young, he had helped his brother to kill his wife taken with a lover. The dead woman had, she told him, long spied upon him, accompanied by her lover's ghost, but the Gods of the Door had always prevented her from entering the house; that night, as she had caught him outside, she had seized her opportunity. Images of the gods, it may be said, are necessary, and mere inscriptions are insufficient.

The God of the Place of the House. The once preponderant importance of the God of the Place (*t'u-ti*) of the house is slight enought to-day; in practice no one takes much notice of him, except in the regions where he is confused with the God of Riches. In the house he has the same part as the other Gods of the Place in their jurisdiction; his special *rôle* is to keep the register of births and deaths. A certain Yin T'ing-hia having been carried away by two infernal satellites, the God of the Place of his house intervened and demanded to be allowed to see the warrant for his taking. "There must be a mistake," he said; "every time a man is born in the Yin family I receive from the Eastern Peak a notification of the duration of his life. Thus I know that Yin T'ing-hia ought to live for seventy-two years. Yet he is only fifty now. How does it come that he has been arrested?" And after the matter was scrutinized it was found that a mistake had been made. Yin returned to life.

This god is, in a general way, the protector of the family. Once upon a time, in the region of Mount Yüan-hêng, the common people used to celebrate the sacrifice to the Sun-god in the second month, drinking all day long, so that by night they were quite drunken. A man of this district, returning home on the night of this festival, fell into a ditch in the middle of the fields. There his body remained, unconscious, but his soul, unaware of this, pursued its way and came to his house. It tried to push the closed door, and was quite astonished to see that it could not budge it, but succeeded in getting in by a chink in the wall. His wife was on her bed, playing with their children, and from time to time broke into scolding against her husband for not coming home. He called out to her, "I am here!" But she did not hear, so that at length he asked himself, "Could I be dead?" And, going to the corner reserved for the Ancestors, he saw his father and his grandfather sitting there. He went up weeping to salute them, when his father said to him, "Do not be afraid! I will call the God of the Place." A white-bearded old man, in a linen garment and straw shoes like a peasant, suddenly appeared; he took the soul away to the place where his body had remained sprawled out. Arriving there, he bade it take possession of its own body while he called it by name several times. The dead man awoke and stood up. Just at this moment certain neighbours dispatched by his wife, who had finally become alarmed at his absence, arrived with lanterns and brought him back to his house.

This function of looking after the registers of the family births and deaths makes him in certain parts considered as giving long life to those who honour him, while his wife is charged with shedding domestic happiness within the house. That is why, in the west of Szechwan, they are called the God of the Place of Long Life, Ch'ang-shêng t'u-ti, and the Noble Lady of Felicity, Jui-k'ing fu-jên.

The Lord and the Lady of the Bed. The house being above all the place dwelt in at night, wherever one's current business may bring one during the day, the bedchamber is the most important part in it. Hence it has its couple of protecting divinities, the Lord of the Bed, Ch'uang-kung, and the Lady of the Bed, Ch'uang-mu, to whom offerings are presented on the last day of the year, or on the morrow of the full moon in the first month, the morrow of the Feast of Lanterns, when women who wish to have a child try to procure one of the ends of the candles that have been used to light up the dragon that is carried in procession through the streets, and light it on the edge of the bed. Their offerings are of cakes and fruits with a cup of tea for the Lord and a cup of wine for the Lady; these dates and offerings vary in different localities.

They are not simply a couple of Gods of the Place; only married people sacrifice to them or have their image; they are the personification of the bed as the power presiding over the engendering of children. In many places young married people entering the nuptial chamber prostrate themselves in their honour. Usually it is the bed itself that is turned to; but sometimes a print is hung up in which they are represented sitting side by side, in official costume, and with their tablet of rank in their hands.

The Goddess of the Privy. One special place in the house, the privies, has its own special deity: she is called the Third Lady of the Privy, K'êng-san-ku, or, more simply, the Third Lady, San-ku, or, again, the Purple Lady, Tsï-ku, or even the Seventh Lady, Ts'i-ku, a name which seems to be a corruption of the preceding one, but which is generally regarded as a false interpretation of another word, *ts'i*, supposed to be her family name, Lady Ts'i. She was, in her lifetime, about the end of the eighth century according to the most widely received legend, the second-rank wife of a sub-prefect; the legitimate wife, a certain Lady Ts'ao, in a fit of jealousy killed her by throwing her into the privy-pit on the day of the Feast of Lanterns; in the sequel the Celestial Emperor took pity on her and made her the deity of this particular spot.

The women, and particularly the girls, of the house make offerings to her in the privies on the fifteenth day of the first month, the anniversary of her death. They make a rough effigy of her with a great ladle; the bowl forms the head, and a human face is drawn on it; to the handle are fastened willow twigs to make the body, and they dress it up with a few bits of cloth. Then they burn incense and call it, saying, "Your husband is away; the Lady Ts'ao is gone; little Lady, you may come forth!" ("Little Lady" is a polite expression for a wife of the second rank.) If one of the women present is a medium, she speedily goes into a trance; they say that the Lady has come and question her about all kinds of things: the next year's harvest, the rearing of silkworms, marriages, etc. The cult of the Purple Lady is very ancient; it can be traced back beyond the T'ang epoch; and already in that epoch the women used to bring her down in the evening of the Feast of Lanterns to ask her to tell fortunes. In the same month and in the same way

Fig. 28. GENERAL PUFFER (HA-TSIANG)
In the Kiai-t'ai sï at Pekin.

they questioned also Lady Basket and Lady Broom, who were represented by an old basket and an old broom dressed up with bits of stuff. These spiritualist seances were very common about the eleventh century in the households of the literati of the Sung court; they were not always satisfied with summoning the Purple Lady in the first month, they called on her throughout the year, and generally she came with no hesitation. Sometimes it was another spirit than that of the Purple Lady who came down, and the séances assumed a more elevated character.

Fig. 29. THE PURPLE LADY
Popular print.

A writer of the eleventh century relates how, about the year 1035, as the wives and daughters of a friend of his father were thus "bringing down the Purple Lady," one of the girls went into trance, and the spirit who took possession of her declared herself one of the wives of the Supreme Emperor, Shang-ti. She wrote remarkable literary compositions, which were even published and much admired. Her writing was very beautiful, but in a style completely unlike that of the earthly calligraphers. During the séances she played the lute, and sang: voice and music were of the most taking charm. She even showed herself once, but only down to the waist, the lower part of her body being hidden by a sort of cloud. These visits came to an end with the girl's marriage.

Another legend of modern origin speaks of three goddesses, three sisters who watch together over the latrine bucket of the house; it is fairly widespread in certain regions, having been popularized by the *Tale of the Investiture of the Gods* (*Fêng shên yen i*); it sprang from a false interpretation of the title K eng-san-ku, which was taken to mean "the Three Ladies of the Privy." Other ancient legends made her a daughter of the mythical Emperor Ti K'u, or even that emperor in person; but they did not prevail and are long forgotten, if they ever even got beyond certain circles of spiritualist literati of the fifth and sixth centuries. To-day this deity is always female; she is in no way a God of the Place; furthermore, she does not preside over the little latrine pavilion, but strictly over the actual pan itself.

The God of Riches (Ts'ai-shên). The God of Riches (Ts'ai-shên) has in our time a considerable importance in popular religion. Every family has at least a label bearing the two characters of his name, Ts'ai-shên, pasted on the door of the principal room in the house; the rich have his image or even his statue. On the anniversary of his birth, the sixteenth day of the third month, he is offered a cock, with the blood of which the threshold of the door is smeared; furthermore many families offer him a meal on the 2nd and the 16th of each month. Sometimes two Gods of Riches are distinguished, the Civil God and the Military God, who both figure side by side in the same rint. Pictures of the Cash Tree, the leaves of which are cash and the fruit ingots, with children at its foot picking up what falls from the tree and heaping it away in sacks, or of the Jewel Casket, which is never exhausted and in which the ingots are replenished as they are taken away, or else simply characters denoting Riches, are also frequently hung up or pasted up in the house.

Fig. 30. THE GOD OF RICHES

The God of Riches is sufficiently important for the *tao-shï* to have made him president over one of the celestial departments, the Ministry of Riches, with a whole staff of officials: the Heaven-honoured One who Discovers Treasures, Chao-pao t'ien-tsun; the Heaven-honoured One who Brings Treasures, Na-chên t'ien-tsun; the Envoy who Discovers Treasures, Chao-pao shï-chê; the Immortal One of Commercial Profits, Li-shï sien-kuan. There is also the God of Riches who Increases Happiness, Tsêng-fu ts'ai-shên, who sometimes, as in Kiangsu, is a distinct god, and sometimes, as in Pekin, is confused with the God of Riches. Unlike most of the secondary gods, who clutter up the celestial ministries of the Taoists, and whose names usually do not go beyond the pages of books nor outside the walls of certain temples, these personages are well known to everybody; it is only that the popular religion hesitates over their respective ranks, and in different localities one or other of them is more especially worshipped and given, along with their titles, personal names and even varying titles. At Pekin the principal one is the God of Riches who Increases Happiness; he has been identified, following the *Tale of the Investiture of the Gods*, with the sage Pi-kan, whom his relative the tyrant Shou-sin, the last Emperor of the Yin dynasty, had, according to the legend, put to death to examine his heart in order to find out whether the heart of a sage is indeed pierced with seven holes. He is represented

FIG. 31. THE GOD OF RICHES WHO INCREASES HAPPINESS
Popular print.

as followed by a servitor, He who Gathers Treasures and Goes to Find Riches, Tsü-pao chao-ts'ai, as well as by Huo and Ho. Beside him there is also the Generalissimo Chao of the Dark (or Northern) Terrace, Hüan-t'an Chao yüan-shuai. In Szechwan it is this same Chao, and not Pi-kan, who is the God of Riches who Increases Happiness, and he is looked upon as the military God of Riches, while the civil god is Kuo Tsï-i, a general of the T'ang epoch, who is elsewhere generally made the God of Happiness, Fu-shên, and not the God of Riches. In

Fig. 32. The God who Increases Riches

Fig. 33. The God of Riches, God of the Place

Kiangsu Chao receives the title of Bodhisattva of the Dark Terrace, Hüan-t'an p'u-sa, and he is made the civil God of Riches, while the military god is the Emperor Kuan; and again it is the Bodhisattva of the Dark Terrace who is the principal God of Riches, and the God of Riches who Increases Happiness is represented as a young man who follows him and serves him (Fig. 32). In Fukien the most widely spread title is that of the Blessed God of Riches Fu-tê ts'ai-shên. Elsewhere is found that of God of Riches of the Five Ways, Wu-lu fu-shên, of which various explanations are given. The legends concerning these personages vary as much as do their titles; they are of no great interest. In some regions the god who takes his title from the Dark Terrace (whether he is called Bodhisattva in Buddhist fashion or Generalissimo in Taoist fashion) is regarded as having been a Muslim; accordingly people carefully refrain from offering him pig's flesh and offer him beef instead. This belief, which is found pretty well everywhere, at Pekin, in Kiangsu, in Szechwan, has brought him the surname of the Muslim God of Riches.

The Ancestors. Besides these very varied deities every family has its recognized protectors in the person of its Ancestors, who are the objects of a regular cult. They are represented in each case by a wooden tablet on which are inscribed the words "Seat of the soul of . . ." with the name of the dead and his titles if he had any; there is often added, right and left, in small characters, the dates of birth and death. The tablets

Fig. 34. THE TABLETS OF THE EMPERORS IN THE TEMPLE OF THE ANCIENT DYNASTIES AT PEKIN

are arranged in a little shrine called the funeral Temple-tabernacle, *ts'i-t'ang*, and set at the right of the Family Tabernacle; in front of it there is placed a little perfume-burner between two candles, but the candles and the incense-sticks are only lighted for ceremonies. All Chinese families (except Christian or Muslim families) have their tabernacle of tablets and pay worship to their Ancestors: it is one of the duties laid down by filial piety. The Emperor used to set the example; in the palace there was the temple of Ancestors, called the Great Temple, *t'ai-miao*, to which at fixed seasons he used to go in order to observe ceremonies in their honour; besides, he paid similar worship to the ancient emperors, the founders and good sovereigns of bygone dynasties, whose tablets were preserved in a special temple (Fig. 34).

From the ritual point of view there are four collective ceremonies, one in each season of the year; but this rule was no longer very strictly observed, except in the imperial cult and sporadically in lettered families of especial orthodoxy. Among the people the four seasonal feasts were almost everywhere swamped in the crowd of regular and occasional small feasts throughout the year. Ordinarily a little collective ceremony is held twice a month before the Tabernacle of the Ancestors, on the day of the new moon and the day of the full moon—that is to say, on the 1st and the 15th of the Chinese month—when the father of the family contents himself with lighting two candles and some incense-sticks after prostrating himself. But besides this there are more serious offerings at each feast; their number and importance vary according to the families, each of which has its own particular customs. A wealthy family of the sub-prefecture of K'un-shan (Kiangsu) with which I was in touch for some time a dozen years ago, regularly offered a piece of cake on New Year's Day for the departure and the return of the God of the Hearth (twelfth month and first month); apricots for the feast of the cleaning of the tombs, *ts'ing-ming* (the second month); medlars and plums for the fifth day of the fifth month, and haricots verts for the summer solstice; new rice for the seventh month, on the feast of Ch'êng-huang; a moon cake at the feast of mid-autumn (the eighth month); a bouquet of chrysanthemums for the ninth day of the ninth month; a crab for the tenth of the tenth month; and blood oranges for the winter solstice (the eleventh month); and furthermore every marriage and every birth was announced to the Ancestors by an oblation. The anniversaries of the birth and the death of each of the last three ancestors were marked by the presenting of a complete meal to the particular ancestor, whose tablet was taken for the occasion from the Tabernacle and placed on the table of offerings. This meal was laid out in ceremonial order; incense-sticks and wax candles were lit, the father of the family made prostration; when the candles were burned out he prostrated himself again, with the whole family, after which the tablet was removed and they ate the meal. In these cases they are careful to give the deceased the dishes they liked in their lifetime: to a grandmother who had taken a vow of fasting they presented only Lenten fare; for an opium-smoking ancestor the pipe and lighted lamps were set on the table, and so forth.

The Family Tabernacle (Kia-T'ang). All families have a little tabernacle in which they place the statuettes, or the images, or the tablets, of certain family divinities, and which is called the Family Tabernacle (*kia-t'ang*). But the custom varies according to localities and individuals. Practically everywhere, however, on the middle of the back is stuck a paper band with an inscription, which serves as a tablet in honour of Heaven, of the Emperor, and the Ancient Masters. One of the most usual formulas is "Seat of the Spirits of Heaven, of Earth, of the Sovereign, of Relations, of the Masters," but still others are used. In Szechwan it occupies the centre of the Tabernacle; to left and right are the four tablets of the Ancestors, the three personal tablets of the latest three Ancestors—father, grandfather, great-grandfather—and the collective tablet dedicated to the first Ancestor of the family and to the five generations before the great-grandfather; below, in front of the tablet of Heaven, is the God of the Place; the perfume-burner, filled with the ashes of the incense-sticks burned in it, must never be emptied. In Fukien it is a little statuette of Kuan-yin that occupies the place of honour, with the tablets of the God of the Hearth and the God of Riches (who is confused with the God of the Place) to its right and its left; in front and in the middle is a statuette or a tablet of K'o Shêng-wêng, a divinity

Fig. 35. GENERAL SNORTER (HÊNG-TSIANG)
In the Kiai-t'ai sï at Pekin.

peculiar to the province of Fukien. In Kiangsu Kuan-yin most frequently occupies the place of honour, but the peasants often enough replace her by the Fierce General, that their fields may be protected against the insects, and in this province hardly any except poor families install the tablets of the Ancestors as well: these usually have a shrine to themselves. A little perfume-burner, or a bowl, filled with ashes to stand the incense-sticks in, with two red wax candles that are only lighted for ceremonies, is placed in front of the Family Tabernacle.

The Gods of the Doors, the God of the Place, etc., in Buddhist Temples

The Buddhist temples, like public buildings and private houses, have gods that guard their entrance-doors, a God of the Place to protect the halls and the monks, a God of the Hearth in the kitchen, a God of the Latrines, etc. But for these deities they have gods peculiar to themselves, Buddhist personages different from the gods of lay houses, and they give them separate names and titles: the Gods of the Doors are the Snorter and the Puffer; the God of the Place bears the title of the God of the Saṅghārāma—*i.e.*, of the monastery—K'ie-lan shên; the God of the Hearth and the God of the Privies themselves are separate Buddhist deities; lastly there are the protecting gods of the four points of the compass, the four kings, and a god who, without being a God of the Doors, is in charge of the entrance, etc. To understand what all these personages do it is essential to have an idea of the general plan of a Buddhist monastery.

We know how they are arranged as a rule in China. The plan is borrowed from that of the palace or from the houses of the nobles, and has no relation to that of the temples of India and Central Asia. Usually there are three blocks of buildings separated by courts. At the entrance is the front hall, generally a simple pavilion with four great statues of the Four Celestial Kings, the guardians of the four points of the compass; along the walls, and in the middle, back to back, Maitreya, the future Buddha, with his great paunch (Ta-pao Mi-lo) and his cheerful face turned to the entrance, and Wei-t'o the porter, knotty cudgel in hand, facing the court. At the far side of the courtyard is the Great Hall, divided by a wall into two unequal parts. In the front part, which is the larger, and against the dividing wall, is an altar with colossal statues, most frequently three in number, accompanied by smaller ones, facing the entrance, and in front of the altar are tables laden with perfume-burners, offerings of flowers, etc. The arrangement and the selection of the personages of the altar varies according to the temples; one of the most frequent places Amitābha in the middle, between Ṣākyamuni and Bhaishajyaguru (Yo-shï-wang), each accompanied by two disciples (Fig. 36), and to right and left of the altar the two Bodhisattvas Mañjuṣrī (Wên-shu) and Samantabhadra (P'u-hien); or it is Ṣākyamuni who occupies the central position, between Amitābha and Vairochana. Again, there is a single Buddha between two Bodhisattvas: Amitābha between Avalokiteṣvara (Kuan-yin) and Mahāsthāmaprāpta (Ta-shï-chê), or Ṣākyamuni between Mañjuṣrī and Samantabhadra. In the back part there is another altar, against the wall, with other statues, usually a Bodhisattva; this is often Kuan-yin with the thousand arms, or any other form of Kuan-yin, or else Mañjuṣrī, or Maitreya, etc. Sometimes there is a group of Bodhisattvas answering to the Buddhas of the front part. And all round the hall are statues ranged along the wall, the eighteen Arhats and the twenty-four *devas*, for example, or a different series, separate niches for different shapes of Kuan-yin, or Ti-tsang, or other Bodhisattvas, as well as little niches containing the God of the Place, etc. Lastly the back hall is often divided into several chapels; in the centre the chapel of a Buddha or a Bodhisattva, and to right and left the chapel containing the funeral tablet of the founder of the temple, the

Fig. 36. Buddhist Triad: Ṣākyamuni between Amitābha on his Right and Bhaishajyaguru on his Left

chapel of Meditation, or that of the Expounding of the Books, according to the sect, and others also. Behind and around these main buildings are the cells of the monks, with the refectory and the kitchens, the guest-chambers, and special chapels of various kinds.

The Great Hall is where the devout especially go to pray; there they find almost all the beings to whom they wish to address themselves. The number of these beings is not, indeed, very large: there are practically only four popular Bodhisattvas in China out of all the crowd mentioned in the books. These are Kuan-yin (Avalokiteṣvara), Wên-shu (Mañjuṣrī), P'u-hien (Samantabhadra), and Ti-tsang (Kshitigarbha). The last named is easily distinguished by the fact that he is generally clad as a bonze; Wên-shu and P'u-hien are recognized by the lion and the elephant on which they are respectively seated; and Kuan-yin is characterized by the fact that in almost all his shapes he wears in his head-dress a tiny statue of Amitābha. To these four great ones, always ready to come to the assistance of whosoever invokes them, popular piety has assigned four places of residence in the four corners of China, thus forcing Buddhism to enter within a purely Chinese frame: Kuan-yin lives in the East, in the island of P'u-t'o (Chekiang), the name of which is an abbreviated transcript of the Sanskrit name of his dwelling-place, Potalaka; Wên-shu is in the North, on the Wu-t'ai-shan (Shansi); P'u-hien in the West, on the O-mei shan (Szechwan), and Ti-tsang in the South, on the Kiu-hua shan (Anhwei), and there are famous great pilgrimages to these places, which are called the Four Mountains of Great Renown.

But it is in the first building that the protector gods are assembled. Two personages

Fig. 37. Vaisramana and Virūpāksha

commonly called the two generals Snorter and Puffer, Hêng Ha êr tsiang, are often painted on the doors, or sometimes their statues are to right and left of the entrance; they are fierce of aspect, their mouths wide open, and each carries a cudgel in his hand. These are the ancient door-wardens of the Hindu Buddhist temples; according to one of the chapters on "Divers Matters" of one of the *Vinaya* in their Chinese translation, the Buddha himself had indicated the way they should be represented to Anāthapindada when the latter, after making the gift of his garden, the Jetavana, to the community, conceived the idea that it was not right not to adorn it with paintings, and went to ask the Buddha for advice. "O Excellent One," was the reply, "on the two sides of the door there should be painted two *yakshas* holding a club!" Here, as for the Gods of the Doors of private houses, a single personage has been duplicated, the *yaksha* Guhyaka, mentioned in other canonical texts, who is also called the Strong One who holds in his hand the thunderbolt,

Vajrapāṇibalin, Kin-kang-li-shï; about the era of the T'ang the Chinese, dividing the name into two parts, had made Kin-kang (Vajra) the name of the *yaksha* with the open mouth and Li-shï (Balin) that of the *yaksha* with the shut mouth. It was said that since the mouth is the "door of the face," in this way it was symbolically indicated that his protection was the same whether the door was open or shut. The present-day names, which are in no respect Buddhist, are popular in origin; they were adopted by the *Tale of the Investiture of the Gods*, which contributed to spread them with the legend it attributes to them, which appears to have been simply invented by the author. They

Fig. 38. Virūdhaka and Dhṛitarāshṭra

were, he relates, two heroes fighting with King Shou of the Yin dynasty against the King of Chou: the first had the power of emitting from his nostrils two jets of white light that sucked up men and slew them, and the second had the power of blowing from his mouth a yellow deadly gas; after their death they were given the task of guarding the doors of the temples.

But in the course of the last few centuries they have seen themselves gradually replaced in their function by the Four Celestial Kings, T'ien-wang. These are four well-known Buddhist gods: Vaiṣramaṇa for the North, holding a banner in his right hand and in his left a *stūpa*; Dhṛitarāshṭra for the East, carrying a species of guitar; Virūdhaka for the South, trampling a demon under his feet, and Virūpāksha for the West, holding in his left hand a jewel in the form of a reliquary and a serpent in his right (Figs. 37 and 38). The wholly Chinese custom of placing them at the entrance of temples as guardians hardly seems to go back further than Ming times; before that they were arranged at the four points of the compass round a *stūpa*, or else they surrounded a group of statues, but no one thought of collecting them in this way in the first building. To-day this arrangement is almost universal, and the ancient guardians have nearly everywhere had to give way to them; but their name Kin-kang-li-shï (Vajrabalin) has to some extent remained attached to the function, and the Four Celestial Kings are often called by the title of the Four (Bearers) of the Thunderbolt, Sï Kin-kang. The Taoists have borrowed these colossal figures, giving them the purely Chinese names of Li, Ma, Chao, and Wên, and they place them sometimes at the entrance to their temples in a position similar to that in the Buddhist temples. As for the popular religion, it has adopted one of them, Vaiṣramaṇa, under his Taoist name of Li; this is Li Tower-bearer, Li T'o-t'a. But the group of four divinities would be completely forgotten if once again the *Tale of the Investiture of the Gods* had not saved it by adopting it in a travestied form. They are the four Mo-li brothers (Māra, but the word is taken as a family name, and not as meaning demon), supporters of the Shang, who were vanquished and slain after various mighty exploits. The eldest, Mo-li Ts'ing, was armed with a sabre that produced devastating whirlwinds and waterspouts. The second, Mo-li Hung, carried a closed parasol; when he opened it the sun and moon were hidden, and the earth was plunged in darkness, and the rain came down. The third, Mo-li Hai, had a guitar whose sounds, in exact accord with the elements, ruled the winds. (We know that in Chinese philosophy the Five Sounds, the Five Savours, the Five Cardinal Points, etc., are brought into relation with the Five Elements, so that to act upon one group reacts upon the others also.) Lastly, the fourth, Mo-li Shou, carried a bag containing the monster Striped Marten, *hua-hu-tiao*, which when let loose devoured men. After their death and the final victory of the King of Chou they received the divine offices of protectors of the pagodas and regulators of wind and rain. It seems that the author of the *Tale of the Investiture of the Gods* drew from the folklore of his own time these popular interpretations of the attributes of the Four Kings: we find the guitar of Dhṛitarāshṭra unchanged in the hands of Mo-li Hai, and Mo-li Hung's parasol seems to me a bad and ignorant interpretation of Vaiṣramaṇa's furled standard; but the other two are

Fig. 39. WEI-T'O
Fa-yüan sï, at Pekin.

not so easy to determine. The author's part consisted less in the invention of the personages themselves than in the fantastic use he made of them in his account of the war between the Shang and the Chou.

Wei-t'o, who also serves as a guardian of the entrance, is shown as a young man clad in the armour of a general, with a helmet on his head, standing with both hands leaning on a knotty club (Fig. 39). He is a god of lesser importance, the chief of the thirty-two celestial generals who are subordinate to the Four Kings; but among the people he is often given the title of Bodhisattva, and the bonzes have long since approved this custom by making him a real Bodhisattva, though not as yet far advanced upon the Way, destined in the end to become the Buddha Lou-chï (Ruchika), the last of the thousand Buddhas of our world-period (*kalpa*), which identified him with the *yaksha* Vajrapāṇi, of whom this prediction was made. The history of this divinity is besides marked with a whole series of misadventures. His very name is the result of a mistake, the confounding of two Chinese characters that are alike in shape, but different in sound; in reality it is an incorrect transcript of Skanda. On the other hand, in the reveries of a seventh-century monk, who, being persecuted with hallucinations, in the last year of his life heard numerous deities who without displaying themselves came to visit and converse with him, he received, by a verbal play on the first character of his name, a purely Chinese family name, and became the Celestial General Wei.

Fig. 40. Maitreya of the Big Belly playing with the Arhats, represented as Children
Fa-yüan sï, at Pekin.

Back to back with his is placed the statue of Mi-lo (Maitreya), the next Buddha, in the shape known as Maitreya of the big belly (Figs. 40 and 41); he is seated or rather 'hunkered,' his right knee up, and the hand leaning on it holding a rosary, the face laughing, with wide-open mouth. This is the shape normally given him, at any rate since the Mongol period, when he accompanies representations of the Sixteen or Eighteen Arhats. The latter, who must await his coming to enter into Nirvāna, sport with him in the Tushita heaven, where he dwells at present, as all the Buddhas of all times have always done before their last existence. But it is not known why nor when this particularly ugly type was chosen to greet visitors at the entrance of Buddhist temples.

The God of the Place, *k'ie-lan shên*, or, in more honorific style, *k'ie-lan p'u-sa* (*k'ie-lan* is the abbreviated transcript of the Sanskrit word *saṅghārāma*, which means 'monastery'), often has a chapel to himself (usually in one of the secondary buildings of the first court, on the right of the entrance, but there is no fixed rule), or, at other times, he has to be content with a niche in the Anterior Hall, or in the Principal Hall, or elsewhere. In the Kuo-ts'ing temple at T'ien-t'ai shan (Chekiang) he has a great chapel of his own in which sick pilgrims spend the night, so that he may indicate to them in a dream the proper remedy. This god is mostly nameless; in certain districts he is declared to be Kuan Yü, the general who helped in founding the Shu Han dynasty in the third century, and who has become elsewhere, under the title of Military Emperor, one of the most powerful gods of the official religion and the popular religion. It is not, on the other hand, uncommon to see in the various halls niches of the God of the Place, the laic *t'u-ti*, independent of and distinct from those of the *k'ie-lan shên*.

Fig. 41. Maitreya of the Big Belly

All parts of the temple have their special god besides. The god who presides over the kitchen is Wei-t'o, the same who is already one of the guardians of the entrance. In the hall of ablutions is placed the image of the arhat Bhadra, one of the Sixteen Arhats who in this world await the coming of Maitreya. The monasteries of India already had to have each of their buildings protected by numerous divinities, but the Chinese have added still more, no doubt in imitation of private houses.

GODS OF PROFESSIONS, TRADES, CORPORATIONS, ETC.

Every profession has its protecting divinity, to whom its members pay worship: he is often the inventor of the craft, or the first who adopted the profession. This is a very ancient custom. In days of antiquity the blind musicians who sang and played on instruments in religious ceremonies reverenced the Blind Ancient, the ancestor of their profession, and K'uei, the one-legged animal of whose skin the Yellow Emperor had made the first drum.

The Civilian Mandarins. Officials have their gods, which are not the same for civilian and for military officials. The first have as their patron mainly the God of Literature, Wên-ch'ang ti-kün, or simply the Emperor of Literature, Wên-ti, and his two attendants, the constellation K'uei-sing and Red Coat, Chu-i; they also pay reverence to

Confucius, but he cannot absolutely be considered as an ordinary patron of a craft (Fig. 42).

Wên-Ch'ang and his Attendants. Wên-ch'ang is a constellation of six stars close to the Great Bear: when it is bright, their literature is prosperous. Its god came down, they say, several times among men, and his seventeen successive lives are recounted in detail in special works that are widely circulated, the *Biography of the Emperor of Literature* (*Wên-ti-pên chuan*) and the *Book of the Transformations of the Emperor of Literature* (*Wên-ti hua shu*). It was after the ninth of his existences, when he had been a certain Chang Ya, that he was charged by the Jade Emperor with keeping the registers of the

Fig. 42. The Great Emperor of Literature, Wên-ch'ang ti-kün, between K'uei-sing and Red Coat

titles and dignities of men, and distinguishing between good and bad literati, rewarding and advancing the first and punishing the second. It seems that at the beginning of this cult there was a very ancient cult of a local Thunder deity among the barbarian peoples of the north of Szechwan. The centre of this was at Tsï-t'ung, a locality the name of which was long borne by the god. There upon the mountain Ts'i-k'ü, until the centuries following the Christian era, there was a temple built of wooden boards to which the people of the country went every year to offer to the Thunder-god ten weavers' shuttles, which vanished and were supposed to be carried off by him. Indeed, this temple still exists, but built in the ordinary fashion: it is called the Temple of Supernatural Succour, Ling-ying miao. The god had appeared, so the story went (and the legend has taken its place in the series of the existences of Wên-ch'ang), in the shape of a serpent in order to frighten the daughter of the Count of Ts'in, who had been sent to the land of Shu (the old name of Szechwan) to marry its prince and pave the way for the conquest of the country, and he had crushed her by causing the mountain to fall on her and her companions. Protector of the region, he had a temple in the capital of the province, Ch'êng-tu, and an inscription dating from the end of the second century of our era relates how the temple of the god of Tsï-t'ung, destroyed with several others by a fire, was restored in A.D. 194 by order of the governor. The T'ang Emperor Hüan-tsung went to Tsï-t'ung when the revolt of An Lu-shan forced him to flee from his capital Ch'ang-an (to-day Si-an fu, Shensi), and take refuge in Ch'êng-tu (A.D. 756): he invested the god with the title of Minister of the Left. About a century later another emperor of the same dynasty was again obliged to flee to Szechwan before another revolt, that of Huang Ch'ao, and on his visit he gave the god of Tsï-t'ung the title of king. It was as local protector again that he appeared in A.D. 1000 on the wall of Ch'êng-tu, the refuge of the rebel Wang Kün, to announce that the city would be taken on the 20th of the month by the Imperial forces. How did this local god of Szechwan come to be confused with the god of the constellation Wên-ch'ang who presides over literature? We only know that this confusion was officially admitted by the Emperor Jên-tsung of the Yüan dynasty when he raised the god to the rank of Benevolent Emperor in charge of official salaries of the constellation Wên-ch'ang which supports the primordial transformation, *Fu-yüan k'ai-hua Wên-ch'ang sï lu-hung ti-kün.*

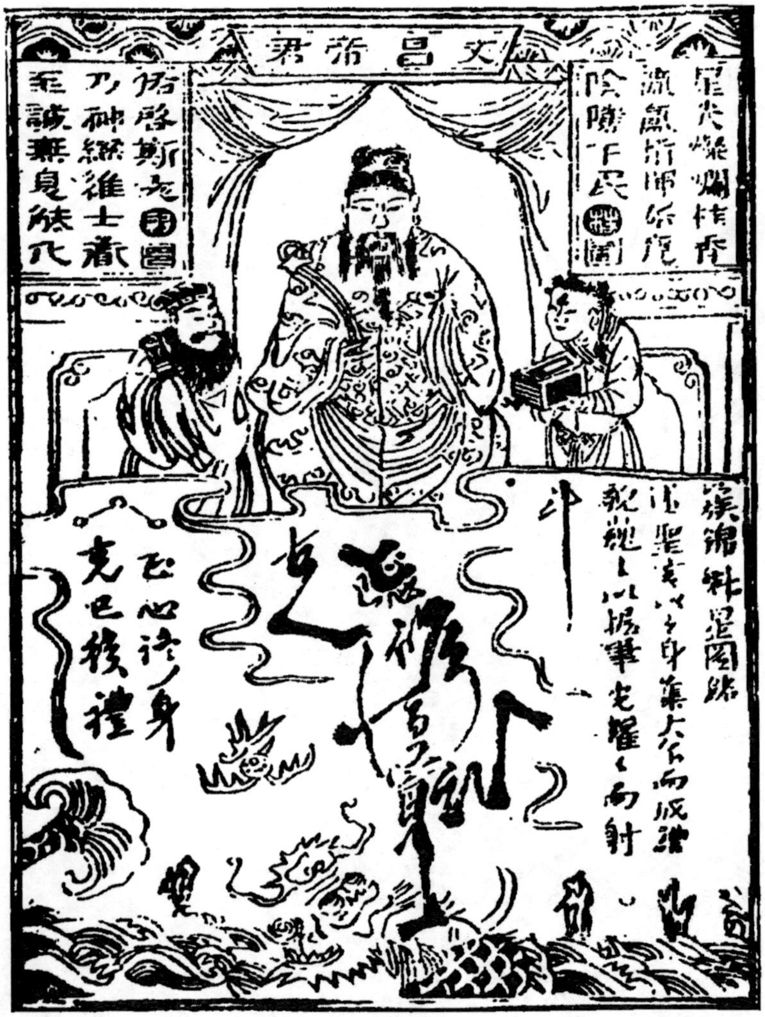

Fig. 43. THE GREAT EMPEROR OF LITERATURE WITH HIS ATTENDANTS
Popular print.

Most lettered families have his tablet, or less often his image or his statue, and pay him worship. He is represented generally in mandarin costume, holding a sceptre (*ju-i*), and with a male and a female servant behind him (Fig. 43). To his left and right are his assistants, K'uei-sing and Red Coat. K'uei-sing is the god of the four stars that make the chariot of the Great Bear. He is represented in a very remarkable posture, standing on his right leg, the left leg raised up behind, brandishing a brush in his right hand over his head, and holding an official seal in his left hand thrust out in front, and with a hideous face.

Fig. 44. K'uei-sing on the Ao Fish

The top of his body is usually naked, and his only clothing is a loincloth and a scarf floating loosely over his shoulders; but sometimes also he wears a vest. Most often he is standing on a fish. It is told that in his lifetime he was so ugly that after his success in his doctorate the Emperor, setting eyes on him, refused him the audience he was in the habit of granting to the first of the year's candidates. In despair he tried to throw himself into the sea, but a huge *ao* fish, having received him on its head, brought him up to the surface and saved him from drowning. Sometimes the fish has a human head; at other times the god is placed astride on its back; but even then the traditional posture is given to his legs and arms. In the print reproduced in Fig. 46 his constellation is shown above his head. He is the distributor of literary grades. He was invoked for success in examinations, and when a young man passed he was given an image or a tablet of the god. One of the most popular ways of representing him is to draw the character that forms his name in such a way as roughly to represent the pose of the god, one arm and one leg lifted, and his fish underneath (Figs. 45 and 43, the lower part). As for Red Coat, Chu-i, he is given the aspect of an old man with a long beard, clad in a red robe; he is the protector of badly prepared candidates, who makes them succeed by pure luck.

FIG. 45. K'UEI-SING IN THE FORM OF A REBUS

It is especially for help in examinations that all these gods, and Wên-ch'ang in especial, are prayed to. In an eighteenth-century tale, which has been translated by Father Wieger, a candidate sees in a dream the Emperor of Literature seated on his throne in his temple supervising the recasting of a certain number of compositions, which, having been placed in crucibles, come out all brilliant; he recognizes his own among them, completely changed by the operation, and learns it by heart. Next day the building where the compositions had been stored is burned down, and the examination has to be begun again: the candidate then produces the composition he had seen in his dream, and passes.

Being God of Literature, it was natural that Wên-ch'ang should write a great deal: his works, revealed by the medium of the divining brush in spiritist séances, are now beyond counting, and considerable collections of them have been put together. One of the most popular is *The Lamp in the Dark Room*, a recent little treatise on all kinds of moral and religious themes (infanticide, filial piety, respect toward Heaven, etc.), which begins with the story of his successive lives related by himself in detail.

Confucius. Then there are few literati who have not a tablet of Confucius, more rarely an image or a statuette: they place these not in the Great Hall where the tablets of the masters and the images of the Gods of Good Fortune are, but in the study or the library, and there they worship them in private. When it is a statuette, he is usually represented seated, in imperial costume (Fig. 47), for he is the "king without a throne," or else simply in the dress of an erudite. One of the most popular images claims to be a reproduction of a picture by the celebrated painter Wu Tao-tsï (eighth century of our era). The original has long since disappeared, but there exists a certain number of stelae that claim to have a reproduction engraved on stone; prints of it are very common. There are also other celebrated portraits that have been similarly engraved on stone, prints of which are very popular.

Fig. 46. K'uei-sing appears to an Examiner in order to destroy the Papers of an Unworthy Candidate

Popular print.

On the other hand, the official religion imposes the public worship of Confucius on all officials. In all the capitals of administrative districts, from those of provinces down to those of the sub-prefectures, there is a temple of Confucius, K'ung-tsï miao, or, more correctly speaking, a temple of literature, Wên-miao, arranged like a princely house with its three buildings, with courts in front of each. Confucius, as everybody knows, is never represented in the temples by a statue, but by a funeral tablet, except in the family temple situated near his tomb in K'ü-fou (Shantung); this was the order of the founder of the Ming dynasty in A.D. 1382.

The principal hall, Ta-ch'êng tien, is at the back of the second court; the tablet of Confucius, the Model and Example for the Ten Thousand Generations, Wan shï shï piao, occupies the place of honour, behind the central altar, facing south, having to the right and the left, and also facing south, those of the Four Saints, Sï-hien, his favourite disciple Yen-tsï and his grandson Tsï-sï on one side, and on the other his two disciples Tsêng-tsï and Mencius, then to right and left, on secondary altars and facing east and west respectively, the Ten Scholars, Shï Chê, who are also ten of his disciples; two large lateral buildings on each side of the court each contain the tablets of seventy-two celebrated disciples of all the ages, from the beginning down to our own day, the seventy-two Sages of the East Wing and the seventy-two Sages of the West Wing. And, lastly, the ancestors of Confucius have their tablets behind in the third building. Quite near the Temple of Confucius, in the capital, is the old Imperial College, Kuo-tsï kien, with its round pond, its pavilions for the doctorate examinations, its classics engraved on stone, etc. It was an almost prehistoric survival in modern China, the old house of initiation for young men of noble birth before their admission into the society of adults. The great feasts are those of mid-spring and mid-autumn; they take place in the second month and the eighth, on the first day marked by the character *ting* in the cycle of sixty days. The head of the administrative district, governor, prefect, or subprefect, presides in person over the ceremony, or delegates somebody to preside in his stead; and all the civilian and military officials present in the headquarters of the administration must be there in person; there are besides many students, and to them are entrusted certain secondary duties in the ceremony. All who take part must prepare for it by a two days' fast. Offerings are presented to Confucius first of all, then to his four assistants, next to the Ten Scholars, whose tablets are in the principal hall of the temple, and lastly to the two companies of seventy-two disciples who have their tablets in the right and left wings; the sacrifice is accompanied with music and civilian dances only. Besides these two great feasts little offerings are made twice a month, at new and full moon: fruits and vegetables on the first and incense on the second day. In the capital it was the Emperor himself, or at least an Imperial delegate, who presided over the spring and autumn sacrifices. The Republic has increased still more, if possible, the honours paid to Confucius, and the President, as of old the Emperor, continues to offer him the prescribed and ritual sacrifices either in person or by a delegate. The ceremony was in no way different from those in the provinces, except perhaps in solemnity.

Fig. 47. Confucius wearing the Imperial Bonnet

This is not the place to set down a detailed biography of Confucius; the oldest work in which it is found, the *Historical Memoirs*, composed by Sï-ma Ts'ien about the end of the second or the beginning of the first century before our era, already gives nothing but a somewhat brief legend; and the fact that it is devoid of any fantastic elements is not enough to guarantee its authenticity. The most current modern work is a kind of illustrated biography, *The Pictures of the Vestiges of the Holy One*; the original version seems to go back to the Mongol period, but popular taste has been responsible for successive versions, each replacing the older by something newer and more up to date, while the preceding ones were forgotten. On page 320 will be found a scene drawn from a series we owe to the great painter of the beginning of the fourteenth century,

Fig. 48. CONFUCIUS
From a print.

Wang Chên-p'êng; to-day the most widely circulated are wood engravings reproducing the hundred and twelve stones of the Temple of Confucius in K'ü-fou (Shantung), which were engraved in 1592. I shall content myself with a brief summary of the traditional legend.

According to this, Confucius was born in 551 B.C., and died in 479 B.C.; and he must, in fact, have lived about that time, at the end of the sixth century and the beginning of the fifth; but the exact dates are far from being certain. He descended, we are told, from the ancient royal family of the Yin, which had preceded the Chou family on the throne of China; his father had married at an advanced age, and died not long after his birth, so that it was his mother who brought him up at K'ü-fou, the capital of the principality of Lu (in the south-west of Shantung), which was his native place. It is told that as a child his chief amusement was to imitate the ritual ceremonies with his companions as well as he could. Growing up, he entered the service of the Prince of Lu, and held various offices at his court; he became Director of Public Works in 503, and of the Department of Justice in 501. About this time, accompanying his sovereign to an interview he had at Kia-ku with the Prince of Ts'i, his neighbour in the north, he saved him by making him dismiss, or even, according to some accounts, execute, under pretext of conforming strictly to the rules and rites of interviews between princes, certain armed dwarfs and dancers who had been charged to make an attempt on his life. But some years after this the people of Ts'i, fearing that the country of Lu, under the good government of Confucius, might become too powerful, sent the prince a gift of a troupe of singing girls, who gradually diverted him from his duties toward the State, so much so that in the end Confucius retired. He determined to leave his country, and set out to travel through the Empire, seeking among the little feudal states that then divided the territory between them a wise prince who might take him for his minister and allow him to put into practice the good government of the holy kings of antiquity. In the course of his pilgrimage he met with a host of adventures, some of which are particularly famous. Once as he was passing through K'uang, on his way from the country of Wei to the country of Ch'ên, the people took him for Yang Ho, the steward of the greatest family of Lu, by whom they had been ill-treated not long before, and kept him in close durance for five days, until one of the disciples who accompanied him succeeded in calming them. During the whole of the time Confucius remained tranquilly seated, playing the lute, unmoved by the threats of the populace.

Another time, as he was going through the duchy of Sung, the minister Huan-t'ui sent men to cut down the tree under which he was resting with his disciples; on this occasion again he refused to allow himself to be afraid. "Heaven wrought the virtue that is in me," he said. "What can Huan-t'ui do to me?"

There is also attributed to him a journey to the royal capital (to-day Ho-an fu), where he had a still famous interview with Lao-tsï, at that time keeper of the archives. After twelve years passed in this fashion, feeling the approach of old age, he went back to his own country and set up in the capital a school in which he taught the doctrine and wisdom of the ancients. It was at this time that he chose the pieces of verse and prose with which he made two anthologies—the *Book of Odes* (*Shï king*) and the *Book of Documents* (*Shu king*)—composed his chronicle of the country of Lu, the *Springtimes and Autumns*

(*Ch'un ts'iu*), wrote little philosophic treatises on a manual of divination, the *Book of Changes* (*Yi king*)—in short, all the literary works attributed to him by ancient tradition, in spite of all likelihood, as it seemed impossible to be reconciled to the fact that the Master who is the Model and the Example of the Ten Thousand Generations left not a single line behind him. In 481 a prodigy warned him of his approaching death—a unicorn appeared and was killed by peasants. He died, in fact, two years after, and was buried near K'ü-fou.

Sufficiently celebrated from the fourth century before our era to be frequently the subject of attacks of every kind, it was nevertheless only from the Han period that Confucius took supreme rank among the masters of thought in China, after the turmoils of the third century before our era, by ruining all the rival schools of philosophy, had allowed only the Confucian and the Taoist schools to survive, for the latter, being altogether speculative, had not the practical interest of the other. Since that time his glory has steadily increased from century to century. His cult went back, it is said, to the actual morrow of his death. His family had made him a funeral temple in which offerings were made to him on fixed dates and in which his relics were preserved; Sï-ma Ts'ien, in the second century B.C., three hundred and fifty years after the Master's death, saw his chariot, his garments, and his ritual utensils. This temple, many times rebuilt, developed gradually and became notable, and to-day is the most important and the wealthiest of the temples of Confucius, and is the only one that has kept the ancient custom of having statues of the Holy One and his disciples, while in all the official temples of the capital and the provinces the statues have been compulsorily replaced by simple funeral tablets. This temple remained for long the only one, and it was on their passing through K'ü-fou that some of the Emperors of the Western Han dynasty offered sacrifices in it. But in A.D. 58, when schools were established in all the commanderies of the Empire, a chapel of Confucius was set up in them. With Confucius was associated from the very beginning the troop of his seventy-two disciples. In the middle of the third century one of the Emperors of the Wei dynasty (the epoch of the Three Kingdoms) detached Yen-tsï from the groups of the seventy-two to associate him more closely with Confucius, thus beginning those changes in the number and the position of the disciples which ended in the present arrangement of two groups of seventy-two, one to the left, one to the right. Ten scholars *shï-chê*, were set apart in 720, then from this group were taken Tsêng-tsï and Tsï-sï, who were given place beside Confucius and Yen-tsï in 1267, and Mencius, who was added to them in 1330, the epoch when their ranks and places were finally established, while a series of new disciples replaced them, and the number of the Scholars was brought up again to ten, among whom a modern, the philosopher Chu Hi, who lived in the twelfth century, was introduced for the first time. An edict of A.D. 739 had fixed the list of the seventy-two disciples who had a right to sacrifices in the Temple of Confucius, with their respective ranks. Little by little additions were made, particularly in 1530 and in 1724, especially of literati of the Sung period, Chang Tsai, Ch'êng I, Sï-ma Kuang, Lü Tsu-k'ien, or of the Ming period, like Wang Shou-jên (the philosopher known by his surname of Yang-ming), Huang Tao-chou, or even of still more recent date, like Lu Lung-k'i (1631–92) and T'ang Pin (1627–87). The list, furthermore, is not closed, and in 1919 the President of the Republic, Sü Shï-ch'ang, introduced two new personages into the Temple of Confucius, Yen Yüan and Li Kung, both of whom lived in the seventeenth century.

Like all the gods of the official religion, Confucius climbed up the rungs of the hierarchical ladder one by one: duke in the first year of the Christian era, king in 739, reduced for a time to the rank of duke in 1075, emperor in 1106. He even kept his rank and his title by a special exception made in his favour when the first Ming emperor abolished all the titles of kings, dukes, etc., conferred upon mountains or rivers, Gods of Walls and Moats, or functionaries of the ancient dynasties admitted to the official religion; but this was only for a time, and on December 4, 1530, the Emperor Shï-tsung

Fig. 49. CONFUCIUS IN THE MIDST OF HIS DISCIPLES
From a painting by Ch'ên-'pêng, fourteenth century.

deprived him of it in order to give him simply the title of Perfectly Holy Ancient Master (Chï-shêng Sien-shï), which he has retained until our own day. Most of the other official gods have at various periods received new titles and new ranks; neither Confucius nor the God of the Eastern Peak (his title of Grand Emperor is not official) have had theirs restored to them. It seems that in recent times this has been looked on as the highest honour that could be paid them, placing them on the same level as Heaven, who has no hierarchical title either.

This lack of titles has had the effect of accentuating the distinction the literati make a point of drawing between Confucius and the other gods of the official religion, all of whom are provided with titles of different degrees of elevation; he appears as in some sort of an essence peculiar to himself, and this impression is strengthened by the fact that his temples are the only ones in which there are no statues. This has contributed to give him that place apart which caused his cult to be officially preserved after the death of Yüan Shï-k'ai, when the other official cults (Heaven, Earth, Sun, Seas, Mountains, and Rivers, etc.) were abolished. Are we to go so far as to declare, with certain modern Europeanized Chinese, that he is not really a god? The quarrel seems to me to lie in the words more than in the realities. In Chinese, which has no common general term to denote beings superior to man, the question could not even be posed, for one would be at a loss for a term to use, since it is impossible to apply to him any of the designations of the Buddhas, of the Bodhisattvas, of the Immortals, or of the local gods. But on the other hand it would be equally impossible to describe him as a *kuei* (the soul of a departed person), like the generality of men. He is certainly a being superior to man; the fact that he lived a purely human life has no importance in China, where all the gods have passed through a terrestrial existence. He is a Holy One, *Shêng*, and this expression, whatever its original significance, has become a religious title which is attributed to many others besides Confucius. We must furthermore make a distinction between the honours paid to Confucius by the pupils of the schools, which are an exact copy of those paid to living Masters (salutations, offerings on the 1st and 15th of every month, etc.) and do not appear to have any definitely religious character in the minds of those who take part in them, barely going beyond a simple form of homage to the Master of the Ten Thousand Generations, and the official cult (the old imperial cult), in which he appears veritably as a protector divinity of the State and a dispenser of peace and good government. I do not know what formulas are addressed to him at times of sacrifice by the Presidents of the Republic in these last few years, but up to the end of the Empire the imperial formulas were real prayers asking his aid to govern well, or even, as for example the prayer of the Emperor K'ien-lung in 1751, asking him to grant fullness of goodhap for ever, with an expression borrowed from a sacrificial ode in the *Shï king*. When there was any serious matter in hand the prayer character became still more manifest, as when K'ang-hi, in 1695, after an earthquake that had devastated Chihli, sent to make a special sacrifice and "on behalf of the people to pray for good fortune," or again, in 1697, announcing his previous year's triumph over the Eleuthes and their chief Galdan, when he declared that now the frontier was pacified, and this "thanks to the efficacious aid of the 'Perfectly Holy Ancient Master.'" These are formulas similar to those employed in the sacrifices to Heaven; the deliberate vagueness and generalizing are due in great part to the necessity of employing in these prayers, which are pieces belonging to a definite literary style, nothing but expressions derived from the Classics. In so far as our term 'god' can be applied to the personages of Chinese mythology, it is therefore clear that Confucius was, at least until quite recently, a god (not of private persons, but of the State) to whom prayers were made and from whom 'good fortune' was expected. But we must add that his influence is not religious in its nature. The cult of which he is the object is the least part of it. It is due above all to the fact that his teaching, as it has been fixed by centuries of commentaries, is marvellously adapted to the Chinese mind, that it has always been supple enough to change with that mind, so much so that still to-day, in these days when the "Occidental sciences" are penetrating everywhere, it can without any trouble remain the foundation of Chinese national education.

The Military Mandarins. The military mandarins render a special and peculiar worship to Kuan-ti, and one of the feasts of this god, that of the twenty-fourth day of the sixth month, is reserved for them. On this day they set up an altar with the statue of the god accompanied by his son and his squire, and place two tables right and left, the first holding a bow and arrows, and the second halberds; then in the corners of the hall they set banners on which his titles are inscribed: "The Great Emperor who Seconds Heaven" on one side, and on the other "The Great Emperor who Protects the State." In front of the altar, on either side, are two horses made of red paper. When all is thus prepared a pig is offered to him, and at night the two horses are burned in his honour.

On the other hand, they are called upon to pay him public worship thrice a year, on a set day in the second months of spring and autumn, and on his birthday, the thirteenth of the fifth month; but this worship is not special or confined to them, and the civilian mandarins of the district take equal share in it: the Great Sacrifice is offered, a pig, a sheep, an ox, with a complete meal, wine, and rolls of silk. Less important offerings are presented also twice a month. The official temples of Kuan-ti, temples of the Soldier Holy One Shêng-wu miao, are composed of two blocks of buildings, each with a courtyard in front; as in the temples of Confucius, the principal building is for the god, and the one behind is for his parents. But their arrangement was modified in 1916 by the President Yüan Shï-k'ai, who seems to have taken the Temples of Confucius as his model. An assessor, General Yo Fei, has been placed on the right hand of Kuan-ti, face to the south, then to the side, facing west and east respectively, two rows of twelve tablets representing twenty-four Exemplary Warriors who have replaced the six officers who till that date served as attendants. These are generals of every period, among whom we find the name of Hulagu, the Mongol conqueror of Persia and Bagdad (1257). The statues of Kuan-ti have been retained on the chief altar, but the new official tablet, from which the title of emperor has disappeared, has been put in front.

The Peasants. The peasants have no particular god who serves them as patron; the official religion is before everything an agrarian religion, and almost all its most important feasts are meant to ensure abundant harvests. Accordingly all the gods are concerned with them. And not merely all the gods, but all the officials as well, so far as they have religious functions alongside their civil duties. The peasants do not individually have to ask the gods to grant them help and protection: it is the mandarins who are officially charged with the duty of praying to the gods on their behalf. They are, with the Emperor and the mandarins, the only persons to whom the official religion assigns a part in its ceremonies; but this part is entirely a passive one: it is never they who perform the rites, it is they on whose behalf the rites are performed by others.

The origin of this special position of the peasants is very ancient. Already in antiquity they had not the right themselves to perform any religious worship: it was the princes and the officials who performed it for them. It was incumbent on the latter to mark, by means of a ceremony performed for the whole community, the beginning of field labours, to notify the Gods of the Soil, of Tillage and the Harvest, to ask for good crops, to pray for rain if it delayed, and so forth. The tillers of the ground made no individual prayers or sacrifices, just as individually they did not own the fields, but worked in common, by groups of eight families, on a certain quantity of land which was allotted to them to maintain their families, and in return for which they paid a tithe of the produce. Although this archaic organization had finally disappeared almost at the very moment when the various authors described it, about the beginning of historic times, in the last centuries before the Christian era, the official religion, and generally the attitude of the Chinese authorities to the peasants, have retained something of it. The Emperors and, in the early days of the Revolution, the President of the Republic made every year, like the kings of antiquity, public sacrifices for agriculture. I have already described the most important of these, the great imperial sacrifice to Heaven in the southern suburb of the capital, *nan kiao*. There were many others: the emperors prayed for rain, for snow, for the harvest, etc. And after them all the local officials, governors of provinces, prefects, sub-prefects, performed similar ceremonies at the times prescribed by the calendar.

And furthermore, work in the fields must not begin without express orders from authority. In principle, it is the first thunderclap of the year that gives the signal; in Kiangsu the villagers await it eagerly, and as soon as it is heard the headman of the village writes officially to the sub-prefect announcing the fact. When the latter has received a sufficient number of announcements from the villages of his district he sends a delegate to each commune with the official poster fixing a solemn day for the beginning of work on the land. The poster is drawn up in the following or similar terms. (I noted the poster I give herewith at the beginning of 1914 in a village of Kiangsu.)

> The time when insects are afraid [this is the name of one of the twenty-four half-monthly periods into which the year is divided] has come. Do you farmers all set to work in the fields. And now I, the sub-prefect, have fixed the seventeenth day of the third month as the due and solemn day to begin work. Let all obey without transgressing, so that the calamities of water, drought, and insects may be avoided!

This beginning of work on the land was marked by the official religion by a solemn feast in the first month of spring, the feast of ploughing. The Emperor himself took the yellow plough yoked to a yellow ox (yellow was the imperial colour under the Manchu dynasty); the President of the Ministry of Finance went on his left with the whip, the governor of Chihli on his right with a bag of seed corn; the Emperor in person traced the first furrow, then the princes and the ministers took his place, and lastly the ploughing was finished by peasants. And it was the grain from this field, situated south of Pekin, just over against the Temple of Heaven, that was used for all the imperial sacrifices of the ensuing year.

The sacrifice of the winter solstice on the Altar of Heaven, that of spring in the temple where prayers were made for the harvest, the feast of ploughing, these were the great imperial ceremonies for the beginning of agricultural labours. It was after these had been performed that the sub-prefects gave orders to the villages. But the officials did not stop at this: they had also to offer regular sacrifices to the Gods of the Soil and the Crops, *shê-tsi*, in spring and autumn, in every district chief town within the uttermost borders of the empire. In the capital the ceremony was performed by the Emperor himself or an imperial delegate. There was no temple; the place of worship was a hillock in the open, in a court surrounded by a low wall, and situated in the palace enclosure to the right of the hall of audience, corresponding to the Temple of the Ancestors situated on the left side (Fig. 50). In a great court there was a rectangular platform, broad but not very high, surrounded by three stone terrace steps, with a stair of four treads in the middle of each side; the top was covered with earth of five colours corresponding with each of the five cardinal points, green to the east, red to the south, white to the west, black to the north, and yellow to the centre; the stone tablet of the god was placed on it facing north (because this god represents the *yin* principle, to which the north answers). For the sacrifice the Emperor did not place himself on the actual hillock of the God of the Soil, as he mounted upon the Altar of Heaven for the *kiao* sacrifice; he remained outside the enclosing wall, on the north side, to face the tablet, and the spectators were behind him or on the other sides of the court, also outside the wall. It was only at the very outset of the ceremony that he went up for a moment upon it to invoke the spirits, prostrating himself and offering incense, but immediately after this he went back to his place and did not leave it again.

Fig. 50. THE ALTAR OF THE GOD OF THE SOIL, AT PEKIN

During the offerings music and songs appropriate to the sacrifices followed one another, as well as civilian and military dances. When the offerings were made, and borne before the tablet by special officials, the Emperor withdrew. Similar sacrifices (but without dances) were performed in every provincial capital, and every chief town of a prefecture or sub-prefecture, by the mandarin of the district (or by one of his subordinates delegated by him to take his place).

Other ceremonies in honour of Heaven or the Gods of the Soil and the Crops took place in summer to obtain rain; in the north they were performed to ask for snow, or in case of unusual circumstances. Whatever the occasion might be the people took no direct part in them: it was the officials who acted in the name of the whole district.

Even when it was not a question of the ceremonies of the official religion, the tendency was for peasant worship to be practised by groups; obviously it would be absurd for an individual to pray for rain for his own field alone, while it is natural that all the villagers should ask it for the whole village. Thus it is by groups that men turn to all the popular divinities who keep watch over each department of cultivation or deal with each incident of farming life. The Celestial Prince Liu received from the Jade Emperor the post of Overseer of the Five Cereals (wheat, barley, millet, sorghum, rice); he protects the harvests and averts drought, and his cult is very widespread in Kiangsu. He has almost entirely ousted the ancient God of the Cereals, the Millet Prince, Hou-tsi, to whom only the official religion pays worship as God of the Crops, associating him with the God of the Soil, and little statuettes such as the one seen in Fig. 51, showing the god in a shape of mingled man and plant, are rather *bibelots* displaying artistic fancy than religious objects. For cotton, a plant of foreign origin, it is the person, man or woman, that first introduced it into China who is reverenced: in Canton, as well as in Fukien, the name is Huang Shï; in Sung-kiang-fu (Kiangsu), where cotton-growing only goes back, it would seem, to the beginning of the fourteenth century, the legend and the name are slightly changed; there they adore Old Huang; she is supposed to have brought cotton from Kwangtung to Kiangsu and to have taught how to grow it and how to weave it; according to others, she only brought the ginning machine from Canton; her principal pagoda is in her native village, Wu-ni-king, near Shanghai. For protection against hail Hu-shên is called upon, the god who makes it fall, and he is offered a sacrifice with the accompaniment of a drama for his birthday, the first day of the seventh month; this is something in the nature of an insurance.

Fig. 51. THE MILLET GOD

One of the most dreaded scourges is the invasion of locusts that devour the harvest in the blade and leave nothing where they have passed. Against them the people invoke the Great King Pa-cha, destroyer of locusts and other harmful insects. "The locusts are summoned before his tribunal and chained," says a very popular inscription in his honour; he shuts them up in his gourd, and in this way destroys them. He is represented with a man's face and a bird's beak, a naked torso, a bell-shaped skirt under which come bird's feet; in his left hand a sabre and in his right the gourd in which he imprisons the evil-doing insects (Fig. 52). He is not invoked at the actual moment when the menace of the insect scourge is feared; that would be too late. Every year, after the harvest, especially if it has been a good one, the village folk bring a sorcerer, at the common expense, to thank the Great Pa-cha for protection granted and to ask him to continue it. The ceremony takes place in the open fields: the sorcerer erects a kind of tent in which he hangs up the images of the Jade Emperor, the Great Emperor of the Eastern Peak, the one the supreme master, the other the terrestrial regent under the orders of the first, and that of the Emperor Kuan, destroyer of evil spirits; then to right and left of this trio, and in an inferior position, those of the God of the Place, the Great King Pa-cha, the God of Riches, etc. He recites incantations, beating on a drum or a gong and burning incense, then he distributes, to all who have joined in paying him to come, amulets consecrated by the incense and the recitation of the formulas. Here is a very curious instance of the popular survival of a once very important rite now rejected by the official religion as lacking in dignity. In days of antiquity, after the reaping, a great harvest-home feast put an end, in the first month of winter, to the work of the fields, and marked the moment after which the earth must not be stirred, just as the feast of ploughing had set the field work going by breaking the winter interdict. It was called Pa-cha, an expression of uncertain meaning, which is traditionally interpreted as signifying " the feast in honour of the eight kinds of spirit that will be sought." Before all else it was a feast of the end of the harvest; its institution was ascribed to the Divine Plougher, the principal spirit was the First Reaper; after him homage was paid to the First Plougher, the First Dike-maker, the First Runnel-maker, the First Builder of Watch-huts. Respects were paid also to the spirits of the cats that destroy rats, the tigers that devour wild-boars; in a word, to all the spirits that by protecting the different stages of farming helped to make the harvest abundant. It was a huge masquerade: the spirits of the cats and the tigers had their representatives, who were men or boys masked and in fancy guise; the feast ended in a great orgy in which all the offerings were consumed, and at which the old men had first place in honour of the old age

Fig. 52. The Great General Pa-cha
Popular print.

of the year. The sacrifice was accompanied by formulas destined to regulate everything for the next year and keep away devouring insects: "Let the fields return to their wont, the waters go back to their channels, let no insects be born, let the weeds hie back to their marshes!" It is this last side of the feast, the expulsion of noxious insects, that alone has survived: the popular religion has made it personal, referring it to one special being charged with this task, the Great King of the Pa-cha Feast, or, as is now understood, the Great King Pa-cha. It went further: from the twelfth or the thirteenth century it had already endowed this individual with a complete civil status and titles. He is the Fierce General Liu, Liu Mêng tsiang-kün, or else the Constable Liu, Liu T'ai-wei, to whom sacrifices were offered in Shantung and in Chihli since the time of the Sungs, and who has been identified with various historical personages according to time and place—Liu I or his brother Liu Jui, two generals of the middle of the twelfth century, or their contemporary Liu Kien, who committed suicide in 1126 at the taking of K'ai-fêng-fu by the Mongols; or with personages whose existence is more or less apocryphal, like Liu Ch'êng-chung, of whom it is told that, holding in the Mongol period an administration in Kianghuai (approximately the present Kiangsu), and seeing the locusts settling on the country under his charge, he drove them away by attacking them sword in hand. The cult of General Liu was officially prohibited at the end of the seventeenth or beginning of the eighteenth century, but it lived on among the people; in certain places he became a personage distinct from the Great King Pa-cha, who was made his lieutenant; in others these are different titles of the same divinity; in others again the new title has driven out the old, which has fallen into oblivion.

Fig. 53. THE GOD OF STOCKBREEDING
Popular print.

On the other hand, besides a God of Stockbreeding in general (Fig. 53), there are particular gods for each breed of beast. They are the personifications of the animal species: the God of Byres, who is called the King of Kine, Niu-wang, is a buffalo; the God of the Sties, who is called the Transcendant Pig, Ling-chu, is a pig; the Lady Horse-head is the silkworm (Fig. 54). In the days of antiquity sacrifice was made at certain periods to the souls of domestic animals, worship was given to the Ancestor of Horses. The modern popular religion, with its habit of humanized divinities, gave a body, a name, a legend, to the objects of this cult.

The Lady Horse-head is a concubine of the Jade Emperor, in memory of the ceremony in which the Empress, followed by the women of the harem, went at the beginning of the third month to the Mulberry Walk in the Palace, to begin with her own hands the gathering of the leaves, after making an offering. She was, according to the tale, a girl who in the times of dim antiquity lived with her parents in Szechwan. One day her father was carried off by pirates; the girl in her filial piety mourned unceasingly and refused to eat. At the end of a year her mother in blank despair took an oath to give her daughter in marriage to the restorer of her husband. Their horse heard this vow; he escaped from the stable, and a few days later came back with his delivered master on his back. But when he learned of his wife's rash vow the man refused to carry it out, and as the horse displayed his indignation he slew him with an arrow, flayed him, and hung the hide to dry at the house door. Not long after the girl passed close by the hide, which rose up and lapped her round and bore her away; ten days after the hide was found hanging on the bough of a mulberry-tree; the girl had turned into a silkworm. The Jade Emperor took her up into heaven and made her one of his concubines.

Fig. 54. The Lady Horse-head
Popular print.

The gods of kine and swine are a little nearer to their origins: instead of being regarded as men turned into animals, they are, on the contrary, animals who were able to turn into men. We know that the Chinese accept this transformation as something completely natural: foxes and tigers can, under certain conditions, take human shape; these are the best known, but not by a long way the only ones that enjoy this power. The foxes, say the Kiangsu peasants, pray every morning to the rising sun and drink in his rays; they kneel on their hind legs, join their fore-paws, and prostrate themselves; when they have done this for several years they can assume human shape, and take advantage of this to mix with men. Similar rites enable serpents to become dragons; wolves, badgers, and numbers of small wild animals are also capable of skin-changing. The domestic animals, oxen and pigs, do not normally possess this faculty; but the King of the Kine and the God of the Sties had in some way acquired it. The author of the *Tale of the Investiture of the Gods* presumably found them picturesque, for he gave them a place among the defenders of the tyrant Shou-sin of the Yin against his adversary the King of Chou, who, having already received the Celestial Mandate, was fighting to de-throne him. The King of the Kine had taken the shape of a giant sixteen feet high (this is the traditional height of the Buddha, and as such has a particular prestige and favour in all folklore), with two horns on his forehead, the mouth and ears of a buffalo, clad in a red robe, protected by a cuirass and a helmet, and armed with a halberd with three points. He defied the warriors of the King of Chou, and slew all who came against him, until the Lady Nü-kua managed to put a wonder-working tether through his nose, and thus forced him to resume his buffalo shape. As for the God of the Sties, he had a black face, with large ears and very long lips, and was clad in black (Chinese pigs are black); he too killed many of the warriors of Chou, but ended by being slain by the hero Êr-lang, the nephew of the Jade Emperor, whom he had gulped down. Both are to-day generally represented in mandarin costume, accompanied one by oxen, buffaloes, and horses, the other by pigs, and their image is placed at the door of the cattle-houses to keep away disease. On their feast offerings are made and crackers set off in their honour.

The rich peasants, again, hold a number of feasts before the altar of the God of Riches: these are the 'birthdays.' The year begins with an important series: the third day of the first month is the birthday of the pigs, the fourth that of the ducks, the fifth of the oxen, the sixth of the horses, the eighth of rice, the ninth of vegetables, the tenth of barley; the twelfth of the third month is the birthday of wheat, and so on. According to the work they are engaged on, the peasants choose some of these days to make offerings and burn incense, usually before the altar of the family God of Riches; a very great number, however, do absolutely nothing of this.

Fig. 55. THE EMPRESS OF HEAVEN, T'IEN-HOU

The Sailors. The Empress of Heaven (T'ien-hou). For protectress the sailors have a goddess who in the last few centuries has taken a considerable position in the Chinese pantheon, thanks to the favour shown her by the Manchu Emperors. This is the Empress of Heaven, T'ien-hou, called also Holy Mother of the Heavens, T'ien-Shang Shêng-mu, or, again, more familiarly, Grandmother, Ma-tsu-p'o. Her cult originated in Fukien, and from there was spread over the whole of China. The sailors of this province have her image on almost all their boats, in a little shrine placed on the left side, and offer it incense morning and evening; before leaving port for a trip they make offerings to her on board, and frequently the crew and the passengers go to her pagoda and burn sticks of incense in her honour. Traders who deal in exports or imports, those who undertake sea-transport, emigrants, simple travellers, sacrifice to her, either regularly or on occasion. The Empress of Heaven is a girl who was born in the island of Mei-chou, near Hing-hua, who lived, according to some, in the eighth century, according to others, in the tenth. She had a particular devotion to Kuan-yin, and refused to marry. Her four brothers engaged in trade on the sea, and each had a ship, and piloted it himself. One night when her brothers were at sea she fell into a trance, and when after long-continued efforts they succeeded in waking her she bewailed that she had been brought back to life too soon. At the time no one could understand what she meant; but a few days later three of her brothers alone returned: a storm had caught their ships and they gave themselves up for lost, when a girl appeared and brought them to shelter; only their eldest brother had not been saved. Her words were then clear; it was she who had gone to the help of her brothers in peril. She died soon after.

The worship of the Empress of Heaven sprang up suddenly at the end of the eleventh century and developed swiftly in the course of the next. According to an inscription set up to her glory in 1228 in her temple at Hangchow, a supernatural light appeared in the night above the coast of Mei-chou, and the inhabitants all dreamed together that a girl said to them: "I am the goddess of Mei-chou, I must be given a dwelling here!" In consequence of this miracle they raised a temple to her on the edge of the sea. The goddess began to be famous some thirty years after by saving a high official, Lu Yün-ti, in a terrible storm, when he was going on an embassy to Korea (1122): she descended upon the mast of the ship and piloted it to safety; on his return in the following year the Emperor Hui-tsung rewarded her by granting her temple the name of the Temple of the Fortunate Crossing, Shun-tsi miao, a title in any event a commonplace one, which was at that period currently given to all temples of sea-deities. In 1155, for a reason that is not known, the goddess was decreed the official title of Princess of Supernatural Favour, Ling-hui-fu-jên; and from that moment there was no cessation in the stream of official honours. She showed herself particularly helpful in the droughts of 1187 and 1190, and besides, she helped on several occasions in the capture of sea-pirates, so that in 1192 she was exalted in rank, and her title of Princess (*fu-jên*) was changed to that of Queen (*fei*), and some years later (1198) this again was altered to Holy Queen (*Shêng fei*). In 1278 the Mongol Emperor Kublai Khan gave her the title of Queen of Heaven, with twelve honorific characters. This title of Queen of Heaven was preserved to her under the Ming dynasty and the beginning of the Manchu dynasty, and was replaced by that of Empress of Heaven (T'ien-hou) by the Emperor K'ien-lung in 1737. And it was not merely her official worship that developed in this way, but her popular worship spread more and more. In the middle of the twelfth century she still had only a single temple, situated where she had appeared for the first time. In 1156 a second was erected a little to the north-east, near the Bridge of the Mouth of the River, and two years after a third about a league to the south-east, near the White Lake, Po-hu. And from this moment her temples multiplied (almost always, it seems, built in consequence of a dream), so that in 1228 the author of the Hangchow inscription could say that she was not adored only in Mei-chou, but that everywhere, in Min (Fukien), in Kuang (Kwangtung), in Chê (Chekiang), in Huai, in Kiang (Kiangsu and Anhwei)—that is to say, in short, in all the maritime provinces of the Sung empire—sacrifices were made to her. In our day her worship has gone beyond these limits, and temples are found in almost all the cities of the coast, as far as Shantung and Chihli; furthermore, the merchants of Fukien who have emigrated and settled in other provinces consider her as a kind of personal patron, and often put up temples to her as a meeting-place for their societies.

The Empress of Heaven is represented under the aspect of a woman sitting upon the waves or upon the clouds, or sometimes, more simply, upon a throne. She is clad in a long robe with a girdle like that of the officials and wears the imperial bonnet with tassels, or sometimes a simple ceremonial bonnet. In her hand she holds a tablet, the sign of the rank of high officers in the sovereign's presence, or else a *ju-i* sceptre: in fact, in spite of her title of Queen or Empress of Heaven, neither the official nor the popular religion ever thought of making her the wife of the Emperor of Heaven (Sovereign On-high, or Jade Emperor, or Monseigneur Heaven): she is a high female dignitary of his court, equal in grade to the male emperors (*Ti*), like Kuan-ti, etc., and like them subordinate to the supreme god.

She is assigned, as subordinates, two personages who help her to see and to hear everything that takes place in this world, and whose names are significant: Ear of a Thousand Li and Eye of a Thousand Li.[1] They are usually represented with outstretched neck, the hand cupped over the ear or the eyes the better to catch sounds or see details of distant scenes; the first has red hair and two horns; the second has a blue face. The *Tale of the Investiture of the Gods* relates that they served in the army of the Tyrant of the Yin (Figs. 56 and 57).

Fig. 56. Thousand-li Ear

Fig. 57. Thousand-li Eyes

Traders and Artisans. Except for the mandarins and the peasants, the official religion sanctions no professional cult. In all times the other professions were reckoned as lower of rank in the traditional hierarchy. They were often obliged to be satisfied with less important divinities.

The traders naturally have the Gods of Riches as their patrons. They do not add more images on this account to those the majority of families maintain, but they pay more frequent worship, making regular offerings twice a month, on the 2nd and the 16th. On these days they present to the particular Gods of Riches that they have adopted a complete meal, which is later distributed to the employees and the clerks. The selection of the god is ordinarily regulated by the customs of the district, but sometimes also by personal devotions. Other causes too may intervene: it is obviously the name of the God of Riches of the Five Roads that caused his adoption as patron by the hotel-keepers of Pekin.

Goldsmiths place in the middle of their show window case the statuette of Mi-lo (Maitreya), the future Buddha, under the current shape of a fat monk with a laughing face, puff-cheeked, big-bellied, half naked, holding a rosary in his hand. He was in fact, it appears, the first goldsmith when in far-off days he fled from the palace of Shï-kia (the Buddha Ṣākyamuni) carrying off ingots of gold and silver, and, taking refuge on earth and hiding among men, earned his living by making jewels out of them for sale. Shï-kia had to send in pursuit the Immortal Lü Tung-pin, who set out to look for him disguised as a beggar, and in the end found him, seized him and bound him with a magic cord, and fetched him back. They keep also in their houses the image of a person sitting on a

[1] The *li* is a measure of length which, while it varies in different provinces, is somewhere about a third of a mile.

chair with his feet on an ingot, whom they call Hua-kuang, and to whom they sometimes give the title of Fo (Buddha). And again many of them pay worship to Tung-fang So, a magician of the second century before our era, because he was an incarnation of the Planet of Metal (Venus), and in consequence presides over all that touches the working of metals. On their part dealers in jade and precious stones have Pien Ho as their patron, who in dim antiquity discovered a piece of marvellous jade that he presented to two kings only to see it unrecognized and declared false, and be punished in each case by the amputation of a foot.

The carpenters and joiners, often too the smiths and the potters, have as their patron Lu Pan, the artisan of genius who made a wooden falcon that could fly, and many other marvels, whose legend was already popular several centuries before our era. His two wives, one red, the other black, are the patronesses of the lacquer-workers (red lac and black lac). He is worshipped twice a year, on the thirteenth day of the fifth month and the twenty-first day of the seventh month.

The butchers address themselves to Fan K'uai, an imaginary personage, who is represented as the friend and the right arm of the founder of the Han dynasty, and who would seem to have begun to earn his living by skinning and cutting up dogs to sell the flesh for food. In other districts their deity is Chang Fei, one of the three sworn Brothers of the Garden of Peach-trees in the *Tale of the Three Kingdoms*: he was a pork-seller when he joined Liu Pei, the founder of the Han dynasty of the country of Shu (Szechwan), and Kuan Yü.

It would be impossible to notice all the gods of the professions: every trade has its own special protector, who varies furthermore according to the country concerned. The patron of the weavers is the God of the Shuttle, whose birthday falls on the 16th of the ninth month; that of the gardeners is the God of the Garden Trees; the god of the brush-makers is Meng T'ien, a general of the end of the third century before our era, who is regarded as the inventor of the brush; the god of the tailors is the mythical yellow Emperor Huang-ti, the inventor of ceremonial garments; the god of the shoemakers is Sun Pin, a general of the fourth century before our era, who, having had his toes cut off as a penalty for some crime, devised and made himself leather boots to hide his defect; similarly the god of the wine-makers is the first maker of wine, I-ti, who discovered it and took a cup to the mythical Emperor Yü the Great during his labours for the drying up of China, which had been covered by a tremendous deluge, or, as the Pekin folk call him, simply, the Immortal One who made wine; the god of the distillers is Tu K'ang, a more or less authentic personage, to whom the discovery of alcohol is attributed, some centuries before our era.

Even the most despised trades have their protectors. The barbers, people of low caste, who before the Revolution were denied the right to present themselves for the examinations, have for patron the Ancestor Lo, whose feast falls on the thirteenth day of the seventh month. He was the first of the barbers, and to him is attributed a manual *What it is necessary to know about Hairdressing* (*Tsing fa sü chï*). At Fukien they appear to have substituted for him, or added to him, the Immortal Lü Tung-pin. This was, they relate, because he came down on earth in the time of the Ming dynasty to shave the head of an emperor whose skin was so sensitive that no one could avoid hurting him. The legend is evidently a recent one, since it was only from the seventeenth century that the Manchu conquerors obliged the Chinese to shave their heads, and in the Ming epoch, to which the story relates, they kept their hair long. As their patron attained the rank of doctor, they fix on the stove on which they heat their water a little reproduction of the red mast, half-way up which are hung special ornaments, that doctors had the privilege of planting at their doors. Public story-tellers have for patron Ts'ang Kie, the legendary inventor of writing; most of the companies of actors in Pekin have Yo Fei, a general of the twelfth century; the public girls have for their patron, in Amoy, Kuan-yin, and, in certain parts of Kiangsu, P'an Kin-lien, a young widow of light morals, who was surprised *flagrante delicto* and killed by her father-in-law. The very thieves themselves have their patrons, who are celebrated brigands of old time. Most frequently, it appears, this is Sung Kiang, who stirred up a very serious revolt in the country situated between the mouths of the Blue River and the Yellow River in 1121, and who has been made popular by the romance *Shui hu chuan*, of which he is the hero. Others address themselves to a still more ancient personage, the brigand Chï, famous on account of the visit that Confucius paid him.

We might in this way run through every profession, every trade, even the least reputable; each one has its god, or gods, who are not always the same in all the provinces of the vast Chinese republic; even the secret societies constituted themselves as a kind of religious brotherhood. The catalogue of names of all these divinities could be continued almost to infinity.

THE GODS CHARGED WITH WATCHING OVER MANKIND INDIVIDUALLY

Kuan-ti. In his *rôle* as regent of the terrestrial world for the Jade Emperor, which has long been his, the Great Emperor of the Eastern Peak is by way of seeing himself supplanted by a divinity of recent origin, but who has assumed a prodigious importance, the Emperor Kuan, Kuan-ti. He is not imagined, like the Eastern Peak, as surrounded by an extensive bureaucracy charged with the duty of registering everything, but rather as a kind of paladin or champion, always ready to intervene against all who disturb the peace of the people, foreign enemies, internal rebels, sorcerers or evil spirits of all kinds, harmful animals. No demon can resist him, every spell is broken directly his name is uttered, the mere sight of an actor representing him in the theatre puts ghosts to flight. He holds a considerable place in the religious life of to-day, and this fact is all the more interesting seeing that his cult is comparatively a modern one. He is a proof how far Buddhism has transformed the religious ideas of the masses of the common people. The conception of the Eastern Peak, a divinity of ancient formation, was modelled on the pattern of the Emperor and his administration; the Emperor Kuan, a recent divinity, was shaped after the model of the Bodhisattvas, whose title, as a matter of fact, he is often given.

The Emperor Kuan is a completely historical person who lived in the third century of our era, the general Kuan Yü, who served the founder of the Shu Han dynasty in the epoch of the Three Kingdoms, and died miserably at the age of fifty-eight in A.D. 220, murdered by order of the Emperor of the rival Wu dynasty, after the capture of the city of Kiang-ling, where he had taken refuge after a defeat. Impossible here to relate the legend of the god in detail; it occupies the greater part of the most famous and most popular of the Chinese novels, the *Tale of the Three Kingdoms*. The most famous scene, the one most frequently shown on the stage, is the "Oath of the Three in the Peach-garden." Liu Pei, the future emperor, founder of the Shu Han dynasty (Szechwan, one of the three kingdoms, the two others being Wei, the basin of the Yellow River and the north of China, and Wu, the lower basin of the Blue River and the southern provinces), was living in poor circumstances with his widow mother, and earning his living by making shoes and mats, when one day he saw a poster calling for brave men to fight the Yellow Turban rebels; and, having read it, he went away sighing, when he heard himself called, and saw an extraordinary man, a colossus, with the head of a leopard, the beard of a tiger, round eyes, and a voice like the rolling of thunder. This was the wealthy butcher and wine-merchant Chang Fei, who proposed that they should join together and answer the appeal of the governor. The pair went into a tavern to discuss their plan, and while they drank there arrived a man of fierce and terrible aspect, who as he entered declared his intention to enrol himself also. Liu Pei and Chang Fei made him sit beside them, and when he had told his name, Kuan Yü, and his history they disclosed their plans to him, after which they all three went to Chang Fei's house. Behind the house was a little garden of peach-trees, and all in bloom. They betook themselves there to talk, then at Chang Fei's proposal they mutually swore brotherhood, offering a white horse to Heaven and a black ox to the Earth. Then they went off to the city of the governor, taking with them a band of young men from their neighbourhood.

Fig. 58. KUAN-TI

We do not know for what reasons and under what form there arose and developed a kind of popular cult of Kuan Yü; but it was already sufficiently widely spread in the seventh century to be adopted by Buddhism: he was, according to the monk Shên-siu, at this time the God of the Place, K'ie-lan shên, of certain temples. His vogue was to go on increasing further during the following centuries, so much so that the superstitious Emperor Hui-tsung, under the influence of his Taoist favourites, received him into the official religion with the high title of King of Military Pacification, Wu-an wang (1102). The success of the *Tale of the Three Kingdoms*, of which he is one of the heroes, carried his glory to the topmost pitch. The Emperor Shên-tsung of the Ming dynasty (1573–1619) raised him to the rank of Grand Emperor, which made him equal with the Eastern Peak, with the title of Just Grand Emperor who Aids the Heaven and Protects the State. The Manchu dynasty raised him higher still: he had, it is said, himself defended the entrance into the imperial apartments on the occasion of the conspiracy of 1813, in which the Emperor Kia-k'ing almost lost his life; hence that prince and his successor Tao-kuang had a special devotion for him. The first conferred on him the title of Military Emperor, *Wu-ti*, and the second decided that he was to be paid honours equal to those paid to Confucius. Temples were erected to him in all cities that were the seats of administration, and until the end of the empire the officials were obliged to go in State procession every year to make offerings on the 13th of the first month and the 13th of the fifth, his feast-days. Innumerable local temples and chapels were erected to him almost everywhere as well.

Fig. 59. KUAN-TI JUDGING A SUPPLIANT
Popular print.

His official *rôle* was to protect the empire against all attack from without and against all rebellion within, and also to concern himself with the military officials, who paid him special worship. The popular religion sees him above all as a great slaughterer of demons, a god who breaks the power of evil spells. He is called the Grand Emperor who Subdues the Demons, Fu-mo-ta-ti, and in this connexion very many anecdotes are related.

A very rich individual having died young, a *tao-shï* presented himself who guaranteed to bring him back to life, but added that, according to the laws of the lower regions, in order that a dead man may return to life there must be a substitute who will die in his place. As none of the wives of the deceased consented to sacrifice herself, an old serving-man came forward. A great devotee of Kuan-ti, he went first of all to his temple to pray for the success of the incantations. In the middle of the ceremony there was a clap of thunder, and the *tao-shï* fell, lightning-smitten; his body bore the following phrase in big characters: "Condemned by Heaven as a corrupter of Religion, a destroyer of the Law, who by changing bodies aimed at wealth; and executed forthwith in accordance with orders received!" The magician had meant not to resuscitate the dead man, but to take his place by sending his own spirit into his body, and Kuan-ti, informed through the prayers of his faithful worshipper, had intervened to chastise him.

In another tale an inhabitant of Pekin, named Ye, having gone to present his good wishes for the birthday of one of his friends who lived on the outskirts of the city, met as evening fell a traveller who presented himself as his friend's cousin and declared that he too was on his way to visit him. Arriving at their host's house, they were very well received, and after dinner were lodged together in a bedchamber in which a servant was installed to attend them. In the middle of the night Ye awoke and saw the cousin sitting on the bed devouring the servant and tossing the gnawed bones on the floor; in terror he called upon the Great Emperor, the Subduer of Demons, and immediately, to the clangour of gongs and drums, Kuan-ti appeared, brandishing his sword, and threw himself upon the demon; the latter turned to a great butterfly and flitted about eluding the sword of the god. Suddenly a peal of thunder rang out, and Kuan-ti and the butterfly both disappeared.

Even the mere appearance of an actor made up like Kuan-ti is enough to break spells. One day a company of famous actors in Pekin saw a servant arrive on horseback with an invitation to go and perform in a mansion situated close to one of the gates of the city. They set out immediately, and as night fell they came to a great house brilliantly lighted and full of company. As he brought them in a servant informed them that his mistress left orders for them not to sing anything but love-songs, and above all to eschew any piece in which a divinity appeared. Barely were they in their places when they began to play; the spectators (men and women sitting in separate parts of the hall, in accordance with custom) formed an extraordinary audience, which was unheard, which talked or laughed or manifested its opinions in a whisper. They were astonished, and even more annoyed, when they saw that the night went by and they were being made to sing without a break and without anyone thinking of offering them refreshments. At last, thoroughly exasperated, they played, in the teeth of their original instructions, a mythological piece, and Kuan-ti came on the stage, sword in hand, to the roll of the drums. At that very instant everything disappeared, lights, spectators, the house itself, and the actors found themselves in a desert place in front of the tomb of a young woman belonging to a wealthy family, recently dead. It was she who had invited them, and they had played all night long before an audience of dead folk who had been able to assume for a space the appearance of life; but at the sight of the actor in the costume of Kuan-ti they had been obliged to return to their true shape.

In another tale it is a fox in human shape that comes to grief. By magic arts he was carrying a man with whom he had made friends through the middle air, when, passing heedlessly above a theatre in which Kuan-ti was on the stage, he lost his powers and dropped his friend in the midst of the audience.

Kuan-ti is not content with acting, he speaks and writes a great deal, which is to say that he is one of the gods that most frequently manifest themselves in spiritist séances. He wields the brush of divination, *ki-pi*, a kind of fork made of peach-wood and lacquered red, the movements of which give the oracle by drawing characters. In all classes of society there are numerous groups of devotees who meet regularly about a medium before the statue of some god or some spirit. They thus form a religious association each member of which in turn is called upon to keep the statue in his house. At every séance they begin by burning a few incense-sticks and presenting a few offerings, then after prostrating themselves they invite the spirit to descend by a prayer in verse, something after the style of the following:

May the expanding of the breaths of Rectitude fill Heaven and Earth!
May the incense we send on high find its way through the Gate of Heaven!
May the Raven of Gold (the Sun) go forth in his flight like the thunderbolt in the clouds!
May the Rabbit of Jade (the Moon) shine in splendour like a chariot-wheel!
May the Star of the South and the Northern Bushel come down together!
May the five-coloured constellation Tsï-wei,
May the constellation Tsï-wei in the midst of its lights opening the true path
Into the grotto of the Spring of the Peachblossom invite the Immortal One!

We, disciples, before the perfume-burner, bow down three times in invitation: we invite Such an One to come down among us. May the divine soldiers [go to fetch them] swift as light, in accordance with orders received!

Then the medium and his assistant stand in their places, each holding one of the branches of the fork of the divining brush. After a moment the god descends into the brush, which, they say, grows heavy, and the medium's right arm begins to contract, as if he was trying to pull the instrument from his assistant. Suddenly the brush lifts up violently and comes down on the tray made ready for writing (usually a lacquered tray covered with grains of rice); it describes a few random movements, then quiets down and begins to draw characters, cursive or abridged or even in regular form. Usually the first signs give the name of the spirit; if not, the persons present ask it insistently, so as to avoid the possibility of entering into communication with evil spirits. The name once obtained, a conversation is begun. The assistant quickly reads the characters as the brush forms them, then he dictates them to one of the associates, who acts as a secretary and writes them down at once. Usually the oracle takes the form of regular verses.

Most spiritist groups have their god or their own familiar spirit, whom they invoke and who habitually comes in answer to their prayers. But sometimes there are unlooked-for manifestations. Most frequently it is evil spirits who, getting possession for a moment of the brush, seize the opportunity to write nonsense or obscenities. Sometimes too it is gods of great importance who take the place of the usual spirit. Among the great divinities who most readily manifest their presence Kuan-ti is one of those who appear most frequently. Sometimes he is content with giving consultations upon individual matters, similar to those given by the ordinary spirits, though naturally with more profound knowledge of the other world; he gives information as to the situation of the soul of a deceased parent, indicates what ceremony should be performed for his salvation, and so on. But he often gives oracles of more general application also, dissertations on the future life and transmigration, with detailed descriptions of the various hells and anecdotes on the retribution following upon deeds through the different existences, or, for that matter, charms against disease, evil influences, and evil spirits. All this is carefully noted and piously preserved by the group that has received the message. Sometimes the text is published in the shape of little tracts, some of which occasionally enjoy a considerable vogue, at least locally, until another similar work replaces them in popular favour.

Kuan-ti is represented as a giant nine feet high, with a beard two feet long, a face red as the jujube fruit, and eyes like those of the phœnix, with eyebrows like the silkworm. His statues generally represent him standing by the side of his horse, wearing his cuirass and armed with his halberd; more rarely he is on horseback. He is accompanied by his son, who carries his seal, and by his squire, halberd in fist. Another type, also fairly common, represents him in the costume of a military mandarin, but without weapons, seated on a chair, caressing his long beard with one hand and with the other opening the *Chronicle of Springs and Autumns* (*Ch'un ts'iu*) of Confucius, that rule of conduct for statesmen of ten thousand generations which he could, they say, recite complete from memory. His son and his squire stand to his left and his right (Fig. 60).

How was the type of Kuan-ti established? It is as difficult to say as it is to follow the vicissitudes of his cult before the time when he suddenly appeared in the official religion. Ancient statues are wanting, as they are for all the non-Buddhist divinities. What is

Fig. 60. KUAN-TI BETWEEN HIS SON AND HIS SQUIRE

certain is that this type was already settled by tradition for the author of the *Tale of the Three Kingdoms*, for he explains it by an anecdote. Kuan Yü, when still young, and not yet having left his native country of Kiai-liang (to-day Kiai-chou, in the south-west of Shansi), one day heard one of his neighbours and his daughter lamenting, and on asking the cause of their tears learned that although the girl was already betrothed the uncle of the mandarin wished to make her his concubine; and the mandarin, who abetted his uncle, had insulted the father when he went to demand justice from him. Kuan Yü in wrath took his sword and ran off on the spot to kill the mandarin and his uncle: then he fled to the west to take refuge in the mountains. But he must needs get through the Pass of T'ung-kuan, guarded by a military post, and feared he would be recognized and taken. He had stopped by a spring to consider this difficulty, when, catching sight of his own face in the water, he saw it was completely changed: it had taken on a red colour that made it unrecognizable. He set out again forthwith, and cleared the pass without trouble.

The probability is that this type came from the theatre and found its way into the novel and the art of the statuary. In any case, in our own times it is the theatre much more than sculpture that has definitely established it and made it widely spread among the people. Kuan-ti is, as a matter of fact, one of the most popular heroes of the stage, for a good half of the repertory of the touring companies is made up of plays taken from the *Tale of the Three Kingdoms*, in which his adventures occupy a prominent place. This influence of the theatre upon the popular conception of Kuan-ti is so strong that in the stories the appearance of the god is very often accompanied by a sound of drums and gongs, not because it is believed that he brings celestial musicians with him, but simply because, on the stage, he always makes his entrance with the crashing noise of these instruments, exactly like every character playing a military part.

Fig. 61. The Supreme Emperor of the Dark Heaven

The Supreme Lord of the Dark Heaven, Hüan-t'ien Shang-ti. Antiquity had set by the side of the Lord on High, Shang-ti, and below him five lords, each master of a sector of the sky, designated only by a title taken from the colour corresponding to the cardinal point under his sway: the Green Lord, Ts'ing-ti (the East); the Red Lord, Ch'ï-ti (the South); the White Lord, Po-ti (the West); the Dark Lord, Hüan-ti (the North); the Yellow Lord, Huang-ti (the Centre). They have almost wholly vanished from modern mythology; there is left practically only the Lord of the North, the Dark Lord, who has survived in a new shape. He has become the Supreme Lord of the Dark Heaven, Hüan-t'ien Shang-ti. called also the Holy Prince Dark Warrior, Hüan-wu Shêng-kün, or the Holy Prince Triumphant Warrior, Chên-wu Shêng-kün, or, finally, and this is his official title, the Holy and Propitious Prince of the North Pole, Pei-ki yu-shêng chên-kün. He rules over the northern quarter of the sky and the world, is the ruler of water among the five elements, and, lastly, drives away evil spirits.

He is usually represented as he appeared to the Emperor Hui-tsung of the Sung dynasty, when the latter had him evoked by his favourite, the *tao-shï* Lin Ling-su, in 1118. The incantation took place at noon in the palace. In the middle of the ceremony the skies were suddenly darkened, and amid thunder and lightnings a great serpent and an enormous tortoise appeared. The Emperor prostrated himself and offered incense; then he prayed the god to deign to show himself in person. In a fresh peal of thunder tortoise and serpent vanished, and a colossal human foot was perceived before the door of the palace. The Emperor prostrated himself afresh, and asked that the god would be pleased to manifest himself in entirety. He then beheld a man more than ten feet in height, with a grave countenance, surrounded with a halo, his loosened hair hanging over his back, his feet bare. He was clad in a black robe, with long sleeves falling down to the ground, covered with a gold cuirass and a girdle of precious stones; in his hand he carried a sword. He stood there for a few moments and then disappeared.

The Emperor, who was a famous painter, had taken advantage, so they say, of these brief moments to draw his portrait, and it is this portrait that has served as model for all the modern pictures. Usually an armed squire is placed behind him, carrying his black banner; the god himself is set on the back of the tortoise encircled by the serpent, and floating on the waters, as is fitting, since he is the ruler of the North, and water is the element corresponding to the northern quarter.

This tortoise and this serpent upon which he rests are interpreted in totally different ways by the various Chinese authors: to some they are two celestial officers placed under his orders; according to others, they are, on the contrary, enemy demons whom he has conquered and whom he is treading under his feet. In point of fact, the wreathed serpent and tortoise are the god himself in his first shape, more ancient than the present anthropomorphic personage. They are met with from the time of the Han dynasty as the symbol of the Northern region of the world in the funeral chambers of the second century, where they face the Red Bird, the symbol of the South, and are opposed to the White Tiger (the West) and the Green Dragon (the East).

The Mother of the Bushel, Tou-mu. In Sagittarius is placed the palace of a goddess who is in charge of the registers of Life and Death, the Mother (of the Constellation) of the (Southern) Bushel, Tou-mu, or, to give her her full title, the Princess Great Holy Mother of the Constellation of the Bushel.[1] "On high she rules the catalogues of the Nine Heavens; in the middle she puts together the lists of the gods; below she keeps the registers of the destiny of men." The Taoist books give her important offices, which nevertheless have not become popular like those of the Eastern Peak. She has a husband, the Father of the Bushel; her nine sons are stars: the eldest are the gods of the South Pole and the North Pole, and in that capacity they settle, the first the date of birth and the latter the date of death. This goddess is a pretty confused mixture of ill-digested Buddhist and Taoist ideas. The *tao-shï* give her the Sanskrit name of Mo-li-chï (Marīchī), which is, properly speaking, the star that goes before the rising sun, but without retaining for her either her Buddhist character or aspect. On the contrary, they give her the face and the eight arms of Chaṇḍī, who is that one of the Six Avalokiteṣvaras who concerns himself specially with human beings, to the exclusion of gods, demons, etc. It seems furthermore that it is on account of this special function of Chaṇḍī that the *tao-shï* have adopted his picture to represent their goddess of the Bushel, who had a similar *rôle*, she too being charged to deal especially with human beings. Chaṇḍī, as a form of Avalokiteṣvara, has become a male personage, in spite of the name, but the Tantric sects, attributing a quite different *rôle* to her, have left her feminine.

She is worshipped with fasting on the 3rd and the 27th of each month; thus it is hoped to obtain from her not a prolongation of life in the strict sense of the word (since its duration has been fixed at birth), but the full completion of the allotted span without

[1] The name of Bushel is given by the Chinese to two constellations: the Northern Bushel is the Great Bear, the Southern Bushel is Sagittarius.

Fig. 62. THE SUPREME EMPEROR OF THE DARK HEAVEN
After a painting of the Sung period.

curtailment. Again, during an attack of a dangerous illness offerings and prayers are often made to her for healing.

The Mother of the Bushel is represented sitting on a lotus, with the crown of the Bodhisattvas on her head. She has three eyes (the middle eye, set vertically in the middle of the forehead, is to the Buddhists and, following them, to the Taoists the eye of supernatural vision, which enables her to see by night and by day all that takes place in all the worlds) and eight arms holding various attributes. This, as I have just said, is a simple Taoist replica of the iconographic type of Chaṇḍī.

Fig. 63. The Three Agents
Popular print.

The Three Agents, San-kuan. The lot of every man depends likewise upon three divinities who have numerous devotees, and hold a sufficiently important place in the moral and religious life of the people, the Great Emperors the Three Agents, San kuan ta-ti, or, more simply, the Three Agents, San-kuan, or, again, the Lords of the Three Worlds, San kiai kung. These are the Agent of Heaven, T'ien-kuan, the Agent of Earth, Ti-kuan, the Agent of Water, Shui-kuan, who keep the register of good and evil actions. Each of them is credited with the power to grant a particular grace: the Agent of Heaven grants happiness, the Agent of Earth remission of sins, the Agent of Water averts misfortune. They are personifications originating in an ancient Taoist ritual that goes back to the Yellow Turbans, and the main lines of which I have already indicated in the introduction with regard to Chang Tao-ling: sick men confessed their faults in writing on three papers which were burned for Heaven, buried for Earth, and drowned for Water. The political power of the Yellow Turbans was broken at the end of the second century of our era, but the influence of their religious ideas was enduring. Purification by confession to Heaven, Earth, and Water gave rise to the cult of the Three Agents, who were the divine officials charged with supervising the performance of rites and with the rewarding of devotees. This new form seems to have emerged from Taoist circles to spread itself among the larger public in the beginning of the fifth century, under the influence of the Celestial Master K'ou Kien-chï.

Devotees of these gods offer them incense, with cakes in the form of a tortoise (the tortoise is a symbol of longevity) or in the shape of chain-links, twice a month, on the 1st and the 15th. But ordinarily it is considered enough to make them offerings on their three great festivals, the 15th of the first month (*shang-yüan*), of the seventh month (*chung-yüan*), and of the tenth month (*hia-yüan*), which are the birthdays of the Agent of Heaven, the Agent of Earth, and the Agent of Water respectively. The first festival is the most important, for it coincides with the Feast of Lanterns, which since the eleventh century it had been the custom (at least in certain regions, Chekiang, Fukien, etc.) to connect with the Agent of Heaven. The Feast of Lanterns is one of the greatest popular feasts of the year. Every family makes an offering to the Three Agents, and the richest and most devout invite a *tao-shï* to conduct a ceremony. During the day the streets of the towns and villages are enlivened with mountebanks showing their tricks on every hand, as well as young men and boys disguised and wearing masks. At nightfall a coloured lantern is lit before the doors of every house, and besides this other lanterns are hung out in profusion; children push about balloon-shaped lanterns that can be rolled along without going out; a dragon is carried about shining and glittering with light in the midst of crackers. It is a general illumination that lasts all night long; in reality it has no connexion at all with the feast of the Agent of Heaven, and originates in ancient ideas altogether different.

Fig. 64. The Agent of Heaven
Musée Guimet.

Sometimes we find images of the Three Agents: they are sitting or standing beside one another in mandarin costume, tablet in hand. But most frequently there is only the image of the Agent of Heaven: he is standing and holds in his two hands a roll, unfolded, with the inscription, "The Agent of Heaven granteth Happiness." This iconographic type seems to come direct from the theatre; every performance, indeed, begins (or rather began until these latter days) with the entrance of the Agent of Heaven, who walked statelily about the stage unfolding a succession of various inscriptions conveying good wishes to the audience. These paper images are universally met with; there is hardly a house without them. Most frequently, indeed, he is confused with the God of Happiness. More rarely little statuettes, like the one reproduced in Fig. 64, are seen. This illustration shows the Agent of Heaven sitting in mandarin dress, holding in his hand the roll of good wishes.

The Three Stars (Gods of Happiness). It is three stellar divinities, "the Three Stars" (*san-sing*), who are the Gods of Happiness of each individual: Star of Happiness, Fu-sing; Star of Dignities, Lu-sing; and Star of Longevity, Shou-sing. There is also another group of the Seven Gods of Happiness, Ts'i-fu-shên; 'ut these seem to have had more vogue in Japan than in China itself. It is generally admitted that the Star

Fig. 65. THE THREE STARS OF HAPPINESS
Gilded wood, eighteenth century. Musée Guimet.

of Happiness is Yang Ch'êng, an official of the sixth century of our era. He was a mandarin in Tao-chou, a country where men were of very small stature, and the emperor of the day, who liked to surround himself with dwarfs as buffoons and comedians, brought every year so many people from Tao-chou that every family was in distress. Yang Ch'êng wrote a petition to the Emperor on this matter, and the Emperor was touched, and thereafter left the inhabitants of Tao-chou in peace. But this function has been assigned to others also, particularly to Kuo Tsï-i, the general who saved the

T'ang dynasty after the revolt of An Lu-shan, in the middle of the eighth century. It is told how one night, the seventh day of the seventh month, as he was about to go to bed, he suddenly saw, in a surrounding light, a woman sitting on a bed; he saluted her, saying, "To-day is the seventh day of the seventh month; surely you are the Celestial Weaving Maiden. I beg you to grant me happiness and riches." She then replied that he was the God of Happiness. This scene is often represented in popular art. Very often the God of Happiness is confused with the Agent of Heaven, and is represented, like the latter, standing, dressed in mandarin costume, holding in his hand a motto promising happiness. For example, "The Agent of Heaven bringeth Happiness as a gift."

When he is accompanied by a child they say it is Kuo Tsï-i bringing his son to court. Often he is surrounded with symbols of happiness, bats flitting about him (the Chinese word for bat is *fu*, pronounced exactly like the word for happiness, *fu*).

Fig. 66. THE GOD OF EMOLUMENTS

The Star of Emoluments (Fig. 66), Lu-sing, who is often called simply the Star of Officials, Kuan-sing, is a personage called Shï Fên, a native of Ho-nei, who attached himself when very young to the fortunes of the founder of the Han dynasty as he passed through his native city after conquering it (205 B.C.), and died more than a hundred years old, in 124 B.C., laden with honours and wealth. He himself and his four children each enjoyed a salary of two thousand *shï* of grain (under the Han dynasty officials' salaries were paid half in grain, half in money, and the total was calculated in measures of about three cubic feet, known as *shï*, approximately equivalent to twenty-five litres), so that he was called Mr Ten Thousand *shï*, Wan-shï kün. According to others, he was the star K'uei. Others again hold that he is the constellation Wên-ch'ang, and that it was the Great Emperor of Literature who is described by this name. Formerly, as a matter of fact, he received the title of Steward of the Dignities and Emoluments of the Living and the Dead.

The God of Longevity, Shou-shên, was also called the Ancient of the South Pole; he is the god of the fine star Canopus of the Ship Argo. It is he who decides the date of every man's death. When the physiognomist Kuan Lo had perceived that Chao Yen would not live beyond twenty years he advised him to go, on a day he appointed, to the southern part of a certain field, to the foot of a great mulberry-tree, taking with him a jar of wine and dried stag's meat, there he would find two men playing draughts, and was to offer them wine and meat, and when they spoke to him be content with saluting them without saying a word. The boy did as he was told, and the two players drank his wine.

When the game was ended one said to the other, "We have drunk his wine. Shall we not show our thanks?" "The official document on this boy's life is completed. What can be done?" replied the other. The first then took the document and, after examining it, changed the order of the characters 'ten' and 'nine' so that out of the 'nineteen' years of life written down in it he made 'ninety' years. Then both of them vanished. When he came back Kuan Lo explained that one was the God of the North Pole, who appoints birth, and the other the God of the South Pole,[1] who appoints death. The God of Longevity has a huge bald skull rising up with very prominent bosses high over the face; he is generally standing, leaning with one hand upon the knotty stick of the Immortals, and in the other holding a peach, the fruit that gives immortality. At his feet there are often placed a mushroom and a tortoise, emblems of long life.

Fig. 67. The Three Stars of Happiness

The three Gods of Happiness are often represented together, the God of Happiness in the middle, having the God of Longevity on his left and the God of Emoluments on his right. Sometimes they are represented symbolically: a pine-tree (longevity) under which are a stag (emoluments) and a bat (happiness); sometimes a mushroom and a crane are added, also emblems of longevity. Again, in families not belonging to the class of literati the God of Emoluments is frequently replaced by the Immortal who Giveth Children, who is set on the right of the God of Happiness, balancing the God of Longevity placed on the left. There are also Taoist images of the Six Gods of Happiness who are the six stars of the Southern Bushel (Sagittarius)—that is to say, the three already described and three others less known, with the Star of Longevity as president. Sometimes they are pasted as pendants on the images of the Seven Gods of the Northern Bushel (the Great Bear). Lastly there are Buddhist images of Seven Gods of Happiness; but this last group is more popular in Japan than in China.

The Eighteen Arhats and the Eight Immortals. These are groups of personages, some Buddhist, others Taoist, whose *rôle* is to protect religion and instruct men. The first are the Eighteen Arhats (*shï-pa lo-han*), or, again, increasing the number, the Five Hundred Arhats; the second are the Eight Immortals (*pa-sien*).

It is related that the Buddha commanded certain of his disciples to remain in the world without entering into Nirvāna until the coming of the future Buddha Maitreya, to protect his Law. The original list contained only sixteen saints, when in the seventh

[1] We are not to take North Pole and South Pole in an astronomical sense, but in a sort of topographical meaning. The North and South Poles are not stars close to the extremes of the imaginary prolongation of the axis of the earth, but constellations situated one to the north (the Great Bear) and the other to the south (Sagittarius) of a Chinese looking up at the sky.

THE EIGHT IMMORTALS (PA HSIEN.)
(Musée Guimet.)

century the celebrated monk Hüan-tsang translated the little book devoted to them. It was in China, about the tenth century, that two others were added. They are usually represented in the guise of monks in various attitudes and with different attributes, sometimes alone, sometimes surrounding Maitreya of the Big Belly. This group has in China had more success in art than in religion itself, and, except for Pindola and Bhadrà, who are in some degree the object of a monastic cult, no one concerns himself about them, either collectively or individually.

The Taoists imitated the Buddhist series to the best of their ability by bringing together eight celebrated Immortals: this is a heterogeneous assembly of personages who have nothing in common. As the Arhats are charged with the duty of protecting the Buddhist Law, they are the protectors of Taoism, going about the world to convert and to save men. Each of them has his legend, which is often reduced to something extremely slight. Of the first among them, Han-chung Li, it is said only that he was the master of the second, Lü Tung-pin; of Chang Kuo-lao it is known that he rode a white donkey which he folded in two like a sheet of paper as soon as he had ceased to need its services, and laid away in a box. Lan Ts'ai-ho was a street-singer, male or female (the legend hesitates on the point of his sex, and makes him sometimes a hermaphrodite, sometimes a girl), who, all clad in rags, used to wander here and there singing, and one fine day mounted to the skies. Han Siang-tsï, they say, was the nephew of Han Yü, one of the greatest poets of the ninth century, and it is claimed that among the uncle's works are found pieces of verse dedicated to him and extolling his magical power; this power was manifested one day when, being yet a child, he caused a clump of peonies in flower to spring up under the eyes of his uncle, who was urging him to apply himself to the study of the Classics. Ts'ao Kuo-kiu is supposed to be the brother of an empress of the Sung dynasty, who in the twelfth century retired into solitude to escape the debauches and the crimes of his elder brother, and was visited by Han-chung Li and Lü Tung-pin, who instructed him. Of the immortal Damsel Ho, Ho-sien-ku, we are told only that she lived long in the mountains and was converted by Lü Tung-pin, who gave her a peach of immortality.

Lastly, Li of the Iron Crutch, T'ie-kuai Li, was an ascetic who was instructed by Lao-tsï himself; he could project his soul out of his body on journeyings that lasted several days. Once when he had set out in this fashion, bidding his disciple to keep his body for six days, and burn it on the seventh if he had not returned, the disciple, suddenly hearing that his mother was ill, burned the body before the appointed date, and when the soul came back it was forced to seek another body, but found only that of an old, ugly, tottering beggar who had just died of cold, and had to be content with that.

The only one whose legend is a little more developed is Lü Tung-pin, who has been put on the stage in a famous play *The Dream of the Bowl of Sorghum Wine.* Lü Tung-pin, a young student on his way to sit for his doctorate at the capital, stops at an inn, where he meets an Immortal in disguise. After conversing with him he falls asleep, and in a few moments dreams a long life of eighteen years. He passes his examination and marries the daughter of one of the ministers; then, being sent to subdue certain rebels, he comes back victorious, but to find his wife in the arms of a lover. In his fury he is about to kill her, when an aged servant succeeds in persuading him to spare her, and he contents himself with repudiating her. Then, being condemned to banishment for some transgression during his expedition, he wanders in distress with his children, stripped of all resources, and ends by being killed by a brigand. At this moment he awakes, and, understanding the vanity of the pleasures of the world, he is converted, and presently becomes an Immortal.

Like the Eighteen Arhats, the Eight Immortals are scarcely the object of a cult: Li of

Fig. 68. FOUR OF THE EIGHT IMMORTALS: LI OF THE IRON CRUTCH, LAN TS'AI-HO, TS'AO KUO-KIU, HAN-CHUNG LI

Eighteenth century. Musée Guimet.

the Iron Crutch often serves as a sign for druggists, but he is not one of their usual patrons; Lü Tung-pin is practically the only popular one; he frequently appears at spiritist séances to indicate remedies or exorcisms. The big collection of his works is very widely known. But even if they have remained outside religion they have often inspired artists. Their type is duly fixed at least since the Mongol period. Han-chung Li, clad in a great mantle, often dilapidated, waves a feather fan; Lü Tung-pin is a young man in the costume of a literatus, with a sword slung at his back and a fly-whisk in his hand; Chang Kuo-lao is mounted back to front on his donkey (sometimes also in the orthodox fashion), with a phœnix-feather in his hand; Lan Ts'ai-ho is a poorly clad adolescent, one foot bare, the other shod, and carrying a flute; Han Siang-tsï is a boy with his hair still tied up in two little knots on either side of his head, carrying a bouquet of flowers or a basket of peaches;

Ts'ao Kuo-kiu is a full-grown man in official bonnet and dress, holding the tablet of a high dignitary akin to the imperial family. Ho-sien-ku (Ho the immortal Damsel) is a girl in elegant costume, wearing upon her shoulder a huge lotus flower. Lastly T'ie-kuai Li (Li of the Iron Crutch) is an ugly old beggar, bald and bearded, lame and leaning on an iron crutch, carrying a gourd, his brow girt with a gold ring that Lao-tsï gave him to bind the few locks he had left. They are often placed on various aquatic animals, in memory of a journey they undertook across the sea, each having a mount of his own,

Fig. 69. Four of the Eight Immortals: Ho-sien-ku, Chang Kuo-lao, Lü Tung-pin, Han Siang-tsï
Eighteenth century. Musée Guimet.

in the course of which they had to contend with the son of the Dragon-king of the Eastern Sea.

The Two Protectresses of Women, Taoist and Buddhist. If the family as a whole has a series of protecting divinities the women have their special patronesses who concern themselves especially about them and their needs. According to the different regions, this patroness is Taoist or Buddhist in type: in the former case it is the Princess of the Motley Clouds; in the second it is the " Bodhisattva that Hearkeneth Rumours "—that is to say, the plaints and prayers of living beings—Kuan-yin p'u-sa (Avalokiteṣvara) under a quite special and unexpected female guise, " Kuan-yin the Giver of Children " (Sung-tsï Kuan-yin).

The Princess of the Motley Clouds. The Princess of the Motley Clouds, Pi-hia yüan-kün, who is often called simply the Holy Mother, Shêng mu, or Madame Lady, Nai-nai niang-niang, is generally regarded as the daughter of the great Emperor of the Eastern Peak, which often brings her, especially in the North, also the title of Lady of T'ai-shan, T'ai-shan niang-niang. Her cult is ancient, and we can trace her legend back to about the Han period. It is related how in the olden time she appeared to King Wu of Chou: he saw her in a dream weeping on a roadway, and she told him that she, the daughter of the Eastern Peak and wedded to the son of the God of the Western Sea, could not go to her husband because she must needs cross the principality of Ts'i, that her train would be accompanied by wind and rain, and that the presence of the Holy Prince of Ts'i, T'ai-kung, forbade the ravaging in this way of the country of which he was the overlord. When the king awoke he remembered his dream and sent for T'ai-kung to come to the Court, so as to allow the goddess to pass. According to others, her husband is Mao Ying, the eldest of the three Mao brothers who attained immortality in the first century before our era upon the mountain Mao, near Nankin. In Fukien it appears that, while keeping her title of Princess of the Motley Clouds, and the same functions, her relationship with the Eastern Peak, all too far away, has been forgotten. She is given the family name of Ch'ên, and various legends are told of her, which, however, are not of any particular interest.

Fig. 70. The Holy Mother
Popular print.

The cult of this goddess is very popular throughout the whole of China, where she is the protectress of women and children: indeed, it is she who gives children and presides generally over childbirth. She is represented with a special headdress made of three birds with outspread wings, one facing to the front and the two others one on either side of the head (Fig. 70); and she is accompanied by two assistants, the Lady of Good Sight, who holds in her hands an enormous eye, and preserves children from diseases of the eyes, and the Lady who Brings Children, Sung-tsï niang-niang, carrying a new-born babe in her hands. She has furthermore a train of six secondary divinities who are in charge of the various phases of childhood: the Lady who Favours the Beginning of Pregnancy, the Princess who Mysteriously Nourishes and Strengthens the Shape of the Embryo, the Lady who Hastens Birth, the Princess who Causes the Rule to be Observed and Protects Infancy, the Lady who Gives Birth, the Princess who Grants Joy and Protects the Accouchement, the Lady of Smallpox, the Princess who Guarantees Tranquillity and Kindness to Childhood, the Lady who Guides Ignorance, the Princess who Guides and Directs Childhood (the last named is sometimes confused with the Lady who Brings Children), the Lady of Suckling, the Princess who Gives to Eat and Nourishes Childhood. All six

Fig. 71. The Holy Mother and her Two Servants
In their temple, at T'ai-shan.

are not always placed at her side: sometimes it is only the Lady who Favours the Beginning of Pregnancy and the Lady who Brings Children who keep her company. The Princess, her two assistants, and her six attendants form the group called collectively the Nine Ladies; numerous temples are erected to them through the whole of China, which are commonly called the Temples of the Lady, Nai-nai-miao, to whom the women, and often the men too, go in pilgrimage in order to have children. One of the most famous is that of T'u-shan, the pilgrimage to which on the eighth day of the fourth month is very popular.

A devotee, after due preparation—only taking a Lenten meal in the morning—that is to say, with neither meat nor fish, nor seasoning of garlic or onion, nor wine—then rinsing the mouth, which is one of the most important Taoist purifications, and obligatory before every prayer, betakes herself to the Temple of the Lady. She prostrates herself before the altar on which is the statue of the Holy Mother between her two assistants, burns incense and silver paper, then prostrates herself anew, making a prayer somewhat in this manner: " O Lady! have pity upon us, wretched childless ones! " while the guardian of the temple strikes a musical stone to draw the attention of the goddess and make her take note of the prayer just made to her. Then she rises and goes on to pass a cord round the neck of one of the children that surround the Lady who Brings Children, one of the assistants of the Princess of the Motley Clouds, or in other temples the Lady who Guides Ignorance, so as to bind it to her and force it to go with her. Sometimes too some carry away one of the pairs of children's shoes, made of paper, that are hung as *ex-voto* offerings around the statue.

Kuan-yin. Kuan-yin to a great extent plays the same *rôle* as the Holy Mother, except, perhaps, as regards accouchements; for the rest she is supposed to bring children, to cure them, etc. The principal difference is that the cult is Buddhist and the temples are served by bonzes and not by *tao-shï*. She is not, it must be added, the only Buddhist personage who is especially applied to for the gift of children: at Canton it is the Mother of the Demons, Kuei-tsï-mu—that is to say, Hārītī—who takes her place; and her statue, surrounded by statuettes of children, which is in the series of the twenty-four *devas*, is always covered with votive offerings of all kinds, paper shoes, etc., brought by the women going to pray. But that is a local matter, and in almost the whole of China the Buddhist 'Children-bringer' is Kuan-yin.

The name of Kuan-yin, or Kuan-shï-yin, is a bad Chinese translation of that of the Bodhisattva Avalokiteṣvara: it came about through a confusion between the Sanskrit words *īṣvara*, 'lord,' and *svara*, 'sound,' 'noise.' Avalokiteṣvara is one of the two assistants of the Buddha Amitābha, the sovereign of the Pure Land of the West; the other, Mahāsthāmaprāpta (Ta-shê-chê), plays no part in the popular religion. He has taken a vow not to become a Buddha until he has saved all living beings: " If in working for the salvation of all beings I feel a single moment of discouragement may my head burst into ten pieces! " He is the Most Compassionate and Most Benevolent, Ta-pei ta-ts'ï. He is represented with a thousand eyes and a thousand arms to save the damned, a horse's head to save the animals, eleven heads among the Asuras, carrying a sceptre among the gods, etc. (Fig. 72). These are the Six Avalokiteṣvaras, each of which is specially concerned with the living beings engaged in each of the six ways of birth and death; but they are not six distinct and separate personages, they are six shapes he takes at once, employing his supernatural powers in his great compassion for all beings. He takes many other shapes besides: Chinese iconography has lists of the Seven Kuan-yins, the Thirty-three Kuan-yins, etc.

Nevertheless it is none of these normal Buddhist forms that became popular in China, but a feminine form that is called Kuan-yin Bringing Children, Sung-tsï Kuan-yin, or, more currently, the Lady who Brings Children, Sung-tsï niang-niang. There have been interminable discussions as to the origin of what is called the change of sex in Avalokiteṣvara, a man in the Buddhist literature of India and a woman in the Chinese popular religion, and sometimes an attempt has been made to discover in this the influence of a great native goddess anterior to Buddhism, who would in this way have survived dressed up with a Buddhist name. The popular images of Kuan-yin the Giver of Children seem to me to present the solution of a problem that in reality has very little substance, except for a European accustomed to the definite shapes and clearly outlined personages of the classical literary mythologies: they often carry the legend of "Bodhisattva in white raiment, Kuan-yin who brings children." Now the expression "Bodhisattva in white raiment," *Po-i ta-shï*, is not a mere casual term due to the artist's caprice: it is the name of a definite form of Kuan-yin, a feminine form of Tantric origin; in fact, it is the Chinese name of the mild aspect of Tārā whom the Thibetans commonly call the White Tārā, but whose Sanskrit name of Pāndaravāsinī ('clad in white') the Chinese have translated with literal exactness. She is represented as clad in a white dress, holding a white lotus flower, to symbolize the pureness of the heart that, having uttered the vow to become Buddha, remains unalterably steadfast to its vow. We know that in the Tantric books the Buddhas and Bodhisattvas appear in multiple shapes, mild and terrible, male and female, of symbolical significance. The mild forms are those that appear to men to instruct them and preach the Law to them: they symbolize the Word—that is to say, the magic formulas that constitute the fundamental part of the Tantric books—the terrible forms are those that repel and destroy the demons, and they symbolize Thought. And, again, the male forms show the personage in his helpful activities for all beings, the female forms represent

Fig. 72. MASCULINE KUAN-YIN (AVALOKITEṢVARA) WITH THE THOUSAND ARMS

his ecstatic meditation (*samādhi*). Avalokiteṣvara, a male form and of mild aspect, has as his fierce counterpart Avalokiteṣvara of the Horse's Head, Ma-t'ou Kuan-yin (Hayagrīva), and has for his female shape Tārā, whose mild aspect is Kuan-yin Clad-in-White (Pāndaravāsinī), and whose terrible aspect is the Green Tārā of the Thibetans, whom the Chinese call simply Tārā, and who is mated with Hayagrīva.

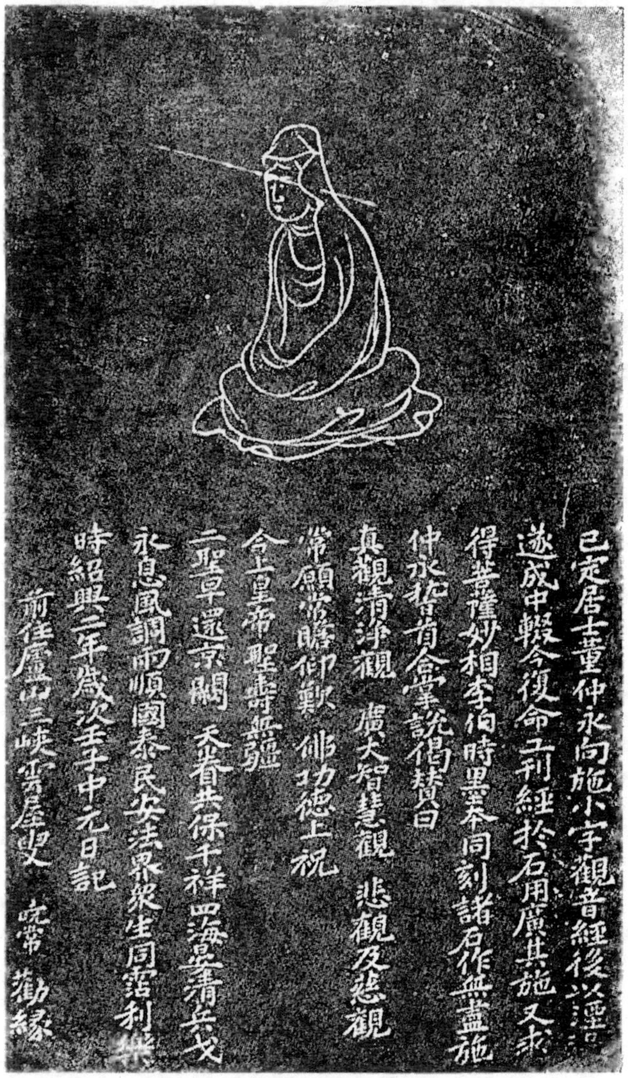

Fig. 73. KUAN-YIN OF THE WHITE GARMENTS
From an eleventh-century drawing by Li Lung-mien.

Kuan-yin Clad-in-White was introduced into China toward the middle of the eighth century with the translation of the *Ta ji king*; but it is seemingly not there that painters and the upper classes turned to find her. She is indissolubly linked with the apparitions and the miracles of the island of P'u-t'o,[1] in the Chu-san archipelago (Chekiang), especially of the Grotto of the Sound of the Waves, Ch'ao-yin tung, and though the texts speak for the most part of a more recent period, I should be glad to think that the speedy development of the island monastery, founded at the beginning of the tenth century, helped to spread this particular type of Kuan-yin. It is, in fact, from that moment that we begin to meet it among the religious painters. Even without reckoning the pictures of Kuan-yin Clad-in-White that we find mentioned among the works of Sin Ch'êng and his contemporary Tu Tsï-huai, as well as among those of Ts'ao Chung-yüan and of Wang Ts'i-han, the painters of the epoch of the Five Dynasties, in the tenth century, and that are now known only from doubtful catalogues, about the end of the eleventh century one of the greatest painters of the Sung dynasty, Li Kung-lin, or, as he is usually called from his surname, Li Lung-mien, had made a charming little drawing of her in Chinese ink, which, by a happy chance, an admirer had reproduced on stone in 1132, not long after the artist's death, as a pious deed at the beginning of the copy of a holy book. And more recent pictures are very numerous (Fig. 73).

This Kuan-yin Clad-in-White, which had been brought by art already away from the setting of Tantrism, was snatched from Buddhism itself by the popular religion, to become the Kuan-yin who Brings Children, representations of which are so widely spread. All the great currents of the Chinese religion contributed to this evolution, which cannot be

[1] The name of the island of P'u-t'o is an abbreviation of Potalaka, the name of the abode of Avalokiteṣvara in the sea of the South.

very ancient; Taoism took part in it to a fairly considerable extent, and the influence of the Princess of the Motley Clouds, already definitely established ever since the Mongol epoch, certainly made itself very strongly felt. In this popular Kuan-yin, to whom those who desire children turn, there remains very little of the Tārā Pāndaravāsinī, who is her prototype, and the change in *rôle* is so extensive that without the survival of the old title, which has been preserved in many pictures to bear witness, and which clearly establishes the affiliation, we might hesitate to link the two together. It seems that a misunderstanding of the Tantric terminology may be at the root of this transformation. Pāndaravāsinī—that is to say, Kuan-yin Clad-in-White—belonged to the "Treasure-of-the-Womb" world, T'ai-tsang kiai (Garbhakoṣadhātu), and it was sufficient to take the symbolical expression literally to proceed to turn this female form of Kuan-yin into a goddess who gives children and protects women. But that was an evolution that belonged exclusively to the modern popular religion; thus the Kuan-yin Giver of Children created by the popular religion never really penetrated into Buddhism; yet Buddhism might have easily justified it, since the Bodhisattvas can assume every kind of appearance, and besides an oft-quoted passage of the *Saddharmapuṇḍarīka* spoke of Avalokiteṣvara as having power to grant children to whosoever should entreat him. But though in practice the bonzes have accepted it, and give a regular explanation of it, the statue is rarely seen in their temples; and if it is sometimes found it is to some extent as a foreigner and a guest, just as we also find Kuan-ti or Wang the Transcendant Official. To find representations of her we must go outside the Buddhist temples to those innumerable crudely coloured prints that are pasted on walls or burned while she is invoked.

Fig. 74. Kuan-yin of the White Garments
After a picture by Ch'ên Hien, seventeenth century.

For this really new personage a legend of her own was needed: the Tantric account of the origin of Tārā, sprung from the ray of light emitted by Avalokiteṣvara, could never become popular, and besides everything in the sacred books was concerned with an Avalokiteṣvara in the form of a man. The elements of a legend relating to a female form of the Bodhisattva were found in one of the collections of revelations of an illuminate of the middle of the seventh century, the monk Tao-süan. Tao-süan, a friend of the pilgrim Hüan-tsang, had been one of the most learned and most eminent men of religion of his time; but in his old age he became insane and imagined himself surrounded by gods who came at every moment to visit and converse with him, giving him revelations on every kind of religious subject, which he hastened to set down in a tremulous and often illegible hand. One of his disciples collected and published those that could be deciphered, and what remains of them is highly curious. It was Tao-süan who was responsible for the introduction of Wei-t'o as guardian in all the temples of China: this name is due to a mistake in the transcription of a Sanskrit word. He seems also to be responsible for the history of Kuan-yin as the third daughter of a king of bygone times, named Miao-shan. The legend, lost sight of in the confused mass of these revelations for centuries, reappeared in the Mongol epoch, when the Taoists laid hold of it and adapted it to their own ideas. For a long time they had been claiming Kuan-yin as belonging to them. A Buddhist writer of the middle of the sixth century spoke of a *tao-shï* who had made a statue of Lao-tsï between two Bodhisattvas, Kuan-yin and Kin-kang-tsang; and one of the Taoist works of which M. Pelliot has discovered manuscript fragments at Tun-huang mentioned, in an enumeration of the Great Immortals, the Great Immortal of Pu-tan-lo-kia (Potalaka), who is clearly Kuan-yin, beside the great Immortal Ti-shï, who is Indra, and the Great Immortal Huo-li-to, who is a male counterpart of Hārītī, the Mother of the Demons.

Fig. 75. KUAN-YIN, THE GIVER OF CHILDREN
Bronze. Musée Guimet.

The most widely spread book to-day is a kind of edifying tale of fairly recent date entitled *Complete Life of Kuan-yin of the Southern Sea.*. In its present form it is, properly speaking, neither Buddhist nor Taoist, but definitely belongs to the popular religion. There was once upon a time, in the country of Hing-lin, situated between India and Siam, a king named Miao-chuang, who, having reached the age of fifty without having children, made great sacrifices to the God of the Western Peak (Hua-shan), which lasted eight days, and after which the queen had, one after the other, three daughters, who were called Miao-ch'êng, Miao-yin, and Miao-shan. When they were grown-up the king decided to marry them, and thereafter to choose a successor from among his sons-in-law. The eldest daughter married a scholar, the second a general; but the third, Miao-shan, refused to marry and requested to be allowed to enter a convent and to lead the life of religion. The king at the outset refused, and placed her in confinement, then in the end authorized her to go to the Monastery of the White Sparrow, but in order to disgust her with monastic life he gave orders that she should be given the task of cooking and washing for the whole convent, which contained five hundred nuns. The Mother of the Great Bear, Tou-mu, seized with pity, ordered the dragon to dig her a well and give her water, the tiger to bring her wood for her fire, and the birds to gather vegetables for her, the God of the Hearth to cook the victuals, the god of the *k'ie-lan* to sweep out the kitchen, so that her work was done by itself. When the king heard of the marvel he ordered the monastery to be burned with all the nuns. It was set on fire, but Miao-shan quenched it by a fresh miracle, and her father, infuriated, commanded that she should be brought to the court to be decapitated. While preparations were being made for the execution the queen, eager to save her daughter's life, built a marvellous pavilion by the roadside to tempt her, but she refused to go into it, and was led to the place of execution, where, as the headsman's sword miraculously broke on touching her neck, she was strangled. Then the Jade Emperor ordered the God of the Place to take the form of a tiger and to carry away her body upon his back into a forest of pines. Her soul wended its way to the world below, the kings of which came in all respect to meet her. As soon as she had entered she began to recite the sacred books, and immediately all pain and suffering were at an end, so that the King Yama, finding himself thenceforth unable to carry out the duties of his post by inflicting punishment on the wicked, decided to send her away; she was taken back to the pine forest, where she found her body again. After some fresh trials the Buddha appeared to her, gave her to eat a Peach of Immortality, then led her to the island of P'u-t'o (Potalaka), on the coast of Chekiang. There after nine years of meditation she was visited by Ti-tsang, who enthroned her as Bodhisattva, making her ascend a lotus throne in the presence of the Dragon-kings, the Gods of the Five Peaks, the ten Kings of the Hells, the Eight Immortals, the Gods of Thunder, etc. Now in the meantime the Jade Emperor had punished King Miao-chuang by ordering the God of Epidemics to send an incurable ulcer upon him. The physicians declared that the only cure must be made from the hands and the eyes of a living person. Miao-shan then plucked out her eyes and had her hands cut off and sent them to her father, who was healed, and became converted forthwith, while Miao-shan miraculously recovered her hands and her eyes. All being thus happily concluded, the Jade Emperor rewarded Miao-shan by sending the god of the Planet Venus to her to confer upon her the title of Most Compassionate and Most Benevolent Bodhisattva, while her sisters, who had been converted, became the Bodhisattvas Mañjuṣrī and Samantabhadra.

Kuan-yin the Giver of Children is usually represented as a woman entirely covered by a great white veil which hides even her hair. She is sitting on a lotus flower, holding a child in her arms. To right and left are placed her two attendants, standing, the Young Man of Excellent Capacities, Shan-ts'ai tung-tsï, and the Daughter of the Dragon-king, Lung-wang nü; a bird brings her her rosary, and a willow-branch is in a vase beside her.

Often she is placed upon the rock of P'u-t'o. Sometimes too the white garment is partly covered by an embroidered robe, or even disappears completely, to give place to a Chinese woman's dress. In this case it is simply the type of the Princess of the Motley Clouds and her attendants that has been adopted and given the name of Kuan-yin. In nearly every house are found crudely coloured prints or even statuettes of her; in Fukien they are even given the place of honour in the family shrine, between the God of the Hearth and the God of the Place. On the festival of her birth, the nineteenth day of the second month, and, in more devout families, on her two other feasts, the nineteenth day of the sixth and the ninth months also, the women present a few dishes of Lenten fare, with sticks of incense.

Outside these regular feasts they pray to her especially to give them children. But as no statue of her is to be found in the majority of the temples, the women go and pray to any Avalokiteṣvara, under whatever shape (always male in the Chinese temples, except for Kuan-yin of the White Garments) he is represented. As they do for the Princess of the Motley Clouds, after burning incense they deposit a little shoe as a votive gift, or, indeed, some carry away one of the shoes already placed there. Some add vows of abstinence from flesh, either perpetual or on certain days, which vary with the individual devotee.

The Immortal Chang who gives Male Children. Besides the two great divinities who are the protectresses of women, there is also a personage who is specially entreated for boy-children, the Immortal Chang, Chang-sien. Like a certain number of popular divinities, he springs from the transformation of an ancient rite of the olden religion, so that the three fundamental sources of the modern Chinese religion, the antique religion, Buddhism, and Taoism, have each contributed their part to the popular worship centring on this particularly important point, the continuation of the family and of its cult. In ancient days when a boy was born they hung a bow of mulberry wood on the left of the door. A few days later, when the child had been formally accepted by the head of the family they took down this bow and shot six wormwood arrows at the sky, the earth, and the four points of the compass, to ward off all calamities. This ceremony, which has gradually died out through almost the whole of China, seems to have survived a long time, in a modified form, in certain parts of Szechwan, where it was personified in the Immortal Chang (the name is due to a play upon words: the expression *chang kung*, 'to bend the bow,' is the same in sound as *Chang kung*, Mr Chang). And, indeed, it is in Szechwan that we see this cult emerge for the first time. According to a famous anecdote, the widow of the King of Shu (Szechwan), who had been taken into the harem of the founder of the Sung dynasty after the conquest of her husband's kingdom at the end of the tenth century, had kept the portrait of her first husband, and when one day the Emperor asked her who it was she replied in fear that it was the picture of the Immortal Chang of the land of Shu, who gives children. The anecdote is not too trustworthy, but about the middle of the following century Su Sün (who lived from 1009 to 1066), a native of Mei-shan, in Szechwan, in a poem attributed to the Immortal Chang the birth of his two sons, the great writers Su Shï and Su Ch'e. A little later another poet who was a native of this province, Li Shï (of the middle of the twelfth century), speaks of the very widely spread paintings in which he is represented shooting with a bow. It seems that the centre of his

Fig. 76. KUAN-YIN, THE GIVER OF CHILDREN
White porcelain.

cult was a temple he had on the mountain Tsing-Ch'êng, in the sub-prefecture of Mei-shan, and that the praises of Su Sün, famous himself, and especially for his sons, contributed in no small degree to spread it beyond his native country. The new god, as a matter of fact, came gradually to be honoured through the whole of the empire, and at the beginning of the Ming period the poet Kao K'i (who was executed at thirty-nine, at the end of the fourteenth century), having no son, received a picture of him from one of his friends, a *tao-shï* and thanked him in verse; but he had not forgotten the provincial origin of him whom he calls the Immortal of Ch'êng-tu.

Fig. 77. The Immortal Chang in the Triad of Happiness

He is represented as a man of ripe age bending a bow or an arbalest with which he shoots up at the sky: often there is placed in the corner of the picture the Celestial Dog fleeing on a cloud. His fundamental *rôle* is, as a matter of fact, to protect children against the Celestial Dog (the star Sirius), who presides over one of the thirty dangerous passages of their life and devours them. Besides this, he is invoked to grant the gift of children, but (this being the last trace of the rite from which he originated) he brings only boys. That is why his image is hung on the wall in the bedroom of young married couples. He is often accompanied by his son Kien t'an, who carries in his arms the child he gives to his worshippers. Some find it more befitting to have the child handed over to the mother by a woman, and add the Lady who Gives Children, Sung-tsï niang-niang, who is also one of the attendants of the Holy Mother (this is one of the titles of the latter as well as of Kuan-yin); at other times it is he himself, in the costume of a literatus, and without his bow, who presents the child, and he is given the place of the God of Emoluments in the Triad of Happiness (Fig. 77). In the temples or chapels dedicated to him (the Temples of the Hundred Sons are consecrated, according to the locality, to the Holy Mother or to the Immortal Chang, like the Chapels of the Hundred Sons which are often found among the numerous halls of the temples of the Gods of Walls and Moats) he is often shown as followed by his son and the Lady who Gives Children, and along the walls, to the right and to the left, are ranged the Twelve Spirits of the Cycle, *shï-êr yüan-kia*, each one of which presides over one of the twelve years, and watches over the children born in his special year. Frequently also, as in the temples of the Holy Mother, there are found the Goddesses of Smallpox and Measles.

In certain regions, on the other hand, he is identified with Chang Kuo-lao, one of the Eight Immortals, and it is the image of this latter, mounted upon his white donkey, that is hung up in the houses.

The Gods of Diseases and the Healing Gods. The *tao-shï* have a Ministry of Epidemics composed of five gods who preside over the epidemics of the five cardinal points and the four seasons. But these divinities are hardly the object of worship, except from the Taoist sorcerers, who give them names and titles according to the regions and the schools to which they belong. So too with the Ministry of Medicine and that of the Driving out of Evil Enchantments, their members are practically only known to doctors and exorcizers.

Among the people the smallpox divinity, Tou-shên, is one of the most dreaded. It is said that she is especially charged with the punishment of infanticide, which is common in certain provinces, where a very large number of girl babies are drowned at birth, and that she prevents the guilty from having posterity. Her image is often found in the little chapels erected at crossroads in the heart of the country, and also in a great number of temples. In certain regions she is a goddess, and is ranged among the attendants of the Princess of the Motley Clouds, with her son, the God of the Black Smallpox, Pan-shên, beside the two deities of Measles, Sha-shên and Chên-shên; in other temples she is a male deity. In either case both pictured images and statues are characterized by an eruption of pustules upon the face. There is also the Goddess of the Plague, the God of Asthma, and the Generalissimo of the Five Dynasties, a God of Boils who seems to be peculiar to Fukien, etc. All these gods and goddesses are invoked as much for protection against the diseases they dispense as for healing, but they are almost invariably only addressed for isolated or not very serious cases, or again in anticipation, following a consultation with a medium or a sorcerer who has advised making an offering to them.

In great epidemics they are too lacking in power to be of much use. In many regions, particularly in Chihli, the feasts of the Day of the Year are celebrated anew, whatever the time of the year may be. The spirits thus misled will suppose that the year is ended and a new year begun, and that the time fixed for the duration of the disease is past, so that it will speedily come to an end. But at the same time the populace goes in crowds to the great temples. In the cities it is above all the temple of the God of Walls and Moats, the official protector of the inhabitants, and responsible for them to the Jade Emperor, that is visited. The local officials used to go there to make official sacrifices, and sometimes the old notion of the responsibility of the sovereign or officials in the ills that befell their subjects or their district gave rise to strange manifestations. I have already told the story of the sub-prefect installing himself in the full sunshine beside the statue of the God of Walls and Moats to decide, by the resistance of his own head and that of the statue, as to which of them was responsible for a calamity. The tale is told almost everywhere; usually it is with reference to a drought (and this is the original form, for the exposure of sorcerers and sorceresses to the sun was one of the ways of bringing down the rain), but sometimes also it is for an epidemic, for the responsibility of the mandarin remains the same whatever the nature of the calamity. The populace makes collections to give a feast to the god; a troupe of actors is engaged, and plays are given in his temple for one day or several. Visits are paid also to the temple of the Eastern Peak, who is the hierarchical superior of the God of Walls and Moats, or to the temple of Kuan-ti, who drives away evil spirits. Or else they go to the great Buddhist temples to appeal to the compassion of the Buddhas and Bodhisattvas, the Most Pitiful and the Most Benevolent, who have taken the vow to save all living beings. In certain regions it is the Buddha Bhaishajyaguru, Yo-shï-wang Fo, whose name means Buddha King-master of Remedies, who then sees worshippers, who are generally few in numbers, thronging at the foot of his altars, for he has taken the vow to " heal the diseases of all living beings," and this vow, which in reality applies to the " disease of ignorance," is taken literally by the crowd. But he is not the only one to whom they address themselves; they go also and burn incense and recite prayers before the statues of Kuan-yin or other Bodhisattvas, often making a vow of pilgrimage to be kept when once the danger is past.

If all this is without avail there remains the resource of a procession. Sometimes it is a god who has ordered this through a medium, and he has indicated also the place from which it is to start, the route to be followed, the offerings to be presented to the principal god and his attendants. It is almost always the local protecting deity who is taken in procession in this way. In the villages it is the patron to whom the principal temple is dedicated, often Kuan-yin of P'u-t'o, in Kiangsu and in Chekiang, or sometimes another Bodhisattva, when the temple is served by a bonze, or again a Taoist divinity or a local hero whose temple is served by lay Taoist masters; in the towns it is the God of Walls and Moats. The procession of the last-mentioned differs from that of his annual feast in practically only a few particulars. At its head are carried charms that destroy demons, and most frequently some of the temple mediums walk before or behind, their hair untied, sword in hand, and go dancing and pursuing the demons of the epidemic all along the way. For the rest, troops of magnates, each one with a lighted stick of incense in his hand, preceding and following the statues, then a train of statues, with gongs, tom-toms, umbrellas, and banners, and last of all bands of maskers disguised as demons of every kind—all this differs from the annual procession only in the numbers taking part.

In the villages of Kiangsu and the north of Chekiang prayers to the patron of the village are preceded by the ceremony of " putting a soul into " the statue. If the god, they think, does not protect the faithful and allows the epidemic to decimate them, that is because his statue is no longer animate and consequently does not know what is going on around it and does not report to him. The ceremony is accordingly intended to restore a soul to it. A procession takes place, in profound silence, in the middle of the night, through the streets and the countryside. The statues, made of dried clay and lacquered, are hollow and have an opening in the back closed by a shutter. On leaving the temple the priest, bonze, or *tao-shï*, opens this shutter; then the statue is borne along in its palanquin while the priest follows reciting the prayers in low tones. Directly he hears the cry of a living creature, a bird, an insect, any animal whatever, he shuts the shutter sharply, and at once leads the procession back to the temple, where the ceremonies begin. It is said that at the moment when the priest has shut the shutter he has captured the soul of the creature that uttered the cry; the creature falls dead, and its soul, shut up inside the statue, animates it; it sees and hears and can give the god information. From that moment it becomes worth while to perform ceremonies.

THE GODS OF THE OTHER WORLD

If the gods who concern themselves with the living, taken as they are right and left from the various mythologies, and assembled in a chaotic fashion by the popular religion, form a somewhat incoherent pantheon, it is not the same with those who govern the dead. Although present-day Chinese ideas on this point also are derived from a mixture of Buddhism and Taoism with old indigenous notions, as Taoism itself borrowed the general framework of its underworld from Buddhism, the whole is relatively fairly well arranged.

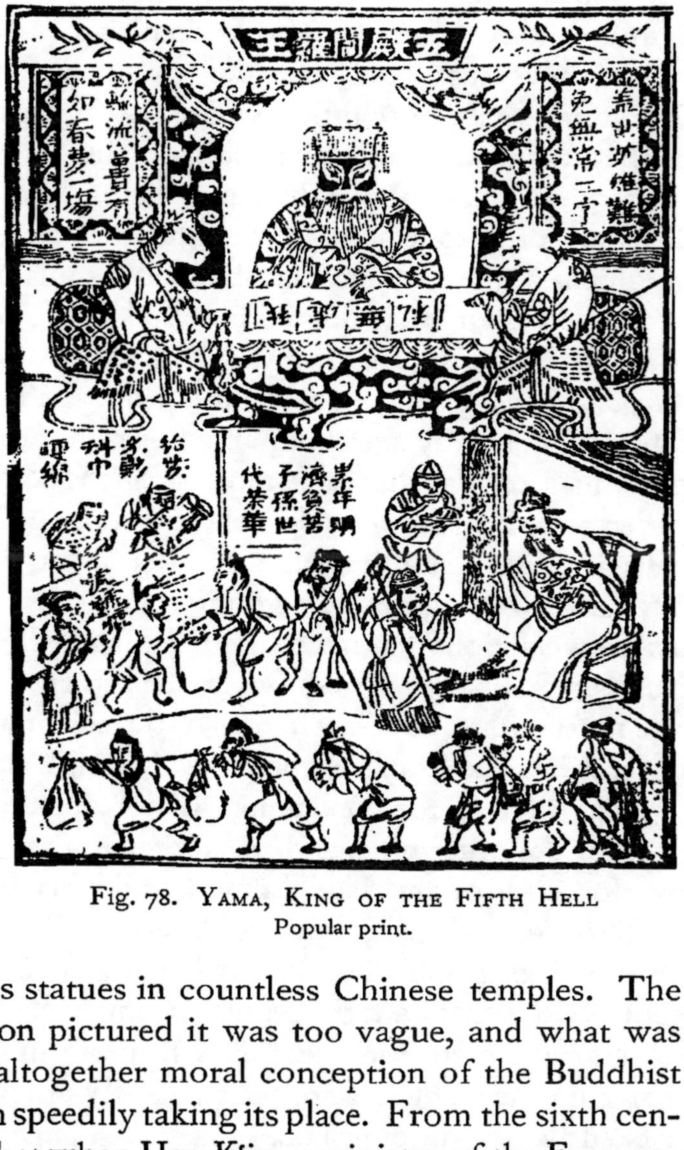

Fig. 78. Yama, King of the Fifth Hell
Popular print.

The Ten Hells and their Kings. The hells, or terrestrial prisons, *ti-yü*, are ten in number, and are governed by ten personages, who are called the Yama-Kings of the Ten Tribunals, *Shï-tien Yen-wang*, or, more simply, the Ten Kings, *Shï-wang*, by itself and without any other title. Each of them is the master of a particular hell, in which, as in the circles of Dante, certain specific sins are punished by definitely fixed penalties.

Buddhism provided the main background of this underworld, and brought with it the ancient Indo-Iranian god of the dead, Yama, so that to-day, while almost forgotten in the lands of his origin, he has his statues in countless Chinese temples. The world of the dead as the old Chinese religion pictured it was too vague, and what was known of it was too aristocratic to keep the altogether moral conception of the Buddhist hells and the precise descriptions of them from speedily taking its place. From the sixth century of our era the new belief was so popular that when Han K'in, a minister of the Emperor of the Sui, died in A.D. 592 the report spread that he had become King Yama in the lower regions. Shortly before his death a neighbour had seen guards before K'in's door in great numbers; in astonishment she had asked what was the matter: "We have come to fetch the king," they replied, and suddenly vanished. Then there was a sick man who came to the house and asked to be brought before the king. "What king?" inquired the servants. "King Yama!" The sons and grandsons of Han K'in wanted to have the man beaten with rods, but he restrained them, saying, "To have been a minister in my lifetime, to be King Yama after my death, that is enough for me!" Soon after he fell sick, was forced to take to his bed, and died.

If the Buddhist books gave a comprehensive picture of the lower regions they differed considerably with regard to the details. In particular they did not agree upon the number and the arrangement of the places of torment: according to some, there are eight hot hells and eight cold; according to others, there are eighteen hells in all; others declare that there are eight great ones, to each of which is attached sixteen lesser, which makes a hundred and thirty-six hells in all, etc., etc. These divergencies did not satisfy the Chinese, who are positive people, and wished to be accurately informed as to the lower regions where they must needs one day dwell, and to familiarize themselves beforehand with everything that goes on there. Hence long ago the Taoists, while copying the main lines of the organization of the Buddhist hells, fixed the number of the infernal judges at ten (the sovereigns of the eight hells, then a king who sits in judgment at the entrance and distributes the souls among the different places of torment, and another king who sits in judgment at the exit and distributes the souls upon the different paths of transmigration), and their system was adopted in a Buddhist book now lost, but which was highly popular in its day, in any case a forgery, the work of a bonze of Ch'eng-tu, the *Book of the Ten Kings, Shï wang king*. To-day it is from similar modern edifying works that the common folk and, generally speaking, all who are not regular members of religious orders, whether Buddhists or Taoists, take most of their notions about the hells and the judges of the lower world. The most complete is the *Yü li ch'ao chuan*, which describes in detail the hells and their subdivisions; another work, equally widely known, relates the descent into the lower regions of a young scholar of pure and blameless life, wrongfully arrested, his conversations with the infernal kings, the scenes he was allowed to see, and finally his dismissal back to earth, where he returned to life after several days of seeming death. We must add to this the chapter of the celebrated novel *The Voyage in the West*, in which is described the T'ang Emperor T'ai-tsung's descent into the nether world.

The first of the Ten Kings is not only the sovereign of the first hell, but also the chief of the other nine, and the supreme master of the infernal world, naturally under the overlordship of the Jade Emperor and his regent on earth, the great Emperor of the Eastern Peak. It was, they say, Yama himself, Yen-lo wang, or Yen-wang, as his name is pronounced in Chinese, who originally occupied the place. But he showed himself too compassionate toward the criminals who came before him: too frequently he allowed them to return to earth for a few days to perform good works and thus redeem their sins, so that the other judges were seeing hardly anybody coming before their tribunals, and the wicked were not punished. The Jade Emperor, to punish him, degraded him from his supreme rank and sent him to govern the fifth hell. To-day it is Ts'in-kuang-wang who holds the office. To him the dead are taken in the first place; he examines the mass of their sins, and those souls whose merits and demerits he finds balancing one another are sent back to be born into this world anew without his inflicting any penalties upon them. As for the souls of the guilty ones, he has them brought to the Terrace of the Mirror of the Wicked, Sie-king t'ai; a huge mirror is presented to them, in which all their victims appear to them, the living beings they have put to death, etc.; then they are taken to the other kings whose duty it is in their turn to judge them and punish them. It is he also who sends the souls of suicides back to earth in the guise of famished demons, until the span of life allotted to them by Heaven, but shortened by their own hand, has been fully accomplished, unless they have a valid excuse to put forward: loyalty to the prince, filial piety, chastity in the case of maidens and widows, etc. On their return they are hurried off to the City of the Dead-by-Accident, Wang-sï ch'êng, whence no one ever comes forth to be born again. However, it is currently believed that they obtain power to come back and be born again on earth when they have found one to take their place, which is why the souls of the dead try to drown those who are crossing the river, the souls of the hanged to persuade all those within their reach to hang themselves, and so on. It is also generally believed, although all the religious tracts, Taoist and Buddhist alike, do everything they can to eradicate this belief, that the same fate awaits not only suicides, but all who die accidentally, however unintentionally. The first king is the great judge, but he punishes no one directly; he nevertheless detains dishonest monks for some time, shutting them up in a dark dungeon and obliging them to finish reciting all the prayers they neglected during life after having pledged themselves to say them.

The second king, Ch'u-kiang wang, punishes dishonest male and female go-betweens (we know that they are absolutely indispensable intermediaries to render a marriage valid in China), fraudulent trustees, ignorant doctors, those who have wounded or mutilated persons or animals, etc. In the sixteen particular minor hells under his jurisdiction the punishments are most various. There is a dungeon of the Famished (the Buddhist *pretas*), over against which has been placed, for the sake of symmetry, a dungeon of the Athirst; there are others in which the dead are cut up like animals in a butcher's shop, where they are devoured by wild beasts, where they are bound to a red-hot pillar, where they are buried in a lake of ice, and so forth.

In the third hell Sung-ti wang punishes unjust mandarins and all who have behaved badly to their superiors, women who were shrews to their husbands, slaves who injured their owners, cheating employees, condemned men who escaped from justice, and also forgers, slanderers, those who sell their family burying-ground. Some have their knees smashed, others their heart or their eyes plucked out, or their feet cut off, or their hands; others are hung up by the heels, others flayed alive, or buried in vermin, and the like.

The fourth hell, under Wu-kuan wang, is the one in which the miserly rich who give no alms are punished, as well as the people who, knowing prescriptions for the cure of diseases, do not divulge them; defrauders, coiners, makers of false weights and measures, or traders who use false money or false weights, those who remove the landmarks of fields, blasphemers, those who steal in pagodas, and so on. The damned are swept away by a torrent, or they are set kneeling on sharpened bamboos, or they must remain sitting on spikes. Some are clad in iron garments; others are crushed under great beams or rocks; others are buried alive; others are made to swallow quicklime or boiling potions. There too is the Lake of Fetid-Blood, in which women who died in childbed are plunged to rise no more; popular belief is harsher than the Buddhist and Taoist theories, which strive in vain to struggle against it, and an attempt is sometimes made to justify it by explaining that for a woman to die in childbed she must have committed most serious crimes, if not in this life, at any rate in a previous one.

The fifth hell is that belonging to King Yama, Yen-lo wang. There are punished the most heinous religious sins, the putting to death of living beings, incredulity, the destructions of books of piety, etc.; the religious who have transgressed their vows, and above all hunters, fishers, butchers, are punished there. There also lust, seduction, rape, and everything connected with prostitution, etc., receive their chastisement. The guilty are first of all sent to the terrace from which one looks toward one's native village, Wang-hiang t'ai. From there they behold the woes that have fallen upon their family since their death, and of which the demerits they have heaped up are the cause. Then they are each taken to one of the sixteen minor hells, where some, sitting on an iron seat and bound to an iron pillar, have their breast opened, their heart torn therefrom, cut into morsels, and thrown to the beasts, while others are cut in pieces under a huge chopper, and so forth and so on.

Fig. 79. The Torments of the Fifth Hell and the Terrace from which One sees One's Native Village

In the sixth hell the King Pien-ch'êng punishes all those who have been guilty of sacrilege: those who curse Heaven, Earth, wind or rain, cold or heat, those who fail in respect for the gods, melt down their statues to turn them into *cash* or to sell the metal, dump refuse near temples or facing the Great Bear, who weave into or print upon materials for profane use the names of the gods, or merely dragons or phœnixes, etc., and those who keep obscene books. The punishments consist of being crushed by a roller, or sawn asunder between two planks, or flayed alive and stuffed; some are plunged into a pond of mud and filth; others are gnawed by rats or devoured by locusts; others have burning torches thrust into their mouths, etc.

The seventh hell belongs to the King of the Eastern Peak, T'ai-shan kün wang, the heir-apparent (*t'ai-tsï*) of King Yama. The name preserves the memory of a time (about the beginning of the Christian era) when the popular religion had made the God of the Eastern Peak, presiding over life and death, the sovereign of a world of the dead that lay underneath his mountain; but this is only a survival in name. To-day the king of the seventh hell is regarded, in spite of the resemblance in the titles, as a totally different divinity. He punishes those who violate graves, who sell or eat human flesh, or use it to make nostrums, those who sell their betrothed as a slave, etc. Some are plunged into cauldrons of boiling oil; others are devoured by beasts: dogs gnaw their limbs; their skin is flayed off and given to the pigs to eat; vultures devour them; mules trample them under their hoofs; demons open the bellies of others and pull out their intestines; and so on.

In the eighth hell, that of the King of P'ing-têng, are punished chiefly those who have fallen short in filial piety. The damned are crushed under chariot-wheels; their

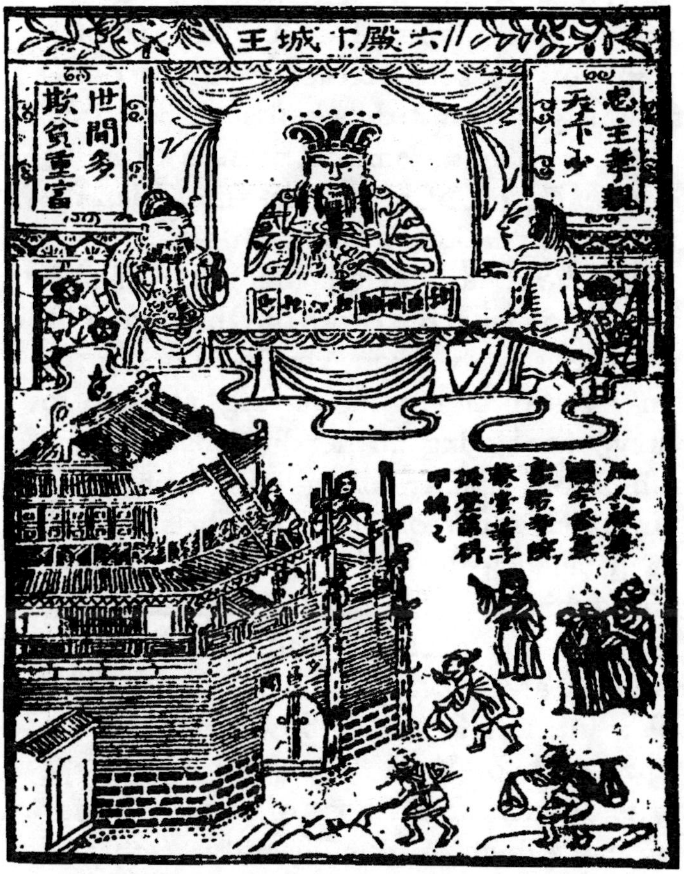

Fig. 80. King Pien-ch'êng of the Sixth Hell
Popular print.

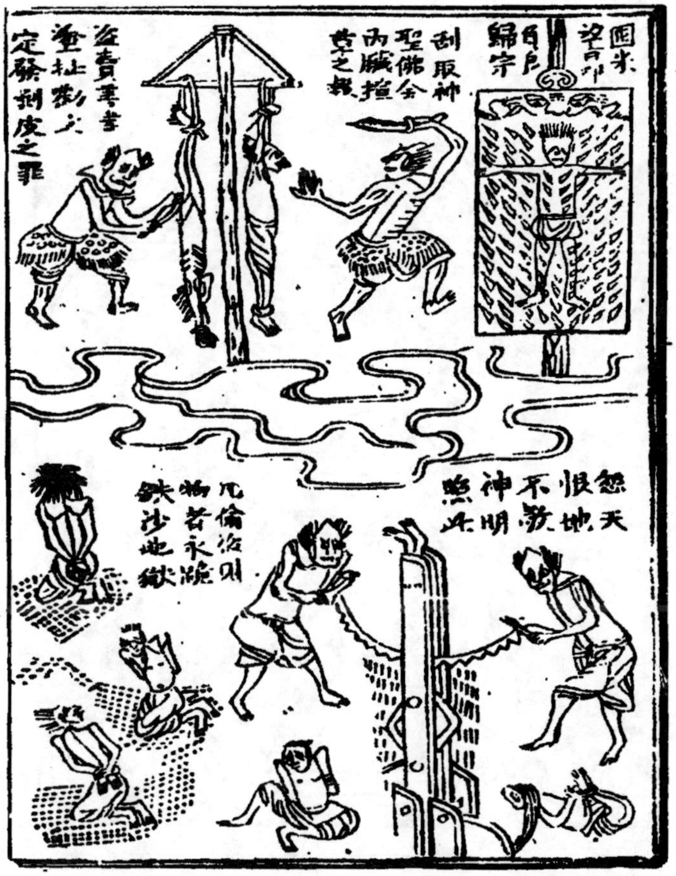

Fig. 81. The Torments of the Sixth Hell: Blasphemers sawn asunder between Two Planks, etc.

tongues are torn out; they are plunged into the latrine pit; nails are driven into their heads; they are cut into a thousand pieces; and so on.

The ninth hell, the domain of the King of Tu-shï, is that of incendiaries, abortionists, obscene painters or writers and those who look at or read their works. Among its sixteen lesser hells there are some where the souls are devoured by wasps, ants, scorpions, serpents; in others they are ground in a grain-mill; or else the demons stew their heads, or take out their brains and put in a hedgehog, and so on. In this king's realm also is the City of the Dead-by-Accident, to which all those who slew themselves without good cause are dispatched. Their punishment consists in for ever re-enacting their suicide and never being born again. Thither too are relegated all the souls who, having committed grave crimes in the lower world, are punished with death, and after their execution cease to be souls, *kuei*, and become shadows of souls, *tsien*, incapable of being born again. The City of the Dead-by-Accident is a place whence none can ever come away: whosoever is imprisoned in it has no longer, as the rest of the damned have, the hope of one day seeing his torment end and of returning to this upper world.

Lastly, the tenth king is the king who turns the Wheel (of transmigration), Chuan-lun wang. Like the first king, he rules over no place of torment: it is he who appoints transmigrations at the soul's departure from the hells. He has eighty offices in which innumerable employees keep the ledgers of reincarnation. As in those of the Eastern Peak, it is spirits of the dead who carry out the duties of these offices. He pronounces on the destiny of the soul according to the deeds previously committed, whether it is to be reborn as man or animal, what is to be its rank, its degree of happiness, etc. Then the soul, leaving the king's judgment-seat, is taken before the Lady Mêng, Mêng-p'o niang-niang, who makes the Broth of Oblivion. The Lady Mêng is a woman who lived under the Han dynasty and who, having refused to marry, and having all her life observed the prohibitions against killing living beings and eating rich food, obtained immortality and was installed at the exit of the lower regions to fulfil this duty. She dwells in a great building, with one principal hall, in which she sits as in a court, and numerous secondary halls; in these latter the bowls of broth are prepared beforehand. Demons divide the spirits of men from those of women; they then make them drink willy-nilly, so that all memory of the nether world is abolished at the moment of their return upon earth to be reborn in some shape or other. The bowl of broth once swallowed, the soul is directed to the Bridge of Pain, K'u-ch'u k'iao, which spans a river of crimson water; there the two demons, Life-is-not-Long and Death-is-Nigh, await it; they hurl it into the waters of the river, which carry it away to a new birth.

Fig. 82. Lady Mêng who gives the Broth of Oblivion
Popular print.

Great mural paintings in the Buddhist temples represent the Wheel of Birth and Life, *shêng-sï-lun*: this is a picture which displays the various rebirths among the various species of living beings, in retribution for the good or evil actions performed in the last existence or in previous existences. According to the majority of the Buddhist books, there are six paths of birth, *liu-ts'ü* (*gati*): three good paths, birth among the gods (great merits), among men (moderate merits), among the Asuras (slight merits), and three evil paths, birth in the nether world, (great demerits), among the famished demons (moderate demerits), among the animals (slight demerits). But certain works reckon only five, which are the same, omitting the Asuras. Thus there are three evil paths and two good.

Fig. 83. The Wheel of Transmigration

This last system is the one adopted by the Hindu painters, and described in the Books of Discipline (Vinaya) as the one the Buddha himself ordered to be painted above certain monastery gates.

> A circle is to be made in the shape of a wheel. In the centre place the hub, then draw five spokes to separate the representations of the five paths: below the hub hell, and on the two sides the famished demons and the animals; above man is to be painted and the gods. The hub should be covered with white colour, and on this background is to be drawn a Buddha, and in front of this Buddha three forms: a pigeon to be the symbol of desire, a serpent to symbolize wrath, a pig to symbolize ignorance. On the felloe there must be represented the twelve causes that produce birth and death. And outside all the great demon Impermanence, with ruffled hair, with open mouth, with outstretched arms, embracing the Wheel.

The Chinese painters generally fall in line with the ritual model: nevertheless they often take pains to have the pictures of the opposite paths correspond, that of paradise in the upper part, with its gardens and pavilions where the gods walk to and fro, opposite that of hell in the lower part, with its tribunal to which the damned are brought and its courts of torment where they are punished; and in this case the picture of the paths of the Famished Demons and the Animals are necessarily both relegated to the same side in order to match that of the path of Men. On page 369 may be seen a good example after a mural painting by Kuang-ts'i sï at Pekin. But this arrangement often gives place to a more symmetrical division into six sections, in which sometimes, though seldom, the Asuras, resuming their place, struggle with the gods. In the popular prints the division in six compartments has got the upper hand, thanks to the symmetrical arrangement it allows of; but the six paths are rarely in accord with the Buddhist tradition; beside the hells, the gods, the human beings, and the animals, which do not change, we often find the Asuras replaced by the Chinese terrestrial divinities and the Pretas (the famished demons) by human beggars; or else hair-clad animals, birds, fishes, and insects, are placed separately in special compartments.

The Existence of the Souls in the Nether Regions. Such is the world to which the souls of the dead go after death. But they do not remain there eternally; they only spend a period of varying length between two earth existences. Only the souls of the greatest criminals or of suicides go to a special corner of the nether world, whence no one ever comes forth to be born again. Even so their pains are not eternal, for these souls will be destroyed at the provisional and temporary end of our world, which, according to the Buddhists (and their imitators the Taoists), separates two of the long periods called *kie* (*kalpas*).

To the Chinese of to-day (except a few scholars who apply literally the celebrated formula attributed to Confucius, "Ye know not life, how could ye know death?" which has long been interpreted as a profession of agnosticism) every man, every living being, is passing through a series of existences in this world, separated from one another by sojourns of longer or shorter duration in the nether world or in various divine appointments. The old Hindu idea of successive rebirths, imported by the Buddhist missionaries from the first or second century of our era, imposed itself upon the Chinese mind, but changed its character in a singular fashion. The term 'metempsychosis,' which is sometimes applied to this theory, and which is absurd with reference to Hindu Buddhism, seeing that this doctrine denies the existence of an individual soul, a continuous *ego*, and only admits in each individual the existence of successive temporary *egos*, each separate and distinct and born one from the other as time elapses, is, on the contrary, very nearly exact when applied to the Chinese popular religion. There is, in fact, a soul (if not in the Christian sense of the word, for to the Chinese souls are material and not purely spiritual) that passes from body to body in each new existence. It brings with it its merits and demerits, which contribute to give it its rank and its 'happiness' in each life; it brings its defects and even its habits. It is endowed with sex, and a man remains always a man from life to life, just as a woman never becomes a man in a subsequent existence; and even if the sins committed entail a rebirth in some animal shape, a dog, a horse, a serpent, etc., the soul of a man becomes a male animal, the soul of a woman a female animal. Those who have lived well are reborn almost immediately upon earth as men and women; this is a reward for them, for the modern Chinese, very unlike the Hindus of old, who had a horror of the idea of setting out again on the endless round of lives and deaths, welcome this notion. Sometimes souls of just persons are given, for their merits, a post as a deity. No one looks on this as an advantage; far from it, indeed, and most people hope rather that they will be born again in a good family, rich and endowed with 'happiness.' But the actions of the previous life set their mark upon the newly born; in Kiangsu when a child is born one-eyed they say that the reason is that he was lustful in his previous life; if he has a hare-lip it is because he insulted people without a cause; if he is dumb or a stammerer, because he was of a contradicting nature, and so forth.

Living man has two groups of souls, the three *hun* and the seven *p'o*. That is an ancient belief, for it is found already mentioned in the works of Ko Hung, one of the great Taoist writers of the end of the third century of our era. To-day every one admits the existence of all these souls; a person in a state of fright, for instance, will exclaim (I borrow this from a play recently played at Shanghai): "How frightened I am! My three *hun* are driven from their places and my seven *p'o* are in utter confusion!" But each of these two groups is regarded as a unit, and the *hun* are not dissociated from each other (neither are the *p'o*), so that actually and practically it is the same as if men had only two souls. They are not alike, and have distinct and separate qualities and attributes. After death they separate from one another: the *p'o* remain near the body in the mortuary chamber, which they cannot leave on account of the Gods of the Doors, while the *hun*, taken away by the satellites of the God of Walls and Moats, whose order to bring them away serves as a pass with the Gods of the Doors, begin their journey to the lower world and future rebirths.

As a matter of fact, when the hour of death comes the God of Walls and Moats, who keeps the register of all the inhabitants of his district, sends two of the satellites of the infernal kings to arrest the soul and bring it before him, the demons Ox-head, Niu-t'ou (Goṣirsa) and Horse-face, Ma-mien (Aṣvamukha). These demons are the souls of those who when alive ate beef or ill-treated their horses, and who in the other world are given their shapes and duties as punishment. And that is why they are represented in all the temples of Walls and Moats with a man's body and the head and feet of an animal, sometimes dressed as mandarins' attendants, one carrying the axe and the other the trident, sometimes naked to the waist and carrying instruments of torture in their hands. However, this *rôle* of conductors of the dead is not exclusively reserved for them, and it also frequently happens that they are two attendants of human shape. They carry the warrant of arrest from the god to the dying man, and the soul follows them forthwith. Every one has the utmost dread of these demons who come to seize the soul. In a play of the "New Theatre" recently performed at Shanghai, *The Three Doubts*, there is seen a servant wakened from his sleep by some one knocking at the door late at night while his master is ill, and refusing to go and open. "It is midnight. How could it be any one knocking at the door? . . . I have it! Probably my master is at the worst, and King Yama has sent two demons to carry away my master's soul. I will not open!" In many places, notably in certain parts of Kiangsu, it is not admitted that demons, even provided with an official order, can by themselves lay hands on a living man and arrest his soul: they are obliged to be aided by the soul of a living man, whose body suddenly falls into a cataleptic trance, while the soul leaves it for a few moments and accompanies the demons, and it is this soul that takes hold of the soul of the dying man and hands it over to the satellites, after which it returns to its own body, which then wakes up. As for the satellites, however they may have taken the dead man's soul, they lead it away to the Temple of Walls and Moats, where it makes a first sojourn for the forty-nine days immediately after the death. The god holds a short inquiry into its conduct, running through his registers, in which he has duly noted the monthly reports of all the Gods of the Hearth, and according to its actions leaves it free or inflicts upon it a greater or lesser punishment, the cangue or beating with sticks.

Fig. 84. The Satellite Ox-head

On the five-and-thirtieth day after death the soul of the dead man is brought back to his house one last time to see his relations. According to some it is the Buddha Shï-kia (Ṣākyamuni) who leads him: as he is not dead, but entered into Nirvāna, he is not a spirit, *kuei*, and consequently is able, thanks to his supernatural power, to pass from the world of the living to the world of the dead, and *vice versa*, which a spirit could not do, even when, like the Gods of Walls and Moats or the gods of the nether world, it is provided with an official position. He leaves the Pure Land of the West, where he dwells with the Buddhas O-mi-t'o (Amitābha) and Ju-lai (Tathāgata), as well as the Bodhisattva Kuan-yin (Avalokiteṣvara), goes up on to the Precious Raft which is the Vessel of Benevolence (the same vessel in which Kuan-yin comes to the aid of those who invoke her), makes the soul enter on it, and in this way takes it from one world to the other. When night comes he brings it back to the Temple of the God of Walls and Moats. And so on this day bonzes are specially invited, at any rate in wealthy families, in Kiangsu. Many, however, do not make the Buddha appear in connexion with this last visit of the soul to its own relatives: it is simply brought back by the infernal satellites.

On the forty-ninth day the dead man's sojourn with the God of Walls and Moats comes to an end: he is then taken to the gods of the nether world, the ten Yama kings, to be judged by them. But first of all the God of Walls and Moats sends the soul itself to the Jade Emperor or to the Great Emperor of the Eastern Peak, or a report on it. It is necessary to ascertain if his life-span is really run out, or if death has not come upon him untimely, either by accident, or by suicide, for in that case he could not enter the underworld before the date appointed by destiny has arrived. When it has been ascertained from the celestial registers that everything is in order the soul finally passes through the portal that divides the earth world from the underworld. This is a pavilion that belongs half to the God of Walls and Moats and half to the infernal kings: on one side it is called the pavilion to which criminals are brought, on the other the pavilion from which criminals are fetched. The satellites of the God of Walls and Moats bring the soul hither on the forty-ninth day and put it in the hands of the infernal satellites, who take it to the first of the Ten Tribunals. It is not, indeed, judged for all its sins in a lump; they have been catalogued, both by the Buddhists and by the Taoists. Ten lists have been drawn up, which have been shared among the ten Yama kings, with the corresponding punishments, and the dead pass in succession before the ten kings so that each may pronounce the sentences attached to the sins the punishment of which is within their province. The ten hells are represented in detail in almost all the temples of the Gods of Walls and Moats: they occupy each a niche in the two sides of the second court of the temple, just before the principal shrine. The infernal kings are represented in mandarin costume sitting behind a judge's table and having in front of them the roll of paper on which they inscribe the sentence, surrounded by their scribes and recorders, judging the dead whom their satellites bring to them in chains or wearing the cangue like criminals, and who are on their knees before them as accused persons used to kneel before earthly judges. These

Fig. 85. AN INFERNAL SATELLITE SEIZES THE SOUL OF A DEAD MAN
Popular print.

are sometimes large mural paintings, sometimes decorative compositions in which, round great statues of the Yen-wang, innumerable little statuettes represent the damned and the demons that torment them. In the big cities the crowd that on certain days throngs the courts of the temple pauses in front of the ten hells, comments on the punishments and the sins committed. This is probably, for many children and even adults, especially among the common people, the most striking and the clearest lesson in morality they will ever have.

Fig. 86. THE GOD OF THE HEARTH HANDS OVER A SOUL TO THE GOD OF THE PLACE
Popular print.

Only after enduring all the penalties that have been assigned to it can the soul be reborn, unless its family has redeemed its sins by appropriate ceremonies and in this way delivered it. But it is generally accepted that it is not reborn before the twenty-eight months of mourning are fulfilled. This is the minimum period it must spend in the lower world. During these two years and four months, if the dead man has no punishments to endure, or if they have been redeemed for him, he leads an existence similar to that of men on the earth. The family has taken care to provide him as soon as he arrived there with a house, with furniture, clothes, money, etc. It is a paper house in two storeys with several rooms; in principle it represents the dead man's abode; an attempt is made to reproduce his chamber exactly as it is in reality with paper furniture. In certain districts it is large enough to enter; in Kiangsu, in wealthy families, it occasionally attains a height of ten or even twenty feet with the roof. Life-sized servants made of paper are placed in it; on their breast are inscribed the names of servants who died in the dead man's service. On the evening of the forty-ninth day, or sometimes of the hundredth day, the bonzes consecrate the house by depositing within it a yellow paper on which they make as many red dots as the number of times they have read the *Book of Great Compassion* (*Ṭa pei king*) for the benefit of the deceased, either on that day or during the three previous days. Then all round are placed bundles of silver paper representing ingots, to create a treasure for the dead man, and the servants set fire to these in the middle of the court of the house. All the time it burns the greatest care is taken not to touch it, for fear of disturbing something and causing it to arrive in the other world in a damaged condition. The fire must not be extinguished, nor must the ashes even be touched before the next day. This is the house the dead man will inhabit in the infernal plains, where with those of the other souls it helps to form cities and townships round the palaces of the Yama kings. Each one continues the kind of existence he led on earth: some are farm-labourers, some are traders, others are given more or less important posts as officials of the underworld.

When the period of sojourning is at an end and the time of rebirth approaches the soul presents itself before the King who Turns the Wheel (Chakravartirāja), the tenth of the kings of the underworld, who arranges births, and according to the soul's merits or sins sends it into the body of a child or of an animal. Some declare that they can remember the sensation of a fall into a dark cell, then the almost immediate return to the light, but in a tiny body and incapable of speech. An eighteenth-century tale, translated by Father Wieger, sets forth in detail the sensations of the moment of birth:

> Everything seemed confused around him; his body was danced here and there by the wind. Suddenly, passing through a vermilion door, he fell into a lake six thousand fathom deep; he felt no pain, but perceived that his body was becoming tiny in length and breadth and was no longer the same. When he had ceased falling his eyes were shut and could not open again; in his ears he heard what seemed the sound of the voices of his father and his mother. He thought he was the plaything of a dream.

When the soul is reborn in the shape of an animal the impression is still more disagreeable.

Such is the lot that awaits souls after death. But for many souls there is a still more rigorous fate. All those who died before accomplishing the life-span fixed by destiny, not having been summoned by regular orders and not having an infernal satellite to be their escort, are unable to find the road to the nether world and transmigration, and their souls remain, vagabond and famished, upon earth. It is for these souls that on the fifteenth day of the seventh month there are performed great ceremonies: the Buddhist ceremony of the *avalambana*, *yü-lan-p'ên*, the Taoist ceremony of the *Chung-yüan* (the day when the Agent of the Earth remits the sins of men), intended to give food to the vagabond souls and bring them back to the way of transmigration. The rites of the *avalambana* were expounded by the Buddha to his disciple Maudgalyāyana (Mu-lien) to allow him to save his mother from the torments of hell, and consist of great offerings accompanied by prayers made at the doors of the houses at night. The lost and abandoned souls are not the only ones to profit by them, for on the first day of the seventh month the nether world is opened and the souls of the damned return upon earth to profit by the offerings generously lavished by the piety of the living, only going back on the last day of the month.

The Bodhisattva Ti-tsang (Kshitigarbha). To deliver the souls of the dead from torment Ti-tsang (the Chinese version of the Sanskrit name Kshitigarbha) is invoked, a Bodhisattva who has received from the Jade Emperor the title of Instructor of the Regions of Darkness, and who travels unceasingly throughout the nether world to succour the damned. Incalculable ages ago Ti-tsang was a young Brahman who, being converted by the Buddha of that time, took a vow himself also to become a Buddha one day, but not before he had saved all beings sunk in sin, had brought them over the river of life and death, and had led them into the Happy Lands. During innumerable lives from existence to existence he sacrificed himself to fulfil his vow. Among other meritorious acts in one of his existences he was a pious girl whose impious mother delighted in killing living beings to eat them. When her mother died she prayed with such intense concentration for her salvation that she fell into trance and saw herself borne to the door of the nether world, where a demon revealed to her that her mother, plunged as she was in the deepest pit of the worst torments, had just been delivered through her prayers. When the present Buddha, Ṣākyamuni, was alive he one day, in a assembly held in the heaven of the Thirty-three Gods, expounded the merits of Kshitigarbha, and ended by addressing him in these terms: "The throng of gods and men now living or to come, I give them to thee in charge henceforward, that by the virtue of thy supernatural power thou mayst leave them not to fall into evil birth for a single day or a single night."

Fig. 87. Ti-tsang (Kshitigarbha) with his Assistants before the Ten Kings of the Hells; behind, the Five Paths of Transmigration
Painting found in Tun-huang. Musée Guimet.

Thus while the other Bodhisattvas are especially concerned with men during their earthly life, Ti-tsang has taken upon himself the task of watching over the worst sinners during their existence in the underworld. He has even adopted six different shapes the better to carry out this *rôle*—one in each of the paths of birth, the nether regions, famished demons, animals, Asuras, men, and gods—and these are known as the Six Ti-tsangs. They are not shapes that he assumes successively in particular cases, when he wishes to save some soul in each of the six paths: they are special shapes that by his supernatural power, that allows him to be present in several places at the same time, he has assumed, all six together, so that he may be always present in the six paths of birth.

He is usually represented standing, less frequently sitting, clad as a bonze, with shaven head. He holds in his right hand the *khakkara*, the metal wand at the top of which are fastened little tinkling rings, and which the Buddha ordered his monks to carry and to shake at house-doors to announce their presence when they go about begging for their food (Fig. 87): it serves to open the doors of the nether world for him. In his left hand he holds the Pearl of Price, whose lustre lights up the dark roads of the lower regions and instantaneously appeases the pangs of the damned. Often, instead of the dress of the

Hindu bonzes, he is clad in the robe of the Chinese bonzes, and on his head is placed the crown worn by them in certain ceremonies. In this case he is sometimes represented standing, sometimes seated upon a throne, and sometimes seated on a lion; fairly frequently he is not alone, but is shown accompanied by two saints, one of whom, Mu-lien (Maudgalyāyana), carries the metal wand and the other holds the Pearl of Price. Sometimes, but this print is not such a popular one, he is represented in the habitual posture and costume of the Bodhisattvas, sitting on a lotus throne and clad in filmy scarves and jewels, the right hand holding the Pearl of Price and the left hand an open lotus flower from the heart of which rises a banner.

Fig. 88. Ti-tsang (Kshitigarbha); around him are the Ten Infernal Tribunals
Tun-huang painting. Musée Guimet.

The Chinese like to regard him as continually going to and fro throughout the nether regions and each time he passes delivering the damned so as to allow them to be born again. Many people have met him among the dead and thereafter been revived. It must not, by the way, be supposed that he is antagonistic to the kings of the underworld and has to war against them; they are under his orders and must obey him. What is the power of a god before that of a Bodhisattva? His mission has been recognized by the Jade Emperor, who has conferred upon him the title of "Instructor of the Regions of Darkness," Yu-ming kiao-shï. On his birthday, the twenty-fourth day of the seventh month, all the kings of the underworld come, with their assistants, to do homage to him, and on this day he distributes favours in profusion to the damned.

Usually the ceremony is carried out on the hundredth day after the death. One or several bonzes come to the house, and before the temporary tablet of the dead man they invoke Ti-tsang, at every word striking on the wooden fish and at the beginning of each verse on the bronze bell.

> O Bodhisattva of the Darkness, whose excellence is ineffable,
> Whose real Transformed Bodies are in all places at once,

So that those that are upon the three [evil] ways among the six paths [of rebirth] may hear the marvellous Law,
And that the ten classes of beings born of the four kinds of birth may be bathed in thy Benevolence,
Thou whose Pearl of Price illumines the ways of the Celestial Palaces,
Whose metal Wand opens the doors of the underworld,
Deign to guide the soul of this departed one,
That upon the Lotus-flower Terrace [*i.e.*, in the Paradise of Amitābha] it may adore the Most Compassionate.

The hymn being finished, they burn incense, reciting a prayer in prose:

Adoration to the Celestial Officers of the Three Worlds, to the kings and princes of Earth, Water, Humanity. Cause the soul of the departed to progress until it come to the Paradise of the West! Respectfully I hold it difficult to escape being reborn to die in the two paths of man and of god, save by a moment of respectful adoration. If the soul of the departed cannot in anywise come hither there is in the storehouse of our Buddhist religion a magic formula [*mantra*] to summon it: I now pronounce it.

And they invite the soul as follows:

Shaking this bell, I invite thee:
Soul of the departed, be not ignorant, hearing it from afar, give ear!
Mayst thou by the power of the Three Jewels be sustained!
On this day, I entreat thee, come hither forthwith!

Then they recite the magic formula in Sanskrit and light incense-sticks before the temporary tablet, saying, "With intense concentration of heart I pray that the fragrance of this incense-stick may penetrate through all the phenomenal worlds (*dharmadhātu*), so that the messengers of the nether world may bring the soul hither!" And they end by a last appeal to the soul: "Thrice I entreat the soul of the departed to come; come back and sit and hearken to the text of the Holy Book!"

The ceremony ends with the reading of the Book that destroys the hells, and with invocations to Amitābha, the master of the Pure Land of the West (Sukhāvatī), where the soul is invited to be born again, and to Ti-tsang, who will help it to reach this paradise. The nether world is represented by a square structure of bamboo upon which sheets of paper or stuff are stretched, set up in the middle of the hall or of the court. A bonze, dressed to represent Ti-tsang and carrying in his hand the sounding-wand, dances in turn before each of its four sides during the recitation of the book, and when dance and reading are over he smashes a rice-bowl with one stroke of the wand, symbolically to demolish the infernal doors and thus to set free the soul of the departed.

The prayers to Ti-tsang are not perhaps essential. According to some, only the wicked are in the hour of death seized by the satellites of Ch'êng-huang and sent before the infernal judges to be chastised according to their sins, while the good see Kuan-yin come and take them away upon a lotus-flower raft to the Paradise of the West; or else it is the great Emperor of the Eastern Peak, Tung-yo ta-ti, who sends them one of his suite, one of the golden lads to men or one of the jade maidens to women, and this messenger carries the banner and leads them to the Lands of Happiness. But it is better to err from too much caution than through negligence; the dead man may have committed grave sins in secret. A scholar who, having died as the result of a mistake on the part of a clerk in one of the infernal tribunals, later came back to life and narrated his journey to the nether world in a work the title of which, impossible to render with the conciseness of the original, may be paraphrased as *Consequences of the Actions performed in Previous Lives with Reference to the Return to Life in this World by Transmigration*, declares that, from what the King of Ts'in-kuang (the first hell) said as he sent him back, out of a thousand souls who appear before him, only one or two are worthy to go to the Celestial Palaces, T'ien-t'ang, and a few others deserve to be sent into the different hells; but nearly all, being neither very good nor very bad, are sent back direct to be reborn in this world as human beings or as animals. He himself, during the few days he remained, saw only three who ascended into Paradise, and some forty who were condemned to various tortures (and, again, among these, ten or so obtained, as a remission of punishment, an inferior human birth), while seven hundred and fifty-two had to resume human existence.

The Paradise of Amitābha. The Paradise to which the souls delivered by Ti-tsang go is the World of Delights of the Western Region, Si-fang ki-lo shï-kiai (in Sanskrit Sukhāvatī, the Happy) or the Pure Earth, Ts'ing-tsing t'u, where the Buddha Amitābha[1] reigns, in consequence of the vow he made when for the first time, countless ages past, he put forth the Thought of Illumination (*p'u-ti-sin*, *bodhichitta*).

We know that to enter on the way that leads to becoming a " Buddha perfectly accomplished " certain conditions are necessary: a Buddha must at the moment be living, and the neophyte, converted by him, must pronounce the vow that he himself will one day, in a future existence, become a Buddha who shall save all living beings. It is this vow that begins the career of the future Buddha; it is from this point that he can receive the title of Bodhisattva; it is thanks to the power of this vow that through ages without number he will at last attain the goal he has set before him. Now this vow is accompanied by conditions the Bodhisattva imposes upon himself before entering into Nirvāna, or that must be fulfilled at the very moment of his entering into Nirvāna. It is through his vow that the Bodhisattva Kshitigarbha (Ti-tsang) became the Saviour of beings born in the evil paths, the hell-born, famished demons, etc.; through his vow Avalokiteṣvara labours incessantly and without discouragement for the salvation of all living beings. It was by virtue of his vow the Buddha Amitābha (O-mi-t'o Fo) so wrought that all living beings were capable of obtaining rebirth in his Paradise of the Pure Earth of the West.

Countless ages ago there was a king who, having heard the Law, was converted and abandoned his kingdom to become a monk. And going to the Buddha of that time he made a vow himself also to become a Buddha perfectly accomplished; then he added: " I make a vow not to take a Land of Buddha that is impure. I declare this vow that when I arrive at Bodhi in my world there shall be no birth in the hells, nor among the famished demons, nor among animals, and that all beings shall be exempt from birth, from death, and from suffering, that all beings shall be the colour of gold, that, being born by transformation, they shall enjoy a life everlasting, that this world shall be pure and without stain." Thus before the Buddha he made eight-and-forty vows with regard to the world of purity whither he wished to go to attain Nirvāna. To the eighteenth vow men owe the power to go to be reborn in this paradise: " I make a vow that if in the worlds of the

[1] We often find him designated by the name of Amida: this is simply the Japanese pronunciation of the Chinese transcript O-mi-t'o of the Sanskrit Amitābha, and there is no reason to use this form when referring to Chinese religion.

other Buddhas there are living beings who, having heard my name and practising good works, make a vow to be born again in my world, conformably with their vow at the end of their life they shall of necessity be granted to be reborn in it, except such as have committed the five unpardonable crimes—to have slain a father, a mother, a child, to have wounded a Buddha, to have caused a schism in the Religion—or have insulted the Buddhas, or have ruined the Law!" When he had finished the Buddha foretold to him in what conditions his vows would be fulfilled. His sons then, having uttered the vow to be Buddhas in their turn, were given predictions also: the eldest was to become the Bodhisattva Avalokiteṣvara, the second the Bodhisattva Mahāsthāmaprāpta, and so on, and they were to reside, with the Buddha Amitābha, in this Pure Land of Sukhāvatī, and help to save all living beings.

This Pure Land of Amitābha is situated to the west of our world, at a distance incalculable. It is separated from it by several millions of worlds like ours, over which preside as many Buddhas. We must not, as some have done, try to find a symbolical and mystical interpretation of this placing of the Paradise of Amitābha in the west: besides the fact of its having its exact counterpart in the Eastern Paradise of the Buddha Bhaihsajyagururājavaidūryaprabhāsa (Yo-shï-wang-liu-li-kuang), almost forgotten to-day in China, but which had its moment of popularity there down till about the end of the T'ang period, everybody places it and has always placed it literally in the west. About A.D. 535, after the death of the holy monk Bodhidharma (the name is generally abridged by the Chinese into Ta-mo), the founder of the Dhyāna school, which to-day has more monasteries than any other, the pilgrim Sung-Yün, who was returning from India, met him in the Mountains of the Onions, on the border of what to-day is Chinese Turkestan: he was going along barefooted, a sandal in his hand, and making in the direction of the west, returning to the Paradise of Amitābha.

This paradise has been described at length in the Buddhist books, and the popular imagination has had nothing to add. "In this world, O Ṣāriputra," explains the Buddha,

> "there is neither bodily pain nor pain of the mind for living beings, and the sources of happiness are innumerable. This world is embellished with seven ranges of terraces, with seven rows of trees and garlands of bells. It is enclosed on every side, magnificent, brilliant with the lustre of the four gems, gold, silver, beryl, crystal. In this world are lotus ponds with margins made of the seven jewels; they are filled to the brim with a limpid, pure, cool water, sweet to the taste, soft to the touch, fertilizing, calm, capable of preventing famine, and the bottom is covered with golden sand. On the four sides of these ponds are magnificent and brilliant steps of the four gems, and all around are wondrous trees shining with the lustre of the seven gems; in these pools grow lotus flowers, blue, yellow, red, and white, large as the wheel of a chariot. In this world a celestial music is always heard; thrice every day and thrice every night it rains *māndārava* flowers. Every day at dawn the beings of this world go and offer flowers to all the Buddhas of the other worlds, and return to their own world at mealtimes. In this world there are marvellous birds, of divers colours, which thrice a day sing deliciously, and from their singing goes up a sound that celebrates the five virtues and the most excellent doctrines. When the men of this world hear this sound they think of the Buddha, of the Law, and of the Community. And say not, O Ṣāriputra, that it is through the effect of sin that these birds are born. Why so? In this world of Buddha even the name of the three evil paths is unknown; how, then, could they exist in reality? These birds are produced by the transformation

of the light of the Buddha, in order to propagate the doctrine. In this world the wind, blowing softly, sways the trees of precious stones as well as the garlands of bells, and causes to be heard delicious sounds as of musical instruments playing a concert; and those who hear these sounds think of the Buddha, of the Law, and of the Community. And furthermore, beings born in this world of Buddha go not back. O Ṣāriputra, 'tis not by virtue of merits acquired by good actions of small importance that one can be born in this world; if virtuous men and virtuous women constantly recite the name of Amitābha for a day, or during two days, or during three days, or during four days, or during five days, or during six days, or during seven days, without their mind becoming distracted, Amitābha, accompanied by the Bodhisattvas, will appear before them at the last moment of their life: when they die their heart will not be troubled; it will be granted them to be born again in the Pure Land of Amitābha."

Thither go, to be born again, the souls of the just, of those who have invoked, were it only once, but with all their heart, the name of Amitābha, and of those also who, already fallen into the evil paths, have been saved by the intervention of Ti-tsang. The just see the Buddha himself come to fetch them in the hour of death, accompanied by the Bodhisattvas, conformably with the nineteenth of his forty-eight vows.

All the beings who take a vow to become Buddhas, who practise meritorious works, who with a perfect heart utter the vow to be born in my world, if when their hour of death approaches I appear not before them accompanied by the throng of my followers, may I not become a Buddha!

And statues are made of "Amitābha going to fetch [the dead]," with arms immeasurably long to show that he is holding them out to the souls of the just. These souls go into the lotus plants on the ponds of this world, and when the flower opens they acquire existence by transformation, in this way avoiding birth and in consequence death. The souls of the just pass into lotuses that bloom immediately; the others remain enfolded for a lesser or greater time in the lotus bud, giving themselves up to meditation, until they are entirely purified and the flower that contains them opens in its turn. In this world there is no stain; there are no sexes, and all living beings live there eternally, mingling the purest pleasures with the adoration of all the Buddhas and meditation.

It suffices to have thought once with concentration upon Amitābha to be saved, and his cult is accordingly widely spread. Fifty years ago Edkins saw in a great temple monks who had themselves shut up for several months in a dark hall to devote themselves more completely to meditation and the repetition of the name of Amitābha.

A dozen or so monks had had themselves shut up of their own accord for a certain number of months or years, during which they must repeat the name of Amitābha night and day without a break. By day they must all fulfil this task; during the night they rest in turns, dividing themselves into groups of watchers so that the invocation never ceases for a moment until morning. They can be freed on their own request, but only after they have spent several months in this sequestration. Most of them seem to be young; some come to the bars of their cage to look at the foreigners; but at the same time they never cease repeating the name of the Buddha.

Laymen often form societies to adore Amitābha.

The Immortals and the Lady-queen of the West, Si-wang-mu. Such is the lot of men after death. But all men do not die. There are some who, after practising the Taoist doctrine all their lives, come to escape death and win eternal life, *ch'ang-shêng*. For this there are various methods: some have attained it through alchemy by making the elixir of long life (Fig. 89), others through asceticism by abstaining from cereals, or, more generally, from cooked food, and by breath-control; some, after having lived as hermits in the mountains, have seen Immortals bring them the Peach of Immortality, etc. As a rule he who has attained this degree of sanctity quits his gross body, which remains as an empty cast-off, thus freeing the subtle body he has made himself by his practices, and which, being endowed with supernatural powers, is capable of flying, of walking on the clouds, of going through water and fire, etc.; he has become Immortal, *sien*. To the common folk he seems to die, but in reality it is something quite different, the Abandoning of the Body, *shï-kiai*: death is, in fact, of necessity followed by rebirth, but he who has made the Abandoning of the Body continues to live without having to be born again. He has escaped from the cycle of transmigrations; and if for any reason subsequently he has to resume a human existence on earth he does not thereby re-enter the cycle, but, his life once ended, he returns among the Immortals. There are also signs by which it is seen that the Abandoning of the Body is not common death: the cast-off body is very light, it does not become corrupt; sometimes even when the coffin is opened no trace of a body can be found.

Fig. 89. THE GOD OF ALCHEMY (RIGHT)

The Immortals go to live on K'un-lun, the mountain in the middle of the world, round which turn the sun and moon, where reigns the Lady-queen of the West, Si-wang-mu, with her husband, the Lord-king of the East, Tung-wang-kung. The former is a very ancient divinity: originally she was the Goddess of Epidemics, dwelling to the west of the world and in command of the demons of the plague. In the Han period she had become the goddess who averts and cures epidemics. About the end of the first century before our era a kind of panic spread throughout the whole northern part of the empire: a terrible epidemic was announced, against which only those would be safe who placed upon their door certain charms of the Lady-queen of the West. It was perhaps after this affair that the custom arose of drawing her on the ridge-beam of houses and funerary temples, as was commonly done at the end of the first century of our era, and this custom was the origin of her mate, the Lord-king of the East. For the latter is, in fact, merely the child of the spirit of symmetry: in houses correctly oriented (with the entrance to the south), the ridge-beam of the principal hall being placed east and west, the figure of Si-wang-mu all the more naturally occupied the side corresponding to the quarter in which she resides, the west, inasmuch as this side being *yin*, a female figure is completely proper there; but the other end of the beam was unprovided with a face. The east being *yang*, a man's face was placed upon it, and in this way was born the person of the Lord-king of the East, whose *rôle* has always remained much in the background.

Fig. 90. THE LADY-QUEEN OF THE WEST, SI-WANG-MU
Bronze. Musée Guimet.

Si-wang-mu had thus become in ancient times the goddess who gives long life: it seems that she plays this part in the *Tale of Mu, Son of Heaven*, the oldest Chinese historical novel (of the fourth century B.C.), which has come down to us in part. This character gradually became definite: she becomes the goddess who cultivates and keeps the Peaches of Immortality in the garden of the Lord On High. So she is described, about the third and fourth centuries of our era, by the author of the *Secret Life of the Emperor Wu of the Han Dynasty*, and fifth-century poets show her and her husband feasting the Immortals on K'un-lun. This character little by little obtained precedence over the rest, especially since the authors of the *Investiture of the Gods* and the *Voyage to the West* took it up and developed it. The Lady-queen of the West and the Lord-king of the East keep the list of the Immortals, govern them, reward or punish them according to their deeds in this new world, which resembles ours, except that there perfect felicity is enjoyed. The gardens of Si-wang-mu are situated on the summit of K'un-lun. There grows the peach-tree whose fruits confer immortality. There is her jade palace of nine storeys, enclosed within a golden wall. The men Immortals live in the right wing, which is watered by the River of the Kingfishers, the women Immortals in the left wing surrounded by the Lake of Pearls. On their arrival they go and pay their respects to the Lady of the West, then to the Lord of the East, and then are taken to do homage to the Three Pure Ones; after which they live in joy and feasting, withdrawn from pain and death, and perform the various duties of the palace. If they commit grave misdemeanours they are excluded from it for a time: they then go down to be born upon earth until, their punishment having been fulfilled, they reascend to resume their rank.

Ancient representations of Si-wang-mu show her as a monster with the teeth of a tiger and the tail of a panther, wearing an aigrette on her head and excelling in roaring.

She has kept only her headgear from these. She is generally shown as a handsome young woman, in court dress, wearing an aigrette; often she is accompanied by a peacock, sometimes even she sits on the bird. In any case these are merely fanciful representation. The cult of Si-wang-mu is long since dead, and has only survived in folklore, and especially in poetry.

HENRI MASPERO

Fig. 91. THE LADY-QUEEN OF THE WEST ON THE TERRACE OF THE JADE PALACE

Fig. 1. THE DEMONS OF DISEASE MAKE THEIR SUBMISSION TO SUSA-NO-WO-NO-MIKOTO
Painting by Hokusai-Katsushita.

THE MYTHOLOGY OF JAPAN

SHINTÔ MYTHOLOGY

THE mythology of Shintô, the national religion of Japan, is founded on legendary stories that appear in two ancient collections, the *Nihongi* and the *Kojiki.*

The "Nihongi" and the "Kojiki." The first part of the *Nihongi* is usually referred to under the title of *Jindaiki* or *Kami-yo-no-maki*, which means "books consecrated to the divine generations."

The *Nihongi*, or more correctly the *Nihonshoki*, annals of Japan, an official history, was published by imperial order in A.D. 720; it is written in Chinese. The *Kojiki* also is written in Chinese characters, but presents peculiarities of syntax that are purely Japanese. This work, really a compilation of older stories, was put together by a high official during the reign of the Empress Gemmyô (A.D. 708–714).

The Emperor Temmu (A.D. 673–686) was not unaware, indeed, that the "chronicles of the emperors" and the original phrases "handed down by the various families," continually corrupted by alterations, "departed more and more from the exact truth." He feared lest these increasing modifications might impair the good order and solidity of the State, and he reckoned that it was time to submit the national traditions to a severe examination, "to eliminate errors and determine the truth in order to transmit [an authentic version] to the ages to come." Accordingly he made Hiyeda-no-Are learn by heart "the successions of emperors" and "the ancient traditions of the past ages."

Thus the *Kojiki* was composed in order to fix in final fashion and set above all controversy, on the one hand the imperial genealogy and on the other the body of Shintô legend, the source of ritual and foundation of the State. " It was, in short, less a question of writing a history than of establishing a settled orthodoxy." [1]

Besides these two works it is proper to mention the *Kogoshûi*, which occupies a preponderant place among secondary sources. It was composed in A.D. 807 or 808 by Imibe-no-Hironari, and is not a comprehensive exposition of the myths of Shintô, but simply a collection of the traditions omitted from the previous books and preserved in the Imibe family.

The numerous local legends that are incorporated in Shintô have been preserved, and, partly in the fragments of the *Fûdoki*, or " descriptions of the Provinces," were composed in the course of the eighth century, at the command of the Empress Gemmyô in A.D. 713.

Lastly, Shintô mythology, and more particularly the Shintô religion, are set forth in the first ten books of the *Engishiki*, a ceremonial dating from A.D. 927.

Foreign Influences. Shintô mythology, undergoing the influence of the cults and beliefs of neighbouring peoples, particularly of China and Korea, was already to some extent changed when it was recorded in the documents that have revealed it to us. Such as we know it, it " is manifestly the result of the fusion and arrangement of innumerable local and family traditions, which had been progressively shaped into a single continuous and all but coherent narrative." [2]

We must not forget that already from the year 405 Chinese writing was officially introduced into Japan, and that Buddhism,

> at the outset greeted with indifference in A.D. 552, made a new attempt in A.D. 557, which was crowned this time with extraordinary success. Enthusiasm came after distrust. The Emperor Yômei (A.D. 585–587) embraced the new faith. Under his successor, Sujun (A.D. 587–592), a converted nobleman, Soga no Umako, and the young Prince Umayado triumphed over the last efforts at resistance.[3]

Now it was merely three hundred and seven years after the official introduction of Chinese writing and a hundred and thirty-five years after the triumph of Buddhism that the *Kojiki* was put together. The different influences were then assimilated by the Japanese people, and " the religious myths, undoubtedly brought to a great extent from a foreign land, no longer showed traces of their primitive local origin, and had ended by becoming incorporated with the very soil of Japan.[4]

The Gods. " The *Kojiki* was before everything written to settle the orthodox tradition in what concerns the origins and the genealogy of the imperial lineage and incidentally of the other notable families." [5] This explains why in Japanese mythology we find few legends properly so called, but rather tales poor in the element of fancy, which relate to us the life of the gods, and in which the forces of nature are deified: mountains, trees, rivers, etc. To the primitive Japanese the divinities were only beings superior to men, *Kami*—that is to say, " beings placed higher." The epithet *chi-haya-buru* given them may be translated as ' powerful.'

[1] Cl. Maitre, " The Historic Literature of Japan from its Beginnings to the Ashikagas," in the *Bulletin de l'École Française d'Extrême-Orient*, October–December 1903, p. 53.

[2] Cl. Maitre, *loc. cit.*

[3] Cl. Maitre, *op. cit.*, p. 23.

[4] Cl. Maitre, *op. cit.*, p. 16.

[5] Cl. Maitre, *op. cit.*, p. 34.

These gods, who despite their power are not omniscient, when in heaven send a messenger to learn what takes place on earth, and to know the future they have recourse to magic.

Heaven. In the texts we frequently meet with the expressions *Ama-tsu-Kami* and *Kuni-tsu-Kami*—that is to say, the 'celestial' gods and the 'terrestrial' gods, which indicates that the gods had two distinct habitations. As a matter of fact the distinction is not always absolute. The majority of the gods and divinities of mountains, rivers, trees, etc., live on the earth. However, certain divinities residing below sometimes go and settle in heaven, or else, indeed, by a reverse process, as in the case of Izanagi and Izanami, they leave the heavens and come down and instal themselves on earth.

Fig. 2. MODEL OF TORII
Musée Guimet.

The word 'Ama,' which we render by 'heaven,' evoked among the Japanese other ideas than our conception of a distant and inaccessible heaven.

The heaven of the ancient Japanese was a vast region peopled by the gods, traversed by a great river, which to-day we call the Milky Way, upon the banks of which the gods assembled to take counsel.

The sky was primevally linked to the earth by a kind of stair, the *Ama-no-hashidate*. According to the *Tango-fûdôki*, it one day collapsed into the sea, forming an elongated isthmus situated to the west of Kyôto, in the province of Tamba. By this stair the gods of the sky were in direct communication with the earth, to which they often descended.

The Underworld. In opposition to the sky there existed beneath the earth a place called Yomi-tsu-kuni (the land of darkness), or Ne-no-kuni (the land of roots), or Soko-no-kuni (the hollow land). A steep break in the ground, still shown in a certain locality in the province of Izumo, next in another place a bottomless abyss, into which plunge the waters of all the seas, and with them the sins the faithful have washed off on the day of the "Great Purification," are the two entrances of the Land of Darkness.

We find only two descriptions of the nether regions in the texts, one on the occasion of the descent of Izanagi to the country of the dead in search of his wife Izanami, the other in the account of the dealings of Okuni-nushi with Susa-no-wo.

As Florenz justly remarks in an excellent article on the religion of the Japanese:[1]

> The important problem with regard to all who, after their death, go down to the lower world finds no explanation when we go back to the earliest origins, and the other traditions of Shintô teach us nothing definite on this point, probably because the followers of Shintô have a horror

[1] "Die Japaner," in *Lehrbuch der Religionsgeschichte, begründet von Chantepie de la Saussaye*, edited by Paul Siebeck (J. C. B. Mohr, fourth edition), vol. i, p. 275.

of everything relating to death and corpses. That is why it is possible that the ancient Japanese never came to any very clear conception of the lot of human beings after death; but it seems to me still more probable that this conception was left in the shade by Buddhism.

The idea of rewards and punishments after death was introduced by Buddhism: the ancient Shintô texts are silent on this subject.

The Celestial Kingdom of Amaterasu

The Invisible Gods. The first deities who engendered the world were, the *Kojiki* says, three in number, but all three invisible. To these there were before long added two others, then two more, equally invisible.

Fig. 3. One of the Oldest Shintô Shrines, at Ise

Now of these seven deities only the last two are mentioned in the *Nihongi.*

Izanagi and Izanami, the Creative Pair. Then the divinities were born in pairs. Each pair comprised a male and a female deity.

Five pairs were created; the last were Izanagi, 'he who invites,' and Izanami, 'she who invites.' Both were to have an especially important destiny. They were, in fact, the ancestors of all the later Shintô deities. They were also the creators of Japan.

The gods having made them the gift of a spear adorned with jewels, Izanagi and Izanami armed themselves with it. At this period the continents were not yet formed, and the world was but a muddy chaôs over which the gods had flung a bridge. Izanagi and Izanami went out on the celestial bridge, then thrust their spear into the chaos. They drew it back all spattered with mud: a little earth came off it and dropped, thus forming the island Onogoro.

Izanagi and Izanami descended on this island and made their dwelling on it.

Izanagi then spoke to Izanami in this wise:

"How is thy body formed?"

"My body," she replied, "grows in all its parts, save only one."

"Mine," rejoined Izanagi, "grows also in all its parts, but one especially. Good were it that I should join this part of my body with that part of thine that grows not. Thus we shall engender countries."

Izanagi then proposed that they should both go round the pillar of their house, but in opposite directions. Soon they found themselves face to face, and were united. Now the first words had been uttered, at this union, by the woman, which was a serious breach of the ritual.

Fig. 4. Temple of Hie-jinja
Shintô religion.

From this conjunction was born Hiruko, an ugly, puny boy. His parents placed him in a basket which they abandoned to the will of the waves. After this they brought the island Awa into the world, but they did not wish to recognize this child.

They addressed themselves to the gods to know the cause of their misfortunes, and the gods consulted the fates; then they declared that these unhappy births were due to the breach of the ritual committed by the goddess Izanami at the moment of her union with her husband.

Having heard the oracles, both went round the pillar once more, and this time it was Izanagi who spoke first to his wife.

In due course from this union were born the eight principal islands of Japan: Awaji, Shikoku, Oki, Tsukushi (Kyûshû), Iki, Tsu, Sado, and Oyamato (the principal island).

The *Kojiki* and the *Nihongi* enumerate in a different order the deities subsequently brought into the world by Izanami—the God of the Sea, Oho-wata-tsu-mi, the God of the Wind, Shima-Tsu-Hiko, the God of the Trees, Kuku-no-shi, the God of the Mountains, Oho-yama tsu-mi, and many others besides.

The last, according to the *Kojiki*, was the God of Fire, who has three different names. His birth having caused his mother's death by the burns he occasioned, Izanagi cut him in pieces with a sword, while from each separate piece, from each drop of the blood of the newly born, there sprang a new deity.

Descent of Izanagi to the Lower Regions. Desiring to bring back his beloved wife to the land of the living, Izanagi went down to the Underworld. But Izanami had already tasted of the food of the subterranean world, which made her return to earth impossible. Nevertheless she went to ask the gods of the Land of Darkness to make an exception in her favour. First of all she had made her husband promise that he would wait for her without trying to see her. The waiting was long, and Izanagi became impatient. At last he arose and determined to make his way into the palace his wife had entered. There a horrible vision greeted him: Izanami's body in a state of decomposition lay on the ground guarded by the Eight Thunders. Nevertheless the corpse spoke to him: "You have humiliated me," she said. The Eight Thunders, joined by the Ugly Females of the Underworld, then darted in pursuit of Izanagi. Long, long, he ran, outstripping his pursuers by but a little, keeping away from them by various devices, then, once he was outside, he shut the exit from the lower regions with a huge rock.

The god Izanagi, feeling himself defiled by this visit to the impure places, purified himself in the waters of the river Woto. He stripped off his clothes, and he cast them far away from him, whereupon the twelve parts of which they were composed were turned into twelve deities. Izanagi plunged into the water, and from this bath were born other gods, among which was the God of the Deep Sea. Washing his nose, he gave birth to the god Take-haya-Susa-no-wo; then in washing his right eye he engendered the Goddess of the Moon, Tsuki-yomi; lastly he washed his left eye, and produced the Goddess of the Sun, Amaterasu.

The Birth of the Gods according to the "Nihongi." The *Nihongi* recounts the birth of the gods after a different fashion. The principal text says nothing of the birth of the God of Fire, but relates the facts as follows: After engendering the eight islands, the rivers, the mountains, the trees, etc., the divine pair desired to create some one who should be the ruler of this land. Having brought into the world the Goddess of the Sun, whom they named Oho-hiru-me-no-muchi, or Amaterasu-oho-hiru-me, they gave her the rule of the kingdom of the sky. Then they begat the God of the Moon.

After these two celestial deities Izanami had two more children: the first, Hiruko, though more than three years old, could not stand upright. His parents put him in a boat and abandoned him to the waves.

The second, Susa-no-wo, was an unruly god. He wept, cried, devastated the wooded mountains, and caused the death of the inhabitants. Displeased with his behaviour, Izanagi and Izanami sent him to rule the subterranean world.[1]

[1] According to one variant, Susa-no-wo had the domain of the sea for his share.

Before leaving the earth Susa-no-wo wished to make his adieux to his sister, the goddess Amaterasu. He started upon his way, but as he journeyed to the palace of the Sun he made such a turmoil that the mountains trembled. At last he caused such destruction that his sister, uneasy, and persuaded that he was coming to seize her kingdom, came out in arms to meet him and asked in sharp tones what his intentions were. Susa-no-wo explained the reason for his visit, and took an oath to her that he had no ulterior motives. He offered her the following proof: if he gave birth miraculously to children

Fig. 5. THE GOD SUSA-NO-WO SPITS FORTH FIVE MALE DEITIES FROM HIS MOUTH
Taken from a volume in the De Halphen Collection.

those he brought into the world would be male of sex, while if he gave birth to girls that would prove his deceitfulness. The Goddess of the Sun, taking Susa-no-wo's long sword, broke it in three pieces. She fell to eating them, then spat them out in the form of a mist, which presently took the shape of three female divinities.

In turn Susa-no-wo received from his sister " the thread with the five hundred jewels." He ate them, then spat them out in the shape of a mist, which assumed the aspect of five male deities (Fig. 5).

Amaterasu recognized as her children the five deities born of her jewels. She gave Susa-no-wo the three female deities. These eight deities were the ancestors of the families of the ancient Japanese nobility.

The Withdrawing of Amaterasu and her Return. Satisfied with the result achieved, Susa-no-wo pointed out to his sister that the children he had brought into the world were five boys, which clearly proved that his intentions were peaceful. Brimming over with joy, he left the palace and lightheartedly fell to committing every kind of misconduct. He cut down the trees, laid waste the rice-fields. Then he went back to the palace and defiled it, leaving disorder everywhere. Finally he laid hold of a celestial horse and flayed it. Seizing it in his arms, he came back to the palace, where all was at peace. In a private apartment, helped by a companion who was holding the web for her, Amaterasu was weaving. Imagine her affright when through the suddenly split ceiling a monstrous creature, flayed alive, burst into the room. Susa-no-wo could not contain himself for joy to see the success of his jest.

Furious, and trembling with fear, the goddess Amaterasu went and hid in a celestial grotto, where she shut herself away. Immediately the whole world was invaded by darkness, and the evil spirits spread over the surface of the earth. Then all the deities assembled in consultation. At the advice of Omohi-Kane cocks were taken up to the grotto so that by their crowing they might give the illusion of the coming of day.

Furthermore, facing the entrance to the cave they placed a great *sakaki*-tree (*Cleyera japonica*). Jewels were hung in its top, and soft white stuffs meant to clothe the gods were fastened to the trunk. Then in the midst of the tree the gods fixed a mirror they had made for the purpose. The deities grouped themselves about the tree in front of the celestial grotto in which the Goddess of the Sun had hidden herself. Near the entrance a god renowned for his physical strength, Ame-no-tajikara-wo, had taken his stand. Then Ama-no-Uzume, who was not beautiful, but had a very comical manner, began to dance (Fig. 6). The goddess uncovered her breasts, discarded her garments one after another, and all this in such a comical fashion that her dancing excited the laughter of all the spectators. Puzzled and interested by this hilarity, Amaterasu, whose curiosity had been strained to the utmost, could not resist the desire to open her door a little. Her surprise became extreme when she saw her own reflection in the mirror. Tajikara-wo took advantage of it to seize Amaterasu by the hand and pull her out of the grotto. Then, holding a plait of straw behind the goddess, the god Tûto-Tamu said to her: " You are not permitted to hide anew." Then, all bathed in sunshine by Amaterasu-Oho-mi-Kami, the world found its light once more.

As for the god Susa-no-wo, a punishment was inflicted upon him, and in addition he was obliged to present to the divine council objects that symbolized the misdeeds he had committed. These objects were thrown into the water and disappeared in the waves, carrying with them the evil of which they had become the containers.

Susa-no-wo and the Serpent. Susa-no-wo, driven away from the sky, came down sadly upon the earth at Tori-Kami, in the province of Izumo. He was following along the river Hi, when he heard the sound of weeping. He made in the direction of the place from which the plaints were coming: there he found an old man and an old woman who kept between them a girl of remarkable beauty, as if they were fain to protect her. The faces of all three were imprinted with great terror. Susa-no-wo went up to them and asked the reason for their distress. Then the old pair told the god, weeping, how every year there came an enormous serpent, the Koshi, and that on each occasion he devoured one of their daughters, that only one survived, and that they wished to save the last one left to them. Susa-no-wo then offered to kill the serpent on condition that they gave him young Kushi-nada-hime in marriage. The parents agreed. Thereupon the god bade them make ready eight cups, fill them with very strong *sake*, and range them before the eight doors of their house. This being done, he waited. Soon the serpent appeared, lifting his eight heads in wrath and spitting foam and fire. When he drew near the house he smelt the *sake;* then after he had come up and with his eight tongues lapped the eight cups of *sake* he fell down dead drunk. Susa-no-wo, coming out of the place where he

Fig. 6. THE GODDESS AMA-NO-UZUME DANCING BEFORE THE GROTTO IN WHICH THE GODDESS AMATERASU IS HIDDEN
From a volume in the De Halphen Collection.

had bestowed himself, cut off his eight heads. Then he opened his belly and found in it a sword that he presented respectfully to Amaterasu. This sword was handed down from generation to generation, and has actually reached our own times. It is now one of the three insignia of the imperial power, and is preserved in several coffers in the temple of Atsuta, near Nagoya.

The Children of Susa-no-wo. Susa-no-wo had children who married local deities. One of his descendants, Oho-kuni-nushi, became lord of Izumo. The *Kojiki* recounts to us the difficulties his brothers stirred up against him, his descent into the underworld, the hard trials he underwent, and lastly his triumphal return to Izumo, with his wife Suseri-bime. To him fell later the rule of the subterranean realms. From his intercourse with a great number of women was born a numerous progeny. Three of his children were to assume particular importance: his daughter Shita-teru-hime, who married the god Ame-waka-hiko, the messenger of Amaterasu on earth, and his sons Koto-shiro-nushi and Take-minakata, who were obliged to hand over the province of Izumo to the grandson of the goddess Amaterasu.

The Conquest of the Earth by Amaterasu

Amaterasu was the unchallenged goddess of the celestial kingdom. But the terrestrial kingdom, if it did not entirely escape her power, was still not organized. This work remained to be done. And to this enterprise she turned her energies.

Descent of the Gods upon the Earth. The second part of the book "of the epoch of the gods" is devoted to the conquest of the earth by the messengers of Amaterasu in the reign of her grandson and during the life of his posterity. The events related by the ancient texts had till then been enacted in heaven, rarely upon the earth. The actors were the celestial gods, come down on earth for a limited time. The projects of Amaterasu were to change the order of things. And if thereafter the action still sometimes takes place in the heaven, most frequently it happens on the surface of the earth, in the province of Izumo, or in the domain of the sea.

Ama-no-Oshiho-mimi. The goddess Amaterasu in the first place addressed herself to her son Ama-no-Oshiho-mimi, and asked him to go and reign over the terrestrial kingdom. The god betook himself to the celestial bridge, from which he examined the earth, and, alarmed by the number of the dissensions among the terrestrial deities, he refused to accept such a responsibility.

Ama-no-Hohi. Amaterasu then consulted the god Taka-mi-Musubi. Together they decided to convene the council of the gods. The council, after deliberating, instructed the god Ama-no-Hohi to betake himself to the earth, to inspect it, and then to come back and report what he had seen. Now three years went by without the gods receiving any news of him.

Ame-waka-hiko. Amaterasu and Taka-mi-Musubi once more convened the deities, who decided to send a second messenger, and armed him with a bow and arrows. They appointed Ame-waka-hiko.

Scarcely had he arrived in Izumo when Ame-waka-hiko met Shita-teru-hime, the daughter of Oho-kuni-nushi, married her, and completely forgot the mission with which he was charged. Eight years passed by. The gods of the sky were still waiting. At last, being uneasy and perturbed, they sent the pheasant Na-naki-me to look for him. The bird soon arrived at the house of Ame-waka-hiko. He perched upon the tree Kazura and began to recite the orders of the gods. Ame-waka-hiko did not know what to do, when Ama-no-sagu-me, his servant-maid, interposed. According to her, the bird had a voice of evil omen; she advised him to kill it. Then Ame-waka-hiko took his bow, adjusted an arrow, and shot it at the pheasant. Now the arrow, having passed through the bird's body, continued on its upward flight. It rose to heaven, piercing through its floor, and fell near the god Taka-mi-Musubi. Surprised, he picked it up, examined it, and recognized where it came from. "Here," he said, "is one of the arrows we gave to

Ame-waka-hiko. If he, in this respect carrying out my orders, has contented himself with slaying the wicked this arrow, which I shall now send back to him, must not touch him. But if he has shot it with impure intent it will bring him misfortune." He sent back the arrow, which struck the god Ame-waka-hiko in the breast in his sleep and killed him.

His widow, Shita-teru-hime, filled space with such bitter lamentation that her tears and moans were heard from heaven. The father of Ame-waka-hiko, accompanied by his first wife and his children, went down to Izumo and gave the god a splendid burial.[1]

Take-mika-zuchi and Futsu-nushi. Resistance of Take-minakata. The Goddess of the Sun yet once more took counsel of the gods to appoint a new messenger. The choice fell upon Take-mika-zuchi, the God of the Thunder, who was given, according to the *Nihongi*, a companion, Futsu-nushi, the God of Fire. Armed with swords, the pair went down to Izumo, and this time immediately entered into negotiations with the lord of the country Oho-kuni-nushi; they asked him to recognize the rights Amaterasu possessed over his lands.

Oho-kuni-nushi reflected; but he would take no decision before consulting his two sons.

The god Futsu-nushi set out to find the eldest son Koto-shiro-nushi. Having found him, he speedily brought him back. In concert with his father he consented to hand the country over to the celestial envoys, then withdrew and disappeared in the sea.

But Take-minakata, the younger son, was minded to resist. Endowed with great physical might, he challenged Take-mika-zuchi to feats of strength. But when the son of Oho-kuni-nushi would have seized the hand of the God of the Thunder the latter turned it to a whetted sword. When it was his turn the god succeeded in gripping the hand of Take-minakata, and crushed it as he would a tender reed. Seized with fear, the young hothead took to flight, pursued by Take-mika-zuchi, and took refuge at Suwa, in the province of Shinano. He was then obliged to consent to hand over the land of Izumo to the celestial gods, and agreed not to leave the province of Shinano on any pretext. On these conditions his life was spared.

His father, Oho-kuni-nushi, learning these things, withdrew beneath the earth to rule over the evil deities and prevent them from harming the living.

Then the gods Take-mika-zuchi and Futsu-nushi, having fulfilled their mission, went up to the sky again, where they gave account to Amaterasu of the success of their undertaking.

Ninigi, the Ancestor of the Emperors of Japan. Once again the god Taka-mi-Musubi and Amaterasu begged Ama-no-Oshiho-mimi, the son of the goddess, to accept the government of the earth. He had a son, Ninigi, and withdrew in his favour.

Then Amaterasu gave him orders to go down to his new kingdom. She presented to him the jewel of Yasaka, the mirror made by the gods at the time of her own retreat into the celestial grotto, and the sword of Susa-no-wo. These three objects were to constitute the insignia of his power. She then said to him: " Consider this mirror as thou wast wont to consider my soul, and honour it as myself." Ninigi, accompanied by five

[1] Here the texts describe the ancient Shintô funeral-rites, with very interesting details.

chiefs and three deities, and equipped with the three insignia of his power (*sanshû no jingi*), set out on his way to the earth. He descended, not on Izumo this time, but on the summit of the mountain Takachiho, situated in the south of Kyûshû. Then he went down to the temple of Kasasa, in the province of Satsuma.

Organization of the Shintô Clergy. There the five chiefs who accompanied him left him to devote themselves to religious tasks. They were to become the ancestors of the families whose successive generations handed down from one to the other the hereditary charges pertaining to the Shintô religion: one was to have the duty of furnishing priests and reciting the ritual incantations and prayers; this other was to be concerned with filling the subordinate posts in the clergy and delivering the timber intended for the building of the temples as well as ritual objects; another was specially to provide members of the clergy for the performance of religious dances; to yet another was entrusted the making of the sacred mirrors; to the last again fell the task of making the jewels belonging to the cult.

The Marriage of Ninigi. Near the temple Ninigi met a girl of rare beauty named Sakuya-hime. She told him she lived in that country with her father and her sister, and that their home was not far from the spot where they had met. Ninigi proposed marriage to her. But Sakuya-hime could not answer: she replied that consent to this lay with her father alone.

Ninigi fell in with this, and asked the father for his daughter in marriage. The father's only reply was to send his two daughters that the god might make his choice. But he found the elder too ugly, and sent her home again. Surprised and displeased, the father went to Ninigi and expressed astonishment at the choice he had made. The children his younger daughter would give him would always, he said, be beautiful but weakly, while by the elder he would have a strong progeny. The god persisted in his resolve, and the father was obliged to acquiesce.

It is to this cause, says the *Kojiki*, that the short life of the Emperors of Japan is due.

After some time Sakuya-hime, being on the point of having a child, informed her husband. Now he expressed doubts as to its paternity. To prove to him that her babe was of celestial origin Sakuya-hime had a house built and shut herself away in it. When the moment of her delivery came Sakuya-hime set fire to the building, but the child, born in the fire, was miraculously saved. He was called Ho-deri.

Ninigi was to have two other sons thereafter, Ho-suseri and Hoho-demi.

Story of Hoho-demi. Ho-deri, the eldest son of Sakuya-hime, had a marvellous hook, which enabled him to take great quantities of fish with the utmost ease. One day Hoho-demi, his brother, who was particularly cunning in the chase, borrowed the hook from Ho-deri. He went a-fishing, but could not catch a single fish, and to add to everything lost the famous hook. Hoho-demi came back to his brother empty-handed. The latter asked for his property, but hearing what had befallen Hoho-demi he fell into a violent rage. Hoho-demi, in despair, wished to make good the loss he had caused him. He broke his sword, and with the fragments made hooks, which he offered to his brother, who refused them.

Sunk in despair, Hoho-demi was sitting weeping on the seashore, when the god

Shiho-tsuchi came to him and asked the cause of his distress. Homo-demi related his misadventures. The god advised him to go to Wata-tsu-mi, the sovereign of the sea, and entreat his aid. Then he built a little boat for him. As soon as the boat was ready Hoho-demi got in and steered for the palace of the God of the Sea. Long he sailed, and at length reaching the goal of his voyage he went ashore. He was wandering round the palace when he was perceived by the handmaids of Toyo-Tama-bime, the daughter of Wata-tsu-mi. These made haste to announce to their mistress the arrival of a stranger; Toyo-Tama-bime went immediately to meet the newcomer, whom she found exceedingly handsome, and brought him to her parents. Hoho-demi, charmed by the girl's grace and delighted with the welcome he had met with, forgot the reason of his journey and had no thought save for the goddess. Being invited to stay at the palace, he lost no time in letting her perceive his feelings. Before long he asked for her hand and married her. In his happiness he did not reckon how the years were passing away. After three full years he recalled the object of his journey. At the memory his face saddened, and he began to sigh. Perturbed, his wife asked why he was sad. Hoho-demi told the story of the quarrel between him and his brother. Then the God of the Sea called together all the fishes, and the hook was found in the mouth of a dorado. The god Wata-tsu-mi laid hold of it, and then, presenting it to Hoho-demi, "Here it is," he said. "When you give this hook back to your brother do not forget to repeat these words to him: 'This hook is bad and defiled.' Then give it to him, keeping your hand behind your back. Your brother will then wish to make rice-fields. If he plants them on high ground make yours down below; if he puts his on low-lying ground put yours on high ground. In this way within three years you will see your brother ruined, while you will become rich, for I direct the streams of water as I will, and can dry up or irrigate whatever region I please. Take also these two jewels: the waters which rise by virtue of the one subside by virtue of the other. If your brother becomes angry and wishes to attack you do not hesitate to drown him; but if he repents, then save his life."

Saying these words, the God of the Sea gave him the hook and the two jewels.

Hoho-demi bade adieu to his wife and his father-in-law. Then he mounted upon a huge shark, which carried him to Japan.

There everything happened as had been foretold: Ho-deri set up rice-plantations and was ruined in three years, while his brother grew rich. Jealous, he attacked Hoho-demi, but the latter, making use of one of the two jewels, made the flood swell and submerge Ho-deri, obliging him to make submission. Then Hoho-demi, having caused the waters to subside by means of the other jewel, became the lord of all the lands thereabout.

One day there arrived the princess Toyo-Tama-bime, who was expecting a child in a little while, and who wished to be with her husband when it was born. She did not want, she said, to bear the child of a celestial god at the bottom of the sea. At her request her husband built her a hut to shelter her for her lying-in. The day of her delivery was at hand. When it came she insisted that her husband should go away so that he should not see her during her travail, then she shut herself up in the hut.

Hoho-demi obeyed, but, being eaten up with curiosity, stayed close by. At length he came up softly and from outside spied on what was going on within: his wife had assumed the aspect of a monster in the form of a shark, covered with scales like a dragon, and was thrashing about terribly! Terrified, Hoho-demi took to flight; but Toyo-Tama-bime, perceiving that she had been seen, was so ashamed that she abandoned her child and went back to her own country.

Jimmu Tennô, First Emperor of Japan. When she had got home she sent her younger sister to the little boy. Tama-yori-bime went and found the child, and brought him up. Then when he had grown to manhood she married him. From this alliance four boys were born. The youngest is known by the name of Toyo-mike-nu. Once grown up, he left Kyûshû and went at the head of his tribe towards the East,[1] reaching the province of Yamato. He received the posthumous name of Jimmu Tennô, and is known in Japanese history as the first emperor, the founder of the dynasty, who according to the tradition occupied the imperial throne from 660 B.C. down to our era.

Fig. 7. BELIEVERS INVOKING THE RISING SUN TO OBTAIN THE RESTORATION OF THE EMPEROR'S HEALTH (NOVEMBER 1926)

With this event ends the official mythology of Shintô. The subsequent documents are devoted to the lives of the emperors, who lived among men and governed them as chiefs of the country. But the narratives they contain still include a considerable proportion of mythology, which gradually disappears to give place to legends, and at length to historical facts.

The Gods of Nature. Besides mythological narratives properly so called there exist a great number of legends, native or foreign in origin, and particular cults. These legends for the most part have no connexion with the Shintô religious tradition, but were invented by the people to explain the phenomena of nature or the manifestations of human life in its various aspects. This is how the Japanese came to create their multiple *Kami*, to be able to venerate everything they saw about them that seemed to surpass the ordinary and average. There were the *Kami* of thunder, of lightning, of fire, rain, springs, mountains, rivers, food, rice, vegetation; the *Kami* of the highway, the stones, the winds; the *Kami* of life; the *Kami* of the hearthside; the *Kami* that explain the origin of geographical names—in a word, the Japanese sets up *Kami* everywhere.

The collection of these deities forms a huge pantheon of eight hundred myriads of *Kami*.

Cult of the Sun. The Sun was adored by the primitive Japanese, and is still worshipped

[1] The direction taken by the tribe of Toyo-mike-nu is extremely curious, and remains perhaps an exceptional case of migration towards the East.

to-day (Fig. 7) as the Amaterasu Ohomi-Kami. The object (the *shintaï*[1]) into which the august soul of the Sun may enter to be present at ceremonies, or to come and hear the prayers addressed to her, is the octagonal mirror (*yata kayami*) (Fig. 8).

The gods had constructed such a mirror when they sought to bring Amaterasu from the grotto in which she had taken refuge. This same mirror, presented by the goddess to her grandson Ninigi, was to be one of the three insignia of his power. It was preserved in the imperial family till the first century before our era. The Emperor Sujin, who reigned from 97 to 30 B.C., not wishing to keep in his palace treasures so precious as the

Fig. 8. SHINTÔ CEREMONY
In the centre is the mirror, the *shintaï* of the Sun.

mirror and the sword of his ancestor Ninigi, had copies of them made and preserved; then to house the originals he built at Kasanui a temple of which his daughter was high-priestess. The next Emperor, Suinin, who reigned from 29 B.C. to A.D. 70, had another temple built at Ise, and had the sacred mirror taken thither, where it would seem it ought still to be. Amaterasu, however, is not the only solar deity worshipped in the Shintô religion.

The *Kojiki* mentions a young sister of Amaterasu who was called Waka-hiru-me, and who became the wife of one of the descendants of Oho-kuni-nushi. Now the *Nihongi* affirms that Waka-hiru-me was weaving with the goddess when Susa-no-wo flung a flayed horse into the room where they were working, which was the cause of Amaterasu's going into retirement. The Japanese scholar Moto-ori (1730–1801) is inclined to interpret this deity as a personification of the Rising Sun.

[1] The *shintaï* is neither a symbol nor the attribute of a deity, but a definite object (a stone, a sword, a mirror, etc.) into which an invisible deity can incorporate himself or herself in order to establish contact with the believers.

Another deity, the god Hiruko, the son of Izanagi and Izanami, a weak and sickly individual, is, according to Professor Florenz, a male solar god.

Aston tells us in his work on Shintô [1] that in comparatively recent times this god was confused with Ebisu, who is one of the seven Gods of Happiness. This god is often represented in Japanese art in ancient national costume, with smiling face, and holding a fishing-line with a dorado hooked on the end of it. Traders have him in high honour, and celebrate his feast on the twentieth day of the tenth month. Many other gods, in the ancient Japanese legends, have links with the cult of the sun. Thus the god who reigned over the province of Yamato before giving it up to the Emperor Jimmu bore a name that the Japanese philosophers translate as the " mild, swift Sun "—that is to say, the morning sun—Nigi-haya-hi.

The sun has always had a preponderant *rôle* among the deities, and the cult is still highly developed in our own times.

Every year his devotees in great numbers make the ascent of Fuji-yama, to salute the rising sun with the profoundest religious respect from the mountain-top. Every morning and every evening the inhabitants of town and country salute the rising sun or the setting sun and address short prayers to him. Places famous for the splendour of dawn or twilight are consequently particularly held in veneration.

Out to sea, not far from the beach of Futami, at Ise, there are seen two rocks, a large one and a small, united by the ritual cord *shime-nawa*, which are called " rocks of the spouses " (*Meoto-ga-Seki*). Now on the beach there is a place from which the sun can be seen rising between these two rocks. The great shrine is actually situated at Ise. Thither the pilgrims betake themselves very early to worship the rising sun. And in it is placed the sacred mirror of Amaterasu.

Nevertheless, in modern Shintô Amaterasu, the solar divinity, is no longer adored as the sun, but as the greatest divinity of all, as the ancestor of the imperial family of Japan.

The sun-deity's attributes are the cock and the raven. Cocks, which proclaim the sun's rising, are still now considered as birds sacred to the luminary. This explains the great number of cocks seen at Ise in the precincts of the temple. The raven (*yata garasu*) is revered as the messenger of Amaterasu.

Cult of the Moon. Less revered than the sun, the moon nevertheless had a cult of its own. The male deity of the moon, Tsuki-yomi, was brought into the world by Izanagi, when on his return from the underworld he was minded to purify himself and washed his right eye. Temples were raised to him, especially at Ise and Kadono. There the god manifests himself through the medium of a mirror.

Every year offerings of live horses are brought to him.

People worship the full moon to-day; two days are consecrated to it—August 15 and September 13. On these days offerings of cakes called *Tsukimi-dango* are made to the moon.

According to the *Yamato-bime-no-mikoto seiki*, a doubtful work of the twelfth century, the god Tsuki-yomi is represented on horseback, clad in a purple coat and armed with a golden sword.

[1] W. G. Aston, *Shintô* (*The Way of the Gods*), p. 133.

In modern iconography we meet with a particularly curious print of the moon. Within a disk is portrayed a scene representing a white rabbit kneading rice dough in a mortar. This print forms a kind of rebus: the full moon is in Japanese *mochi-zuki;* now to pound in a mortar the dough intended for making the cakes called *mochi* is also *mochi-zuki.* Hence the symbol.

Star Worship. One version of the *Nihongi* speaks, with reference to the descent of two celestial deities to the earth in order to bring the land of Oho-kuni-nushi under the sway of Amaterasu, of an evil stellar deity, Ama-tsu-mika-hoshi.

Fig. 9. The God of the Wind

Recent mythology knows the feast of Tanabata, celebrated in honour of the star the Weaving Maiden, on July 15. This cult originates from a Chinese legend according to which the star of the Oxherd meets that of the Weaving Maiden above the Milky Way once a year.

With these two exceptions the stars seem to have a very subordinate part in Shintô mythology. The late Professor Haga gives an excellent reason to account for this: the Japanese, he tells us, were an agricultural people. As they went early to bed they had little opportunity for star-gazing.

The God of the Storm and of Love. The God of the Tempest and Lord of the Waters of the Ocean, Susa-no-wo, who plays a very important part in the ancient myths, has, in the course of the ages, lost his stormy character. He has become the god of love and of marriage. The common people to-day call him Gozu-Tennô, the ox-headed Emperor. This god is regarded as one of the metamorphoses of Bhaishajyaguru. He is worshipped in the Yasaka-jinja temple and in the Temple of Gion, which was formerly consecrated to Buddhism.

The Gods of the Winds. In the foremost place among the manifestations of nature, the winds, so frequent in Japan, were explained by the intervention of the gods.

The *Nihongi* teaches us that from the breath of Izanagi was born the God of the Wind, Shina-tsu-hiko. Another version tells us that Izanagi, after the creation of the world, wished to scatter with his breath the morning mist that covered the country, and gave birth to the goddess Shina-to-be.

Two deities of the wind, a male deity, Shina-tsu-hiko, and a female, Shina-to-be, are quoted in one of the *norito.*[1] Two subordinate gods are under their orders: the god Tatsuta-hiko and the goddess Tatsuta-hime. This same *norito* tells us that the God of the

[1] A kind of incantation.

Wind has the task of filling the void that divides the earth from the sky and of holding up the sky.

Many prayers are addressed to these deities; messengers were often sent to Tatsuta to entreat him to be propitious to the harvests. The belief in the God of the Wind is still alive in Japan, and the sea-coast population of the Osaka district come to Tatsuno to pray to him and to obtain charms against wind and tempest.

Fig. 10. Gohei, a Shintô Symbol
Musée Guimet.

Besides the Gods of the Wind there is also a God of the Whirlwind, known by the name of Haya-ji, or Haya-tsu-muji-no-Kami. His origin is of great antiquity: when the arrow that had pierced the pheasant Na-naki returned to strike Ame-waka-hiko, and killed him, the lamentations of his wife, Shita-teru-hime, were heard in heaven. Amaterasu understood what had taken place, and sent the God of the Whirlwind to earth, and he brought back the dead body to heaven. In the iconography of the Ryôbu-Shintô the God of the Wind is represented under the form of a devil holding on his back a great bag from which he is squeezing the wind (Fig. 9).

In front of the temples dedicated to them can be seen the statues of the Gods of the Wind and the Thunder, the first bent under the weight of his wind-bag, the second laden with drums meant to give out the rolling noise of the thunder.

The Gods of the Rain. There are two rain-gods. One, Taka-okami, dwells upon the mountains; the other, Kura-okami, the God of Rain and Snow, dwells in the valleys. Both have the shape of a serpent or a dragon.

But the Shintô priests do not apply to them to bring rain. When a drought arrives the peasants get up a procession at the head of which walks the priest carrying a *gohei* (Fig. 10). He is followed by a peasant who blows a huge shell. Next comes a group of worshippers carrying a kind of dragon made of bamboo and plaited straw. Immediately after these march men holding banners the inscriptions on which are prayers addressed to the king of the dragons. Last come the throng of peasants playing on drums and making a terrific noise. The procession takes its way to a river or a lake, where the ceremony is completed by immersing the effigy of the dragon in the water. According to the *Izumo Fûdoki*, west of the mountain Kaminabi there was a stone deity. Near this stone came into the world the God of the waterfall, Taki-tsu-hiko, and the stone became the soul (*mi-tama*) of this god. If he is applied to in time of drought he causes rain to fall.

The *Engishiki*, which contains the ceremonies of the Engi period (901–922), and which was published in 927, enumerates the eighty-five temples to which messengers from the Imperial Court were sent with prayers requesting the gods to cause it to rain.

The Gods of the Springs. Springs and wells are also inhabited by *Kami.* These are called the Mi-wi-no-kami. They make the water of the earth gush forth. It is necessary to purify the water of a newly dug well, for which purpose it suffices to throw salt into it in the course of the ceremony.

The Gods of the Rivers. In a mountainous country like Japan the rivers in spring

Fig. 11. General View of the Shrine of Itsuku-shima, dedicated to the God of the Sea

often leave their beds and cause great damage. That is why every region traversed by any considerable stream adored a god of the river that was a menace to it.

The mouths of these streams had their deities too, the Minato-no-kami.

According to an old popular belief, every river is inhabited by a dwarf with streaming hair, whose head presents a curious malformation: his skull at one point forms a tonsured hollow that always contains a little water. This deity is called Kappa. He is sometimes very malignant, and can do a great deal of harm to men. If by chance anyone meets with this Kappa he must make him a very low bow: the dwarf returns his bow, and as he bends his head he spills the water in the hollow on top of his skull. And at the same time he loses his strength and the power to injure the man.

The Gods of the Sea. The famous sanctuary of Itsuku-shima is dedicated to the deity of the sea (Figs. 11, 12, and 13). But there are several sea-deities. Two of them, Oho-wata-tsu-mi and Shiho-tsuchi, rule as lords over the maritime realm. The shark (*wani*) and the crocodile are their messengers.

The Gods of the Sea, as we have seen, possess jewels capable of bringing about the ebb and flow of the tide at their pleasure. It was jewels of this kind that were given to Hoho-demi.

When Shintô was joined with Buddhism under the form of Ryôbu-Shintô the priests

Fig. 12. Torii (Gateway) of the Shrine of Itsuku-shima at High Tide

associated the Hindu god Varuṇa with the local deity of Sumiyoshi, near Osaka. Thus they made a new sea-god, who was given the name of Sui-Tengu.

This is the deity to whom the mariners pray to protect them from shipwreck.

Later the god Sui-Tengu was associated with the memory of the young Emperor Antoku, who perished with his nurse in the bay of Dan, near Shimonoseki, in 1185. To-day the god is often represented in the shape of a woman holding a child in her arms: this is Nii-no-ama, the widow of Kiyomori, and her grandson, the little Emperor Antoku.

The Gods of Vegetation. The fields are inhabited by the divinity called No-no-kami, to whom is joined the Goddess of the Herbs, Kaya-nu-bime, called also Nuzuchi, or

Kaya-no-mi-oya-no-kami. The god Ku-ku-no-chi is the father of the boles of trees. The leaves are under the protection of the god Ha-mori.

In Japan, where the mountains are covered with splendid forests, trees of great size and great age are highly revered. The peasants protect them and surround their trunks with the sacred cord *shime-nawa*. It is not unusual to see little chapels made of wood, called *hokora*, in front of these noble woodland specimens. Before the Shintô temples

Fig. 13. Torii (Gateway) of the Shrine of Itsuku-shima at Low Tide

there are planted divine trees (*kami-gi*), among which the *sakaki* (*Cleyera japonica*) and the *hinoki* (*Chamæcyparis obtusa*), a kind of cypress, are especially held in reverence.

Echo. The Japanese regarded the echo as a manifestation of life; they thought that the trees were endowed with speech and that they were answering the call, in this way making the echo, which explains the name they gave it, Ko-dama, the soul of the tree.

The Divinity of Food. The divinity of food, who in the ancient texts is designated by different names, holds a very important place in Japanese mythology. According to a legend related in the *Nihongi*, Amaterasu sent to earth the Goddess of the Moon, Tsuki-yomi, to find the Goddess of Food, Ukemochi-no-kami, or "she who possesses (*mochi*) [1] food (*uke*)." Tsuki-yomi soon met the goddess, who invited her to dinner.

[1] *Mochi*, from the verb *motsu*, 'to possess,' 'to have.'

During the meal Ukemochi-no-kami behaved in a way that to Tsuki-yomi appeared unpleasant and unseemly: she made cooked rice and quantities of other dishes come out of her mouth. Annoyed by these goings-on, Tsuki-yomi could not restrain herself; she got up and killed the goddess Ukemochi-no-kami.

According to another legend, the solar deity Amaterasu appeared in a dream to the Emperor Yûryaku, and complained to him that she had no companion at Ise; she bade him, therefore, send her the goddess Aga-mi-ketsu-no-kami—that is to say, "the divinity of the food that is offered to me (Amaterasu)." The temple Gekû (Fig. 14) was built at Ise in honour of this goddess, who thenceforward was worshipped in it.

Fig. 14. One of the Gateways of the Temple of Gekû, at Ise
A primitive form of *torii*.

Inari, the God of Rice. Often the God of Rice, Inari, is confused with the goddess Ukemochi-no-kami. The cult of Inari is very widely spread. And for that reason it has undergone many alterations. Thus this god, venerated as the protector of food, becomes the god of prosperity in every form: he brings aid in all the difficulties of life; he protects lovers and married people; he recovers and restores stolen objects. From early times he was regarded as the patron of swordsmiths. Now he is revered by all Japanese traders.

The god Inari is generally represented as balanced on the back of a fox, holding a bag of rice under each arm or on his shoulder. He wears a long beard (Fig. 15). He is sometimes represented with the features of a woman. The fox is his companion and his ordinary messenger. So much is this animal's existence linked with his that popular belief has confused them, and often adores the god Inari in the shape of a fox.

Temples dedicated to the rice-god are exceedingly numerous; an ancient saying declares that in Edo (the ancient Tôkyô) there are as many temples of Inari as dog-droppings. The principal temple erected in his honour is at Fushimi, near Kyôto. It is characterized by a great number of gates (*torii*) painted red. A round stone is placed in front of the temple. This is the *shintaï* (residence of the god). This *shintaï* is generally flanked by two statues representing foxes.

The Gods of the Mountains. The ancient Japanese having had feelings of respect for everything great, they could not fail to venerate the many mountains of their own land. The texts mention a deity of the mountains named Yama-tsu-mi, of whom, however, they say very little. Still, he was approached before the trees necessary for the construction of temples and palaces were cut down.

THE GODDESS OF FUJI-YAMA
(Musee Guimet.)

The mountains had each its own deity: thus Sengen Sama dwelt on Fuji-yama, the highest peak in Japan. Mount Ontake, in the province of Shinano, Mount Nantai, near Lake Chûzenji, the volcano Aso, in the province of Higo, also had theirs.

The Japanese are given to making ascents of the sacred mountains; in summer pilgrimages are organized for these, especially to the top of Mount Fuji.

The Cult of Stones. The Japanese revere stones, for they are often great and unchanging. Thus they adore the great God of the Rock, Oho-iwa Dai-myô-jin, in the form of a rock.

Fig. 15. Inari, the God of Rice
Musée Guimet.

Stones are also the *shintaï* of certain deities. Certain temples consist of three huge stones surrounded by *sakaki*-trees. Such, for instance, is the Hime-goso temple, the dwelling of the princess Akaru, who, according to the *Kojiki*, was obliged to flee from Korea in the third century of our era.

An old legend tells us that the Empress Jingô (A.D. 170–269), just at the point of giving birth to a child, had to go on campaign against Korea. To postpone her travail she put stones on her belly and was able to fight at the head of her troops. These stones were objects of veneration thereafter. In the Hizen province, not far from the place called Fukue, there is a temple of the stones that lighten travail—Chinkwai-seki-no-yashiro.

And we have seen how a stone became the soul of the god Taki-tsu-hiko, the god of the waterfall of Mount Kaminabi.

The Gods of the Thunder. The ancient myths tell us of eight Gods of the Thunder. Ika-zuchi, who guarded the corpse of Izanami and pursued Izanagi when the latter, who had gone down into the lower world in search of his wife, sought to bring her back to earth. But these Gods of the Thunder seem rather to personify the maladies that emanate from a decomposing body, or the subterranean noises that are to be heard in the vicinity of volcanoes and during earthquakes.

The sky thunder is called Kami-nari, the divine muttering. It is also met with under the name of Naru-kami, the thundering god. He personifies thunder and lightning together,

The God of the Thunder was regarded as the patron of the craftsmen who made arrows, and when they feared a foreign invasion the emperors would send envoys to his temples to pray.

Furthermore this god is the friend and protector of the trees, and thus hostile to wood-cutters. A legend of the year 618 tells us how an envoy of the Emperor Kawabe-no-Omi, in the province of Aki, having set about cutting down a tree on imperial service to make boats, a deity appeared to him and told him that the tree he was about to fell was a "tree of the thunder" and that he ought to respect it. The imperial envoy persisted and had the tree cut down. Immediately a violent storm broke out, accompanied by torrential rain and terrible rattlings of thunder.

Fig. 16. Shintô God

Even to-day trees struck by lightning are looked on as holy. They are called *Kantoki-no-ki*, "the trees cloven by the god," and they are left untouched.

The *shintaï* of the thunder-god is the sword. The offerings pleasing to him are horses. The temple of Kashima is consecrated to him.

The Gods of Fire. The *Nihongi* tells us that Izanami died in giving birth to the God of Fire, burned up by her last son. He was called Kagutsuchi, but in the ritual prayers he is always invoked under the name of Homusubi, "he who starts fire."

Since very distant antiquity the Japanese have dreaded fire. Twice a year an imperial service Ho-shizume-no-matsuri, was held to appease and soothe fire. During these ceremonies the priests read a *norito* recounting the fire myth and mentioning the objects capable of conjuring it.

Besides the fire that brings destruction there is the pure fire of the ritual, which the priests use in the temple. This fire was procured by rubbing pieces of *hinoki* wood together; in this case it was given the name of *kiri-bi*.

To-day this fire is obtained by a shorter method, which consists in striking a hard stone with a piece of steel. The fire thus obtained is purifying, and protects those it has touched. In this way they purify the holders of certain functions in religious feasts or ceremonies. The protecting fire is also caused to spark forth over the head of *geishas* going to exercise their profession.

The Gods of the Road. The deities of the road and the highway form a somewhat important group in Shintô mythology. They are known under the name of Sae-no-kami,

Fig. 17. Statue of Hachiman Sai-bosatsu (Divine Manifestation of the Emperor Ojin)
Ryôbu-Shintô art.

or Dôsojin. They sometimes bear the name of Chimata-no-kami, the God of the Road, and Yachimata-hiko, the man of countless roads.

They were created by Izanagi after a journey to the nether world, when, being pursued by the thunders, he flung his stick, *kunado-no-kami*, across the path, crying out, "the thunders shall come no farther."

The Sae-no-kami protect travellers and keep them from evil spirits. Hence two days before the arrival of Chinese or Korean envoys in the Japanese capital ceremonies were held in honour of the Sae-no-kami gods, that they might guard Japan against the arrival of evil spirits in company with the foreign ambassadors.

Fig. 18. SHINTÔ GOD

The *shintai* of these deities is a stick.

The Phallic Cult. We read in the *Fusô-ryakki*, a historical work dating from the year 939 of our era, that the Japanese worshipped deities in the shape of the male and female genital organs. Mr Deguchi, in an article on phallic worship in Japan, thinks that, though both represented in the shape of a stick, the deities of the road and those of the phallus were of different origin.

The cult of the phallus, of extreme antiquity, was relegated to a secondary place in official Shintô. None the less it got into Ryôbu-Shintô.

To-day the authorities have issued orders to remove the emblems of this cult into unfrequented spots, to avoid shocking people's susceptibilities. But in the popular belief this cult is maintained, and temples consecrated to this deity are still found. Such is the Ebishima-jinja at Ishikoshi, to the north of the city of Sendai, and the Iwato-jinja in the island of Shikoku.

The Gods of the Hearth. And finally in the Shintô religion, as in all primitive mythologies, there are the Gods of the Hearth. Thus there is the God of the Hall Door, the God of the Kitchen Stove, who is revered in palaces and in cottages alike. There is even a God of the Privies, who must not be neglected, for he can send evil genii carrying diseases.

Deified Men. Our brief sketch has enabled us to enumerate the most important of the deities worshipped by the Shintô religion. But the study of these gods is far from taking in the whole of the colossal mythological pantheon of Japan, and now for a long time emperors and men who by their skill, their intellect, or their courage rendered service to their country have been regarded in Japan as *Kami* (Figs. 16, 17, and 18). In certain cases even temples were erected to the glory of living persons. But this is a theme that leaves the domain of mythology to enter that of history.

Fig. 19. Acolyte of the God Hachiman

Fig. 20. Fudô reascends to Heaven after performing a Miracle in favour of the Monk Shyôku

BUDDHIST MYTHOLOGY

INFLUENCE OF BUDDHISM IN MODERN JAPAN

Of all the countries in which Buddhism took hold and spread Japan is perhaps the one in which the religion of Buddha remains most alive. It is the great Buddhist universities of Tôkyô, Kyôto, Mount Kôya, that furnish the superior clergy, and these great intellectual centres have preserved the traditional study of the Sanskrit and particularly the Chinese texts that treat of the Buddhist religion. The Buddhist canon was even published on several occasions in its Chinese version by Japanese scholars.

And furthermore the influence of Buddhism makes itself definitely felt in Japanese art; the modern painters continue to show it; there are art journals specially devoted to it.

Finally, the mind of the masses is impregnated with Buddhist ideas, which are expressed in concrete fashion in the manners and customs of the Japanese people.

The true believers, to whatever sect they belong, go to the temples to worship the deities of many shapes brought by the priests from China and Korea.

Origins and Development of Japanese Buddhism

Buddhism appears to have been brought to Japan by Korean or Chinese monks long before the sixth century, the official date of its introduction.

Two currents of Buddhism had at this time been propagated in the Western world—the Hīnayāna and the Mahāyāna. This latter especially was widespread in China, where it had undergone important modifications; its pantheon had besides been enriched by a great number of deities. It was this form that spread in Japan.

In the year A.D. 552, the Emperor Syöng-myöng, who ruled over the kingdom of

Pakchoi, situated in the south of the Korean peninsula, sent to Kimmei, the Emperor of Japan (A.D. 540–571), ambassadors whose mission was to present him with a statue of Buddha in gilt bronze, several volumes of *Sūtras*, various articles belonging to the cult, and a treatise containing an apologia for the Buddhist doctrine.

The Emperor Kimmei was deeply moved by the discourses of the Korean ambassadors; but as in Shintô, the national religion of Japan, he held a position that obliged him to take part in the religious rites celebrated in honour of the national divinities, and as, on the other hand, he observed that the hereditary priestly caste of the Nakatomi and a great part of the people would be hostile to a religion coming from abroad, he displayed no enthusiasm for being converted. At the same time he authorized the head of the Soga family to accept the gifts of the Koreans and to attempt to make trial of the new religion. Soga Iname took the statue of Buddha and installed the first Buddhist temple in his own house.

This innovation was very severely condemned by the nationalists of the time.

In A.D. 577 the King of Pakchoi sent to Prince Owaka, the Japanese ambassador, on his return to his own country, a considerable quantity of Buddhist books, and sent a number of monks, a sculptor, and an architect to accompany him. Presently Prince Owaka was given an imperial authorization to build a Buddhist temple on Japanese soil.

In A.D. 579 another little Korean kingdom, Silla, also sent to Japan the statue of a Buddha. A few months after the death of the Emperor Yomei, in 587, a struggle broke out between the Soga family, which practised Buddhism, and the national party, which was hostile to the foreign doctrine, and the victory remained with the Sogas and Prince Umayado, better known under his posthumous name of Shôtoku Taishi. And when in A.D. 592 the Empress Suiko (A.D. 592–628) ascended the throne, Prince Shôtoku was declared heir to the crown, and was virtually in the position of regent.

Shôtoku Taishi was a fervent Buddhist, and fostered the sudden development of religious art in Japan. The Hôryûji temple and its treasures are masterpieces that allow us to judge of the beauty of the architecture of this distant period (the seventh century). Buddhism was thenceforth adopted by Japan. The consequences of this acceptance were of real importance from the point of view of internal politics, of diplomatic, commercial, and other relations with foreign countries of the same religion, from which Japan was to derive her own civilization. The priests did, indeed, distinguish some differences in dogma between the various sects, but as a matter of fact Buddhism was considered by the imperial court as a perfectly homogeneous religion, possessing a fundamental unity of doctrine wherever it held sway.

The Sects of Nara

The next period of the history of Japanese Buddhism is closely linked with the history of the ancient capital Nara, and is known as the "period of the six ancient sects of Nara."

The first Buddhist sect, according to the historical tradition, was only introduced into Japan in A.D. 625. This was that of Sanron, or "the doctrine of the three *Śāstras*."

We cannot here write a detailed history of Japanese Buddhism, and we must pass the other sects of Nara by in silence. We shall indicate only the one that was introduced in

A.D. 736 by a Chinese bonze, and which was the first strictly Mahayanist sect. It is known as Kegon-shû, the Japanese pronunciation of the title of the Chinese version of the *Avatamsaka-sūtra*.

These six sects of Nara popularized among the Japanese sculptural representations of the Buddha, of Buddhist saints, of the disciples of Ṣākyamuni, and of Buddhist divinities created by the imagination of the Hindus. In this period Japan saw for the first time the statues of Fudô, of Jizô, of Binzuru, of Emma-Ô, and of several deities such as Kwannon and others that have since become very popular, and of which we shall speak in detail farther on.

THE NEW SECTS

The Buddhist pantheon was especially enriched by the Tendai and Shingon sects.

In 794 the capital was finally transferred to the plain, at the foot of Mount Hiei. It received the name of Heianjô—the capital of Peace—which later became Kyôto.

The Emperor Kwammu (782–805) found in the monk Dengyô Daishi, who lived on Mount Hiei, very near the new capital, the man he was seeking to reform the Church. In A.D. 804 he sent him to China. There Dengyô Daishi studied the secret doctrines on Mount T'ien-t'ai. On his return to Japan he built the great Enryakuji monastery, and introduced new iconographic forms.

SHINGON

A young monk who accompanied Dengyô Daishi on his visit to China had studied with special attention in the Chinese monasteries the doctrines of the mystical sect Mikkyô, which was also called Shingon, the simple translation of the Sanskrit word *mantra*, which signifies the 'true word.' Kôbô Daishi (such was the posthumous name of the monk) on his return to Japan spread this new doctrine.

This mystic sect became one of the most popular, not on account of its esoteric aspect, but because of the beauty of its religious ceremonies. And it has exercised a very notable influence on the Buddhist art of Japan.

The Shingon sect calls itself the mystic sect, because it declares itself in possession of the secret that allows man during his terrestrial life to attain to the Buddha nature. According to this doctrine, there are two methods of attaining the essence of truth, the one spiritual, the other moral. The first indicates the stages that must be passed through to reach the absolute, the other lays down in principle the commandments that point out the way of salvation.

The world is explained by two schemas, which are called the *mandalas* (in Japanese *mandaras*).

One of the *mandalas* is called Kongôkai (Vajradhātu): it is the ideal aspect of universal life in which fundamental and indestructible ideas are presented in the eternally serene soul of the Great Enlightener, Dhyāni-Buddha-Vairochana.[1]

The pictorial representations of this *mandala* show us the Great Enlightener plunged in the profoundest contemplation and with a white aureole. He is surrounded by various

[1] M. Anesaki, *Quelques pages de l'histoire religieuse du Japon*, pp. 45 *et seq.*

saints, his emanations, likewise with white aureole and sitting upon white lotus flowers, emblems of serenity. Persons and symbols ranged in eight squares round about the central square represent other emanations of the Great Enlightener.

In this pictorial representation of the world of ideas the centre is occupied by the Dhyāni-Buddha-Vairochana and everything converges on this centre, aiming at the absolute.

The world of forms is represented by the *mandala*, called by the Japanese Taizôkai (Garbhadhātu), in which the various groups of divinities and other creations find a place according to the nature of the powers and intentions they respectively embody. In the centre a lotus flower, with its stigma and eight petals, symbolizes the heart of the universe. The whole forms a counterpart to the nine squares contained in the *mandala* of the world of ideas. The stigma of the lotus is the seat of the Dhyāni-Buddha-Vairochana, who appears sitting on a pedestal of diverse-coloured lotus, surrounded by a double halo of red disks, emblems of activity. The other manifestations may be divided into two categories corresponding to the wisdom and the love of Vairochana: the Wisdom that enlightens us in the truth of universal communion and subdues our vices; Love that embraces all existences in the compassionate beneficence of the lord of the cosmos. In this schema of the world of forms the centre also is formed by the Dhyāni-Buddha-Vairochana, but the movement is directed outward from the centre. From the Dhyāni-Buddha-Vairochana emanate other Buddhas, from these in turn emanate Bodhisattvas, who give life to other deities, and so on until the whole world of forms is constituted. This is to prove that the primordial source of all existence is the eternal Vairochana, and that all other beings have a relative existence subordinated to him.

Thus the universe seen in these two aspects, potential and dynamic, is nothing else but the life of the Dhyāni-Buddha-Vairochana, the lord of the cosmos, while the other emanations are incarnations of the inexhaustible fullness of his wisdom and his love.

The Shingon sect absorbed the Buddhist deities, then it produced a very elaborate pantheon to justify all the emanations of Vairochana. The same deities appear in the *mandala* under different forms and situations to indicate the various manifestations of the lord of the cosmos.

We shall speak again later of the principal deities of the Shingon sect, which appear very frequently in Japanese art.

The Joining of Buddhism with Shintô: the Ryôbu-Shintô

Besides creating the Shingon sect, Kôbô Daishi holds a special place in the history of Japanese Buddhism, for he succeeded in amalgamating Shintô with Buddhism. The theories relating to the origin of the Shingon sect represent the gods of Shintô as a temporal manifestation of the Buddhist deities. The Goddess of the Sun, Amaterasu, was then neither more nor less than a temporal manifestation of Vairochana. In this way a struggle between the two religions was avoided. Ideas of this nature were not in any case wholly foreign to Buddhism, which in its journey across Asia had already incorporated a goodly number of local deities in its pantheon. Kôbô Daishi crystallized the ideas that were already in the air at the time by assuming the identity of numerous Shintô deities with those of Buddhism. Shintô joined with the Shingon sect received the name of Ryôbu-Shintô, " Shintô with two faces." It became a very popular doctrine. A new iconography was created, the architectural style of the Shintô temples underwent modifications, and this state of things continued as late as 1868, when after the restoration of the imperial power it was sought to purify the Shintô doctrine by a clean separation from the Buddhist doctrine. In the great mass of the Japanese people, however, the Ryôbu-Shintô has remained alive; these gods are still worshipped, and many families belong to two congregations, one Buddhist, the other Shintô.

The Zen and Jôdo-shû Sects

For more than three centuries there were no important changes in the religious life of Japan. A new sect made its appearance about the end of the twelfth century: the Zen sect, introduced into Japan by the monk Eisai, who had studied it in China. From the point of view of iconography and mythology Zen presents no interest whatever. " Zen was a simple intuitive method of spiritual exercise; its followers set before them as their aim the attaining of purity of soul, and consequently to keep themselves aloof from the turmoil of human life." [1]

At the same period there was established in Japan another sect founded by the monk Genkū (1133–1212), better known by his posthumous name of Hônen Shônin. Contrary to the Zen, this sect relied for the salvation of men on the Buddhist deities, and not on man's spiritual strength. It assumed the name of Jôdo-shû, " sect of the pure earth." Its doctrine was that salvation was impossible outside the Buddha Amida (Fig. 23). This Buddha of " the eternal light," who also bears the name of Amitāyus, " eternal life," is the Dhyāni-Buddha—that is to say, the immaterial part of the eternal light of Gautama Buddha—Vairochana being the abstraction of ideal purity. In the popular creeds this emanation, the Buddha Amida, is regarded as a divine personage. Belief in Amida is closely linked with the belief in the existence of a paradise and a hell. The Gokuraku-Lekai " the world of the supreme pleasure," Jôdo, " the pure earth," is situated in the West (Fig. 24). This Western paradise is what for the common people takes the place of Nirvāna, for it is there that human beings find the reward for their good actions. The description of the Buddhist paradise is found in several *sūtras*, as well as in that well-known work the *Fushisôgô* of the monk Kôa Shônin (fourteenth century).

Since there was a paradise for the good, there must needs be a hell for the wicked. Hell (in Japanese Jigoku) was situated, according to popular beliefs, under the earth, and was divided into eight hot and eight cold regions. Besides this there were secondary hells and preliminary hells. The soul after death appeared before the principal divinity of the underworld, Emma-Ô (Yama-rāja). In a book placed in front of him were entered the sins of the departed. A female head (*miru-me*), endowed with the faculty of perceiving the most secret faults, and a male head (*kagu-hana*), with the gift of smelling out the scent of all misdeeds,[2] were ranged on either side of the supreme judge.

[1] M. Anesaki, *op. cit.*, pp. 117–118.

[2] See the colour plate opposite.

EMMA-O (YAMA-RAJA)
(Musee Guimet.)

The dead man then passed before a mirror that reflected all the deeds of his earthly life.

Emma-Ô pronounced his judgment, and handed over the condemned to the demons, who tormented him by administering the penalties proportioned to his degree of guilt (Figs. 30 and 31).

But in the realms of Emma-Ô there is no eternal suffering: damnation is but for a fixed period; one can even be delivered before the prescribed term by the power of prayers and offerings from the priests. The hells and the judging of the departed by Emma-Ô and by the Ten Judges are often represented in art.

Sects of Jôdo-shin and Nichiren

In the thirteenth century a new sect, an offshoot of the Jôdo-shû (whence its name of Jôdo-Shinshû, " the true sect of the pure earth ") and founded by Shinran Shônin (1173–1262), brought certain modifications into the doctrines of the Jôdo sect. For Shinran the one and only Buddha was Amida. That is why in the Shinshû temples only statues of this god are to be seen.

It was in the thirteenth century also that the priest Nichiren founded a sect that based itself upon the doctrines of the *Saddharmapuṇḍarīka Sūtra* (" Sūtra of the Lotus of the Good Law "). But from the point of view of iconography and mythology these sects are without interest. The Nichiren was the last of the modern sects.

In this brief sketch we have cited only the most important sects. Twelve sects of Japanese Buddhism are often spoken of; this number has no relation to the facts.

Fig. 21. Butsumo Dai-Kuyaku-myô-ô (Mahā-may ra)
From Butsuzô zue.

AN ICONOGRAPHY OF JAPANESE BUDDHISM

THE Buddhist deities introduced into Japan by China and Korea are exceedingly numerous; some have maintained themselves to our own day, and have kept a certain popularity, the others have fallen into oblivion.

We shall speak here of the most important and most popular of these deities, arranging them in alphabetical order; indeed, it is all but impossible to embark on a summary study of them otherwise, on account of their simultaneous adoption into the pantheon of the various sects.

AIZEN-MYÔÔ (RĀGA-VIDYARĀJA)

This is a deity 'impregnated' with love for human beings. He calms evil passions. His aspect is terrible, but his heart is good. Regarded as secret by the Shingon sect, he manifests *samâdhi*, the state during which agitation (*kleṣa*) becomes enlightenment (*bodhi*), and in which the great passion of love changes into infinite compassion for everything that lives (*sattva*). The *Yugikyô sūtra* tells how, during an assembly of deities, an 'agitation' was suddenly manifested. It was not of celestial origin, it did not come from the earth, nor from any other quarter whatever, it was a spontaneous 'agitation.' All the Bodhisattvas were disturbed at it, and in their perturbation they seemed like men drunken; and they did not understand the cause of this apparition. Then the Bhagavat smiled, and, addressing himself to the Vajrasattvas and to all the Bodhisattvas, he said, "It is immaterial to know whence comes this manifestation of 'agitation': it is the primordial cause of an enlightenment, it is the agitation of the hidden qualities of the *sattva*. It comes without having had a beginning, it is a vital agitation of hidden qualities, it is born spontaneously of the 'ego.' It is the fundamental *chakra* furnished with hidden qualities that has neither origin nor beginning." At this moment the agitation took the form of a Vajrasattva: it was Aizen-myôô.

This deity is usually represented with a ferocious visage. He has three eyes, the third is placed on his forehead, vertically, between the two eyebrows. He has on his head a lion's head with bristling mane, surmounted by a *vajra*, a kind of five-pointed thunderbolt, a weapon that drives away guilty desires and manifests the wisdom of the deity. Its five points are symbolical of the centre and the four quarters of the world of ideas (Vajradhātu). Aizen-myôô is the only deity that wears such an ornament on his head. Five-hued Mâllikâ flowers fall in garlands upon his shoulders. He has six arms; in one of his left hands he holds a metal bell, in one of his right hands a five-pointed *vajra*; in the second left hand a bow, and in the corresponding right hand a quiver; in the third left hand he holds, according to the particular iconographic influence that presided over the conception, a wheel (*chakra*), or a man's head, or a hook, etc. In the third right hand is a lotus flower. Aizen-myôô is seated cross-legged on a red lotus flower placed in a vase (Fig. 22). In

Fig. 22. AIZEN-MYÔÔ (RĀGA-VIDYARĀJA)
Musée Guimet.

certain prints of this god treasures of various kinds may be seen escaping from the two sides of the vase.

Japanese iconography knows several forms of Aizen-myôô, with two, four, or six arms. There are also images of Aizen-myôô with two heads, and the Shingon sect has created a pictorial representation—what is called the *mandala*—the centre of which is occupied by Aizen-myôô. The Buddhist books of Japan give numerous explanations of his iconography: if his body is red it is because Compassion and Pity issue from every pore in drops of blood like sweat. He has three eyes to behold the three worlds. He wears a lion's head head-dress because he is like a lion, which is the king of animals; the bell he holds in one of his hands is intended to awaken enlightenment. The 'thunderbolt' symbolizes the pure heart ready for *bodhi*. The bow and the arrow drive away forgetfulness, and the lotus calms the agitation of guilt.

Fig. 23. AMIDA (AMITĀBHA)
Musée Guimet.

AMIDA

The esoteric sects distinguish between three Amidas: Muryôju (Amitāyus), Muryôkô (Amitābha), and Kanro-ô (Amṛita).

In the *mandala* of the World of Forms (Taizôkai) Muryôju is placed in the central group, immediately underneath the Dainichi-nyorai; in the *mandala* of the World of Ideas (Kongôkai) he is above the head of Dainichi. But it is not in the secret sects that Amida plays the most important part; it is the others, principally the Shinshû and Jôdo-shû sects, that have made Amida the great saviour of humanity. Indeed, it is he who comes to the aid of all who believe in him and address sincere prayers to him. He gives to every human being the possibility of being born again in his Paradise of the West. Among the esoteric sects the Buddha Amida is represented seated (Fig. 23); but among the exoteric sects we see him always standing, with head uncovered, clad in Indian fashion, one arm bent, pointing with his fingers to the sky, and the other arm extended, with the fingers directed to the earth, thus taking earth and heaven as witnesses of his vow not to enter Nirvāna until he had saved all human beings.

Fig. 24. Taema-mandara, the Paradise of Amida
Musée Guimet.

We also find Amida enthroned in the middle of the Sukhāvatī Paradise, in which are born again all those who, before dying, have addressed their prayer to him, pronouncing the sacred formula " Namu Amida Butsu."

The appellation "Kuhon no Mida" designates the Amida of the pure earth, of the paradise of nine degrees (Kuhon) reserved for the blessed. In the Japanese iconography there are two very widespread forms: Yamagoshi no Amida, Amida appearing behind the mountains, and Kuwarishiki no Amida, Amida with crossed legs and red of hue, red being the colour of the West, in which this deity's paradise is placed. An image of this form is preserved among the treasures of the Chi-on-in temple at Kyôto.

Ashuku (or sometimes Ashiku) Nyorai (in Sanskrit Akshobhya-tathāgata)

This is one of the four Buddhas. In the *mandala* of the World of Ideas (Kongôkai) he is immediately underneath Dainichi-nyorai. In the *mandala* of the dynamic aspect of

Fig. 25. Atago-Gongen. On his Right, at the Back of the Shrine, the God Jizô
Musée Guimet.

the world (Taizôkai) he bears the name of Tenkurai onbutsu (in Sanskrit Divyadundu bhimeghanir-ghosha), and he is placed on the right of Dainichi—that is to say, to the north. He is represented under the aspect of a Buddha sitting upon a lotus, his legs crossed, the right foot placed on his left knee, the left hand closed, the right hand held out, with the fingers turned toward the earth. His head is without headdress, his body usually the colour of gold. In Japan there is no cult of Ashuku, and he is only met with in groups of deities or on *mandalas*.

Atago-Gongen

This was a deity of Ryôbu-Shintô until the moment when the Japanese Government expelled Buddhism from the Shintô shrines (beginning of the Meiji period). This deity bears the name of the mountain Atago, in the province of Yamashiro, on the summit of which he manifested himself; his temple is there. Tradition has it that he is a patron deity of fire. Some claim that he is the god Kagutsuchi no kami, others that he is Susa-no-wo, Izanami, or another deity of thunder or fire. In A.D. 781 the bonze Keishun explained that the deity Atago-gongen was a deity who preserves fire. It was this same bonze who raised on the summit of Mount Atago a Buddhist temple consecrated to "Jizô of the Victorious Army." This aspect of Jizô became very popular among the military caste, and numerous warriors came to pray to this god. The iconography of Jizô of the Victorious Army influenced the monks of Mount Atago, who gave their deity the same aspect of a Chinese warrior on horseback, and the same emblems—the pearl of price and the crozier.

Fig. 26. DAI ITOKU-MYÔÔ (YAMĀNTAKA)
Musée Guimet.

BINZURU HARADA (IN SANSKRIT PIṆḌOLA BHARADVĀJA)

Binzuru is his name, Harada his surname. He is the first of the sixteen Rakans (Arhats), disciples of Buddha. He is represented in pictures as an old man with white hair and long eyebrows. Because in youth he had broken his vow of chastity Buddha had forbidden him to enter into Nirvāna. He dwelt on Mount Marishi (Mārīchi), and came to the aid of men. A wooden statue of Binzuru is often placed on the threshold of temples. The sick pray to him while rubbing with their hands the part of the statue corresponding with the place where they are suffering. In this way they hope to obtain a cure.

DAI ITOKU-MYÔÔ (YAMĀNTAKA)

This is the terrible manifestation of Amida; one of the five great *myôô*. He is placed in the region of the west. He is ordinarily represented with six heads, six arms, and six legs, and mounted on a white ox. He is always surrounded by flames. There are prints also in which the Dai itoku is sitting on a rock. The three right feet are set on the earth, the three left legs are folded. Two hands are joined, making a *mudrā*: one of the right arms holds a sceptre, the other is raised, and the hand holds a sword; in one of the left hands he holds the wheel, and in the other a sort of trident with a long shaft. The six faces wear a terrible aspect, and the hair is all bristling (Fig. 26). This *myôô* fights against illness and poisons, and he is more powerful than the dragon.

He also bears the name of Gôemmason, for he has vanquished Emma-Ô, King of the Underworld. Dai itoku-myôô is also the terrible form that corresponds on the one hand to the form of Monju-bosatsu, and on the other to Amida-nyorai.

There are also images of Dai itoku-myôô with only one head and two arms. He is then represented sitting on a rock in front of a background of flames, with legs crossed, holding in his right hand a long stick with a trident at each end, and the *vajra* in his left hand. The face has three eyes. The hair is bristling (Fig. 26).

Dainichi-nyorai (in Sanskrit Mahā-Vairochana Tathāgata)

This is the fundamental deity of the esoteric sects. He transmitted, through the Bodhisattva Vajrasattva and the great Hindu Nagārjuna, the secret doctrine that forms the basis of the Tendai, the Shingon, the Kegon, and other sects. Eminent Japanese priests, Jikaku, who went to China from A.D. 838 to 847, and Chishō, who went from A.D. 853 to 858, brought back to Japan the Chinese works relating to the doctrines of Dainichi-nyorai. There are two forms of the Dainichi. When he occupies the centre of the *mandala* of the world of ideas (Vajradhātu) he is seated, with legs crossed, on a lotus, a crown on his head, clothed as the Bodhisattvas always are. He holds in his right hand the forefinger of his left: this is the *mudrā* of the Six Elements, in which the five fingers of the right hand symbolize the five fundamental elements, earth, water, fire, air, and the ether, while the forefinger of the left hand symbolizes the intellectual element (*chi*) (Fig. 27). The Dainichi-nyorai is also placed in the centre of the *mandala* of the World of Forms (Taizôkai-mandara); then while keeping the aspect of a Bodhisattva he has his hands joined in *dhyāna-mudrā*, and they rest upon his crossed legs.

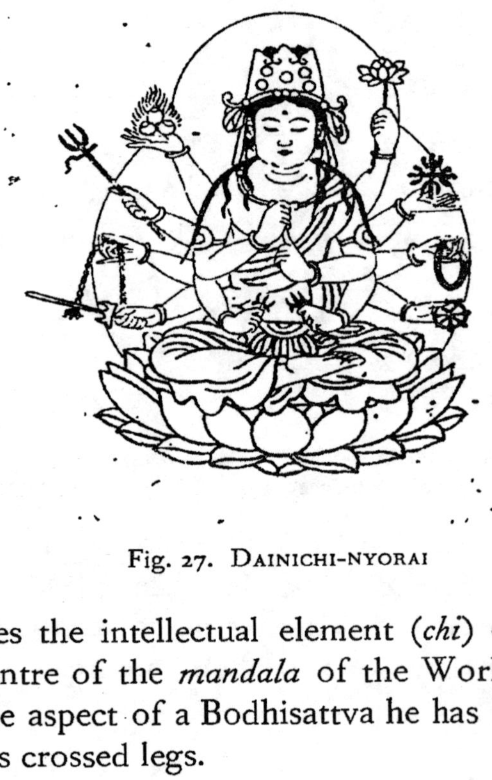

Fig. 27. Dainichi-nyorai

Emma-Ô (Yama-rāja)

South of the province Embushi (Jambūdvīpa), beyond the Iron Mountains, is the Buddhist underworld. There reigns Emma-Ô, surrounded by eighteen generals and eighty thousand soldiers, who are under his orders. It is Emma-Ô who judges sinners and who sends them, according to the gravity of their offences, to the different parts of the hells, where the demons inflict various torments upon them. According to one tradition,

Emma-Ô has a sister younger than himself who judges the women, while he judges only the men. If we are to credit another legend, three times by day and by night one of his soldiers seizes Emma-Ô and stretches him out on red-hot iron. Opening his mouth with an iron hook, he pours into it molten brass, but his body does not burn, and after this torment he resumes his ordinary life and enjoys himself with the other deities of the hells. In popular representations of the nether regions the Emma-Ô is always clad in the costume of a Chinese judge, and wears a bonnet on which are written the characters Emma; his face is fierce of expression.[1]

The esoteric sects have a *mandala* in which the Emma occupies the centre, and in which he is surrounded with deities who are akin to him: this is called the Emmaten-mandara. There are three versions of it, but the central figure of Emmaten (Yamadeva) is always seated on a buffalo and holds a stick with a human head on the end. The Chinese origin of this *mandala* is clearly demonstrated by the costume of the deities and the presence of a Taoist deity in the lower part of it.

Fudô-myôô
(in Sanskrit Arya achalanātha)

He is the most important of the five great myôô — Fudô-myôô, Gozanze-myôô (Trailokya-vijaya), Gundari-myôô (Amṛita Kuṇḍika), Dai itoku-myôô (Yamāntaka), Kongô-yasha-myôô (Vajra-yaksha)—and is one of the incarnations of Dainichi-nyorai (Vairochana). He is represented sometimes standing, sometimes seated, with legs crossed, upon a conventionalized rock. His body is greenish-black. Behind him rise flames that symbolize benevolence and the virtues and destroy all agitation (*kleṣa*). His hair is long, one great lock falls from the left side of his head. His face has a fierce expression; his right hand holds a sword, the symbol of wisdom and compassion. With this weapon he fights the "three poisons"—avarice, anger, folly. In his left hand he holds a cord to bind those who might oppose the Buddha (Fig. 28).

Fig. 28. Fudô-myôô (Achala)
Musée Guimet.

[1] See the colour plate facing p. 416.

Fudô-myôô is often represented with two acolytes, Kongara (Kinkara) and Seitaka (Chetaka).

The cult of Fudô-myôô is sufficiently widespread. Temples are dedicated to him, a notable one being that of Shin-shôji in the town of Narita, in the province of Shimôsa. According to the tradition of this temple, the statue of this deity was carved by Kôbô-Daishi (A.D. 774–835), if it was not simply brought by him from China. Which proves that the cult of Fudô-myôô is an ancient one. But it was particularly in the course of the seventeenth century that Fudô-myôô became highly popular. When Taira Masakado raised a rebellion, in A.D. 935, against the Government of Kyôto he withdrew into the north-east of Japan, and began to make war in that district. At the command of the Emperor the bonze Kwancho took the statue thither. Thanks to the intervention of the deity the rebels were defeated in A.D. 940. Then the bonze wished to take the statue back to the Takao temple, where it had been before the expedition, but all his efforts to carry it away were in vain. A dream revealed to him that Fudô-myôô desired to remain at Narita. The Emperor Shujaku (A.D. 931–946) had a handsome temple built, granted lands for its upkeep, and presented a sword to the deity. The present building dates from 1704. The sword presented by the Emperor Shujaku has been preserved. The mere touch of this sword cures madness and delivers persons possessed by the fox spirit.

Fugen-bosatsu (in Sanskrit Samantabhadra)

He is at the summit of the Way of the Extinguishing of Errors. Everywhere he propagates the essence of his character, and therefore he has been given the name of Samanta (*fu*). As in suppressing errors he approaches the highest sanctity, he receives the name of Bhadra (*gen*). Among the Bodhisattvas Fugen is regarded as one of the most important; with Monju-bosatsu (Mañjuṣrī) he forms a pair: the first represents compassion (Karunā), constancy, cordiality, the second wisdom, intelligence, comprehension. Fugen, representing constancy in contemplation, is always the same in his acts of compassion. In his relations with living beings it is he who understands the motives of all their acts, thanks to his profound heart. This faculty of ruling the manifestations of the human heart is symbolized by the image of Fugen seated on a white elephant; he is also credited with the power to prolong human life, and there are special prayers to ask him for the gift of longevity.

Japanese iconography represents Fugen under various aspects. Usually he is seated on a lotus, legs crossed, holding in his left hand a lotus surmounted by a sword surrounded with flames; the right arm is slightly upraised, breast high, the palm of the hand is turned upwards, the fingers are stretched out, except the fourth and the fifth fingers, which are bent; he wears a crown. There are also Fugens with multiple arms, especially one with twenty; every hand then holds some symbol. We also meet with the image of Fugen as a youth, seated on an elephant and holding a manuscript in his hand. But in the majority of representations Fugen is seated on a lotus upheld by one elephant or by several (Fig. 29).

Go-chi-nyorai

This is the name given to the five *nyorai* placed in the central square of the pictorial schema of the World of Ideas (Vajradhātu). In the centre is the Dainichi-nyorai (Mahā Vairochana). Below him there is shown Ashuku-nyorai (Akshobhya). On the right is Hôshô-nyorai (Ratnasambhava), on the left Fukû jôjû-nyorai (Amoghasiddhi), and above the central deity Muryôju-nyorai (Amitāyus).

Godaison

This is the popular name of the five great *myôô* (Godai-myôô): Fudô-myôô (Arya achalanātha), Gozanze-myôô (Trailokya-vijaya-rāja), Gundari-myôô (Kuṇḍalī), Dai itoku-myôô (Yamāntaka), Kongô-yasha-myôô (Vajra-yaksha).

These five *myôô* are the agents of the wills of the five great Buddhas, which we will enumerate in the same order as the *myôô*—that is to say, Dainichi (Mahāvairochana), Ashuku (Akshobhya), Hôshô (Ratnasambhava), Mida (Amitābha), and Fukû (Amoghavajra).

Fig. 29. Fugen-bosatsu (Samantabhadra)
Musée Guimet.

Gokuraku-jôdo

The Sukhāvatī paradise, which is in the west, according to sects like the Jôdo-shû (sect of the pure earth), is the residence of Amida; he is enthroned in the centre, having at his sides Kwan-on-bosatsu and Seishi-bosatsu, while higher than Amida, on clouds, are placed to his right Monju-bosatsu, and on his left Fugen-bosatsu.

According to the doctrines of these sects, who believe that human beings can be saved by the power of Amida, this deity, followed by Kwan-on and Seishi, comes at the last hour to fetch the soul of the believer, who, according to the piety he displayed during his earthly life, will be born again in one of the nine states (*kuhon*) of the Paradise of Amida. There he will be happy and safe against all suffering.

Japanese iconography knows two representations of Paradise, one the Kwangyô-mandara, the other the Taema-mandara (Fig. 24).

Gôzanze-myôô (Trailokya vijaya)

This is one of the five *myôô*. A deity of terrible aspect, he dwells in the region of the east, and is usually regarded as a manifestation of Ashuku (Akshobhya). Represented with four faces, all with a fierce expression, a forehead eye, and bristling hair, he has eight arms; two of the hands are joined breast high; the lowest right hand holds a sword, the second an arrow, the third a *vajra*; the left hands hold a stick, a bow, and a lance. The left foot tramples vigorously on Jizaiten (Maheṣvara) while the right foot presses lightly on the hand of Umahi (Umā), the wife of Jizaiten. In the *mandala* of the World of Forms (Taizôkai) there are also representations of Gôzanze seated on a lotus flower, in front of a background of flames.

Gundari-myôô (Amṛita Kuṇḍika, or Amṛita Kuṇḍalin)

He is one of the five *myôô*, and is a manifestation of Hôshô (Ratnasambhava). He also bears the names of Nampô Gundari Yasha, because he dwells south of Mount Sumeru, and Kanro (Amṛita), because he distributes the celestial nectar to poor human beings. His aspect is terrible: standing, with his feet on lotuses, his left foot is sometimes raised and his body in the act of leaping. He has three eyes; his hair bristling; fangs stick out from his mouth. On his headdress is a human skull. His red body has eight arms; serpents are frequently wreathed round his ankles and his wrists. Two hands are crossed upon his breast; the lowest right hand is open and pointing to the earth; the second in the *mudrā* position; the third holds a *vajra*. One left hand, near the knee, holds a kind of axe, another a long stick ending in a trident, and the third, at the height of the head, a wheel.

In the *mandalas* of the esoteric sects this deity occupies three different places, from which are derived his three names: Kanro-Gundari, Kongô-Gundari, and Renge-Gundari. The first is regarded as a manifestation of Kokûzô-bosatsu (Akāṣagarbha), the second of the Kwanjizai-bosatsu (Avalokiteṣvara), and the third of the Kongô-bosatsu (Vajrasattva).

Gwakkô-bosatsu (in Sanskrit Chandra-prabha)

One of the two acolytes of Yakushi-nyorai (Bhaishajyaguru) is the personification of the moon; the other companion of Yakushi-nyorai is the Nikkô-bosatsu, the personification of the sun. In the Buddhist iconography Gwakkô-bosatsu is represented as a youth with long hair dressed in three knots. He is seated cross-legged on a red lotus; his body is yellow; in his left hand he holds a lotus-bud; in the right a blue lotus (*utpala*), upon which is placed a crescent moon.

The Hells (Jigoku)

According to the popular Buddhist beliefs, the hells are underneath the earth. There are eight hot hells where souls endure the torments of fire and eight frozen hells where they endure the pangs of cold; furthermore, each of the eight hot hells is divided into sixteen distinct hells, which makes one hundred and twenty-eight hells of fire. These eight hells are the principal ones; there are also hells named *kimpen jigoku*, which are divided into four (placed at the cardinal points of each principal hell), and hells called *Kôdoku-jigoku*, which can suddenly manifest themselves, in the mountains, in the meadows, under the trees, and in the air.

But for the popular beliefs, as well as for Japanese art, it is the fire-hells that are the real hells. Figs. 30 and 31 show us the eight hells. The sinners are before Emma-Ô, who

Fig. 30. JIGOKU. PICTURE OF THE BUDDHIST HELLS (UPPER SECTION)
Musée Guimet.

has to right and left of him two heads, each on a supporting stand: the female head is Miru-me, who sees all the sinner's acts, and from whom nothing can be concealed; the male head to the right of Emma-Ô is called Kagu-hana, or "the nose that smells," so named because it smells out the very smallest sin. Then the demon leads the sinner to a mirror that reflects all his past sins before his eyes. His sins are then weighed. Sentence having been given, he goes straight to one of the eight hells, or he may have to spend a period in several in succession. The prayers of the living, addressed to a Bodhisattva through a Buddhist priest, may save the sinner. The compassionate deity then goes down into the hells and brings back the rescued wretch, who is born again on earth or in a paradise.

Hôshô-nyorai (Ratnasambhava)

This third Tathāgata of the *mandala* of the World of Ideas (Kongô mandara) is steward of all treasures. He is represented seated on a lotus cross-legged; the right

Fig. 31. Jigoku. Picture of the Buddhist Hells (Lower Section)
Musée Guimet.

shoulder is bare, the right arm slightly bent, and the right hand making a *mudrā* gesture; the left hand is closed and resting upon the knee. His body is always gilded.

There are other forms in which the hands of Hôshô-nyorai make other *mudrās*, and there are others which represent him standing.

Ida-ten (in Chinese Wei-t'o)

This is a Buddhist deity of no great importance, who has become sufficiently popular in China and in Japan. Statues of Ida-ten began to be placed in the Chinese temples in the time of the Emperor Kao-tsung (A.D. 650–683), and Ida-ten was worshipped as the protector of the Law and the monks.

The Chinese monk Tao-Süan (A.D. 596–667), celebrated for his pious life, his works, and the rules he drew up for the organization of the monasteries, had visions toward the end of his life. Celestial personages appeared to him and conversed with him. Among these the General Wei played the most important part. He was

> the first of the thirty-two generals of the four *devarājas*, placed under the direct command of the *devarāja* of the South, Virūdhaka, the protector of Buddhism, and particularly of the monasteries and the monks, in the three regions of the South, the East, and the West, endowed with absolute purity and freed from all passion.

One of the celestial personages who appeared to Tao-Süan spoke as follows of this deity:

> Among the thirty-two generals the General Wei is the one who wields the greatest protection. If the sons and daughters of Māra desire to divert themselves with monks whose virtue is weak and to trouble them the General hastens up with great solicitude and repels them as circumstances may call for it. When any event takes place he goes to the place where the four kings dwell; and, seeing him, the kings all rise, because the General Wei practises pure works and protects the upright Law.

Fig. 32. IDA-TEN (WEI T'O)
Musée Guimet.

When General Wei—that is to say, Ida-ten—appeared to Tao-Süan they discussed various questions, notably those "relating to the Buddha, to temples, to celebrated statues, and to points of discipline." The monk Tao-Süan wrote several volumes recounting these conversations.

> Tao-Süan's authority was great, especially in everything concerning discipline, the ordering of the monasteries, and the practices that were to be observed in them. His instructions had the authority of Wei t'o, who had dictated or approved them, Wei t'o, to whom he pointed as the great protector the Buddha himself had given to the monasteries and the monks. That is amply sufficient to explain why everywhere and wholeheartedly statues have been erected to him and worship paid him.

From China Wei t'o passed to Japan, where he became Ida-ten and was very popular.

The current expression *Ida-ten bashiri*, "running like Ida-ten," which is used to describe great swiftness, refers to a legend of which the following is the Japanese version:

> At the moment of the death of the Buddha, before the gold coffin had been shut, a demon named Shôshikki drew near in disguise under the two trees, snatched one of the holy teeth and bore it away. The four classes of disciples, stupefied at the sight, endeavoured to stop him, but in an instant he cleared forty thousand *yojana* at a bound, rising in his flight half as high as Sumeru, where the four *devarājas* dwell. Ida-ten pursued him and took back from him the Buddha's tooth.

In statuary Ida-ten (or Wei t'o) is

> represented as a young man, in the costume of a Chinese general, clad in armour and wearing a helmet, both hands leaning on a weapon (a sword, or a kind of sceptre or more or less knotty stick) one end of which stands on the ground, or again with hands joined, and this weapon lying across his arms. The first form appears to be most widespread in China; the second is better known in Japan.[1]

M. N. Péri has published a copiously documented article on the god Wei t'o in the *Bulletin de l'École Française d'Extrême-Orient* (vol. xvi, No. 3, 1916), on which we have drawn freely.

JIGOKU—*see* HELLS

JIZÔ-BOSATSU (KSHITIGARBHA)

This is a deity little known in Indian Buddhism; his popularity began in Central Asia and developed in China; but it was in Japan above all that his cult expanded. Although temples consecrated to Jizô-bosatsu were erected in Japan from the eighth and ninth centuries, it was only in the twelfth century that this deity became popular. His iconography has undergone certain modifications in the course of the years. In the old Japanese pictures and sculptures Jizô is seated cross-legged, or standing. Lightly clad, the torso often bare, like that of the Bodhisattvas, sometimes he is holding the pearl in his right hand, and a lotus flower in the left, sometimes the left hand holds the pearl, while the right arm is lowered, with the fingers pointing to the earth. Later, and under certain definite influences, this form was modified, and Jizô was represented under the aspect of a Buddhist priest, standing or seated, holding a crozier (*khakkara*) in his right hand and a pearl of price in the left (Fig. 33). In Japan, in the Nara period (A.D. 645–781), we frequently find images of Jizô without attributes; his left hand is making the *abhayamudrā*; his right hand the *varadamudrā*. In the ninth, tenth, eleventh, and twelfth centuries he appears with the pearl of price in his left hand and his right hand in the *abhayamudrā* gesture. Then at the end of the twelfth century he takes the form that is now the most widespread—that of a Buddhist monk holding the pearl in his left hand and the crozier in the right; his head is surrounded by a halo.

Numerous temples and shrines are consecrated to him, and his image carved in stone is often placed by the side of the highways in Japan. Jizô is considered under different aspects, and there are various Jizôs. Thus there were created the six Jizôs who protect the six ways (*gati*): the way of the Hells, that of the Famished Demons (*gaki*), that of the World of Animals, that of the Asura Demons, that of Man, and that of the *devas*.

[1] See Fig. 32.

Fig. 33. Jizô
Japanese painting of the twelfth century. Berlin.

These six Jizôs, according to the doctrines, bore different names. In the manifold Japanese texts we often encounter tales about Jizô: now he saves the life of the great warrior Toshihira, now he appears in a dream and predicts fires, thus enabling the proper counter-measures to be taken. Sand from his temple at Mibu eases the pains of women in labour if they are careful to place a little on their belly. In the province of Awa, in the Rikkôji temple, there is a Jizô called Koyasu no Jizô, " the Jizô that procures easy labour." There is a Jizô " who sweeps away the snow," and this is the legend. The prior of the Jurin-in temple was aware that early every morning the Jizô of his temple went out to succour men in distress. So he ordered his servant every morning to sweep the snow from the god's path. But one day, being weary, the servant uttered a prayer that the deity might carry out this task himself. Next day when he arrived he found upon the path already cleared traces of little wet feet, turned in the direction of the altar dedicated to Jizô.

Among the numerous Jizôs there is one who bears the name of " Jizô of the Victorious Army " (Shôgun-Jizô). The celebrated priest Enchin (who died A.D. 798) received in the Kiyomizu temple at Kyôto a visit from the famous general Sakanoe Tamuramaro, who by imperial command was going into the north to put down the rebellion of Takamura. The priest promised to pray to the Buddhist deities to come to his assistance. The general was in the first instance defeated by the rebels and forced to retire; but, being pursued by the enemy, found himself obliged to give battle again. His arrows giving out, he was beginning to despair, when he beheld a little Buddhist priest, assisted by a young man, picking up the arrows on the battlefield and handing them to his soldiers. Then Tamuramaro renewed the fight, slew Takamura, and quelled the rebellion. Returning to Kyôto, the general went to see the priest Enchin and thank him for his prayers. As he inquired who were the saints that had helped him, he learned that it was the Shôgun-Jizô and Vaiṣramaṇa, the " Vanquisher of Enemies " (Shôteki-Bishamon). The general thus discovered who had been his protectors, and worshipped them with the deepest reverence.

Later on, when Shintô was absorbed by Buddhism in the form of Ryôbu-Shintô, it was declared that the deity of the great manifestation of Mount Atago was no other than the Shôgun-Jizô. Representations of this Jizô are found in Japan: he is on horseback in the dress of a Chinese general. In his right hand he holds the crozier, and in the other the pearl of price. In Fig. 25 may be seen a group in the midst of which is an equestrian representation of the deity of Mount Atago. On his right is a second Jizô in the guise of a Buddhist monk.

After the seventeenth century the popularity of Jizô went on increasing, for it is he who has power to get sinful souls out of Hell and lead them to Paradise; it is he too who protects the souls of dead children that play on the bank of the river of the nether regions. Parents address their prayers to him, casting pebbles at his feet, for him to give them to the departed children. The Shintô God of the Highway, Sae no kami, was replaced by the effigies of Jizô, and the little stones that travellers used to place at his feet to obtain a pleasant journey are now offered to Jizô for another purpose.

The image of Jizô is also found very frequently on the tombstones of children.

He is the great protector of all human beings that suffer, and particularly of children.

NILAMBARA-VAJRAPANI
(JAPANESE FORM.)

Kishimojin (Hārītī)

Kishimojin is a female deity imported into Japan, and in the Shingon mystical sect kept her original name, being called Kariteimo. According to the legend, she dwells in China; she was a demon-woman who devoured children, but who after her conversion by the Buddha became their protectress and the protectress of women in childbirth. Kishimojin was popularized by the Nichiren sect, and in Japan to-day numerous temples are consecrated to her. She is represented either standing, holding a baby in her bosom, and with the Flower of Happiness in her right hand, or else sitting in the Western fashion surrounded by children. Japanese mothers make their prayers to Kishimojin when their children are sick or when an epidemic threatens them.

Kokûzô-bosatsu (Akāsagarbha)

This Bodhisattva dwells in the Kôjû world and possesses all the virtues; he is full of compassion for human beings. Japan has preserved several ancient images of him, notably a statue in the Tôji temple of Kyôto. The lotus on which Kokûzô is seated rests on the back of a lion; the deity has his legs crossed, is crowned, and holds in his left hand a lance and in the right hand the Sacred Jewel (*chintāmani*). A picture preserved in the Godai-Sambô-in temple represents Kokûzô lightly clad, wearing necklaces, bracelets, and crown, the Sacred Jewel in his left hand, the right palm turned out, with the fingers pointing to the earth. There are also images of Kokûzô holding in his right hand a sword surrounded with flames and in his left hand a lotus flower, upon which lies the Sacred Jewel. Sometimes for the sword is substituted a fly-whisk.

Kompira, or Kubira (Kuvera)

Kompira is a fairly popular deity in Japan. In the volume *Bukkyômondôshû* (a collection of questions and answers concerning Buddhism) several *sūtras* are quoted, giving various information about this deity, who was originally a demon converted to Buddhism, and who became a God of Happiness. According to other texts, he was one of the twelve generals, the protectors of Buddhism, named in the *sūtra* Yakushi Rurikwô-nyorai-hongwan-kudokukyô. Others again make him one of the twenty-eight Nakshatra deities.

The centre of the Kompira cult is the village of Kotohira, in the Sanuki province, in the island of Shikoku. Here is the great temple to which hundreds of pilgrims come to invoke him under the name of Namu-Zôzusen-Kompira-Daigongen. The cult of Kompira spread most of all in the Tokugawa period, particularly among the sailors of the inner Sea of Japan. When the storm is raging a sailor cuts off his hair, casts it into the sea . . . Kompira is invoked, and the winds and the sea subside. The pilgrims who come to his temple are given an amulet. This is a little tablet on which the Chinese character for 'gold' is inscribed in coarse script, enclosed in a circle. This is because Kompira is regarded not merely as a patron god of sailors, but also as a god of prosperity. The images represent him as a big-bellied man, sitting cross-legged. He is ugly, his skin is black, and he holds a purse.

KONGARA-DOJI

He is the acolyte of Fudô-myôô; he is placed on his right hand, clad in the Indian fashion. He shares with Seitaka the office of servant and messenger to the god.

KONGO-YASHA-MYÔÔ (VAJRA-YAKSHA)

This is one of the five great *myôô*: the terrible manifestation of the Bodhisattva Fukû (Amogha vajra). He protects the north, and is represented with three heads and six arms, or one head and four arms. This *myôô* stands on two lotus blossoms, his left leg is raised, and his foot is in the air, he is surrounded by flames. In the lowest of his right hands he holds an arrow; in the one near his breast a *vajra*, and in the third, which is uplifted, a sword; in his left hands he holds a bell, a bow, and a small wheel. He wears bracelets on legs and arms. His three heads of hair are bristling. His front face has five eyes, a peculiarity not found in any other deity.

Fig. 34. BUTSU MO DAI KUJAKU-MYÔÔ
Musée Guimet.

KUJAKU-MYÔÔ (MAHĀMĀYŪRĪ)

This is a deity with the aspect of a Bodhisattva. He is always represented sitting on a peacock, whence his name (Kujaku means peacock). Although he is a *myôô* he is not of terrible aspect. Kujaku-myôô dwells in the centre of the Tushita heaven, where he is seated upon an eight-petalled lotus. His face is turned to the east, his body is white, his garments are white and transparent; he is adorned with necklaces and earrings and wears a crown. He has four arms. In the lower right hand he holds a fully opened lotus flower; in the next a fruit of the Bijapûraka plant; in the hand level with his left breast he bears the Fruit of Happiness (Kichijôkwa), and in the fourth hand a peacock's feather (Fig. 34). The lotus upon which he sits is white, or occasionally blue, and rests upon a peacock, which is often gilded. According to the tradition of the esoteric sects, this deity is a manifestation of Ṣākyamuni. Kujaku-myôô protects from calamity, and in times of drought is prayed to for rain.

Kwangiden, or Kwangiten

He is also called Daishô Kwangiden, Daishôden, or, popularly, Shôden sama, as well as Tenson sama. He is a protector god, and dispenses riches: thus he is especially invoked by those who wish to make their fortune. This deity is regarded as secret, and the temples that possess images of him do not display them to the eyes of the believers. Kwangiden is represented in two aspects: sometimes it is two human figures with elephant heads that stand embraced, sometimes one human figure with an elephant head. Buddhist mythology knows two *devas*, Gaṇapati and Vināyaka; in the secret sect these two deities are joined in one.

In Japan the reproductions of the first form of Kwangiden is usually in metal, and takes the shape of a statuette nine inches high at the most. Sometimes it is even smaller. The two personages have elephant heads, but one is a male deity and the other a female deity. Each lays the head on the other's right shoulder. The trunk, tusks, and eyes of the man are often larger than those of the woman, and a piece of stuff is thrown over his shoulders. The female deity has bare shoulders, but wears a headdress of precious stones. The hips of both deities are draped, their feet naked. The female deity has bracelets on her ankles, and her toes are placed on those of the male deity. They are embracing, and their fingers meet behind each other's back (Fig. 35). The two bodies are white in colour.

Fig. 35. Kwangiden
Musée Guimet.

The other shape, less popular, represents Kwangiden alone, with a human body and elephant's head. In this guise he may have two, four, or six arms; in the first case his left hand holds a radish root and the right hand a ball. When he is represented with four arms he has four legs also. In one of the right hands he holds a kind of long-handled axe, in the other a platter with a ball, in one of the left hands a tusk, in the other the stick of treasure. When he is represented with six arms he has a whole tusk on the left side of his head, slightly turned to the left; on the right side the tusk is broken. The trunk is curled upwards; and the body of Kwangiden is then yellow-red. In one of his left hands he holds a sword, in the second a dish of fruits, in the third a wheel; in one of the right hands he holds a stick, in the second a cord, in the third an elephant-tusk.

One of the variants of the legend tells us that the god Maheṣvara married Umā and with her had three thousand children; the eldest son was called Vināyaka. He was a cruel and violent god, given over to evil. One of their daughters Sannāyaka, on the contrary, was gentle and beneficent; she was a manifestation of Avalokiteṣvara. To soften Vināyaka's character she became his wife, and gave him so many delights that his heart was soothed and he became peaceful. This pair of deities is always represented in an embrace, and is called Kwangiden (in Sanskrit Gaṇapati). There is still to-day a secret worship paid to them in wealthy households. Rather more than a litre of refined hemp-seed oil is poured into a bronze basin; prayers are read and the oil is consecrated a hundred and eight times. It is then heated, and the two deities are plunged in it and subsequently are stood up in the middle of the basin. With a bronze ladle with a copper handle the oil is then dipped up and poured a hundred and eight times over the heads of Kwangiden, while prayers are addressed to him.

Kwan-on- (or Kwannon-) bosatsu (Avalokiteṣvara)

Avalokiteṣvara bears in Chinese the name of Kuan-yin; the two Chinese characters that make up this name read in Japanese as *Kwan-on*, pronounced *Kwannon*, or *Kannon*. He is one of the Bodhisattvas most revered in Japan, and great temples are consecrated to him. Japanese literature abounds in miracles due to the power of Kwan-on.

The date of the introduction of the first statue of Kwan-on into Japan is hard to determine, but it is certain that the cult goes back to the beginning of the propagation of Buddhism. Prince Shôtoku (A.D. 572–621) was a fervent worshipper of Kwan-on, and the monastery of Hôryûji possessed a fine bronze statue that is preserved in the imperial treasury. This statue, which shows the Bosatsu standing and holding a small phial, must be dated from A.D. 651; it is the oldest statue of Kwan-on in Japan.

The Kwan-on-bosatsu and the Daiseishi-bosatsu (Mahāsthāmaprāpta) are the two companions of Amida. According to the doctrines of the exoteric sects, this Bosatsu is a pupil of Amida, while, according to the Shingon secret sect, Kwan-on is regarded as a manifestation of Amida. This explains the presence of the image of this god on the head or on the diadem of Kwan-on.

In the triad of which Amida occupies the middle Kwan-on is placed on his left hand and Daiseishi on his right. The iconography of Kwan-on is very rich, and it would be impossible to enumerate here all the images of this popular deity. There are groups of Kwan-ons, differing in composition according to the sects, such as the six Kwan-ons, the seven Kwan-ons, the thirty-three Kwan-ons.

The Emperor Kwazan (A.D. 968–1008), who reigned only from 985 to 986, built no fewer than thirty-three temples consecrated to the different Kwan-ons of the group of seven. The form with a thousand arms is worshipped as the principal god in seventeen of these temples. Here are a few indications as to the seven forms of Kwan-on most widespread in Japan. In the first rank must be placed Senjû-Kwan-on (Kwan-on of the thousand arms, Sahasrabhuja sahasranetra), usually represented with forty arms, each hand holding different attributes and making *mudrā* gestures, while a thousand hands form an aureole for the god; in each palm an eye is set. There are images of Senjû-Kwan-on with three eyes, the principal head of which is surmounted by twenty-seven other heads; but the meaning of this peculiarity is not known.

Nyo-i-rin Kwan-on (*Chintāmanichakra*) is one of the forms of Kwan-on with six arms. He is seated; one of his arms is propped on the bended right knee, and his chin supported on the palm; the hand of the corresponding arm on the left side rests on the lotus that serves the god as a seat. The other left hands hold a lotus flower and a wheel; the right hands a rosary and the *chintāmini*, the symbol of the fulfilment of prayers (Figs. 36 and 37). Believers are assured that their prayers addressed to Nyo-i-rin Kwan-on will be heard, for this deity is in possession of the *chintāmini* that confers upon him this mystic power. The Nyo-i-rin Kwan-on wears a kind of tiara adorned with the effigy of Amida. Each of his hands protects one of the Six Paths: that which supports his head preserves creatures from the Way of the Hells; that which carries the *chintāmani* aids those foreordained to the Way of the *Pretas* (*gaki*); that which holds the rosary saves human beings from the Way of Animals; that which rests on the lotus succours beings on the Way of the Asuras; that which holds a lotus flower those on the Way of Human Beings. That which holds a wheel is the beneficent hand of the Way of Heaven. Besides this six-armed form, which is the most widespread, there are images of the Bosatsu with two arms; the *chintāmini* is then in his right hand, and a full-blown lotus in his left. There are still other forms, but less common, with eight, ten, or twelve arms.

Fig. 36. Nyo-i-rin Kwan-on
Musée Guimet.

Ju-ichimen-Kwan-on (*Ekādaṣamukha*) has eleven heads, the arrangement of which varies according to different schools: sometimes the principal head carries others grouped in three rows of three surmounted by one isolated head; sometimes the principal head supports a group of five smaller heads, then a group of four, and then the last one; sometimes, as in the Hôryûji statue, ten heads are arranged as a crown upon the principal head. There are slight variations in the descriptions given in the different *sūtras*, but in general they give the same indications. The statue of a Bodhisattva with eleven heads is standing and may have two arms or four; the Hôryûji one has two arms and is without attributes, the fingers making the *mudrā* gesture, while the statue of the Toganji temple bears a small vase in its left hand. According to the indications of the *sūtras*, three faces, those placed in the middle and looking to the front, should have the expression of the Bodhisattvas; the three faces to the left a furious expression, the three to the right a Bodhisattva expression; but the canine teeth should project from the mouth. The face at the back of the Bodhisattva's head is laughing. The one at the top is the face of a Buddha, or, according to other sources, that of a *nyorai* (*tathāgata*). Each of these heads wears the image of Amida on his diadem. Frequently the left hand of the statue holds a little vase containing a lotus flower. From the right arm, which points to the earth, hang strings of precious stones ornamented with coral. The three faces on the left, with the angry look, represent the section of Vajra (*Kongô-bu*), the frontal Bodhisattva faces the section of the Treasure (*Hôbu*); the Bodhisattva faces with the canine teeth represent the section of the Lotus (*Renge-bu*), the canines being the symbol of the power of Amida over the Six Ways of metempsychosis; the smiling backward face represents the section of Karma (*Katsuma-bu*); finally, the head set at the top, being that of a Buddha, represents the section of the Buddhas (*butsu-bu*), the whole representing the five sections of the Vajra world (Kongôkai). As for the three different series of expressions of these eleven faces, they should be linked up with the three sections of the Garbha world (Taizôkai).

Fig. 37. Nyo-i-rin Kwan-on

Shô-Kwan-on (*Avalokiteṣvara*) is to the right of Dainichi, in the *mandala* of the World of Forms (Taizôkai), in which the "various groups of deities and other creations find place according to the nature of the power and intention they embody respectively." In the *mandala* of the World of Ideas (Kongôkai) this Bodhisattva bears the appellation of Kongôhô-bosatsu; he is the repository of all the virtues arising from the sentiment of Compassion; he hears prayers, and at once comes to the aid of him who prays. He is seated cross-legged. He wears a crown; his long hair falls over his shoulders; the palm of his left hand is turned out, and his right hand holds a pink lotus flower. There are also images in which the Bodhisattva, head slightly inclined to the left, looks at the lotus in his left hand, while with the right he pulls open the petals of the flower. On his diadem is an effigy of Amitāyus.

Batô-Kwan-on (*Hayagrīva: "Kwan-on of the horse's head"*) is one of the Kwan-ons of the World of Forms (Taizôkai). Among the six Kwan-ons it is he who protects beings on the Path of Animals. He is the manifestation of Amida under a terrible aspect. He is seated upon a lotus, on which his left knee is resting, the right knee is raised, the arms bent, and the hands at the height of the breast making a *mudrā* gesture; his fierce face has a third eye, and fangs project from his shut mouth. This Bodhisattva has no crown, but a horse's head placed on his hair. He is regarded also as a *myôô*. The horse's head is an allusion to the noble steed of Chakravarti-rāja, which galloped in the four directions without ever tiring; in like manner this Bodhisattva traverses the four seas, subduing the demons and succouring human beings. China has preserved several legends about him, which are not current in Japan.

Jundei-Kwan-on (*Sunde*) is regarded as having infinite virtues. Whether a man be monk or layman, be he pure or a sinner, it matters little, he saves him. In the esoteric sects he is named Sonna-bosatsu (Chunda). Seated cross-legged on a lotus, he is clad to the waist in a white material and another covered with flowers. His shoulders are covered with a light shawl. On his head is a tiara. He wears a bracelet on each arm. This is the rarest of the forms of Kwan-on.

We must also mention Fukû-kensaku-kwan-on (Amoghapāṣa). This Kwan-ôn is a deity of the World of Forms (Taizôkai). Represented most frequently with two, four, or six arms, when he has more than two arms he has three faces too, and each is furnished with a third eye. This Kwan-on is seated on a lotus flower, is cross-legged, and holds in his hands various attributes, such as the cord, the lotus, the phial, and the rosary for the form with four arms.

We have enumerated the different Kwan-ons in the order of their popularity to-day. But the Buddhist believer does not stop at these varieties of forms. He attaches very little importance to all these iconographical details. It is solely the compassionate nature of a Kwan-on that draws him to the many temples dedicated to this divinity and visited by pilgrims in great numbers.

Marishi-ten (Mārīchi-deva)

Is sometimes also called Marishi-bosatsu. He is a *deva*, and is invisible. Usually he takes precedence of the sun and wields vast power. When this deity is invoked protection against fire is assured. He is also regarded as the protector of warriors. The Buddhist iconography of Japan has preserved traces of the Chinese origins of this *deva*, and represents him under a female guise. His costume is that of a Chinese lady. His right arm is extended, and the hand is open, with palm turned out. His left arm is bent, the hand at the height of the breast holds a fan in the shape of a large leaf, upon which is frequently traced the *swastika* character. The head is slightly inclined to the right and wears a diadem.

Miroku-bosatsu (Maitreya)

This is the future Buddha, who will come down on earth 5670 million years after the entry of the Buddha into Nirvāna. Miroku is at present in the Tushita heaven. Thither the great Asanga repaired to receive direct from Miroku the secret doctrines of the Mahāyāna; hence the popularity of this deity among the esoteric sects. Images of Miroku are found among the ancient statues in Korea and in the Buddhist art of Japan. He is often represented with his left foot on the ground, the right foot placed on his left knee, his right elbow on his right knee, and his right hand supporting his chin, the head slightly bent forward, his left hand on his right ankle. On his crown is a little *stūpa*. There are also images of Miroku, like that in the Tôdaiji temple at Nara: the future Buddha wears no ornament, his hair forms an *ushṇīsha*, the hands make the *mudrās* of charity and argument, his legs are crossed. Miroku is standing, or seated upon a lotus. Sometimes he is represented sitting and holding a *stūpa* in his joined hands; sometimes he has a vase in his left hand, while the right arm is extended; sometimes again he holds in his right hand the stem of a lotus flower upon which there stands a little vase.

Monju-bosatsu (Mañjuśrī)

He was very popular in Japan, and we read that the Emperor Nimmyô (834–850) instituted a special ceremony in honour of this Bodhisattva, which was celebrated for the first time in A.D. 834, in the two great temples of Nara, at Tôdaiji and Saidaiji. He is the deity of the intellect. He is frequently found in a group in which Shaka-nyorai occupies the centre, Fugen-bosatsu the right, and Monju the left. The iconography of this Bosatsu offers a variety of forms. He is most frequently represented holding in his right hand the sword of the intellect (which cleaves the darkness of ignorance), and in his left hand a book or roll. He is seated on a lotus, generally supported on a lion, which is the animal peculiar to this Bodhisattva. Sometimes he is seated cross-legged, sometimes with one leg on the ground. The hands of the statue of Monju in the Daigôji temple are in the *mudrā* posture and hold no attribute. In the picture in the Tôfukuji temple Monju is represented seated on a lion couchant, his left foot on the ground, holding a roll in his left hand and the monks' sceptre, Nyoi, in the right. A fairly well-known form in Japan is that in which Monju is clad in a coat made of cord. We also find Monju clothed as a monk.

Nijuhachi-bushu

These are the twenty-eight protecting deities sometimes regarded as the servants of Kwan-on. They symbolize the twenty-eight constellations. Their iconographic peculiarities are not invariable, but usually this group is composed of the following deities: Basosennin, Daibenzaiten, Naraen, Misshakukongô, Daibonten, Teishakuten, Makeshura, Tôhôten, Konshiki-kujaku, Zôchôten, Bishamon-ten, Kômoku-ten, Mawaraten, Manzenshaô, Shimmôten, Gobujô, Nandaryû-ô, Karura-ô, Kinnara-ô, Magora-ô, Ashira-ô, Konda-ô, Kendatsuba, Shakara-ô, Kompira-ô, Mansen-ô, Sanshi-taishô, and Hibakara-ô.

Nio

These two statues of Vajrapāṇi are placed on the two sides of the entrance-door of temples. They are the two protectors of Buddhism, and in the journal Kôbô Daishi (A.D. 779–835) wrote during his stay in China we may read as follows:

> The Vajra is reason, and by the power of this reason all agitation (*kleṣa*) is destroyed; the power of this Vajra consists in being able to penetrate within all objects as well as the human heart,

and by means of reason to cause it to open; it is on account of this that the Vajrapāṇi are placed near the door and the Buddha in the heart of the temple.

Although there are two of them, the legend knows but one guardian of the Buddha; he bears the name of Misshaku-kongô. It relates how, in days of old, there was a king who had two wives. The first bore a thousand children who all became monks and followed the way of Buddha. The second had two sons: the elder, the Kongôrikishi, protected his brothers, who practised Buddhism, the younger became the Bon-ô and helped his brothers in their religious practices. Out of this protecting deity—Kongôrikishi—iconography made two Vajrapāṇi, who are frequently red in colour. Their contracted muscles and the scarves floating around them are symbols of their tremendous strength.

One of them is named Fukaotsu. He raises his left hand open to the level of his face; the right arm is lowered and the hand holds a great *vajra*. The second is called Sôkô. His right arm is raised, the hand closed, the left arm lowered with open hand and fingers contracted. These two guardians are represented sometimes scantily clad, with the upper part of the body naked, sometimes panoplied in beautiful armour of the T'ang period.

Nyorai (in Sanskrit Tathāgata)

The Japanese dictionaries explain this as follows:

> It is one of the ten appellations of Buddha; it is he who follows the way of Bhūtatathata (*shinnyô*). He is travelling from the cause (*in*) toward the effect (*gwa*). And because he has obtained *Sambhodi* he is called *Nyorai*. *Nyo* is *dharmakāya*—that is to say, the state of true existence, the state of the absolute—it is the body represented by the aggregate of *dharmas* in their state of super-existence. *Rai* is the *sambhoga-kāya*, which means that a Buddha, although arrived at the state of Nirvāna, continues to have an existence of his own in order to be able to enter into relations with the Bodhisattvas, which is called *sambhoga-kāya*. The two united bodies (*nyo + rai*) form the *nirmānā-kāya* body, one of the forms by which the Buddha manifests himself to save the human race.

Oni (Devils, Demons)

In ancient times in Japan the word *oni* did not exist; the words *shikome* and *mono* were used, which mean rather " deities that are causes of disasters."

In the Nara period (A.D. 645–781), when Chinese and Indian ideas penetrated into Japan, they strongly influenced the conception the Japanese had of the demon; a new iconography was created. We find images of *oni* on one of the faces of the well-known reliquary of Hôryûji, the Tamamushi no zushi; a devil is seen there with a human body and a wild-beast head. Later on, in the Heian period (A.D. 782–897), belief in demons was very widespread, and the numbers of *oni* were greatly multiplied. A clear distinction can be found between the *oni* of the nether regions and the *oni* living in the upper world. The *oni* of the nether regions introduced by Buddhism have a red body (*aka-oni*), or a green body (*ao-oni*), and the head of an ox or a horse. They drive in fiery chariots and come to fetch the sinner and take him to the nether regions, before Emma-Ô. There are also demons called *gaki* (*preta*), always tormented by hunger and thirst, with huge bellies.

Among men live maleficent demons, who take sometimes an animal form, sometimes that of inanimate objects. Thus a demon turned himself into a little vessel full of oil, and by this means managed to make his way into a house, where he wrought much harm. The tales of this period also tell us of invisible demons, though they are audible, for they sing, whistle, or speak. The invisible demon could seize the soul of a dead man and appear in his shape to his parents. Numerous tales of the Heian period relate the transformation of girls or women into demons under the influence of a strong sentiment of jealousy or distress.

The idea of nefarious powers, which was introduced into Japan with the Chinese doctrines of the *yang* and the *yin*, was modified, later on; these powers were regarded as *oni* demons. The demon Akuma, born of Buddhist conceptions, since he represented the materialization of our desires, an obstacle to progress in the way of salvation, resembled a Garuḍa (*tengu*), and flew like a bird. Epidemic diseases were also looked upon as the result of the activities of demons, and the *oni* of the various diseases were represented clad in red.

Fig. 38. SHARIDEN TEMPLE OF THE BUDDHIST CONVENT ENGAKUJI, AT KAMAKURA
Thirteenth century.

The Japanese of this period, founding their ideas on the Chinese doctrines of *yang* and *yin*, believed that very virtuous persons could on certain days see the processions of demons invisible to ordinary mortals.

In the following period (Kamakura, 1186–1393), the ideas of Buddhism having been disseminated among all classes of the Japanese nation (Fig. 38), and the type of devil belonging to the nether regions having become preponderant, the *oni* of the diseases became assimilated to this type, and were always clad in red. The illuminated rolls of this period (*e-makimono*) give us fine specimens of the *oni* of the different diseases.[1]

Subsequently the various classes of *oni* tend to disappear, and from the seventeenth century they are reduced, in general, to two, those of the nether regions and women turned into *oni* by jealousy or distress.

The *oni* represent evil especially, hence the comparison, common at this period, of a very strong and cruel warrior, of a woman devoid of all gentleness and sentiment, or a creature of extreme ugliness, to an *oni*.

[1] See the headpiece on p. 385.

Fig. 39. Oni grown old and converted to Buddhism
Musée Guimet.

However, as the power of the devil remains far below that of the true believer,[1] the *oni* have never been considered by the Japanese as particularly formidable beings. The temperate climate of the country, the absence of ferocious beasts and poisonous serpents, are possibly the cause of this mild character. The demons themselves are capable of conversion, as is proved by those popular statuettes in which we recognize under the garb of the mendicant monk an *oni* converted to Buddhism (Fig. 39).

SEIT KA-DOJI

This is the acolyte of Fudô-myôô. He is placed on the right hand of the deity, clad in Indian costume. His left hand holds a *vajra* and his right a stick. He is a servant and a messenger of Fudô-myôô like Kongara.

SHICHI FUKUJIN (THE SEVEN GODS OF HAPPINESS)

According to the Japanese tradition, one of the painters of the Kano family executed for the first time, at the request of Tokugawa Ieyasu (A.D. 1542–1616), a picture representing the seven Gods of Happiness.

These deities are of different origin. Some come from Buddhism, others come from the *Kami* of Shintô; others are of Chinese origin. Different groups of the Gods of Happiness are found, but in our days they are usually the following: *Ebisu*, *Daikoku*, *Benzaiten*, *Bishamon*, *Fukurokuju*, *Jurôjin*, and *Hôtei-oshô*.

Ebisu is probably of Japanese origin; he is the patron of work. He wears a Japanese headdress and Japanese costume. The lobes of his ears are swollen, his right hand holds a fishing-line and his left a big dorado hanging from the end of the line.

Daikoku is the God of Prosperity; he too is of Japanese origin and also presents the peculiar feature of the swollen lobes of the ear. In his right hand he carries the hammer of riches, and has a big sack on his back. He stands on two bags of rice.

Benzaiten is a woman. Goddess of love, she is often represented playing on the *biwa* (a kind of guitar). She rides upon a dragon, and the serpent is her messenger. This deity is of Hindu origin, like the next god, Bishamonten, the God of Happiness and War; he is accordingly represented in full armour, holding in his right hand a small pagoda and a lance in his left.

The next three gods are of Chinese origin. Fukurokuju is the God of Wisdom and Longevity. His skull is of disproportionate height; he is accompanied by a stork. Jurôjin, also God of Happiness and Longevity, holds a long stick; he is accompanied by a stag. Lastly Hôtei-oshô is represented in the guise of a Buddhist priest, ill-shaven, bald, the ear-lobes swollen, and very big of paunch. He holds a screen in his right hand, and sits on a big sack; in Europe he is known by the name of Pusa.

SHITENNÔ

The four celestial guardian-kings: 1. *Jikoku* (Dhṛitarāshṭra); 2. *Zôchô* (Virūdhaka); 3. *Kômoku* (Virūpāksha); 4. *Tamon* (Vaiṣramaṇa).

[1] At the popular feast of spring they are driven away with beans (Fig. 40).

These celestial guardians are very tall; their stature attains half a *yojana*; they are five hundred years old; they dwell forty thousand *yojana* from this world, half-way up the slope of Mount Sumeru. Under their orders are placed eight generals, who are also protecting gods. Jikoku protects the region of the East, Zôchô that of the South, Kômoku the West, and Tamon the North; they are vassals of Taishaku-ten (Ṣakra devānām Indra), who reigns over the Tôri (Trāyastriṃṣā) and dwells on the summit of Mount Sumeru.

Representations of these celestial guardians are very common throughout Japan; they are found in a great number of temples in the guise of Chinese warriors clad in cuirasses and trampling upon demons. They are distinguished by the help of their attributes. Jikoku holds a sword in his left hand and carries in the palm of his right hand a little ossuary. His name may be translated "protector of the earth." Zôchô has a sword in his left hand, and his right hand holds up a buckler resting on the ground. In certain statues the buckler is missing and the sword is in the right hand. Zôchô destroys evil and dispenses good.

Kômoku holds a lance in his upraised right hand; his left hand is placed on his hip. The iconography of this celestial guardian includes variations. Thus the lance may be replaced by a brush; in this case the left hand holds a sword-sheath.

Tamon, better known under the name of Bishamon, is represented holding in his right hand a sceptre, and in the palm of the left hand there sits a little ossuary in the shape of a pagoda.

The best-known statues of the celestial guardians are those of the Tôdaiji temple of Nara.

Yakushi-Rurikwô-nyorai

More often called Yakushi-nyorai (in Sanskrit Bhaishajyaguru), this is a god who became very popular in Japan from the Nara period (A.D. 645-781), and especially during the Heian epoch (A.D. 782–1183). He is the great healer, the divine physician; he governs the land of Jôruri, which lies in the East; he protects human beings against diseases and heals unknown maladies.

The *sūtra* Yakushikyô is devoted to him. This text was translated into Chinese by five separate bonzes, which proves the interest it aroused.

The bonze Ninkai (954–1046), who was a fervent apostle of the mystical doctrines, says that Yakushi-nyorai is the same deity as Ashuku-nyorai, and he introduced Yakushi among the five Buddhas of the Vajradhātu *mandala*. In the Garbhadhātu *mandala* he was identified with Dainichi (Vairochana).

Among the national treasures of Japan is included the statue of Yakushi belonging to the temple consecrated to this god at Nara. It represents him standing with the face of a Buddha, the right arm bent with open hand, making the *semui mudrā*, the attestation of the coming preaching of Buddhism. The left arm is hanging down, and the hand holds a little pot containing remedies. This attribute is peculiar to Yakushi, and is not met with in representations of the other Buddhas or Bodhisattvas.

The statue of Yakushi in the temple that bears his name, in the province of Yamato, represents him seated with legs crossed. In his left hand he holds the medicine-pot. The right hand, uplifted, makes the *semui mudrā*; but this time the forefinger is slightly bent. There are numerous statues of Yakushi in Japan. They offer variations in the *mudrās* and in the attributes; sometimes the medicine-pot is replaced by a bunch of grapes.

Yakushi-nyorai is often represented between two deities: Gwakwô-bosatsu, the image of the moon, and Nikkwō-bosatsu, the image of the sun.

There is also a group of the seven Bhaishajyaguru Buddhas (Shichi-Butsu Yakushi), among which Yakushi-Rurikwô-nyorai is the most important.

In the *sūtra* devoted to Bhaishajyaguru there is mention of Yakushi-Hachidai-bosatsu, the eight great Bodhisattvas and Yakushi. It is said that when this deity departed from, life eight Bodhisattvas appeared and accompanied him to paradise. The *sūtra* does not give the names of these Bodhisattvas.

According to the legend, Yakushi-nyorai has under his orders twelve generals, who protect true believers; in Japanese they are called Yakushi jûni shinshô.

SERGE ELISEEV

Fig. 40. ONIYARAI: THE EXPELLING OF THE DEMONS BY MEANS OF BEANS

Popular feast of spring.

THE WAR FOR THE RELICS
From Sānchī.

INDEX

INDEX

ṢIVA DANCING
Musée Guimet.